WALKING IN THE ARDENNES
WALLONIA - BELGIUM

Reflections in the River Semois at Bouillon

WALKING IN THE ARDENNES

ARDENNES

Wallonia - Belgium

by
ALAN CASTLE

CICERONE PRESS
MILNTHORPE, CUMBRIA

© Alan Castle 1996
ISBN 1 85284 213 X
A catalogue record for this book is available from the British Library

There is something about walking which
stimulates and enlivens my thoughts
Jean-Jacques Rousseau 1712-1778

Solvitur Ambulando

To my wife - for being there

Photographs and illustrations by the author

By the same author:
Tour of the Queyras (French & Italian Alps)
A Pyrenean Trail (GR 10)
The Robert Louis Stevenson Trail (Cévennes, France)
Walks in Volcano Country (Auvergne and Velay, France)
The Corsican High Level Route
Walking the French Gorges (Provence and the Ardèche)
The Brittany Coastal Path

Front Cover: Bouillon and the River Semois in evening sunlight

CONTENTS

INTRODUCTION 9
   THE ARDENNES - BACKGROUND, WALKING IN THE ARDENNES, ...
      CLIMATE - WHEN TO GO 9
   TRAVELLING TO THE ARDENNES, LOCAL TRANSPORT, ...
      ACCOMMODATION 17
   TOURIST OFFICES, EATING OUT - BELGIAN FOOD 27
   EQUIPMENT, MAPS, WAYMARKING AND NAVIGATION, GRANDES .....
      RANDONNEES 28
   FLORA AND FAUNA, HUNTING, DIFFICULTIES (HAZARDS AND
      SAFETY) 35
   PHOTOGRAPHY, LANGUAGE, MONEY - BANKS AND POST OFFICES, ...
      INSURANCE 38
   TELEPHONE BETWEEN BRITAIN AND BELGIUM, TIME IN BELGIUM, ...
      PUBLIC HOLIDAYS IN BELGIUM 40
   VARIOUS TYPES OF WALKING AND OUTDOOR HOLIDAYS IN THE ....
      ARDENNES, NOTES ON USING THE GUIDEBOOK 41

GUIDE
   SUMMARY TABLE: PROVINCES, CENTRES AND WALKS 46
   KEY TO MAPS 46

PROVINCE OF NAMUR 47
NAMUR 47
   WALK 1. NAMUR: A TOUR OF THE CITADEL - 2.5 miles (4.0kms) 50
   WALK 2. NAMUR: A TOWN TRAIL - 2.0 miles (3.2kms) 53

DINANT AND ENVIRONS - THE MEUSE AND THE LESSE 55
   WALK 3. FALMIGNOUL AND THE RIVER MEUSE -
      7.5 miles (12.0kms) 58
   WALK 4. FALMAGNE AND THE RIVER LESSE - 8.1 miles (13.0kms) ... 62
   WALK 5. THE FURFOOZ NATIONAL PARK - 2.2 miles (3.5kms) 67

ROCHEFORT AND HAN-SUR-LESSE 69
   WALK 6. THE ROND DU ROI (SENTIER ROI ALBERT) -
      3.1 miles (5.0kms) 74
   WALK 7. THE ROCHEFORT AND HAN-SUR-LESSE GRAND CIRCUIT -
      10.4 miles (16.7kms) 76
   WALK 8. HAN-SUR-LESSE, BELVAUX AND THE NIAU & GRIGNAUX ......
      NATURE RESERVES - 6.5 miles (10.5kms) 80
   WALK 9. BOUVREUILS - 3.7 miles (6.0kms) 84
   WALK 10. HAN-SUR-LESSE, LESSIVE, EPRAVE AND LES ....
      BERGERONNETTES - 12.6 miles (20.2kms) 86
   WALK 11. THE FOND DE TION - 6.1 miles (9.8kms) 91

VRESSE-SUR-SEMOIS AND ALLE-SUR-SEMOIS 94
WALK 12. VRESSE, BOHAN AND THE RIVER SEMOIS -
9.9 miles (16.0kms) 96
WALK 13. ALLE, THE VIREE DES MALHEURS AND THE GRAND ....
OPIMONT - 11.2 miles (18.0kms) 100

PROVINCE OF LUXEMBOURG 105
BOUILLON AND THE SEMOIS 105
WALK 14. BOUILLON, SENSENRUTH, THE GRAND RUISSEAU,
THE TOMBEAU DE GEANT AND THE RIVER SEMOIS -
9.3 miles (15.0kms) 109
WALK 15. BOUILLON, BUHAN AND THE RIVER SEMOIS -
8.7 miles (14.0kms) 115
WALK 16. DOHAN, DAMPIREE, THE COTE DU HAVET AND THE
ROCHER LECOMTE - 9.3 miles (15.0kms) 118
WALK 17. DOHAN, LA CORNETTE, THE RUISSEAU DES ALEINES,
MAKA AND THE ROCHE PERCEE - 8.1 miles (13.0kms) 120
WALK 18. PROMENADE DE LA SCHEVAUCHEE - 4.0 miles (6.5kms) 124
WALK 19. ROCHEHAUT, POUPEHAN AND FRAHAN - THE LADDER ....
WALK - 9.6 miles (15.5kms) 127

SAINT-HUBERT 131
WALK 20. SAINT-HUBERT, THE PARC A GIBIER AND FOURNEAU
SAINT-MICHEL - 12.6 miles (20.2kms) 134
WALK 21. SAINT-HUBERT AND THE HURTEBISE MONASTERY -
8.4 miles (13.5kms) 140

HOTTON AND THE OURTHE 143
WALK 22. HOTTON, WAHARDAY AND MENIL-FAVAY, WITH AN ....
OPTIONAL TOUR OF HOTTON CAVES - 9.6 miles (15.5kms) 146
WALK 23. HOTTON CRAGS: MELINES, TRINAL, WERPIN AND
HOTTON - 10.1 miles (16.2kms) 151
WALK 24. MELREUX, THE CHATEAU DE DEULIN AND THE OURTHE
VALLEY - 11.5 miles (18.5kms) 155

LA ROCHE-EN-ARDENNE 158
WALK 25. LA ROCHE AND SAMREE - 9.5 miles (15.3kms) 162
WALK 26. LA ROCHE, MABOGE AND THE RIVER OURTHE -
8.4 miles (13.5kms) 165
WALK 27. THE VALLEE DES TOMBES, HIVES AND BUISSON -
8.4 miles (13.5kms) 168
WALK 28. LA ROCHE, HIVES AND BEAUSAINT -
7.5 miles (12.1kms) 171

WALK 29. LA ROCHE, VECPRE AND BEAUSAINT -
7.5 miles (12.0kms) 174
WALK 30. LA ROCHE, CIELLE AND SAINTE MARGUERITE -
8.1 miles (13.1kms) 176

VIELSALM AND THE SALM VALLEY 179
WALK 31. VIELSALM, FARNIERES, GORONNE AND
SALMCHATEAU - 12.4 miles (20.0kms) 181
WALK 32. VIELSALM, GRAND HALLEUX AND THE ROCHER
DE HOURT - 10.3 miles (16.5kms) 187
WALK 33. VIELSALM, BECHE AND THE GRAND BOIS -
8.7 miles (14.0kms) 191

PROVINCE OF LIEGE 195
SPA 195
WALK 34. FEUILLEE JEAN D'ARDENNE AND CREPPE -
5.6 miles (9.0kms) 200
WALK 35. SPA, THE BOIS DU CHINCUL AND THE VAL DU BROXOU -
7.1 miles (11.5kms) 202
WALK 36. SPA AND THE ETANG DE CHAWION - 6.0 miles (9.5kms) 207
WALK 37. THE GRAND CIRCUIT OF THE HILLS OF SPA - THE LAC DE ....
WARFAAZ - 8.1 miles (13.0kms) 209
WALK 38. THE PROMENADE DES ARTISTES & THE ARBORETUM DE .....
TAHAN - 4.4 miles (7.0kms) 212
WALK 39. GERONSTERE AND THE HAUTES FAGNES -
7.5 miles (12.0kms) 215

STAVELOT AND COO 218
WALK 40. STAVELOT, AMERMONT AND RENARDMONT -
6.8 miles (11.0kms) 222
WALK 41. STAVELOT, THE MAGIRU STREAM AND THE
CROIX-COLLIN - 8.7 miles (14.0kms) 225
WALK 42. THE FALLS OF COO, THE PROMENADE DU POINT DE
VUE DE STER AND COO RESERVOIR - 6.5 miles (10.5kms) 229
WALK 43. A CIRCUIT OF COO LAKES - 7.5 miles (12.1kms) 233

CANTONS DE L'EST 239
MALMEDY AND ENVIRONS 239
WALK 44. MALMÉDY AND LIGNEUVILLE - 11.8 miles (19.0kms) 243
WALK 45. MALMÉDY, GEROMONT AND ARIMONT -
6.2 miles (10.0kms) 247
WALK 46. ROBERTVILLE AND THE VALLEE DE BAYEHON -
10.3 miles (16.5kms) 250

WALK 47. WAIMES, CHIVREMONT, GROSBOIS AND REMACREUX -
5.0 miles (8.0kms) 254
WALK 48. WAIMES, TRO DES POYES AND LIBOMONT -
5.0 miles (8.0kms) 257

SANKT VITH 259
WALK 49. SANKT VITH, NEUNDORF AND KAPELLEN -
12.7 miles (20.5kms) 262
WALK 50. SANKT VITH AND HUNNINGEN - 6.1 miles (9.8kms) 266
WALK 51. SANKT VITH, LOMMERSWEILER AND THE GERMAN
BORDER - 14.0 miles (22.5kms) 267

BURG-REULAND 272
WALK 52. BURG-REULAND, LASCHEID AND DURLER -
9.0 miles (14.5kms) 275
WALK 53. OUDLER, ESPELER AND THOMMEN - 8.1 miles (13.0kms)278

APPENDICES
1:   FRENCH, DUTCH, GERMAN AND ENGLISH PLACE NAMES IN THE ....
BELGIAN ARDENNES, AND SURROUNDING REGIONS 282
2:   USEFUL FRENCH AND FLEMISH WORDS 284
3:   TOURIST OFFICES IN THE BELGIAN ARDENNES 289
4:   YOUTH HOSTELS IN THE BELGIAN ARDENNES, BRUSSELS &
OSTEND 291
5:   GR TRAILS IN THE BELGIAN ARDENNES 203
6:   USEFUL ADDRESSES 295

INDEX OF WALKS 297

INTRODUCTION

THE ARDENNES - BACKGROUND

The Ardennes (*Les Ardennes* in French and *De Ardennen* in Flemish) is a huge area of forest, hills and meandering river valleys stretching across north-western Europe, from northern France, across south-east Belgium as far as the Meuse between Namur and Liège, and into the Grand Duchy of Luxembourg, and even further eastwards into Germany, where the range changes its name to the Eifel (Fig A). The largest and best known area of the Ardennes lies within Belgium, where it covers much of the Provinces of Namur, in the west, Luxembourg, in the south, and Liège in the east. This book covers the Belgian Ardennes exclusively.

The Belgian Ardennes (Fig B) forms the major part of Wallonia, the French-speaking southern part of Belgium, home of the Walloons. The Walloons are celtic in origin, the descendants of tribes that migrated eastwards from the British Isles in prehistoric times - the Dutch (Flemish) word for Walloon is *Waelsch*, meaning foreign, and is derived from the same root as the word "Welsh". The extreme east of the country, the Cantons de l'Est, or Ostkantone, is predominantly German speaking.

The area now known as the Ardennes was first brought into being some 600 million years ago by a series of colossal earth movements which occurred beneath the sea that covered the whole of north-western Europe at that period. A gigantic V-shaped fold in the earth's crust (the Hercynian Fold) was the result, forming three major mountain ranges: the Massif Central at the foot of the V, the Armorican Massif (Brittany) to the north-west, and the Vosges and the Ardennes on its north-eastern arm. Erosion of the latter over aeons of time has reduced the original mountains into the high-level plateaux and hills seen today.

The word "Ardennes" comes from a celtic root meaning "dark" or "obscure", which may be a reference to its wild, harsh landscape, or perhaps also to its unenviable reputation as the battleground of this part of Europe. The area has long been forested: it was well known to the Romans, who called it Arduenna Silva. Today extensive tracts of mature, deciduous woodland (beech, oak, birch and alder predominate), interspersed with areas of spruce and other introduced conifer species, are broken by open heath and moorland, and in the valleys by numerous rural farmsteads, hamlets and villages. The landscape is riven by several deep, wooded, sinuous gorges and attractive narrow valleys. The principal river is the Meuse (*Maas* in Flemish) which flows through the region from the French border to Dinant, Namur, Huy and Liège on its way north to Holland and the North Sea. Into this wide river flow several of the well-known meandering rivers of the Ardennes, in particular the Semois in the south, the Lesse in the west and the Ourthe further to the east, all of which rise in the uplands of the Ardennes forest. The Amblève, the Salm and the Warche are

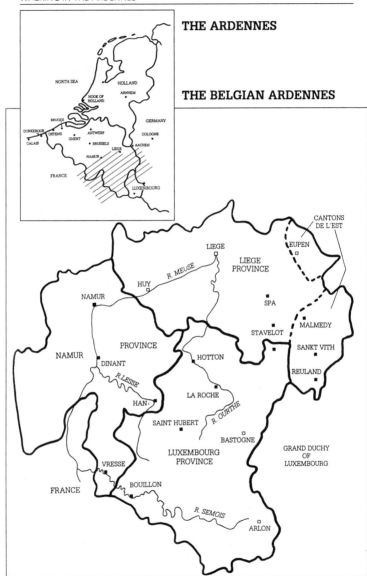

THE ARDENNES

THE BELGIAN ARDENNES

other important Ardennes rivers which have carved out valleys, each of which have their own special character. The rivers and their numerous tributary streams disappear underground in some areas. These subterranean waterways have frequently sculptured, over countless millennia, cave systems, sometimes of labyrinthine proportions, the limestone formations within often of exquisite beauty. Above the valleys are vistas of rolling, green hillscapes and forests, seemingly stretching into infinity.

The Ardennes, although lacking the many art treasures of the eastern half of Belgium, is without doubt the scenic highlight of the country. The charming town of Namur is the traditional gateway to the Ardennes, from where it is possible to travel by boat along the picturesque Meuse valley to Dinant and beyond towards the French border. The often narrow and winding Lesse valley stretches from near Dinant south-eastwards and upwards towards Han-sur-Lesse, where the famous Han Grottoes are some of the most spectacular of the many show caves in the Ardennes. Other worthwhile cave systems to visit are at Remouchamps, Goyet, Rochefort and Dinant. Saint-Hubert, in the heart of the Belgian Ardennes, is a renowned hunting centre, famous for its historic abbey, as too is Stavelot further east, home of a unique and most celebrated Lenten Carnival.

The large and rather industrial city of Liège, which nevertheless possesses some fine museums and art galleries, guards the north-eastern entrance to the Belgian Ardennes. From here the Ourthe valley winds past attractive sylvan landscapes to Hotton and on to La Roche, a most picturesquely situated town, famous for its smoked ham, the justly deserved "capital" of the Ardennes. The Semois valley in the south of the region is deep, wooded and highly meandering. On its banks lies the appealing town of Bouillon, close to the French border, with its picturesque citadel perched high above the river. Farther east is the Gaume or Belgian Lorraine, a forested area occupying the southernmost tip of Belgium. To the north-east of the Ardennes lies elegant Spa, a town which was to lend its name to so many other health resorts throughout Europe. Despite its popularity as a holiday centre the Ardennes is large and wild enough to absorb any tourist crowds, and it is always possible to find peace and tranquillity in its woods and hills, particularly if enjoyed on foot.

The highest part of the Ardennes is the Hautes Fagnes (Hohes Venn, Hoge Venen or High Fens) a vast area of upland forest, peat bog, marsh, moor and heathland, situated above the towns of Spa and Malmédy in the east of the country. This tundra-like landscape was left behind after the retreat of the Scandinavian ice sheets at the end of the last Ice Age. Belgium's highest point, the Signal de Botrange at 2275ft (694m), is located in the heart of the Hautes Fagnes, north of Malmédy. Numerous wayside pillars and crosses will be found along the many ancient paths and trackways across the Hautes Fagnes, some of them dating back to Roman times and beyond. Large areas of these wild, sombre, windswept heights, where winters are often harsh, have been designated *réserves naturelles*, home to deer and wild boar.

History

The Belgian Ardennes is French speaking, with the exception of a far eastern pocket of the country known as the Cantons de l'Est or Eastern Cantons (*Ostkantone* in German and *Oostkantons* in Flemish). In these three cantons (Eupen, Malmédy and Sankt Vith) the language is predominantly German. Bounded by Germany to the east and the Grand Duchy of Luxembourg to the south, the region has a rich and often tragic history. Prior to the end of the 18th century the area was divided among a number of rulers, including the Ecclesiastical Principality of Stavelot-Malmédy, the Duchy of Luxembourg and the Prince Bishopric of Trèves (Trier). After the French Revolution the Belgian Ardennes, including what is now the Cantons de l'Est, passed into French hands, but by the Congress of Vienna in 1815 the cantons were ceded to Germany. After a century of Germanisation the territory was granted to Belgium after the First World War by the 1919 Treaty of Versailles. Apart from the period 1940 to 1945, when it became part of the Third Reich, the Cantons de l'Est have remained in Belgium. Nevertheless the language, culture and general atmosphere of the region is distinctly Germanic. It is an area of upland forest, lakes, reservoirs and an abundance of pleasant rural hamlets, villages and small towns.

The rather unfortunate geographical location of the Ardennes, between the great Germanic states to the north and east, and the French powers to the south and west, has resulted in the area becoming the battleground of north-western Europe many times over the centuries, with innumerable foreign armies staging bloody campaigns through its forests and valleys. Time and again its towns and villages have been destroyed and rebuilt. The Roman legions were here, Caesar having great respect for its huge size and wildness, which offered refuge to local guerrilla forces defying the might of the Empire. But the greatest ravages of war in the Ardennes were felt during the 20th century. During the First World War the German and French armies collided at full strength in the Ardennes at the end of 1914, with fierce fighting and the loss of much life. Again the Ardennes featured as a major theatre of war during the Second World War.

The Ardennes was the scene of some of the fiercest fighting in the latter stages of the Second World War. Six months after the D-Day landings in Normandy, Belgium had been completely liberated and the Allied line was poised to advance into German territory. Hitler, in one last desperate attempt to avoid defeat, decided to wage a counter-offensive at the weakest point on the Allied line, which stretched between Maastricht and Alsace. This was in the central portion of the line, in the region of the Belgian Ardennes. The aim was to breach the Allied lines, creating a "bulge" in the Ardennes, and then with great speed continue west to take Antwerp and so drive back the Allied armies.

The Battle of the Ardennes, sometimes referred to as the Battle of the Bulge, commenced just before Christmas, 1944. On the 16th December the Germans, under the General Von Rundstedt, made a surprise attack on the Allied lines, and by Christmas Day the bulge had been formed, the Germans reaching a position close to Dinant and to Liège. However, by the beginning of 1945 the Allied counter-attack began with American forces under Patton striking from the south and the British under Montgomery advancing from the north. By the end of January the Germans had been pushed back to their former position, Belgium being liberated for a second time, but not without the loss of some 120,000 German soldiers and 77,000 Americans. There were a number of atrocities to local civilians during the campaign, which was staged during severe winter conditions. Ramblers will be sure to see many memorials to those horrendous days whilst walking in the Ardennes, in the many villages and towns that were devastated and alongside numerous footpaths and quiet country lanes, where many ambushes took place.

The life of the hardy people of the Ardennes has never been easy, even in peacetime. A poor region, rugged and relatively undeveloped, much of the land is unsuitable for growing crops. Old industries, such as slate mining, have now largely died out. The Ardennes depends today on forestry and particularly on tourism and various commercial outdoor pursuits. The Ardennes receives not only holidaymakers who stay for a week or longer, but many of its visitors come just for a day from nearby Liège or from Brussels; many others come for weekends or other short breaks from other parts of Belgium and from neighbouring Holland, Germany and France. Outdoor pursuits such as walking, climbing, caving, canoeing, mountain biking and cross-country skiing are all very popular, activities which promote the sort of "Green Tourism" on which the future of the region will depend.

WALKING IN THE ARDENNES

Of all the outdoor pursuits undertaken in the Ardennes walking is perhaps the most popular. Every area of the Belgian Ardennes has many miles of waymarked walking trails, and almost every tourist office in the region has produced a map specifically designed for use by walkers, facts that are indications of the importance placed on walking as a leisure activity in the region. In addition to the many local trails there is an extensive network of long distance paths criss-crossing the Ardennes.

The 53 walks described in this book, varying from 2 miles up to 14 miles in length, are representative of the variety of landscape found in the Ardennes and the types of walks available. There are long walks through extensive forests and tramps over undulating green hills; rambles along and above deep-sided meandering river valleys past towering limestone crags, strolls through natures reserves, and town trails past castles, cathedrals and ancient monuments. Some are gentle walks along quiet country lanes whilst others include a number of steep narrow paths, with just a few involving the fording of streams and some easy scrambling for the more experienced and adventurous walker - there is even a "ladder walk" which involves some exposed scrambling over steep rocks high above a river's edge! There is something for everyone in the Ardennes, from the adventurous and enthusiastic walker who wishes to spend all of his or her time walking the hills, river valleys and forests, to the family rambler and the holidaymaker who likes to mix a walk in beautiful surroundings with general sightseeing. Many of the walks are suitable for children, accompanied by an adult. The introductory sections to each walk in the book, describing the nature, length, places of interest passed and facilities available en route, should give a good indication.

Fourteen varied walking centres are covered in the book, sampling some of the best walking to be had in the region. However, as the Ardennes covers such a large area, a single guidebook can only give a taste of the walking to be found in the district. The Ardennes could be visited annually for twenty years or longer and there would still be new and interesting corners to explore, particularly on foot. After most of the walks described in this book have been completed the walker should know the Belgian Ardennes reasonably well, but it is perfectly feasible to continue to discover more by purchasing a local tourist office map of another region and walking the local waymarked trails with the aid of this map. By combining sections of the various local trails, your own walk itineraries of preferred length, character and difficulty can easily be devised. Or even one of the long distance trails could be attempted, many of which can form the basis of excellent one and two-week walking holidays.

Although it is very easy to "get away from it all" in the woods and hills of the region, the walker will rarely be far from civilisation in the Ardennes, from a warm café or welcoming hotel or restaurant. The elaborate system of waymarked walking trails means that the modern wayfarer is unlikely to become seriously lost. In days gone by, wayside crosses, calvaries and shrines were often erected in this Catholic country to mark cross-tracks and give encouragement and protection to the traveller in a land where ambush from highwaymen was not uncommon. Many of these ancient shrines remain and several will be passed when following the walks described in this book. Another charming feature of the Belgian countryside and towns, which will be frequently seen by the walker, is the numerous and rather elaborate large free-standing letter boxes outside many of the cottages: they are often made of metal, decorated and brightly painted, often in red or black.

The Ardennes can also satisfy the rambler who prefers to walk with and meet other like-minded people on organised walking events. The Walk of Remembrance and Friendship, organised by the 3e Chasseurs Ardennais, takes place over a four-day period ending on the last Saturday in June. Participants (usually 4000-5000 in number) come from all over Belgium and abroad and range in age from the young to the most senior of senior citizens. Tent villages are erected at the end of each day stage at Bastogne, Houffalize and Vielsalm. For further information contact the Secretariat de la Marche du Souvenir et de l'Amiti, 3e Chasseurs Ardennais, Caserne Ratz, B-6690 Vielsalm (tel (080) 21 71 20 or (080) 21 67 83, ext 206).

This guidebook provides some information on places of interest in the 14 walking centres featured in the book, especially those encountered on the described walks. For more detailed information the reader should consult a general tourist guide to the region. Although there is no ideal tourist guide in English to the Ardennes, the following two guidebooks are worthy of consideration:

1. *The Blue Guide to Belgium and Luxembourg* by Bernard McDonagh (A. & C. Black). A fairly comprehensive tourist guidebook to the two countries, with art and architecture heavily emphasised. A moderately sized section of the book is devoted to the Ardennes.

2. *The Rough Guide to Holland, Belgium and Luxembourg*. A good buy for those intending to visit the three Benelux countries during their stay. However the treatment of the Ardennes is rather superficial.

In addition the tourist offices in Belgium produce an annual publication in English, usually entitled *Guide to the Tourist Attractions and Museums in Belgium*. This is packed with information on places to visit whilst on holiday in the area. It is usually provided free of charge on request, but a few tourist offices make a small charge. Namur and Luxembourg Provinces also produce their own similar publications which are even more detailed for their particular areas (perhaps the Province of Liège will do likewise in the future?). Ask at local tourist offices.

CLIMATE - WHEN TO GO
The Ardennes has a climate not dissimilar from that of Britain, that is a temperate climate with rain possible at any time of the year. The average daily temperatures for Belgium are 1 degree Celsius in January and 19 degrees Celsius in July. The weather tends to be slightly more extreme in Wallonia than in the Flemish part of Belgium for two reasons: firstly, the Ardennes, being farther to the east, is more affected by the typical continental weather pattern of hot summers and cold winters; secondly, much of the Ardennes, particularly the Hautes Fagnes around Spa, Stavelot and Malmédy, lies at a relatively high altitude, so that winter temperatures in particular tend to be fairly low, with snowfall quite common.

Winters during the latter part of the 1980s and for the first five years of the 1990s have been relatively mild, perhaps a consequence of global warming, the result being disastrous for the cross-country skiing tourist industry in the area, as snowfall has been slight. However, it should be stressed that winters in the Ardennes can be severe, with heavy snowfall and low temperature persisting for weeks on end.

Rainfall can be heavy and persistent at times, particularly during the spring and autumn, and over the higher ground in the region. This leads to muddy paths and tracks, a feature of walking in the Ardennes between October and April. The rate of drying of these muddy trails is slowed in areas where there is dense tree cover, which decreases the rate of evaporation of water from the ground - conditions are often worse in the vicinity of a riding school, where horses churn up the mud. (There is generally no distinction between footpaths and bridleways in the Ardennes, although in areas where there is much horse riding the trail is often partitioned into walkers and riders only sections.) Heavy and persistent rainfall leads on occasions to flooding in some of the more low-lying river valleys. Of particular note in recent times was the severe flooding that occurred in Dinant when the River Meuse burst its banks in January and February, 1995, during one of the worst floods in Belgium, France, Holland and Germany this century. A few of the walks featured in this book cover sections close to major rivers in the Meuse, Lesse, Ourthe and Semois valleys. Obviously to attempt these routes during times of flood would be highly dangerous and an act of great folly. Just one or two walks in the book involve fording streams or small rivers, which in normal dry conditions are shallow and slow-moving, but which after heavy and prolonged rain could become deep, fast-flowing and dangerous. Adequate warnings about such crossings, and how to avoid them, are given in the text of the relevant walks. Provided common sense is exercised at all times the walker should not place him or herself in danger.

Summers generally tend to be warm without being hot, similar to those in the south-east of England, but perhaps generally a degree or two warmer. Sunshine levels between the two locations are also not dissimilar.

Walking in the Ardennes is an enjoyable experience during all of the seasons: the freshness of spring with the trees bursting into leaf above a ground covering of spring flowers; the sunshine, warmth and luxuriant growth of summer in the forests and river valleys; the mellowness of autumn with acres of purple heathland and the rich, golden tints of the turning leaves; the crisp, cold winters, when snow decorates the landscape and streams and lakes are often frozen. Certainly a winter walking holiday should not be discounted. Views are generally more extensive in winter when the leaves are off the trees, and much of the available accommodation remains open throughout the year, as do many of the tourist offices.

A more important consideration, perhaps, than the climate is the availability of accommodation. Many of the hotels in the Ardennes, and particularly in the more popular tourist areas, are fully booked during the main summer holiday period, and over Christmas, Easter and the other bank holidays, so that advance booking is recommended at these times. Some of the campsites also become full during these periods, although this would be less of a problem for those with their own transport, who could easily "move on" to find somewhere else to stay.

At other times of the year finding accommodation is rarely a problem (with the exception of Friday and Saturday nights in the popular cross-country ski areas, during times when snow conditions are good). Many of the hotels remain open throughout the year, although some close for a few weeks in the winter whilst the owners enjoy their own holidays. Most of the campsites in the Ardennes close during the wintertime, but the hardy camper will still find some of them open all year. Youth hostels and *gîtes d'étape* (private hostels) vary somewhat in their opening dates, some remaining open all year, whilst others close down for a period during the winter, or open only at weekends during the winter months. April, May and June are excellent months to visit the Ardennes, as are September and October, although in the latter case walkers will have to take heed of hunting activities in some areas (see "Hunting" below).

TRAVELLING TO THE ARDENNES
Public Transport
There are basically two ways of reaching the Ardennes by public transport:

1) By air, followed by train and/or bus to reach the final destination.

2) By train or coach, crossing to the Continent by means of either a ferry or the Channel Tunnel.

When consulting timetables remember that Belgium is one hour ahead of Britain for most of the year.

By Air
The best airport to fly to from the UK is undoubtedly Brussels. There are several flights daily from most major British airports, and a few services from some smaller airports. The major carriers are British Airways, and Sabena Airlines, the Belgian national carrier. Prices are generally competitive, so be sure to shop around. APEX fares are available. Brussels Airport (Zaventem - Tel (+32) (02) 723 60 10) is 17kms from the city centre. There are bus, train and taxi services to the city centre from the airport: buses leave approximately every 30mins with a journey time of about 40mins; trains also leave approximately every 30mins with a journey time of about 18mins. There is a very good train service from Brussels to Namur (70kms, journey time approximately 50mins; about 40 trains per day) and to Liège (100kms, journey time approximately 1hr; about 40 trains per day) from where most of the centres in the Ardennes can be reached by public transport (see "Transport" below).

The other option is to fly to Liège, which is admittedly closer to the Ardennes than Brussels but there are few direct flights from Britain and the cost is generally greater. Other airports to consider are Luxembourg City (eg. only 110kms from Malmédy), which has a good train service through the Ardennes to Namur, and Cologne, which has a good train service to Liège (approximately 120kms). However, none of them can compete with Brussels for the sheer number of flights available and for general convenience.

One disadvantage of flying is that the return home often has to be booked in advance.

By Train

The introduction of the Eurostar Service between London and Brussels via the Channel Tunnel has greatly facilitated travel to this part of Europe. There are two services a day from the International Terminal at Waterloo Station to Brussels Midi Station, but frequency is eventually expected to reach one an

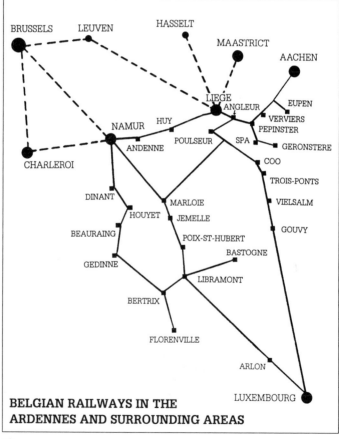

BELGIAN RAILWAYS IN THE ARDENNES AND SURROUNDING AREAS

hour. The journey time is 3hrs 15mins, so that with a good connection one could be in Namur and the Ardennes about 4½hrs after leaving central London. When a new high speed line is opened in Belgium (trains will travel at over 100mph) the journey time by Eurostar to Brussels will be reduced by 30mins. There are also direct services from the Midlands, northern England and Scotland. The use of Eurostar to Brussels, particularly for those living in the south-east of England, can be recommended. In terms of speed, cost and convenience the Eurostar train service will compete very favourably with the airlines.

There are several traditional train and ferry services operating daily between London Victoria and Belgium, via the port of Ostend. Connecting trains from the latter depart directly for Liège (Guillemins Station) via Bruges, Gent, Brussels (Midi and Nord - change at either station for connections to Namur) and Leuven. Journey time through to Liège from London is approximately 10hrs (for example there is a very convenient service that leaves London just after 8am and arrives in either Liège or Namur just before 7pm local time). Note that there are three principal railway stations in Brussels: Brussels Midi (or Zuid), Brussels Central and Brussels Nord. Several services to Namur and Liège stop at all of these stations, but it is best to check timetables first (see Appendix 6).

By Coach
The cheapest way to travel to Belgium by public transport is by long distance coach. Eurolines, the arm of the National Express coach company operating to Europe, operate services from London's Victoria Coach Station to Brussels, once or twice daily, usually via Bruges and Antwerp. The journey time is about 11hrs. From Brussels there is a Eurolines connection to Liège (see Appendix 6).

Private Transport
The use of a car would certainly be a benefit if it is intended to visit several centres in one holiday, or to combine walking with general sightseeing. Local travel in the Ardennes is considerably easier by car than by the sometimes infrequent bus services. Another possibility is to travel to Brussels, Namur or Liège by plane and/or train, and then hire a car. Caravan and camping enthusiasts are very well catered for in the Ardennes, with many sites in the area (see "Accommodation" information for each walking centre).

Ferries to the Continent
The most direct car ferry service to Belgium is that from Dover to Ostend, operated by P & O European Ferries. There are generally 6 or more sailings per day, with a crossing time of about 4hrs. The Dover to Zeebrugge P & O service is a close contender with almost as many sailings and a crossing time of 4hrs 30mins.

The shortest Channel crossings, but which involve longer drives once on the

Continent, are to the Pas de Calais in northern France. There are services between Dover and Calais (Sealink-Stena and P & O), Dover and Boulogne (P & O), Folkestone and Boulogne (Hoverspeed - by SeaCat) and between Ramsgate and Dunkerque (Sally Line). Crossing times vary between 1hr and 1hr 40mins, except for the Sally Line service which takes 2hrs 30mins. Of the three Continental ports Dunkerque is the nearest to Belgium, but the drive to the Ardennes from any of them is not over long.

Those living in the north of England and in Scotland might find the overnight Hull to Zeebrugge service (14hrs) operated by North Sea Ferries to be the most useful and the standard of both ferry and service is very high. North Sea Ferries also operate a service between Hull and Rotterdam (Europort). Another option is the relatively new service (started May, 1995) operated by Scandinavian Seaways between Newcastle-upon-Tyne and Amsterdam (from Tyne Commission Quay to a new terminal at Ijmuiden, 30mins by car from the centre of Amsterdam). A third route to the Netherlands is the well established twice daily service between Harwich and the Hook of Holland (Stena-Sealink). Note that the Olau Line ferry service between Sheerness and Vlissengen in southern Holland ceased operation in 1994. (For ferry companies see Appendix 6.)

Note that the fares for taking a car to the continent on a cross-Channel or North Sea ferry vary considerably with season, day of the week and time of day. Be sure to check price structures outlined in the company brochures with care!

Le Shuttle
For speed and convenience there is little to beat Le Shuttle crossing by the Channel Tunnel. When fully operational Le Shuttle service will run every 15mins during peak times. From the M20 in Kent leave the motorway at junction 11a to follow the signposts into the terminal at Folkestone. It is not possible to make a reservation: simply turn up, buy a ticket at the tollbooths, proceed past customs and passport control and drive onto the train. The train travels at up to 100mph; within 35mins you should have joined the French motorway network near to the village of Sangatte (see below). When driving towards the Tunnel on the British side it is possible to check for any delays by tuning into Channel Tunnel Radio on 101.2 FM. Le Shuttle operates 24hrs a day, 365 days of the year. Further details can be obtained from Le Shuttle, tel (01303) 271100.

Driving in Belgium
Radar speed traps operate in Belgium, France and Holland and police can inflict on-the-spot fines. Seat belts are compulsory on both rear and front seats. It is obligatory to carry a red warning triangle in case of accident or puncture and British drivers are strongly advised to obtain a Green Card level of insurance. On some town and city roads priority is still "on the right": this does not apply where an orange diamond shaped roadsign occurs along the road.

The speed limits in Belgium are as follows: 50kms/hr in built-up areas,

90kms/hr on single carriageway roads and 120kms/hr on dual carriageways and motorways.

When driving across the Flemish half of Belgium from the Channel ports or across Holland from the North Sea ports, signs are in Dutch. In the Ardennes signs are in French. The most important ones to note are as follows:

Through Traffic: *Toutes Directions* (French); *Doorgaand Verkeer* or *Alle Richtingen* (Dutch).

Diversion: *Déviation* (French); *Omleiding* (Dutch).

Roadworks: *Chantier* (French); *Werk in Uitvoering* (Dutch).

Place names often differ considerably in the two languages (see Appendix 1).

A roads or Autoroutes (motorways) carry both a red A number and a green E number (International European Number). The latter are given preference in Belgium and are the ones to memorise and follow when driving through the country (if driving in the Netherlands note that the A numbers are generally given preference). Road maps prior to 1986 should not be used, as the road numbering system in Belgium was changed at that time. N (National) roads, which can be double or single carriageways, are roughly equivalent to British A roads.

Driving Routes to the Ardennes
The Ardennes is easily reached from the Channel and North Sea Ports, for the most part on a network of well-maintained motorways. Suggested routes are given below. The times given are approximate and assume travel on motorways for the most part at the maximum legal speed limit. Traffic jams can, of course, be expected during main holiday periods and at peak times.

From Ostend/Zeebrugge to the Ardennes:
From Zeebrugge south on the N31 to meet the E40 (A10) motorway south of Bruges. From Ostend east along the E40 (A10) motorway. Follow the E40 (A10) past Gent to meet the Brussels "Ring". Drive north around this to reach the E40 (A3) motorway to Liège. Those driving to Namur should continue around the Brussels Ring (it loses its motorway status for a few miles) to reach the start of the E411 (A4) motorway heading south-east to Namur, Dinant and beyond. Journey time is about 3-4hrs.

From Boulogne/Sangatte/Calais/Dunkerque to the Ardennes:
From the three ports or the Channel Tunnel exit join the new motorway heading eastwards parallel with the coast. At the time of writing there is a break in the motorway network for about 10 miles near to the Belgian border. Enter Belgium and continue past Veurne on the E40 (A18) motorway. This joins the E40 (A10) motorway east of Ostend, from where the route is as above. Journey time is about 4-6hrs.

From Hook of Holland/Rotterdam/Amsterdam to the Ardennes:
From Europort head east along the N15 and then the A15 motorway to meet the A16 motorway south of Rotterdam. From the Hook take the N20 and then the A20 motorway to join the Rotterdam Ring - turn onto the A16 motorway signposted to Dordrecht. From Amsterdam take the A4 motorway to the point where it joins the A13 motorway between Den Haag and Delft - now follow the A13 to drive around the Rotterdam Ring to take the A16 motorway signposted to Dordrecht. Remain on the A16 past Breda to cross into Belgium, where the motorway becomes the E19 (A1). On reaching the Antwerp Ring take the E313 (A13) motorway if travelling to Liège, or, if driving to Namur or Dinant, continue around the Ring to take the E19 (A1) motorway signposted to Brussels via Mechelan. Drive around the Brussels Ring to take the E411 (A4) to Namur. The journey time is about 3½ to 4hrs from the Rotterdam area (add 45mins if coming from the outskirts of Amsterdam).

Note that if driving into the Ardennes beyond Liège, the motorway (A27) that links Verviers to Spa, and on towards Malmédy and Sankt Vith, is referred to as the E42 on some road maps and as the E421 on others.

LOCAL TRANSPORT
All of the walking centres featured in this book can be reached by means of public transport, though most accessible are those that lie on a railway line. For details of the rail network in the Belgian Ardennes see the map of the Belgian Railways in the Ardennes and Surrounding Areas - Fig C. Namur, Dinant, Hotton, Spa, Coo and Vielsalm are very easy to reach by train. La Roche, Saint-Hubert, Rochefort, Han-sur-Lesse, Bouillon, Stavelot, Malmédy, Sankt Vith and Burg-Reuland are all accessible by a combination of bus and train. The majority of the walks described start and finish in a town or village centre, and, as all of them are circular walks, there are no problems of returning to base at the end of the day. For the few walks which are located some way from a town or village centre, access details are given in the write-up to those walks. Details of the bus and train possibilities in all 14 walking centres can be found under "Transport" in each section, and reference should be made to this when making plans to visit each area. It is certainly possible for those without private transport to enjoy a walking holiday in the Ardennes.

Details of train services throughout Belgium can be obtained at most of the manned railway stations in the country and at many local tourist offices. The train timetable numbers for the lines serving the areas described in this book are as follows:

Brussels to Liège: No. 36.   Liège to Verviers to Cologne (Kln): No. 37.
Brussels to Namur: No. 161.   Namur to Dinant: No. 154.
Verviers to Spa: No. 44.   Ostend to Brussels: No. 50A.

Public transport in the Belgian Ardennes has suffered a similar fate to that in Britain. With an increasing reliance on the car, many bus and local train services have been cut or severely curtailed. However, the public transport network is still reasonably good in several of the areas covered by this guidebook, better than in many areas of rural Britain. Many of the towns and villages in the Ardennes that do not have a railway station are often linked to the railway network by bus - though there are often only a few buses a day and usually an inferior service at weekends, particularly on Sundays. If relying solely on public transport it would be prudent to journey from one walking centre to a new base on a weekday because of the superior bus and train services. Generally winter timetables are inferior to those of the summer. Some bus services only operate during the main summer tourist season (mid-June to mid-September, or sometimes only in July and August) whilst several others run only on certain days of the week (eg. on market days) or during school terms. Tourist offices supply up-to-date information or if this is closed try the principal bus stops in a town or village, where bus timetables are often displayed. If all else fails a local taxi service will probably charge less than for a comparable journey in the UK.

Local transport problems can be partially alleviated by hiring bicycles wherever possible. There are facilities for this at several centres in the Ardennes, and occasionally from railway stations. Ask at the tourist office or keep a look-out for signs indicating bicycle hire.

Motorists will find driving in the Ardennes relatively easy. Except during popular holiday periods the traffic on motorways and major roads, several of which are dual carriageways, is relatively light, the roads being far less busy than those in the industrial Flemish half of the country. There is an excellent network of motorways and major roads which allows fast and easy travel around the district. Of particular use to users of this guidebook are the E42 (A15) motorway between Namur and Liège, the E411 (A4) motorway linking Namur, Dinant, Han-sur-Lesse and places further south, the E25 (A26) motorway running south from Liège passing La Roche, the E421 (A27) motorway linking Verviers, Spa, Malmédy and Sankt Vith, the N4 dual carriageway running south-east from Namur, and the N89, much of which is dual carriageway, between La Roche and Bouillon. Some of the minor roads in the Ardennes can be narrow, steep, with many bends in them, so extra care is required.

ACCOMMODATION

Hotels

Hotels are plentiful in the Belgian Ardennes, and are generally less expensive than their equivalents in the UK. Hotels in Belgium are star graded on a system very similar to that in Britain. The basic hotel is a one-star and this is usually reasonably priced, clean and comfortable. The two-star generally offers more comfort and facilities, although, as is so often the case with such grading systems, the good one-star hotel with friendly and helpful staff can offer a better stay than the less welcoming two-star establishment. One and two-star hotels can be found everywhere in the Ardennes in considerable numbers. Rooms come either with or without a shower (*douche*); some of the more expensive rooms have a bath. Although it is customary to pay for the room, rather than per person, the cost of a single room in a hotel is often considerably less than a room for two. This is not always the case, however, so it is worth the lone walker shopping around. There are also many three-star hotels, particularly in the larger, more popular resorts and towns. These offer considerable luxury and usually, a first-class restaurant. In one or two places even higher grade establishments can be found, which, although expensive, are generally less so than their equivalents in Britain.

Sometimes the price of the room includes breakfast, but remember that this will be continental in style. It is a legal requirement in Belgium that room prices must be clearly displayed in each room in hotels. It is advisable to settle on the price for an overnight stay at the outset, and always inspect the room first before accepting (it is customary to be shown the room on making an enquiry in a hotel in Belgium; in the unlikely event that a request to inspect the room is denied then move on to another hotel). Some establishments levy a small surcharge to cover extra laundry costs, to visitors who stay for only one night. It is possible in some hotels to obtain half-board (includes dinner and breakfast), usually for a worthwhile saving. It is often worth enquiring if this is available, although several hotels will only offer half-board if the customer agrees to stay a minimum number of nights (often three).

It is rarely necessary to book hotel accommodation in advance outside the main holiday periods. Most centres featured in this book (but not all - see the chapter on Burg-Reuland) have a number of hotels so that even the walker using public transport should have few problems. During July and August, at Easter and certain other holiday periods (note that bank holidays are often different from those in the UK - see Public Holidays in Belgium below) the situation is very different, with many hotels fully booked. If intending to visit the area during these periods it is advisable to make reservations. The easiest way to do this is to contact the tourist offices of the centres that you intend to visit, preferably well in advance of your trip (see Appendix 3) to request a brochure detailing the hotels in their areas. If sending a written request keep your letter short, in French if possible. The brochure will list all the hotels and their facilities in the region. Send a reservation either directly to the hotel, or ask the tourist office staff to do this on your behalf (there is sometimes a small fee for this). The alternative method of booking a hotel in the Ardennes, and indeed anywhere else in Belgium, is via the free Belgian Tourist Reservations service, based in Brussels (see Appendix 6).

Chambres d'Hôte, Private Rooms and Holiday Homes

In addition to hotels many of the centres have a number of private rooms available for visitors. *Chambres d'hôte*, or Bed and Breakfast establishments, although becoming increasingly popular in the Ardennes, are not found in the sort of numbers now common in many parts of Britain. The term *chambre d'hôte* is the one generally used to advertise this type of accommodation, but occasionally the word *chambre* (room) can be seen in a front window or garden, or even the more descriptive *chambre avec petit déjeuner* (room with breakfast). Because there are so many Flemish, Dutch and German visitors to the Ardennes, B&B signs will also often indicate *Kamers met Ontbijt* (Dutch) or *Zimmer mit Frühstück* (German). Local tourist offices keep lists of *chambres d'hôte* and other private rooms. If stuck for accommodation it is always worthwhile to enquire in a local bar or café. Sometimes these have rooms above the premises that are available for hire on a nightly basis, often at very reasonable rates.

Although a stay in a *chambre d'hôte* can be a pleasant experience, often providing a better opportunity to experience Belgian family life than is possible in the more impersonal hotel, it should be realised that, unlike the situation in Britain where the B&B is at the cheaper end of the accommodation market, the *chambre d'hôte* is likely to cost as much as the average one-star hotel. So opting for the *chambre d'hote* is not necessarily a means of economising on accommodation though occasionally prices in private rooms are considerably lower than in nearby hotels - it is always worth checking. However, it must also be borne in mind that the average price of a one or even two-star hotel in the Ardennes is in the same price range as the average B&B in Britain: it is the low-star hotel that is the standard form of overnight accommodation in Belgium, not the B&B.

If intending to stay in one centre for more than a week, another option to consider is the *gîte rural* or holiday home. These are generally booked on a weekly basis. The local tourist office can provide details.

Youth Hostels and Gîtes d'Etape

There are youth hostels at Bouillon, Champlon, Herbeumont, Huy, Liège, Malmédy, Namur, Sankt Vith and Givet. These all belong to the Belgian YHA organisation (with the exception of Givet which is part of the French YHA network). In addition there are a number of private hostels known as *gîtes d'étape*. Details of some of these are given in the relevant sections, but for a full list of *gîtes d'étape* in the Ardennes consult the latest edition of the French publication *Gîtes d'étape de Randonnée et Refuges, France et Frontières* by Annick and Serge Mouraret (La Cadole, 6th edition, 1994). This invaluable book lists over 3600 simple establishments, suitable for walkers and other outdoor types, throughout France but also including regions that border France, including the Belgian Ardennes. The publication is in French but has an English lexicon.

It is advisable to book hostel accommodation in advance for the main holiday season or bank holidays. Bookings can be made through the Belgian

YHA for any of the 32 youth hostels in Belgium under their jurisdiction (or contact the youth hostels direct - see Appendix 4). To book accommodation in one of the private *gîtes d'étape* in the Ardennes, either look them up in *Gîtes et Refuges* (see above) or contact the local tourist office. Note that if booking hostel or *gîte d'étape* accommodation by phone, say a few days before (ie. without sending advance payment), then a bed for the night will normally only be reserved until a certain time in the early evening (you will be informed of the exact time).

Belgian youth hostels are similar in character to those in Britain and offer dormitory accommodation at comparable prices to their counterparts at home. Remember to take your YHA card with you, although it is possible for a visitor to join the Belgian YHA on the spot when arriving at a hostel. Private *gîtes d'étape* are similar in many ways to the "official" hostels, but it is not necessary to be a member of any organisation to stay at them. Prices are similar to those for youth hostels.

Camping and Caravanning
There are over 400 campsites in tiny Belgium, a large proportion of which are located in the Ardennes. The facilities at Belgian campsites vary from spartan (merely a water tap) to luxurious, with bars, restaurants, swimming pools, games & TV rooms and various sports facilities. Most of the campsites in the Ardennes lie somewhere between these two extremes. Virtually all campsites provide hot showers. A star grading system is in operation for official campsites throughout the country: One-star is the least pretentious, four-star has all mod cons. It is usually necessary to provide passport details and complete a registration form.

Details of campsites at each walking centre featured in this guidebook can be found under "Accommodation" in each section, but further and up-to-date information is available from local tourist offices. A small brochure listing many of the recognised campsites in Belgium, with addresses and telephone numbers, is usually available from tourist offices. This is normally updated annually, but there are often many other campsites to be found in the Ardennes, of every level of sophistication, that are not featured in this brochure - these will be discovered easily whilst on your travels.

There are commonly more caravanners than tent campers on most of the sites. It is possible to rent static caravans on a weekly basis, but also, particularly out of the main holiday season, some sites will have a few caravans to rent out on on a nightly basis, usually at reasonable rates (a sleeping bag is usually required for short-term bookings).

Campervans are extremely popular, particularly with Belgian, Dutch and German tourists, the great majority of the campsites in the Ardennes catering both for campervans and for touring caravans.

The Ardennes is not suitable for wild camping (*camping sauvage*). In many areas it is strictly illegal and several *Camping Interdit* (No Camping) signs will be seen. If intending to camp anywhere other than on an official campsite it is essential first to obtain permission from the landowner.

TOURIST OFFICES

Every town and many of the villages and other small centres in the Ardennes have a tourist office (*office du tourisme* or *syndicat d'initiative*). Virtually every tourist office in the Ardennes will have at least one walking map of the area, and often small pamphlets describing local walks. The most suitable maps for walking in the locality will nearly always be on sale in the tourist office, but rarely elsewhere. (These maps are in fact often tourist office publications.) The local *syndicat d'initiative* is also often responsible for erecting the signposts and waymarks for the official walking trails in the region.

In summary, the local tourist office can provide the following:

1. Full details of all types of accommodation (*hôtels*, *chambres d'hôte*, private rooms, *gîtes rural*, *gîtes d'étape*, youth hostels and campsites) available in the area. Staff in most offices will also book accommodation on your behalf.
2. Details of local bus, train and taxi services.
3. Walking maps of the local area.
4. A small selection of walking guide booklets to the region, and to long distance trails that pass through the town or village (these are usually in French, but some are also in Dutch - none, to the author's knowledge, have been produced in English).
5. General tourist information on things to see and places to visit in the area.
6. Details of local events, carnivals and fêtes, etc.
7. Information on organised and independent outdoor activities (canoe-kayaking, rock climbing, mountain biking, horse riding, pony trekking, etc).

The addresses and telephone numbers of all of the relevant tourist offices can be found in Appendix 3.

EATING OUT - BELGIAN FOOD

Belgium is justly famous for the quality of its cuisine, second only to France in all of Europe. As an added bonus, eating out in Belgium is generally somewhat cheaper than in Britain. Food in the Ardennes is basically French in style. Most restaurants have a range of fixed-price menus, as well as *à la carte*. The average fixed-price menu is usually of three or four courses and consists of a choice of hors d'oeuvre, a main course (usually a meat or fish dish) and sweet, fruit and/or cheese. Wine is generally extra and is somewhat more expensive than in France. Many restaurants in Belgium are hotel-restaurants, but meals are almost always available to non-residents. Quite often a restaurant will double as a café or bar and will serve drinks and snacks to customers not requiring a meal. Food in youth hostels or *gîtes d'étape*, where provided (see Appendix 4), is generally of the same quality and price as in the more basic restaurant. Vegetarians will find life generally a little more difficult in Belgium than in Britain, although vegetarian meals are slowly becoming more widespread these days. If there is none on the menu a vegetarian alternative will nearly always be provided on request.

There are a great number of bars and cafés in this holiday area. On several of the walks described cafés, restaurants and food shops are passed en route, but where there is no possibility of obtaining refreshment this fact is made clear under the heading "Refreshments" in the walk write-up. In some of the more popular centres, such as La Roche, many of the shops, including food shops, are open on Sundays, even during the winter months. Some of the smaller cafés in the countryside open principally to serve a particular trade. For example the several bars and cafés along the Lower Lesse that cater for the summer kayak enthusiasts (Walk 4) close when this season comes to an end; other establishments that lie along cross-country ski trails may only open in wintertime on weekends when there is good snow for skiing, when trade is likely to be brisk.

Several of the better quality hotel-restaurants in the Ardennes offer special "Gastronomic weekends", particularly outside the high season when they are trying to tempt clients in order to fill their establishments. These offers often represent good value for money. Local tourist offices will have details.

The Ardennes is renowned for its paté and smoked hams, and for its game, particularly wild boar and venison. Belgium is home to some 500 different brands of beer, mainly lager in type, many of them brewed by small local breweries. Beer is the national drink: it is to Belgium what wine is to France. The country is also famous for the high quality of its chocolates. Finally, mention must be made of waffles (*gaufres* in French and *wafels* in Dutch/Flemish), a Belgian speciality.

EQUIPMENT

As the climate of the Ardennes is not dissimilar from that of Britain, clothing suitable for walking in, say, the Yorkshire Dales or the Cotswolds would be appropriate. Except for some of the walks in the Hautes Fagnes, on the higher stretches of moorland, the terrain is not particularly rugged or exposed to the elements, so that full mountain gear, as would be carried in the Lake District or Scotland, for example, is not generally required, although if walking during the winter months do remember that severe weather conditions can be encountered.

A small day-sac for waterproofs, spare clothes, food and drink etc. will be sufficient for the walks described in this book. A compass is useful, although not always necessary. Remember a small first-aid kit and suntan cream.

A few of the walks described in this book can be walked in good quality trainers or stout shoes. However, this is only advisable during a period of prolonged dry weather, and remember that these types of footwear give little or no ankle support. For the majority of walks described, however, lightweight walking boots are the most suitable form of footwear, preferably well worn in and with a good grip. Heavyweight mountain boots are not required for walking in the Ardennes. Unfortunately, many types of lightweight boots are far from waterproof. Gaiters are sensible when conditions are muddy or wet, and particularly for the couple of walks that may involve fording streams.

Some of the terrain of the Ardennes, particularly in the Hautes Fagnes and along some of the narrow, stream-filled valleys, tends to be rather wet and muddy outside the summer season. At such times the "Nokia" boot, known generally in Britain as the bogtrotter, a superior form of wellington boot, is excellent. These are Scandinavian in origin, much shorter in length than the standard Wellington, and if fitted with a Sorbothane insole are quite comfortable for many of the day walks detailed in this book, although they are not recommended for multi-day treks, such as the GR 5, nor for day walks exceeding about 10 miles. They also have a reasonable grip on the sole and heal, although boots with good grips are preferable on steep, loose or slippery ground. The author is presently using his second pair of bogtrotters, having possessed a previous pair for about seven years, during which time he walked many hundreds of miles in them before they finally fell apart. Bogtrotters are perfectly waterproof and although they are priced far above the average pair of wellington boots, the cost is much lower than for most walking boots.

Footwear advice is given under "Footwear" in the introduction to each walk.

MAPS
Walkers' Maps of the Ardennes
The maps of most use to the walker in the Belgian Ardennes are those generally produced, published and sold by the various tourist offices. A map suitable for walkers, at an appropriate scale and with all the local, regional and long distance trails overlaid on it, is referred to as a *Carte des Promenades* in French, a *Wandelkaart* in Flemish/Dutch and a *Wanderkarte* in German. These maps vary considerably in design, style and quality - there is no uniformity in the mapping of the various regions of the Ardennes. The majority of the maps are in colour, but one or two may appear in black and white. Some have detailed contouring and shading, with topographical features and local numbered walking trails clearly marked on them, whilst others are uncontoured and unclear with regard to the exact routes of some of the trails. Some of the better quality maps are accurate and easy to use, the maps of the Bouillon, Vresse-sur-Semois and La Roche areas being good examples of this category. The mapping for these high-quality maps is usually carried out by the IGN, the national mapping authority (see "IGN Maps" below). Other walkers' maps, unfortunately, are little more than sketch maps and leave a lot to be desired. One of the

problems with the poorer quality walkers' maps is that underlying details and features, such as roads and the exact location of villages, cannot always be easily deciphered. However, the majority of the tourist office maps, when used in conjunction with the local waymarking (which itself varies greatly in standard from area to area - see "Waymarking and Navigation" below) are satisfactory. Most of the tourist office walkers' maps are at a scale of 1:25,000, a few at an even larger scale of 1:20,000. Local walking trails are often overlaid on the maps with a continuous or dashed, red or black line.

New editions of tourist office walkers' maps may appear with time, not only from a need to improve quality, but also when a trail network is altered significantly, with changes to the trail numbering systems, or when new trails are developed and added to the network. Sometimes changes will be made to an existing map when the stocks of one edition have all been sold: slight changes may then be made before the map is reprinted. Generally, however, the trails in most areas of the Ardennes are now well established, so that there are likely, in most cases, to be only relatively minor changes in the future.

The 53 walks, in 14 centres, described in this book are covered by the following tourist office (or similar) maps for walkers:

1. Street map of Namur (Namur Tourist Office)
2. *Promenades dans l'Entité de Dinant: Falmagne, Falmignoul*; maps inside this folder at 1:25,000 scale to *Itinéraire Orange*, *Itinéraire Rouge* and *Itinéraire Bleu* (Dinant Tourist Office).
3. *Carte du Parc de Furfooz et des Sites notables jalonnant la Promenade* (available at the Furfooz National Park entrance).
4. *Rochefort - à Pied, à Cheval, à Bicyclette*. 1:25,000 scale map (Rochefort and Han-sur-Lesse Tourist Offices).
5. *Promenades Balisées - La Haute Lesse et Rochefort - Carte No. 2*, at a scale of 1:25,000 (Rochefort and Han-sur-Lesse Tourist Offices).
6. *Carte Promenades: Lessive, Eprave, Jamblinne, Villers/Lesse*, at a scale of 1:10,000 (Rochefort and Han-sur-Lesse Tourist Offices).
7. *Carte des Promenades de Vresse-sur-Semois*, at a scale of 1:25,000 (Vresse-sur-Semois Tourist Office).
8. *Carte des Promenades du Grand Bouillon*, at a scale of 1:25,000 (Bouillon Tourist Office).
9. *Carte des Promenades Pédestres*, at a scale of 1:25,000 (Saint-Hubert Tourist Office).
10. Sketch map of the Open Air Musée de la Vie Rurale en Wallonie (available at the entrance to the museum in Fourneau Saint-Hubert).
11. *Promenades*, at a scale of 1:25,000 (Hotton Tourist Office).
12. *La Roche-en-Ardenne*, at a scale of 1:25,000 (La Roche Tourist Office).
13. *Carte des Promenades Pédestres*, at a scale of 1:25,000 (Vielsalm Tourist Office).
14. *La Carte du Promeneur*, at a scale of 1:20,000 (Spa Tourist Office).

15. *Carte des Promenades de Stavelot (Stavelot et Coo)*, at a scale of 1:20,000 (Stavelot Tourist Office).
16. *Trois-Ponts en Ardenne - Promenades, Wandelingen*, at a scale of 1:25,000 (Trois-Ponts Tourist Office).
17. *Promenades Malmédy - Waimes*, at a scale of 1:25,000 (Malmédy Tourist Office).
18. *St Vith Wanderkarte*, at a scale of 1:25,000 (Sankt Vith Tourist Office).
19. *Reuland, Ouren, Burg-Reuland: Wanderkarte, Cartes des Promenades, Wandelingen*, at a scale of 1:25,000 (Sankt Vith Tourist Office).

For further details of specific maps see "Maps" in the write-up to each walk. See Appendix 3 for addresses and telephone numbers of all relevant tourist offices.

IGN Maps

The Belgian Institut Géographique National (IGN), the equivalent of the British Ordnance Survey, has a full National Survey, the entire country being covered by 72 sheets at a scale of 1:50,000. The country is also completely covered by IGN maps at 1:25,000 scale, most of the areas covered by one 1:50,000 sheet being divided into 4 sheets at 1:25,000. Although these maps are cartographically accurate, they are of limited use to the walker in the Ardennes as they do not indicate walking trails as such. Furthermore, each sheet is more expensive than any of the tourist office walkers' maps described above. Nevertheless, for completeness the IGN maps of the National Survey at a scale of 1:50,000 have been given for each walk described, for those who wish to use the most accurate maps available.

The 53 walks described are all covered by the following eight IGN maps in the 1:50,000 scale series: sheet numbers 49, 50, 54, 55, 56, 59, 60 and 61.

Walk Booklets

Should you wish to do some additional walks to the ones described in this book, it is relatively easy to devise your own by use of the local tourist office walkers' maps or the booklets to local walks. The booklets vary greatly in quality, some having quite reasonable IGN or sketch maps, so that the route can be easily followed if you are unable to read the text (they are often published in both French and Dutch, but never, to the author's knowledge, in English). However, some of them contain very poor sketch maps, or even only descriptions of walks in French or Dutch without a map of any sort. The booklets describe a range of walks, from day and half-day rambles to short strolls of an hour or less, and are available at several of the walking centres in the Ardennes.

Maps to Long Distance Paths - Topo Guides

There are a large number of long distance (GR) trails in the Ardennes (see section on Grandes Randonnées, and also Appendix 5) and a few readers may wish to sample some of them. The best maps to use for these trails are those in the special Topo guides that describe the trails. These booklets can be purchased locally or from the Belgian Long Distance Path organisations (see Appendix 6 for addresses). One Topo Guide usually covers one Grande Randonnée, or sometimes two or three relatively short trails. The maps in the guides are usually official IGN maps, at a scale of 1:25,000 or 1:50,000, with the route of the GR trail overlaid in red. There is an accompanying text, usually in French, or sometimes in Dutch (never in English), which includes details of accommodation en route and availability of public transport.

General Map of the Ardennes

The best general map of the Ardennes for planning purposes, and for use when travelling around the area, either on public transport or by private transport, is the one published by Geocart, at a scale of 1:150,000, entitled *Les Ardennes - De Ardennen*. This map is recommended for several reasons: 1) It is extremely useful for general planning, showing the whole region at a glance. 2) It is more detailed than most road maps, so is useful when driving along some of the minor and less frequented roads in the region. 3) It shows the positions of tourist facilities and amenities, such as campsites and youth hostels. 4) The locations of tourist information centres are given. 5) Areas for *ski de fond* (langlauf or cross-country skiing), canoeing, sailing, tennis, rock climbing, etc, are indicated. 6) Long distance (GR) trails are marked. 7) General tourist attractions, such as show caves, museums, churches, castles, etc, are marked. 8) Several larger scale maps of the principal towns and large villages in the Ardennes are included on the sheet. 9) The whole of the Grand Duchy of Luxembourg is included on the map. This map is not, however, suitable for use as a walkers' map to follow the walks described in this book, or any others in the region.

Road Map of Belgium

There are several road maps and road atlases of Belgium available, some of which cover the whole of the Low Countries, ie. including Holland and the Grand Duchy of Luxembourg. The one that the author would recommend, for its clarity and ease of use, is the Michelin road map of Belgium and Luxembourg, at a scale of 1:350,000 (Sheet No. 409). The motorways (with exit numbers) and other trunk and main roads are shown and numbered clearly, and even the minor roads are generally easy to distinguish, which is not the case with all of the road maps available. Those arriving at one of the Dutch ports will also need a road map of Holland - the sister Michelin map of the Netherlands, at a scale of 1:400,000 (Sheet No. 408), can be recommended (this has an insert at a larger scale of 1:100,000 for the Europort/Hook of Holland area, which is very useful for those arriving at these ports). Drivers who plan to arrive at one of the French Channel ports will also need a road map of the north-western tip of

France for the 50kms or so before entering Belgium.

WAYMARKING AND NAVIGATION

Walking trails in Europe are generally waymarked more thoroughly than those in Britain. The situation in the Ardennes is no exception. However, although trail waymarking is extensive, there is no uniformity of the waymarking of the local trails in the various regions of the Ardennes. The long distance trails (GR routes) are an exception: the standard waymarking system used throughout the Ardennes (and indeed throughout Belgium, Holland and France) is that of red and white painted stripes, which occur, usually in a horizontal position with white above red, on rocks, boulders, trees, posts, fences, telegraph poles, etc. But for local walking trails each centre has adopted its own system of numbering and waymarking. Some are far superior to others, both quality and style differing considerably. For example, in Rochefort and Han-sur-Lesse district there are diamond-shaped metal waymarks which bear the name of the local walking trails, whereas the Spa district authority has opted for a very professional system using easily recognisable yellow signboards. There are no signposts in Malmédy and the surrounding area, but their walks are recognised by yellow waymarks which bear the letter M (for Malmédy) followed by a number. The Stavelot and Coo authorities have used symbols such as fish, birds, and animals. The rather poor system in the Burg-Reuland area compares very unfavourably with the excellent signboards used in the vicinity of Spa. The waymarking in each area is unique to that district.

Whatever trail identification system is used, the trail waymarks on the ground will always correspond with those identified on the local tourist office walkers' map, a principal reason why these maps are recommended in preference to the IGN National Survey maps (see "Maps" above). Remember not to confuse the local trail numbering system with the Walk Numbers used in this book (ie. from Walk 1 to Walk 53 in the "Guide" section below).

The local trails themselves also vary considerably. Walking trails are sometimes much longer in one area than in a neighbouring district. In some regions nearly all the trails consist of forest paths and tracks, whilst in others considerable use has been made of quiet country lanes for walking. Sometimes the system is one of an interlacing network of trails, whereas in other areas each route is waymarked as a separate entity.

It must be emphasised that Belgium does not have the sort of "rights of way" network that is familiar to the British walker. Ramblers must restrict their walking to the waymarked walking trails, for other paths are usually privately owned and not open to the public. There are also some areas of the Ardennes that are nature reserves where the public are generally forbidden to wander. Always keep a look-out for signs prohibiting access (see below) and please obey them. It is unlikely that in the future any of the routes described in this guidebook will be closed to the public, except on a temporary basis (eg. on certain days during the hunting season - see "Hunting" below), although it is certainly not inconceivable that a landowner may decide to close a particular path. If such an unlikely event does occur then the fact will be made obvious on the ground, with barriers and *Acces Interdit* or similar notices. In such a case the local authorities will almost certainly provide an alternative waymarked route. If in any doubt then please do not trespass, but return if possible to the local tourist office to enquire about the situation.

It should be possible for much of the time to remain on the trail by following waymarks and making use of the route descriptions and sketch maps provided in this book. However, it would be foolish to ignore the use of map and compass. These should always be carried and one's position on the map checked frequently. A compass, although not always essential, will enable bearings given in the text to be checked and will certainly be an aid, when used in conjunction with the map, in relocating the correct trail if this is inadvertently lost. It should be stressed that navigation on most of the trails used in this book is generally not difficult, the majority of the walks being suitable for the novice navigator.

Certain notices should be understood. *Propriété Privée* or *Défense d'Entrer* means that the area is private and entry forbidden. *Chemin Privée* means that the footpath or track is private and access not allowed. *Acces Interdit* also means means no entry. The signs *Réserve du Chasse* and *Chasse Privée* do not refer to walkers, but indicate that hunting rights are reserved for the owner of the land.

GRANDES RANDONNEES

Belgium has an extensive network of long distance paths (LDPs) called *Grandes Randonnées* in the French speaking regions and *Grote Routepaden* in the Flemish areas (literally Big Walks in both languages). The abbreviation "GR" is commonly used to denote a long distance path. Each GR route has been designated a number, eg. GR 5, GR 14, GR 572, etc, the system adopted being very similar to that used in the extensive long distance path network found in neighbouring France. Sometimes an alternative or *variante* route of a GR trail is qualified with an alphabetical letter after the GR number. For example the GR 579A is a variant route of part of the GR 579; similarly the 12B is a variant route of a section of the GR 12. The majority of GR trails are linear walking routes, but some are circular in nature, these being generally referred to as *Tours* in Belgium and France, eg. the 81 mile (130km) circuit of the GR 563 (GR H) in the Ardennes is known as the Tour du Pays de Herve.

Although nearly all Belgian GR trails have been assigned an identification number, it is often the case in the Ardennes that a GR route is known more usually, not by their designated number, but by the initials of their full name or title. For example the GR 56 is more widely known as the GR E (GR of the Cantons de l'Est), the GR 57 as the GR O (GR Ourthe) and the GR 577 as the

GR LL (GR of the Lesse et Lomme). The abbreviations GR E, GR LL, etc, will be seen on waymarks usually more frequently than their respective GR numbers. One of the more famous GR trails in the Ardennes does not in fact carry a number at all, but is known simply as the GR AE, which stands for Ardennes-Eifel; this LDP links the Ardennes with the neighbouring Eifel range of wooded hills in Germany. Several of the above-mentioned GR trails and others will be encountered on the walks featured in this guidebook, and small sections of some of them are utilised as parts of our walks. The most well-known and venerated long distance path in the Belgian Ardennes, one that traverses the entire region form north to south, is the GR 5 or E 2 ultra-long distance European Path. (See Appendix 5 for a reference list of the principal GR trails in the Belgian Ardennes.)

For more information on the E 2 and the other European Long Distance E Footpaths contact the European Ramblers' Association (see Appendix 6 for address).

FLORA AND FAUNA

The Ardennes is covered in extensive tracts of mature woodland, the predominant indigenous trees being beech, oak, birch and alder. Spruce, an introduced species, is commonly seen. Heather covers considerable areas of high heathland and moorland, its purple flowers making walking a delight during the late summer and early autumn. Broom and gorse are also common and alpine plants are frequently seen. The soil at the higher altitudes in the Hautes Fagnes is poor and acidic in character. There are areas of peat bogs and sphagnum moss holds considerable quantities of the very pure water for which the region is famous.

Prehistoric tribes hunted in the area now known as the Ardennes for bison, tarpan (a type of wild horse), lynx and brown bear. These animals are now all extinct in the Ardennes, but examples of them can be seen in the several wildlife parks (*parcs à gibier*) found in the region (for example at Han-sur-Lesse, Walks 7, 8, 10 and 11, and near Vielsalm, Walk 32). The modern huntsman shoots for deer, which are present in the forests in considerable numbers, for pheasant and for wild boar, the latter a speciality on the menus of many Ardennes restaurants. Walkers who may be concerned at the thought of meeting an aggressive wild boar whilst walking in the Ardennes forests should rest assured that the chance of such an encounter is very unlikely (of more danger perhaps are trigger happy huntsmen! - see "Hunting" below). Rabbits are very common and other small mammals, such as hedgehogs and badgers, live in the region. Red squirrels are also not uncommon. The often muddy floor of the Ardennes forest is ideal for making paw prints of the various animal species that roam the woods, most of which are very secretive, and with a little patience and diligence several of these can be recognised. There are publications available in the region that provide the shape and size of these animal prints.

HUNTING

Hunting, mainly for deer, wild boar and pheasant, takes place in the Ardennes, and during the time an organised hunt is in progress it is forbidden to walk on the trails affected. Occasionally certain areas, particularly woodland areas, are closed off to the general public for one or a few days for shooting/hunting purposes, usually during the autumn months, typically between mid-September and the end of December. On these occasions even the roads in the area, as well as the walking and riding trails, can be closed to the public. This is made evident by police notices posted up at appropriate points, past which it is prohibited to proceed, and the periods to which it applies (in French, of course!). If planning to walk in the Ardennes during the autumn months it is therefore advisable to enquire at the local tourist offices whether hunting is to be staged during the period that you intend to walk, and if so to which areas and walking trails it applies. If a shoot is being held it is likely to affect only a few of the many trails normally available in an area, and the tourist office will be only too pleased to advise and tell you where you may safely walk. These rules, which are strictly enforced, are designed to protect the general public. Each area used for hunting is only usually affected on a few days per month throughout the hunting season, typically at weekends. Only a relatively small percentage of the total huge area of the Ardennes forest is affected by organised hunting.

Perhaps of more danger to the walker than the large organised hunt is the lone huntsman who is out shooting informally. Always keep an eye and ear open for shooting if walking in the forests, particularly during the autumn months, and if you inadvertently walk into an area where shooting is in progress make your presence immediately known, before beating a hasty and safe retreat. The notice *Tir à Balles* warns of possible shooting in the area.

During the many days that the author has spent walking in the Ardennes he has only been affected once by hunting activities, and that was because he had not bothered to check beforehand that a shoot had been organised for that day in the area that he had planned to walk. Even on that occasion it was a very simple matter to choose a route that avoided the hunting area.

DIFFICULTIES, HAZARDS AND SAFETY

The majority of the walks described in this guidebook could in no way be described as hazardous, being in woodland and gentle hill country, rarely very far from civilisation. However, on just a few of the rambles it may be necessary to ford streams. The severity of such crossings will vary considerably, from a stroll across an almost unnoticed dry stream bed during a long dry summer, to a demanding crossing of a fast flowing and moderately deep stretch of water after continual heavy rainfall during a very wet period in spring, autumn or winter. It cannot be stressed too strongly that when rivers and streams are in flood no attempt should be made to cross them, unless the walker is very experienced in such matters, has the correct equipment and clothing, and is accompanied by similarly experienced and equipped companions. But this caution only applies to two or three of the walks in this book, where a warning of the possibility of a difficult stream crossing under wet conditions is clearly given under the heading "Special Problems" in the write-up to the walk.

With the exception of one itinerary, none of the walks described in this book requires scrambling ability. Most of the rambles follow forest tracks, footpaths and quiet country lanes and are relatively undemanding in terms of physical effort and navigational skills required. Many of the gradients in the Ardennes are quite gentle, although there are the occasional steeper climbs. A particular note is generally made in the write-up to the walk where the route involves more ascent and descent than most, and where some of the climbs are quite steep. It is not easy to compare the landscape and walking in the Ardennes to any area in the British Isles, but as a rough guideline the walking is closer in nature and severity to that found in, say, the Cotswolds, South Downs or New Forest, than to the terrain and walking often encountered in, for example, the Pennines or Brecon Beacons. Several of the walks, particularly the shorter length ones, are suitable for families with children. The one walk described in this book where a head for heights and the ability to move safely on steep ground is required is the "ladder walk" from Rochehaut (Walk No. 19).

There is relatively little danger on the walks described in this book of being far from assistance in the event of an accident, so the main threat to the lone walker could come from other human beings. As the trails often follow quite lonely stretches of woodland and hillside that are rarely very far from centres of population, the possibility of being attacked or robbed is certainly a real one, although the chances of such an occurrence are fairly small, and certainly no greater than those to be expected in the popular walking regions of the UK. Walkers should be aware of the dangers, however slight, and decide for themselves whether they consider the risks acceptable or otherwise.

A warning should be given of the possibility of encountering ticks in the undergrowth of the Ardennes, particularly during the late spring and summer months. Ticks are small arachnids (they have eight legs and are related to the spider) which are found on a variety of vegetation, but which attach themselves with considerable tenacity to passing mammals, including deer, sheep and man.

During the summer months, the skin should be inspected from time to time whilst walking in the Ardennes (or elsewhere in Europe for that matter, including Britain) for signs of ticks. If they become a problem then long walking trousers should be worn rather than shorts, and particular care taken with bare arms, avoiding arm contact with vegetation wherever possible.

Ticks, to my knowledge, are no more prevalent in the Ardennes than they are in other areas of Europe, and the threat of encountering them should not deter walkers from walking there or elsewhere.

The walker in the Ardennes should also be aware of the dangers of bracken.

This plant will be encountered occasionally, although it grows perhaps not as rampantly as it does in some areas of Britain. Apart from being a favourite habitat of ticks, the spores of the bracken plant are thought to be carcinogenic. Therefore the wise and informed walker will avoid contact with the fronds of the plant, particularly during the autumn when the spores on the under surface are in the process of dispersal. Walkers wearing shorts should be especially careful.

Other dangers of walking in the Ardennes are similar to those found in the UK. Hypothermia, sunburn, dehydration and exhaustion are all potential problems, though not especially so in the Ardennes.

Dogs
Guard dogs are very occasionally a problem when encountered on some of the isolated properties passed on a few of these walks. The majority of dogs are more "bark than bite", but they can be unnerving at times. They are often chained, but frequently on a long chain, so be sure to keep more than a chain length away from them. Some walkers advocate the use of a stout stick to fend off an attack, but this may simply anger the animal. Never run or walk quickly past an unfriendly dog, as this may release its chase response. Walk slowly, backwards if necessary, facing the animal, keeping it in sight at all times. However, do not stare at the dog, as staring is a threat and the animal may read it as a challenge and is thus more likely to attack. If a bite is sustained, however slight, it is important to seek medical advice as soon as possible. More advice on how to deal with a potentially dangerous dog will be found in the leaflet *How should you cope with an unfriendly dog?*, produced and issued free by the RSPCA (send SAE to RSPCA, Causeway, Horsham, West Sussex RH12 1HG).

PHOTOGRAPHY
The best type of camera to take is probably the 35mm SLR; with a good quality medium zoom lens (eg. 28-80mm). This would obviate the need to change lenses continually, though zoom lenses are themselves heavier than prime lenses. Weight can be radically reduced by using a good quality 35mm compact camera with a zoom lens. The quality can be almost as good as an SLR camera, but the compact camera is light and small, easily fitting into a pocket.

Both used and unused film should be protected from heat by placing it well inside the rucksac. It is advisable to take all exposed film home rather than risk loss or damage by posting it back to Britain to be processed.

LANGUAGE
The region covered by this guidebook is all within the French-speaking area of Belgium, known as Wallonia. The Walloons actually speak a dialect of French, but those who speak standard French should have no problems in communicating with the locals. English is fairly widely understood, nonetheless, particularly by

the younger generation, and by people in the tourist industry. If any language problems are by chance experienced when travelling through the Flemish-speaking areas of Belgium en route for the Ardennes, then the glossary of Flemish words in Appendix 3 should be useful. No doubt many Dutch-speaking walkers will be met during your stay in the Ardennes, and if there are any problems using English then once again Appendix 3 should be of some assistance.

German is the predominant language in the so-called Eastern Cantons (Ostkantone, Cantons de l'Est or Oostkantons), which lie on the extreme eastern edge of the country, bordering Germany to the east, and to the north of the Grand Duchy of Luxembourg. Those with a knowledge of German will find this language of use when walking in the Cantons de l'Est, although French is understood by a considerable number of the population of these areas.

MONEY - BANKS AND POST OFFICES

The unit of currency is the Belgian franc, commonly abbreviated to BF or BEF. Although the Belgian franc is divided into 100 centimes, the value of the latter is so low as to be impracticable. Common banknotes are 100, 500, 1000 and 5000BF. Besides cash, Eurocheques, travellers' cheques and credit cards are all widely used in Belgium. (Belgian banks can levy a fairly high service charge for cashing travellers' cheques.) Mastercards (Access), Visa cards and other well-known credit cards are widely accepted in Belgium and are a useful form of payment for hotel bills, restaurant meals and rail tickets.

The Eurocheque card will be accepted in many cash dispensers in Belgium. Contact your bank at home before leaving for Belgium to ensure that you have the correct card and that the bank participates in the international scheme. Several of the towns included in this guidebook have such facilities for obtaining cash.

Banks will be found in all of the major centres featured in this guidebook. Normal banking hours in Belgium are from around 9am until midday and from 2pm until 4pm, on weekdays, although opening times of individual banks do vary, so that it is wise to check. Some banks stay open at lunchtime and increasingly now banks are open on Saturday mornings. Exchange facilities, open from early in the morning until late at night, will be found at the major border crossings along the motorways.

With a Girobank account, cash can be obtained at most Belgian post offices. You need a Postcheque card and a book of Postcheques (no charge is levied). The Girobank account in Britain is debited after the documents reach Girobank headquarters. Opening hours of post offices in Belgium are normally from 9am until midday and from 2pm to 5pm, weekdays, although some larger branches may stay open over lunchtime. Post offices are usually closed on Saturdays.

The French franc may sometimes be accepted as payment in the Belgian

Ardennes, although if paying for services with this currency then don't expect a good rate of exchange. On occasions car parking metres will accept French, Dutch and German, as well as Belgian coins!

Walkers intending to visit the Grand Duchy of Luxembourg whilst in the area should note that Belgian francs are legal tender in Luxembourg, the two currencies being tied, with the same rate of exchange against all other currencies. Change, however, will invariably be given in Luxembourg francs, which are not normally accepted back in Belgium.

INSURANCE

It is advisable to take out travel and medical insurance for the duration of the holiday as medical, and particularly hospitalisation, charges are very expensive in Belgium. Ensure that the policy has an adequate medical sum insured. Several companies issue cover within Europe for "hillwalking, rambling, scrambling and camping". Such a policy would be more than adequate for the walks described in this book. A good general policy designed for the independent traveller would be suitable, although it is always advisable to check first with the insurance company that your activities (viz. walking in the Ardennes) would not invalidate a claim. Drivers are strongly advised to obtain a Green Card level of insurance.

There are certain reciprocal rights available for British subjects in Belgium under the National Health Service arrangements within the EEC. Information concerning eligibility for medical cover under this scheme and the necessary E111 form can be obtained from local DHSS offices or from main post offices. It is not, however, advisable to rely solely on Form E111.

TELEPHONE BETWEEN BRITAIN AND BELGIUM

Public telephones in Belgium, as in the UK, are a mixture of payphones and those requiring a phonecard. They are fairly numerous in the Ardennes, being found in most of the villages and towns and even in some of the small rural hamlets.

If intending to make several phone calls whilst in Belgium it is better to use the cardphones, which can be purchased from most post offices and some shops (newsagents and the like) and at certain other advertised outlets. Payment direct to a cashier can sometimes be made at post offices for use of a phone. A call made from a phone in a hotel, café or restaurant will be more expensive than from a public phonebox.

The procedure for placing a call to the UK. is very simple. Lift the receiver and insert the appropriate coins or phonecard, after which a dialling tone will be heard. A digital exchange system has been in operation in Belgium for a considerable time. First dial 00 (the code for an international line) and pause until a second dialling tone is heard. Next dial 44 (the code for the UK). Pause again before dialling the STD code of the number required, but minus the initial zero. Lastly, dial the number of the line required. For example, to phone a number in Glasgow (STD code 0141) dial: 00, pause, 44, pause, 141 123 4567.

If phoning Belgium from Britain the code is 00 (for an international line), followed by 32 (the code for Belgium) and then the individual number. The initial zero of the area, city or town code is omitted when phoning a Belgian number from abroad. For example, to phone the Belgian National Tourist Office in Brussels (see Appendix 3) dial 00 32 2 504 03 90 from Britain, dial 02 504 03 90 when in Belgium but outside the capital, and dial 504 03 90 when in Brussels.

TIME IN BELGIUM
Belgium follows Central European Time (CET). For most of the year Belgian time is one hour ahead of the time in Britain, ie. Belgian summer time is one hour ahead of BST and French winter time is one hour ahead of GMT. For about four weeks of the year, (liable to change) usually from the last week in September to the last week in October, Britain and Belgium are on the same time, ie. the clocks in Belgium go back one hour at the end of September (whereas in Britain the clocks go back at the end of October), and go forward one hour at the end of March (the latter on the same day as the clocks change in the UK.). This situation will change if CET is eventually introduced into Britain, in which case Belgium and Britain should have the same time throughout the year. The neighbouring countries of France, Holland and Germany are also on CET and follow the same time changes as Belgium in March and September.

PUBLIC HOLIDAYS IN BELGIUM
Belgium has somewhat more public holidays than Britain. Fortunately between June and October there are only two to consider, viz. National Day on July 21st and the Fête of the Assumption on August 15th. On both of these days the public transport system is considerably affected and banks and several shops are closed, so it is well to bear these days in mind and to plan accordingly. In the spring there are public holidays in Belgium at Easter and on May 1st (Labour Day), Ascension Day and Whit Monday. In the autumn there are bank holidays on November 1st (All Saints Day) and November 11th (1918 Armistice Day). November 15th, the Fête de la Dynastie, the old King's birthday, is a partial holiday (official and governmental), but few facilities are affected. Christmas Day (but not December 26th) and New Year's Day are also public holidays.

VARIOUS TYPES OF WALKING AND OUTDOOR HOLIDAYS IN THE ARDENNES
One, Two or Multi-Centre Holidays
A visit to one or two of the walking centres featured in this book would make an ideal one week holiday in the Ardennes, perhaps mixing walking with general sightseeing or another outdoor activity (see below). For a two week holiday some people will wish to stay at just one centre for the whole period, although there should be ample time to visit two, three or even four centres.

It is a good idea to select centres which are different in character from each other in order to get a good overview of the Ardennes during one holiday. Reference to the introductory sections for each centre in this book will help you to make a choice of centres. Some walkers, particularly those who have their own private transport, could easily spend just a couple of days each in a number of centres over their holiday period, as driving times between the areas covered by this book are moderately short. However, for a more relaxing holiday it is advisable to explore a few areas in depth and at a leisurely pace. The closeness of the Ardennes to Britain means that a weekend or long weekend break in the Ardennes is easily possible, particularly for those living in the south-east of England.

Walking Combined with Sightseeing Holidays

It would be rather a pity if the walker concentrated all of his or her time on walking, good though it may be in the Ardennes, without visiting some of the places of interest for which the area is justly famous. A holiday in the Ardennes without visiting one of the spectacular show caves in the area is almost unthinkable. As some of the best of these (eg. the caves at Han-sur-Lesse, Rochefort and Dinant) are found at some of the walking centres featured in this book, it would be easy to combine a visit to one of the caves with a half-day ramble in the area. For the historically and architecturally minded there are numerous museums, castles, cathedrals and churches to visit, whilst for those with an interest in science and astronomy there is even a space and telecommunications centre in the heart of the Ardennes (see Walk 10 - Lessive). Brief details of some of these various attractions are given under "Places of Interest" for each walk, but for more detailed information consult a general tourist guidebook and/or local tourist office.

Walking Combined with Another Outdoor Pursuit

The Ardennes is essentially a holiday area for outdoor enthusiasts. Apart from walking, other popular activities include canoe-kayaking, river rafting, mountain biking, rock climbing, horse riding, pony trekking, and during the winter *ski de fond* (cross-country skiing). Equipment for all of these activities can be hired from a number of centres in the Ardennes, and instruction is available in most cases, although the language of instruction is usually either French or Dutch (enquire at the tourist offices).

The main outdoor attraction, apart from walking, in the Ardennes during the summer months is canoeing-kayaking. There are three main rivers on which the activity is very popular: the Lesse, Ourthe and the Semois. The principal centres for canoeing are from Anseremme (near Dinant) and from Han-sur-Lesse on the River Lesse, from La Roche and from Hotton on the River Ourthe, and from Bouillon and Alle on the River Semois. All of these centres are featured in this book. Canoe-kayaking takes place between April and October when the rivers are generally low enough to make the activity relatively safe, even for absolute beginners. For non-swimmers life-jackets are usually available for a small fee, although the water level is often very shallow. No previous experience is necessary: although instruction is generally not given, most people teach themselves the rudiments of paddling and steering the craft, usually within about the first 10mins or so. There are several companies in each location who generally offer a day or half-day package, which includes transport out from a base to a starting point upstream, and the hire of a canoe on arrival. One or two-seater canoes are usually available. The canoe is then paddled downstream back to base. There is usually a choice of distances: absolute beginners should not be too ambitious. A sense of humour is imperative!

For further information see the introductory sections for the chapters on Dinant, Bouillon and La Roche.

Mountain biking is also very popular in the Ardennes. There are marked trails designed for the mountain biker, which are shown on special maps usually available from tourist offices. Enthusiasts need not bring their own bikes as these can be hired from a number of centres.

Keep-fit enthusiasts can try their hand at the several "fitness areas" or *parcours sportifs*, where simple apparatus to increase fitness and tone various muscle groups is permanently laid out in the woods, often alongside the walking trails (eg. see the chapters on Namur and Spa). The use of these areas is free to members of the public.

The author would recommend that an active outdoor person going to the Ardennes for a walking holiday for the first time should devote about 60 percent of his or her time to walking, 25 percent of the total holiday to general sightseeing, as there is much in the area of interest, and the remaining time to trying one or more of the other outdoor pursuits on offer in the area. If at all possible include a visit to one of the local carnivals.

NOTES ON USING THE GUIDEBOOK
Layout of Guide:
Provinces, Regions and Centres of the Belgian Ardennes
The Guide is divided into three major sections, each corresponding to the three Provinces of Belgium in which the Ardennes is situated: these are, from west to east, the Province of Namur, the Province of Luxembourg and the Province of Liège. This last section has a further subdivision into the predominantly German-speaking Cantons de l'Est, which, although not a separate administrative area of the country, is a distinct and well recognised regional entity. Each section describes the walking from a number of centres within each Province, arranged in an approximate geographical sequence from west to east: four centres in the Province of Namur (Namur, Dinant & Environs - the Meuse & the Lesse, Rochefort & Han-sur-Lesse, and Vresse & Alle-sur-Semois), five centres in the Province of Luxembourg (Bouillon & the Semois, Saint-Hubert, Hotton & the

Ourthe, La Roche-en-Ardenne and Vielsalm & the Salm valley) and five centres in the Province of Liège (Spa, Stavelot & Coo, Malmédy & Environs, Sankt Vith and Burg-Reuland - the last three centres are located within the Cantons de l'Est). Between two and six walks are described for each centre, which, it is hoped, demonstrate the quality and variety of the landscape in each area: there are 13 walks described in the Province of Namur, 20 walks in the Province of Luxembourg and 20 walks in the Province of Liège, of which 10 are situated in the Cantons de l'Est. In all, 53 walks are described, ranging in length from 14 miles (22.5kms) to 2 miles (3.2kms), totaling 425 miles (684kms) of trail. (See the Summary Table: Provinces, Centres and Walks, and the Index of Walks.)

Centres

Each walking centre in the book is the subject of a separate chapter. Each chapter begins with an introduction to the centre, which is subdivided into General Information and Places of Interest, Accommodation, Transport, and the Official Waymarked Trails in the Area. After this follows a full description of a number of walks from the centre, under the heading Walks. The General Information and Places of Interest section provides an overview of the centre, its main features and characteristics. The type and abundance or otherwise of available accommodation in a centre can be seen at a glance by reference to the Accommodation section, whilst the Transport section provides not only details of the relevant train and bus services, but also advice on travelling to the region for those with private transport. Finally, the official, waymarked walking trails from each centre are listed, both for information and so that the walker can identify them when walking.

Walks

The 53 walks described are all circular in nature, starting and finishing at the same point. They are all truly circular in that the return route is always different from the outward part of the walk, ie. the return journey is never merely a return along the same route (except for a very few short repeated sections). The majority of the walks start and finish in the heart of the 14 centres featured in the book, but most of those that do begin some way from a main centre can be reached fairly easily by public transport (this is indicated where necessary).

The information contained under the various subheadings, prior to the route description, has two principal functions. First, it helps you to choose a suitable walk; second, it provides essential information at a glance for those about to embark on the walk. Each walk is then accompanied by a detailed route description which should be read in conjunction with the accompanying sketch map, tourist office map or other map, and with due regard to the waymarking on the ground. All the walks have a sketch map of the route, with the exceptions of Walk 1 and Walk 5 where a map is unnecessary.

Distances - Metric and Imperial:

The length of each walk is given in miles because most English-speaking walkers are familiar with this unit of length, but also in kilometres as all the maps of Belgium have a metric scale. The mileage was calculated arithmetically from distances in kilometres taken from the maps.

To avoid tedious repetition in the description of the route, metric distances only, metres and kilometres, are given in the text of the route descriptions, for example "turn left in 400 metres". This should present no problems if the description of the route is followed using the metric maps. Do not assume that such distances carry a high degree of accuracy; they merely give an indication of when you should look out for the change of direction.

Miscellaneous Notes:

1. Reference to "right" and "left" in the route descriptions refers to the direction of travel when on the walk. However, reference to "right" and "left" banks of rivers and streams relates to their direction of flow. For example, if you are walking up-stream on the left bank of a river then the water will be on your left, but if you are walking down-stream on the left bank of a river then the water will be on your right.

2. Where there are two or more spellings for place names, either French or Flemish, the French name is the one generally given in this book, as the Ardennes lies solely within the French-speaking area of Belgium. The main exceptions to this rule will be found in the chapters on the Cantons de L'Est (Ostkantone), in particular Sankt Vith and Burg-Reuland, which are predominantly German speaking. In these areas the German names, by which they are usually known today, are generally quoted (see Appendix 1 for a list of French, Flemish and German place names).

    The spellings of place names used in the book are generally those given on the official IGN maps. The only exception to this rule is on the very few occasions where a signpost is encountered which gives a somewhat different spelling of a place name to that on the map. In this case the signpost spelling is given at this point in the text, so that there can be no confusion when reading the description of the route.

3. The walks described in this book should not be confused with the numbered local trails in the various regions of the Ardennes. The walks featured in this book are always referred to as Walk 1, Walk 2 whereas local trails are referred to as Trail No. 1, Trail No. 2, or sometimes as Route No. 1.

GUIDE

SUMMARY TABLE: PROVINCES, CENTRES AND WALKS			
NAMUR	LUXEMBOURG*	LIEGE	CANTONS DE L'EST
Namur (2) Dinant (3) Rochefort/ Han-sur-Lesse (6) Vresse/Alle (2)	Bouillon (6) Saint-Hubert (2) Hotton (3) La Roche (6) Vielsalm (3)	Spa (6) Stavelot/Coo (4)	Malmédy (5) Sankt Vith (3) Burg-Reuland (2)
5 Centres 13 Walks 85.8 miles (137.9kms)	5 Centres 20 Walks 182.0 miles (292.9kms)	2 Centres 10 Walks 68.2 miles (109.6kms)	3 Centres 10 Walks 88.2 miles (141.8kms)
Total: 53 Walks in 14 Centres. 424.2 miles (682.2kms).			

* The Province of Luxembourg in Belgium, not the Grand Duchy.

Each column represents a Province of the Belgian Ardennes, except for the Cantons de l'Est which is a Region within the Province of Liège. Listed in each column are the Centres featured within that Province or Region. The figure in brackets is the number of walks described for each Centre.

KEY TO SKETCH MAPS

➡	=	route of walk with direction arrow
– – – – –	=	other tracks and roads
⟶	=	river or stream with direction of flow
··············	=	alternative route
⊬⊬⊬⊬⊓⊬⊬⊬⊬	=	railway with station
●	=	town
•	=	village
➤	=	start/finish point of walk

Province of Namur

NAMUR
General Information and Places of Interest

Namur (*Namen* in Flemish), "Gateway to the Ardennes", is a medium-sized town with a population just over 100,000, the capital of the Province that bears its name. Originally dating from before the 10th century, Namur has a rich history. Between 1792 and 1815 it was the capital of one of France's northern *départements*. Because of its size, importance, location and good road and rail connections it is the place that a first time visitor to the Ardennes is likely to reach first, particularly those arriving from the west, from Flanders and the Channel ports. It would be a mistake for walkers eager to encounter the woods, hills and deep river gorges for which the Ardennes is justly famous to bypass Namur, as it is a most elegant town, with a great deal to interest the visitor. It has a very fine collection of 17th and 18th century houses and mansions, many of which have been expertly restored to their former elegance. In addition there are a number of interesting museums, and the huge citadel, which dominates the town and its twin rivers, is a major attraction. All in all Namur is one of Belgium's finest towns, in great contrast to the many industrial cities further west.

No visitor to Namur can fail to miss the citadel, strategically sited on a small area of land between the Rivers Meuse and Sambre at their confluence, in the heart of the town, an area known as the Grognon or "pig's snout". Dating originally from the early Middle Ages, and latterly consolidated by both Vauban, the famous French military architect, and the Dutch who also held the town for a period, the fortress became one of the most important strongholds in Europe. This immense complex, which has only been open to the public since 1978, is best explored on foot (Walk 1). Whilst on the walk you may be lucky to spot, as the author was, one or more red squirrels: these animals are far more common on this side of the Channel than they are in most parts of Britain these days. More information on the citadel can be obtained from the local guidebooks to the fortress, on sale at the site and in Namur town.

Other parts of Namur can be explored by following the Town Trail (Walk 2). There are some interesting museums, several of them holding very beautiful objects of art and medieval craft. There are many fine, old houses and elegant mansions and churches.

Museums:

Musée Félicien Rops contains many of the works of the 19th century painter and engraver (1833-1898) who was born in Namur. Musée des Arts Anciens du Namurois contains examples of the work of local gold and silversmiths as well as a number of stone and wood carvings. These two museums are housed in the Hôtel de Gaiffier d'Hestroy, one of Namur's most elegant mansions. The Maison des Soeurs de Notre Dame houses the Trésor d'Oignies, a superb collection, dating from the 13th century, of gold and silver work by a local craftsman. The Hôtel de Croix is a luxury mansion where items of 17th and 18th century art are on display in the Musée de Groesbeek de Croix. There is also an archaeological museum in the town. The Musée de la Forêt (fauna and flora of the Ardennes) and the Musée d'Armes et d'Histoire (local military history) are situated in the citadel complex.

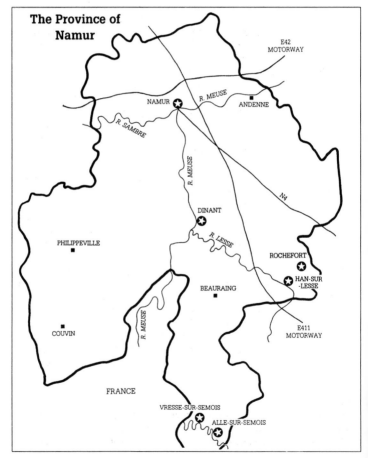

Ecclesiastical Buildings:
Namur Cathedral, the neoclassical Cathédrale Saint-Aubain, is built of both stone and brick. There is a hugh domed interior and highly ornate carving around the walls and on the ceiling. The paintings are from the School of Rubens. Of particular note is the large, ornately carved wooden pulpit. The cathedral treasury is in the attached Musée Diocésain. The baroque Eglise St Loup, the Eglise Notre-Dame and the Eglise St Joshep are three notable churches in the town.

Old houses:
The Rue des Brasseurs has a particularly fine collection of restored 17th and 18th century houses, including that of Félicien Rops (see Museums above). The Hôtel de Ville, dating from the 18th century, is on the Rue de Fer. Namur has some of the finest examples of houses and town mansions of these periods in all Belgium. The several sieges experienced by the town during medieval times destroyed all the houses of note built prior to the 17th century.

The arsenal was built by Vauban and dates from the 17th century.

Between May and September you can take a boat cruise on the Meuse and the Sambre. The trip lasts about 45mins.

Accommodation
The largest of the centres featured in this guide, Namur has quite a number of hotels so that finding accommodation is rarely a problem outside of the main season. Do remember to book, however, in the height of the summer season. The tourist office (see Appendix 3) has lists of hotels, and private rooms. There is also a youth hostel, albeit some way out of the city centre (see Appendix 4). The nearest campsites are several miles from the town, at Malonne and Lives-sur-Meuse.

Namur has a wide selection of bistros, cafés and restaurants serving Belgian, French and foreign cuisines.

Transport
Namur is easily accessible by public transport. Although there are bus services connecting Namur with other towns and villages, near and far, most people will find the train the most convenient means of reaching Namur, from Brussels, or from Flanders and the Channels ports to the west. Main train lines radiate from Namur to Brussels in the north-west, Liège to the east-north-east, Luxembourg City in the south-east and Charleroi to the west-south-west. The lines to Liège and to Luxembourg, both of which have several intermediary stations, are particularly important for those seeking access to the Ardennes. Another useful train line is that heading south from Namur to Dinant, Houyet and beyond (see map of the Belgian Railways in the Ardennes and Surrounding Areas).

The railway station is situated on the northern edge of the town, on the

Avenue de la Gare, with information on national and international train services. Details of bus services are available from the tourist office, which is located in a chalet close to the railway station in the Square de l'Europe Unie.

The E411 (A4) motorway linking Brussels with Luxembourg City passes within a few kilometres of the centre of Namur. The E42 (A15) motorway from Lille and Charleroi to Liège passes just to the north of Namur.

Namur is the only centre featured in this book where parking can be a problem. There is parking on the earthen verge to the side of the road which runs alongside the railway line on the eastern approach to the railway station. A major city car park (700 cars) will be found just off the roundabout (Place Leopold), a short distance to the east of the railway station; this should be easily reached if entering the town from the direction of Brussels. A convenient car park for the walks described below will be found at the point where the Rivers Meuse and Sambre meet, on the south side of the Pont du Musée.

Official Walking Trails in Namur

A booklet describing 12 walks in the neighbourhood of Namur, between 4 and 13kms in length, can be purchased from the tourist office, available in either French or Dutch. An ability to read one of these languages is required, as no sketch maps are provided.

Walks

The walks in Namur are naturally urban in character, and as such are quite unlike the other walks described in this book. Nevertheless, there is a definite rural "feel" to the place, and from the high citadel the close proximity of the woods, rivers and hills of the surrounding Ardennes is very evident.

Two Walks in Namur are described below.

WALK 1:
Namur: A Tour of the Citadel

Start/Finish: The walk starts from the car park in the centre of Namur near to the junction of the Meuse and Sambre rivers, on the south side of the Pont du Musée (see sketch map). This is less than a mile, south-east, from the central railway station. There is a small tourist office in this car park.

Distance: About 2.5 miles (4.0kms).

Time: Allow 2hrs plus at least an extra 2hrs if the fortress itself, with its museums, displays and underground passages (guided tours), is to be visited.

Map: A map is unnecessary for this simple walk through the grounds of the fortress above Namur town. Sketch maps of the citadel are sometimes available from the entrance kiosk.

Footwear: Trainers or good shoes are adequate.

Refreshments: Several cafés and restaurants are passed en route within the grounds of the citadel.

Options: The route may be shortened by taking the cable car (*téléphérique*) either for the ascent to the citadel, or on the descent. Note that the *téléphérique* operates all through the year (10am to 7pm), but only at the weekends during the winter months (from 1st October to the end of March). Another alternative is to take a bus (service number 3) from the railway station to the top *téléphérique* terminus, or conversely, the walk could be terminated from here by returning to the town on the bus (a bus stop is near the Château de Namur hotel, close to the *téléphérique* terminus on the summit).

Citadel Opening: The walk described can be made at any time of the year, and at any time of the day, whether the fortress is open or not. The roads, tracks and paths around the fortress are always open to the public. The fortress itself, for which there is a moderate entrance fee, is open daily in July and August (10am to 6pm), in the afternoons only in June and September (1pm to 5pm), and weekend afternoons only (Sat and Sun, 1pm to 5pm) in April, May and October. It is closed from the end of October until April.

Parfumerie
and Gardens: These are situated on the citadel at Le Château des Comtes and are passed on the walk. There are guided tours of the Guy Delforge parfumerie and associated museum, daily during the summer and at weekends in the wintertime. These tours last about 70mins and include a visit to the factory as well as an audio-visual show. The adjacent gardens (Les Jardins de Médiane) are the venue for an annual *son et lumière*. There is a different theme each year for the event which is held every spring (usually from mid-April to the end of May). There are around 22,000 flowers arranged in thematic tableaux. Worth a visit.

Fitness Circuit: A short *parcours sportif* (fitness circuit) has been laid out on the citadel. This will be encountered on the walk. It is intended for runners, joggers or walkers who wish to exercise a number of different muscle groups. Use of the equipment is free.

Tourist Train: A *petit train touristique* operates during the summer months from the main car park outside the entrance to the Citadel Fortress. This provides a tour of the grounds of the citadel.

Route
Cross the road outside the car park and take the steps, located by the *téléphérique* entrance, leading up towards the citadel. A sign for the GR N long distance trail will be seen here (this is the GR Namurois which has come from

Brussels and is heading along the valley of the Meuse to Dinant and on to the Lesse valley). The red and white waymarks of this trail lead the way upwards to reach a good viewpoint above the Sambre river. The elegant buildings of the old town are seen to good effect from here, as is the junction of the Meuse and the Sambre rivers at the Grognon or "pig's snout". The huge domed cathedral is the most prominent building on view. It is possible to trace the route of the Town Trail (Walk 2) from this viewpoint.

The GR N continues ahead, but leave the red and white waymarks here to take steps up to the left leading to the Château des Comtes (a restaurant) and continue to a parfumerie, from where there is a splendid view down to the River Meuse and the surrounding countryside of the Ardennes (a bench is provided from which to admire the scene). From here a tour of the parfumerie can be made or the adjacent gardens visited (see Parfumerie and Gardens above).

Little description of the route is required from here. Simply continue uphill along the peripheral road of the citadel, with the Meuse down below to the left. Continue to the large car park, which accommodates visitors to the Citadel Fortress. Here will be found the entrance to the citadel (admission charge).

Take the steps up behind the car park, noting the *parcours sportif* that you will now have joined (see above). Following this circuit will lead back to the Citadel Fortress car park. The citadel complex covers a large area and is a veritable maze of ditches, banks and escarpments, which were designed for defensive purposes in times gone by. The easiest way to progress is to continue upwards along the periphery road, admiring the Meuse with its many bridges below, and the surrounding Ardennes countryside. About 150 metres after passing under the wires of the *téléphérique* take the footpath off to the right which ascends above the road beneath the crags of the citadel. This soon leads to an upper road at a sports stadium where there are more cafés and ice-cream stalls. Continue to the top of the hill where there is a very exclusive (and expensive!) hotel and restaurant, the Château de Namur, a most impressive building which has been in view for some time.

From here there are three means of returning to the starting point of the walk: a) the *téléphérique* (the top terminus station is near to the hotel, adjacent to a café), b) take bus No. 3 back to the railway station (the bus stop is also near to the Château de Namur), c) walk back over the citadel by the numerous tracks, paths and roads that abound, either by the same route as used on the ascent, or by any number of minor alternatives. There should be no problem in choosing a route and very little chance of getting lost. To give one example: return along the periphery road, but leave it just before reaching the *téléphérique* wires spanning the road, by taking a gently descending, partly stepped, track off to the right which heads down towards the River Meuse, with steep wooded slopes down to the right. This eventually meets another surfaced road; continue, following the line of the *téléphérique*, which is now above to the left. Descend, soon taking another path down to the left which leads to the main road at the riverside opposite the casino. Follow the course of the Meuse down the Rue Notre Dame back to the Pont du Musée and the car park.

WALK 2:
Namur: A Town Trail

Start/Finish: The starting point is the same as for Walk 1, ie. the walk starts from the car park in the centre of Namur near to the junction of the Meuse and Sambre rivers, on the south side of the Pont du Musée. This is less than a mile, south-east, from the central railway station. As the Saint-Aubain Cathedral is closer to the railway station than the car park, walkers arriving by train may wish to start the ramble at the cathedral. To reach the cathedral from the railway station, walk south from the station along Rue Goderfroid to the Rue de Bruxelles. Turn right here and then take the next major road to the left (the Rue Lellevre) which leads to the cathedral. Then pick up the route description at the asterisk (*) in the text.

Distance: About 2.0 miles (3.2kms).

Time: Allow 1¹/₂hrs for the actual walk plus an extra 15mins to visit the cathedral, and several more hours depending on how many of the museums passed en route are visited.

Map: An adequate street map of Namur can be obtained from the tourist office in the Square de l'Europe Unie, near the railway station.

Footwear: Trainers or good shoes are adequate. The walking is all on the level.

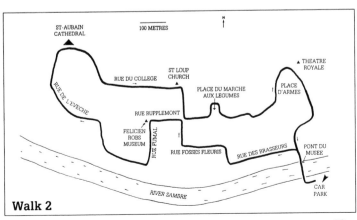

Walk 2

Refreshments: Many cafés, restaurants and shops of all descriptions are passed on the Town Trail, whilst very many others are to be found within the limits of the city.

Museums: The major museums of Namur are passed en route. These are, in order of visiting whilst on the walk, the Archaeological Museum (Musée Archéologique), the Musée Félicien Rops, the Musée de Grosbeech de Croix and the Musée Trésor d'Oignies. The Musée des Arts Anciens du Namurois is a short detour from the route (about 5mins walk to the north-east from the Church of Saint Loup). If intending to visit several of the museums in Namur it may be more economic to purchase a museum pass (enquire at the tourist office).

Cathedral: The main point of interest on the walk is perhaps the Cathédrale Saint-Aubain (see Introduction). There is also a church of note passed en route, viz. the Eglise Saint Loup in the Rue du College, which has an elegant curved roof, but entrance is unfortunately forbidden.

Route

From the car park cross the bridge over the River Meuse to reach the Archaeological Museum. In 30 metres turn left down the Rue des Brasseurs. Continue to the Place Maurice Servais, turning right into this square, where there is often a small fruit market. Cross to the far left-hand corner of this square, being sure to look back up for the view of the citadel before leaving it. Take the pedestrianised Rue Fosses Flueris to reach a T-junction at the Rue du President. Turn right and take the first left, the Rue Rupplemont. At the next T-junction the road emerges opposite the Musée Félicien Rops. Turn left here, walking down the narrow, straight Rue Fumal, heading towards the citadel seen ahead and above. On reaching a T-junction turn right, once more on the Rue des Brasseurs. Turn right again on reaching the Rue Joseph Saintraint, taking the first left opposite the Maison de la Culture, down the Rue de l'Eveche. Turn right at the Rue du Seminaire to reach the large, dominating Cathedral of Saint-Aubain, which is most certainly worth a visit.

Standing on the steps of the cathedral with your back to the building (*), bear to the right across the Place Saint-Aubain, to locate and follow the Rue du College. Just after the church and street of Saint Loup on the left, turn right along the Rue du President. Take the first left turn on the Rue Saint-Jean which leads to the ancient Place du Marché aux Legumes and the church of Saint Jean Baptiste (note the stone plinth in the centre of this square which has carved vegetables on it, marking the trade that has taken place here for many centuries. The square was excavated during 1992/93 to reveal its ancient foundations and a well thousands of years old. Some of the pottery finds, together with photos of the excavations should still be on display in one of the shop windows in the square).

Leave the square to locate the Rue des Frippiers on the left, which leads to one of the main shopping streets of Namur. Walk obliquely right across this to take the pedestrianised Rue de la Monnaie. At the end of this street note the interesting fountain, with stone snails. By these sculptured snails turn left on the Rue du Beffroi, bear to the right through a cobbled street to reach the Rue Emile Cuvelier opposite the Théâtre Royal de Namur. Turn right at the theatre to follow the Rue de la Tour to the Marché Saint Remy, where turn right and in 80 metres turn left down the Rue du Pont which leads to the Pont du Musée and the car park.

DINANT AND ENVIRONS - THE MEUSE AND THE LESSE
General Information and Places of Interest

Dinant, the "Pearl of the Meuse", is a picturesque town situated in a large rocky defile in the Meuse valley. A small (population c7000) and ancient town which has a rich, unsettled history, but which nowadays is a popular tourist centre. Perhaps Dinant's most famous son was Adolphe Sax (1814-1894) who invented the saxophone in 1846. The town was almost destroyed by the Germans in August, 1914, and there was again much damage during the Second World War. In recent times the town suffered a near catastrophe during the severe flooding of January and February, 1995.

The town is squeezed between the River Meuse and a high steep cliff on top of which, at over 100 metres above the river, sits the citadel, the town's

Canoeists in action on the River Lesse

most distinctive landmark and tourist attraction. The fortress dates from around 1050, although there is evidence of even earlier fortifications on the rock. A number of strongholds have been built, destroyed and rebuilt on this strategic site in the various wars that have troubled the region for the last 900 years. The French did the last major damage to the fortress in 1703, the present buildings dating from the Dutch period (1818-1821). There is a marvellous view of the town, Meuse valley and surrounding hills from this lofty perch, which can be reached from the town by either a chair-lift or via a flight of over 400 steps (built in 1577). Unfortunately the citadel can only be seen on a conducted tour, which lasts about half an hour. It is a very popular excursion during the summer months.

Dinant's most distinctive building is the Eglise Notre-Dame, Gothic in design with a large bulbous spire, and situated immediately below the cliff and citadel. Dating from 1240 it has been destroyed several times during the intervening centuries, but always re-built to the original design.

Other places of interest in Dinant include the Grotte de Montfort (prehistoric cave in the hillside), the 14th century Tour (Tower) de Montfort, the Grotte La Merveilleuse (open April to September - guided visits - delicate white stalactites) and Mont-Fat Parc, whose gardens overlook the Meuse and offer a good view of Dinant citadel and church.

This is one of the most picturesque stretches of the River Meuse, a 900km (560 mile) long river which rises in France, and after passing through Dinant, Namur and Liège enters Holland near Maastricht, where, as the Maas, it flows into the Waal, thereby reaching the great Dutch Rhine delta which pours into the North Sea. It is possible to take boat excursions along the River Meuse to Namur, and also to Anseremme at the confluence of the Meuse and the River Lesse. Other boat trips explore the Meuse further South from Anseremme to Waulsourt and Hastière. Part of the River Meuse and the wooded hills that rise up steeply from its banks can be explored on Walk 3.

The Meuse is wide and graceful, but its tributary, the Lesse, is the more attractive of the two rivers, as it meanders below steep, wooded hills, through the heart of the Ardennes. Scenically the best section of the Lower Lesse is where the river passes beneath the Furfooz National Park (Walk 5) past the crags much frequented by rock climbers, and under the 13th century château of Walsin (Walk 4). These sections can be enjoyed on our two walks, and also, from a different perspective, by paddling a canoe on the river itself. The descent of the Lesse by canoe-kayak is a very popular pastime, one for which it is not necessary to have had any previous canoeing experience. Three canoe-kayak companies operate between May and September on this stretch of the river, with similar prices and standards of hired canoe. Tickets are bought in Anseremme from where the morning train is taken to Houyet. A single or a double seater kayak is collected here and paddled downstream the 21kms back to Anseremme, a journey which will take the average person about 5hrs of paddling. There are many places to stop along the way for refreshment, and the scenery is a delight, so it provides a very full and exciting day out. This experience is highly recommended, but try if possible to go mid-week, outside the main summer holiday period, as it can become extremely busy on the river at these times, with canoe jams and pile-ups! For the less athletic a trip on a crewed boat is also possible.

Accommodation

The tourist office will be found on the High Street. There are a fair number of hotels in most price ranges. Some of the cafés and bistros in the town are worth trying for accommodation, as a few of these have rooms above the establishment at reasonable rates; the tourist office keeps a list of private rooms.

There is no youth hostel in Dinant, but several campsites will be found in the locality:

Dinant: Camping de Bouvignes (2kms to the north of the town centre) and Camping La Vallée (both of these campsites are situated on the Chaussée d'Yvoir). Anseremme (a couple of kilometres south of Dinant by the confluence of the Meuse and Lesse): Camping Villatoile by the Barrage de Pont-à-Lesse. Falmignoul: there are two campsites here (Au Cheval Blanc and Camping de l'Agougeois) which are ideally located for those following Walks 3 and/or 4, below. Furfooz: Camping Paradiso - convenient for those taking Walk 5. Houyet: Camping La Lesse, particularly convenient for those canoeing on the Lesse.

Transport

The easiest way to reach Dinant is by train from Namur. Several trains a day ply south down the Meuse valley from Namur, via Profondeville and Yvoir, to Dinant. Dinant Railway Station is situated on the opposite side of river to the town centre, which is easily accessible by way of Dinant Bridge. From Dinant the line continues farther south to Anseremme, Houyet, Beauraing, Gedinne, Paliseul, Bertrix and Florenville. Buses also make the run between Namur and Dinant, usually four times a day.

There are several buses to destinations up and down the Meuse valley: north to Namur and south to Givet in France, via Freyr, Waulsourt and Hastière, places worth visiting in their own right. There are also buses to Beauraing which stop at Falmignoul, the starting point for Walks 3 and 4 below. For up-to-date bus timetables and services contact the tourist office (see Appendix 3).

For those with private cars the fastest road access to Dinant is via the E411 (A4) motorway from Namur: leave at Exit No. 20 to follow the N97 (a dual-carriageway) west towards Dinant. Alternatively, the N96 follows the west bank of the River Meuse south from Namur via Profondeville to Dinant, along perhaps one of the most attractive stretches of the River Meuse.

Official Walking Trails in the Falmagne/Falmignoul Region, Dinant

There are three official, waymarked, circular walking trails in the Falmagne/
Falmignoul region, south of Anseremme, near Dinant. The routes of these trails
are shown on individual 1:25,000 scale maps in the publication *Promenades
dans l'Entité de Dinant (Wandelingen in Dinant): Falmagne, Falmignoul*,
available from the tourist office. The three trails are as follows:

Itinéraire Rouge: Falmagne - Chaleux - Walzin: 11.2 or 13kms.

Itinéraire Orange: Falmignoul - Les Cuves - Le Drapeau et les Cascatelles: 6.0
or 12.0kms.

Itinéraire Bleu: Falmignoul - Falmagne: 6.3kms.

Walks

Three walks are featured in this region, all to the south of Dinant, near to the
point where the River Lesse drains into the wide River Meuse, an area which
offers some of the most varied and attractive walking in the district. The first
walk features the undulating wooded hills which rise steeply above the River
Meuse, whilst the second visits some of the most dramatic stretches of the
Lower Lesse, an area beloved of both canoeists and rock climbers. The third
walk is quite different in character: a visit to a tiny National Park, above the River
Lesse, where there are many limestone cave formations.

WALK 3:
Falmignoul and the River Meuse

Description: An excellent walk, but quite a demanding one, following a
steeply undulating trail above the River Meuse, south of Dinant. The highlights
include fine views of the River Meuse, a visit to the ruins of the Château Thierry,
and a delightful cascading stream that is followed during the final ascent
through the forest that lines the precipitous banks of the Meuse.

Location: To the south of Dinant, between the villages of Falmignoul
and Waulsort, and on the southern border of the River Meuse.

Start/Finish: Place Roger Bodart in the village of Falmignoul, 8kms south
of Dinant. This is adjacent to the main road from Dinant (the N95) and opposite
a small campsite. There is ample space for parking a car here. The start of the
walk can most easily be reached by car from Dinant, south along the N95,
although there are buses from Dinant which stop at the village (enquire at the
tourist office for an up-to-date timetable).

Distance: 7.5 miles (12.0kms)

Time: Allow 5hrs.

Maps: The publication entitled *Promenades dans l'Entité de Dinant*

(Wandelingen in Dinant): Falmagne, Falmignoul, obtainable from the Tourist Office. The map inside this folder, at a scale of 1:25,000, entitled *Itinéraire Orange (Oranje Reisweg)*. The route of the walk is overlaid on this map.

IGN 1:50,000 series: sheet number 53.

Waymarking: The route is well waymarked throughout with orange waymarks, which appear in two forms: a pair of orange triangles or an orange "walking man" symbol.

Terrain: This is a fairly hard walk which involves several steep sections along a rather tortuous trail, although the latter stages provide straightforward and easy walking along tracks, across fields back to Falmignoul. The majority of the walk is through woodland over the steep-sided hills which line the banks of the river Meuse in this region. Particular care is required when conditions are wet or icy underfoot, as the steep paths, often covered with tree roots, stones and protruding rocks, are then usually very slippery. The severity of the walk is considerably increased under bad weather conditions. The dramatic views down to the river Meuse are perhaps best seen during the wintertime when there is little foliage on the trees.

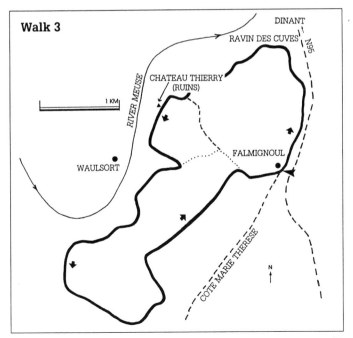

Footwear: Boots with a good grip are recommended.

Options: The walk can be shortened to about half its length (ie. to approximately 3.7 miles, 6kms) by following the northern part of the circuit only, returning eastwards back to Falmignoul where indicated in the text below. Fit and experienced walkers might like to combine this walk with Walk 4 to form a long and very fine walk linking the Rivers Meuse and Lesse.

Refreshments: There is no possibility of obtaining refreshments on the walk itself, but Falmignoul, where the walk begins and ends, has a grocer's shop and a *boulangerie/pâtisserie*.

Route

From the car park in Place Roger Bodart in Falmignoul, walk away from the main road for 75 metres to a road junction, where orange waymarks point to the right and blue ones to the left. Turn right here following the orange waymarks along the Rue de la Draisienne. In 100 metres or so turn right on a driveway immediately before a large house. Cross a footbridge over a small stream and follow a narrow footpath alongside it to a second footbridge: left over this and along the footpath to reach the end of a road where a blue waymarked trail goes off to the left - here bear right to cross a third footbridge, still following orange waymarks. Continue on the footpath heading northwards alongside the stream and then alongside a caravan site.

After the caravan site a track T-junction is reached: here turn left for 20 metres and then right across a grassy field where indicated by the orange waymarks painted on a tree. Keep to the left-hand edge of the field to pick up a footpath on the left which soon enters trees. The path begins to undulate and becomes interesting: there is soon a steep drop to the right. The trail can be slippery in wet conditions, so that extra care is required from hereon to prevent mishap on slippery tree roots or half-submerged rocks. Continue on this narrow path ignoring a few side turnings (the correct trail is quite obvious and is well waymarked with orange triangles). Eventually a vantage point is reached high above the River Meuse, at a wide curve in the latter. The view down to the river, with its steep banks and towering cliffs, is excellent, although leaves often obscure the full glory of it during the summertime. There are one or two better vantage points just off the path, but these are precariously positioned close to the edge of a very steep drop down towards the river, so that extreme care must be exercised if these are visited.

The narrow path continues through the trees, now heading generally in a south-westerly direction, following the course of the River Meuse, but remaining high above it. The path eventually widens a little and becomes somewhat grassy and easier to negotiate, before descending slightly to reach a clear track at a T-junction. Turn left here, heading towards the south. After only about 75 metres leave the track by turning right downhill on a path through trees. Cross a steep-sided ditch, taking especial care here in wet or icy conditions, as the trail can be treacherously slippery. The narrow path continues to reach the ruins of Château Thierry, a classified site which is worth an exploration before continuing on the walk: descend the stone steps ahead to do so (these are behind the wooden fencing, rather hidden from view at first). The castle was built on the site of a large rock outcrop and remains of its walls are clearly seen.

The trail, however, does not descend these steps, but rather turns left, uphill, in front of the château, and then soon bears to the right above the ruins, before descending steeply and re-ascending as indicated by the waymarks. The path continues, still with a steep bank down to the right, to reach another viewpoint of the river Meuse, this time looking down onto the village of Waulsort on the opposite bank, a splendid vantage point. Continue on a narrow path along the edge of a grassy field to your left, to reach a small bench at a second viewpoint of the same scene. Bear left here to continue along the path, which eventually reaches a narrow track at a T-junction. Turn left here (east) alongside a grassy field if wanting a quick return to Falmignoul (the route is tagged with orange waymarks: it is about 1.3kms from this point back to Falmignoul by this route - see sketch map).

However, for the full circuit turn right downhill on the track, following orange waymarks in the shape of a walking man, now heading towards the west. After a few hundred metres leave this track by taking the waymarked path down to the left. In a few metres this bears left to cross a steep-sided gully. The path, as tortuous as ever, soon follows a stream, which is down on your left, and begins to climb into a nature reserve. Another viewpoint over Waulsort is passed. Soon after this the path descends very steeply (particular care is again required) to cross a gully along which runs a narrow stream. Continue ahead, now climbing steeply following the course of a stream bed down to the right. The path continues, climbing occasionally, to reach another viewpoint over the river, this time where the latter sweeps widely to the right. Take the path leading away from the river at this point, soon descending steeply (care once more, particularly when it is wet or icy) to the left of a wooded gully. Descend to a path T-junction, a little above a series of small waterfalls on the stream below.

Turn left here, uphill on the path following the course of this pleasantly cascading stream. Soon cross the stream (usually easily fordable) and continue uphill on the path on its left bank. Later re-cross the stream and continue uphill on its right bank. Higher up cross the stream yet again to continue once more along its left bank, this time crossing three of its small tributaries on the ascent. The trail eventually levels, becomes somewhat easier underfoot, and then reaches the edge of the woodland, where it bears to the left to follow the edge of the wood, with grassland to the right, heading gently uphill to reach a track at a corner of the woods. From here on the "going" is much easier back to Falmignoul.

Follow this track, with fields to the left and right, heading in a north-easterly direction, but take great care not to miss a left turn onto another track, a few hundred metres after the corner of the wood, so that now you are heading in a north-north-westerly direction. Continue to a track T-junction, a few hundred metres before the wood seen ahead. Here turn right heading again in a north-easterly direction. This straight track provides easy walking across the open fields, back towards the village of Falmignoul. The track eventually reaches a metalled road on the outskirts of the village, opposite a covered shrine to the Virgin. Here there is a choice of routes, to the left or right as waymarked. I have chosen the trail to the right, heading towards the church. Descend through the village to return to the car park in Place Roger Bodart, where the walk began.

WALK 4:
Falmagne and the River Lesse

Description: An opportunity to explore on foot what is perhaps the most scenic section of the Lower Lesse, one of the more dramatic of the rivers of the Ardennes. The walk offers three contrasting aspects of the area: the impressive precipitous crags of the deep, meandering limestone gorge of the Lower Lesse, the pleasant woods that fringe the river, and the open fields of the plateau above the Lesse valley. Other outdoor folk will probably be encountered on the circuit, particularly canoeists and rock climbing enthusiasts, the activities of both of which give added interest to the walk. Apart from the muddy paths which will no doubt have to be endured in places, the walk is a fairly easy and relaxing one.

Location: To the south of Dinant, between the villages of Falmignoul, Falmagne and Hulsonniaux, and along the River Lesse south-east of Anseremme.

Start/Finish: Place Roger Bodart in the village of Falmignoul, 8kms south of Dinant. For further details see under "Start/Finish" for Walk 3.

Distance: 8.1 miles (13.0kms).

Time: Allow 5hrs.

Maps: The publication entitled *Promenades dans l'Entité de Dinant (Wandelingen in Dinant): Falmagne, Falmignoul,* obtainable from the tourist office. The maps inside this folder, at a scale of 1:25,000, entitled *Itinéraire Rouge (Rode Reisweg)* and *Itinéraire Bleu (Blauwe Reisweg)*. The route of our walk consists of the majority of *Itinéraire Rouge* combined with much of *Itinéraire Bleu*, the trails of which are overlaid on these maps.
        IGN 1:50,000 series: sheet number 53.

Waymarking: Blue and red triangle arrowheads, and blue and red "walking man" waymarks.

A crag towering above the River Lesse south of Dinant

Terrain: A good mixture of small villages, open countryside, woods and riverbank. A few of the paths and tracks used (warning is given at the relevant points in the route description below) are very muddy for much of the year, due to the frequent riding of horses along them.

Footwear: Boots or bogtrotters are recommended, as some of the paths can be very muddy.

Options: The route can be shorted by about a mile (1.6kms) by starting and finishing the walk at Falmagne, returning directly to Falmagne from the Nawagne cross-tracks by following the red triangle waymarks as indicated in the text below.

Refreshments: There are shops in Falmignoul at the start/end of the trail, and on the main road outside Falmagne, 1km into the walk. A café where drinks and snacks may be purchased is passed on the bank of the River Lesse a little over halfway through the walk. This is an ideal spot for lunch, where the antics of the canoeists on the river can be observed, but note that this establishment is normally only open during the kayak season (May to September).

Route
From the car park at Place Roger Bodart in the village of Falmignoul, walk away from the main road following the blue triangles (arrowheads) to the left. Climb the hill, passing to the right of the large village pond. Turn left about 20 metres before reaching the roadsign that indicates the limit of the village of Falmignoul, but do not take the stony track here, which climbs gently to the left of a house,

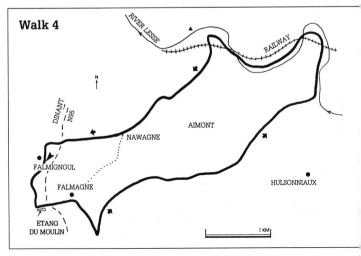

The wooded hills above La Roche
La Roche nestles on a steep bank of a wide sweep of the River Ourthe

The Château de Walzin high above the River Lesse (Walk 4)
Rochefort seen from the Rond de Roi (Walk 6)

but instead turn sharp left passing to the left of a garage (blue waymark). This soon becomes an enclosed path between trees. On reaching the low concrete retaining wall of the dried-out Etang du Moulin, turn left in front of this "pond" on a track which climbs back to the main road (ignore left fork before the final steep ascent to the main road). At the point where the track meets the main road there is a small shop where refreshments may be purchased.

Cross over the main road to take the cobbled road opposite, to the left of a large barn, and in 40 metres take the right fork to follow Ruelle Levreau. Turn right on reaching a T-junction at a minor road, heading south-east away from the church of the village of Falmagne. Walk gently uphill past the houses of the village, now picking up red triangle (arrowhead) waymarks as well as the blue ones. This is the Rue du Grand Cortil. Note the small stone shrine on the right seen immediately on leaving the village. On reaching a T-junction a few metres after a concrete telegraph pole, turn sharp left, heading towards buildings. Continue ahead to meet a cross-tracks at the small Chapelle Saint Donat. Walk ahead, along a "no through road", at this point leaving the blue waymarks (which point to the left) to follow the red triangle arrowheads and red "walking man" waymarks only. This stony track traverses a gentle rise (marked on the map as 262.5m above sea level) before descending towards woodland (keep to the main stony track on the right where there is a minor fork to the left by a copse of trees).

The track eventually runs alongside the wood before bending to the left to enter the trees (can be muddy here) where it soon narrows to a path. This path is following the course of the River Vesse, a tributary of the Lesse, little more than a peaceful babbling brook here. This rather muddy trail, often used by horseriders, ends at a small footbridge over the Vesse. Turn left on the poorly surfaced track found on the far side of the bridge. The track follows the course of the stream, passing to the left of a large stone and brick built house, site of the old mill of Falmagne. Where this surfaced track curves left to go uphill, bear right (ie. straight ahead) on an earthen track (again often muddy) heading once more into trees, and still following the stream on your left. The worst of the very muddy section ahead can be avoided by taking the footpath on the bank to the right of the main track. This footpath leads to a plank bridge over the stream: over this to follow the left bank of the tributary. A second muddy section can be avoided firstly by taking a path on the steep bank to the left of the trail, and then on a thin path to the right of the track, down near to the river (horses are the major culprit in churning up the mud on this trail).

The track leads to a minor road at a T-junction by a collection of small wooden buildings. Turn left on this road, now heading north in the valley of the Lesse, with the River Lesse over to your right. During the summer months cries of glee from the canoeists on the river will no doubt be heard here, as considerable numbers of them descend the Lesse from Houyet to Anseremme, particularly at weekends: the scene may even inspire you to try your hand at this most enjoyable activity. Continue on this riverside lane to pass under the railway bridge and arrive at a large *buvette* (cafeteria), a popular stop for those kayaking down the Lesse. This is a good spot for lunch, a vantage point from which to observe the rock gymnasts practising their sport on the most impressive crags which tower above the river at this point.

Walk down to the river bank and turn left along it. Immediately after passing under the railway bridge climb the steps on the left to reach the top of the bridge. Cross over it by way of the railed path to the left of the railway line. Descend the steps on the opposite bank to turn left along a stony track, now with the River Lesse over to your left. This track, muddy in parts, continues to a point where the railway crosses the river for a second time. Climb up the bank on the near side of the bridge, using the latter to cross back over to the left bank of the River Lesse. Descend to pass under the railway bridge to follow the path on the left bank of the river. This soon leaves the river, which curves away to the right. Soon the château de Walzin comes into view, perched high on a limestone crag above the River Lesse, now a hundred metres or so over to the right. Reach a T-junction of tracks, at a point where the Château is over to your right. Turn left on this track, soon re-crossing the railway, this time on a cobbled brick footbridge. The trail enters a dark avenue of pine trees, but the path soon begins a gentle climb through pleasant mixed woodland. The red and white waymarks that have been seen for some time, accompanying the red triangles and red "walking man" symbol of our trail, are those of the GR 126 (Brussels to the Semois long distance path). The trail climbs out of the woods onto open grazing pastureland, and continues as a track to the Nawagne cross-tracks, where there are a pair of trees emblazoned with a multitude of paint marks, depicting various walking routes. The track to the left, waymarked with the red triangle arrowheads, leads directly to the church at Falmagne, whereas we are to leave the "red itinerary" at his point to follow the track to the right, waymarked with the blue triangles once again. This heads to the west towards the church of Falmignoul seen in the distance. The track leads back to the main Dinant to Beauraing road, the N95. Bear left along this road for 50 metres before sloping down to the right on a minor lane. Cross a small footbridge and follow the path to the left of the small stream. At the metalled road bear left uphill on it away from the stream, following the direction of the blue triangles. At the Rue de la Draisienne turn left (ie. leaving the blue waymarked trail which continues ahead at this point). This leads back to the car park where the walk began.

WALK 5:
The Furfooz National Park

Description: A short but extremely interesting walk in very attractive countryside on the northern shore of the Lower Lesse, amidst caves and limestone cliffs, in what is possibly the world's smallest National Park. The park can only be visited on foot, by following the official Park Trail. This is the shortest country walk described in this book and is suitable for families, even those with quite small children. Although access to the trail is restricted to the park's opening times (see below) and a small admission fee is payable, no excuse is offered for including the walk in this guidebook, as the park can be highly recommended. It will particularly delight cavers, climbers, amateur geologists, archaeologists and botanists.

Location: About 4 miles (6.4kms) south-east of Dinant, between the village of Furfooz and the northern (right) bank of the River Lesse.

Access: There are three possible modes of access to the park: car, train and canoe. The main entrance to the park is situated south of the village of Furfooz, where there is a large car park, but note that there is no bus service to this point. A subsidiary entrance to the park is from the cafeteria (Buvettes des Grottes) on the right bank of the River Lesse, from where entrance tickets, sketch maps and the official guidebook can also be purchased. This can be reached in one of two ways: by train from Dinant (Anseremme) along the Lesse valley, direction Houyet, alighting at the Gare de Gendron-Celles and walking along the riverside footpath (part of the GR 126 - the GR de la Lesse) to reach the buvette. Alternatively, there is a landing stage at the buvette where canoes can be tied up whilst visiting the park (see "Start/Finish" below).

Opening Times: The usual opening times of the park are as follows:
April and May: 10am to 5pm, every day.
June, July and August: 10am to 6pm, every day.
September and October: 10am to 4.30pm, every day.

November to mid-December: open on Saturdays and Sundays, but by reservation only (tel 082/22 47 65, or by letter: Parc de Furfooz, 8 Rue des Croisers, 5000 Namur).

Christmas and New Year period (usually 19 December to 4 January): 10am to 3.30pm, every day.

Mid-February to the end of March: open Saturdays, Sundays and Bank holidays only, by prior arrangement (as for November to mid-December, above).

If visiting outside the period between June and October, then the opening dates and times should first be confirmed at the tourist office.

Annual Closure: The park is closed completely for about a six week period in the middle of the winter, usually between 5 January and 15 February.

Start/Finish   Entrance to the park: Rue du Camp Romain (tel number of the on-site office at the entrance: 082/22 34 77). This is situated south of the village of Furfooz - the route to the entrance is signposted from the village.

The trail could also be started and finished from the Buvettes des Grottes on the shore of the River Lesse, at the foot of the limestone cliffs. It is possible to purchase an entrance ticket from this alternative entrance to the park, but note that its only access is by foot along the GR 126 path, or by canoe-kayak. It is therefore feasible for those canoeing down the Lesse from Houyet to Anseremme (see details above under the general information for Dinant) to tie up their canoes here and spend a couple of hours walking the Park Trail, but note that this would require a very full day. When canoeing down the Lesse look for the signposts indicating the Buvettes des Grottes and the Furfooz National Park (park visitors standing in the Trou du Grand Duc above the precipitous drop down to the river are usually clearly visible to canoeists on the river below).

Entrance Fee: There is a small entrance fee to the park (lower price for children, students and group members).

Distance: 2.2 miles (3.5kms).

Time: Allow 2hrs for a visit to the park.

Map: *Carte du Parc de Furfooz et des Sites notables jalonnant la Promenade*. This sketch map is supplied on payment of the entrance fee to the park (it is all that is required to follow the walk and so a sketch map is not provided in this guidebook).

Guidebook: *A Practical Guidebook to Furfooz Park*. This 14 page booklet, in English (French, Dutch and German editions also available), is published by the Ardenne et Gaume Association and is available at the park entrances and in certain other outlets locally. For a full appreciation of the park the purchase of this booklet is recommended.

Waymarking: Clear direction arrows indicate the route of the National Park Trail, and "checkpoint" numbers indicate one's position along the trail with reference to the park's sketch map.

Terrain: Numerous caves and limestone cliffs above the meandering River Lesse. There are a few steep paths, but the trail is well engineered and protected with hand rails in all necessary places. The park is a nature reserve, where many protected species of trees and wild flowers can be seen.

Footwear: Trainers or stout shoes are normally suitable for this walk, except under severe weather conditions.

Refreshments: The Buvettes des Grottes, the National Park cafeteria, on the right bank of the River Lesse, at the halfway point in the walk for those starting from the park's main entrance, provides snacks and drinks. Note that this café, which is well frequented by those canoeing down the Lesse, is normally only open during the main summer months.

The Park

The National Park is administered by Ardenne et Gaume, a non-profit making organisation, whose brief is to conserve sites in Wallonia of special scientific or archaeological interest, particularly in areas of great natural beauty. The role of the organisation is both to protect the environment and to encourage access by the public. The organisation was founded in 1948 and much of the restoration and reconstruction work in the park was carried out in the late 1950s. Major archaeological excavations in the park were undertaken between 1974 and 1976. The caves are the real highlight of this limestone park, particularly the Trou du Grand Duc, whose riverside entrance stands out dramatically some 160ft (49m) vertically above the River Lesse: it is best seen from below from a kayak or boat on the river.

The Walk

The route will not be described in detail here because this is not necessary, as it is very obvious on the ground, is well waymarked and can be followed quite easily by means of the sketch map supplied with the entrance ticket. Starting from the main entrance the principal items of interest passed on the trail are as follows: heated Roman Baths, a Roman and Medieval Fortress, the Trou (cave or "hole") du Grand Duc (which provides a dramatic viewpoint high above the Lesse), the Trou qui Fume (the "smoke" is water vapour which is commonly seen in winter), the Trou des Nutons (prehistoric caves inhabited between 4500 and 2500BC), the Trou du Frontal and the Trou de la Mâchoire, the Buvettes des Grottes at "checkpoint" No. 9 on the official sketch map, the Grotte de la Gatte d'Or (cave of the Golden Goat), the Trou Collard and the Trou Reuviau. Full details of all these aspects of the park are described in the official guidebook to the park (see above).

ROCHEFORT AND HAN-SUR-LESSE

General Information and Places of Interest

This area, one of the loveliest in all the Ardennes, is well known for its extensive and spectacular cave systems, the most impressive in Belgium, and indeed the Grottes de Han rank highly amongst any of those found in northern Europe. It is the region where the River Lhomme, the river on which Rochefort is built, joins the River Lesse. The Lesse and the Lhomme form two prominent valley systems which dominate the topography of the district.

The caves at Rochefort, discovered in 1865, have both marble and limestone formations, and include the vast Salle du Sabbat whose ceiling is 85 metres above the floor of the cave. The Grotte de Rochefort is open from the beginning of April to mid-November, usually from 9.45am to 4.30 or 5.15pm. A visit lasts for approximately one hour.

Opposite the cave entrance in Rochefort are the ruins of the feudal castle of Comtal, which was once the largest fortress in the region (open to the public from Easter onwards). Nearby is a monument to La Fayette who was arrested here by the Austrians in 1792. All these items of interest in Rochefort are passed on the walks described below. There is also a small local country museum in Rochefort and a *train touristique* runs during the summer months. Finally the town is known for its local beer, brewed originally by Trappist monks.

Han-sur-Lesse is a small town which survives solely on tourism, which it is able to do because of the spectacular caves situated nearby. The Grottes de Han are certainly the grandest in the Ardennes, so if you only have time to visit one of the show caves in Belgium, then make it this one. The immense cave system, sculptured over millions of years by the subterranean River Lesse, and discovered in 1814, consists of a long series of limestone galleries, 8.7 miles (14kms) in length. The show caves are open to the public and offer an underground walk of almost 3kms. The entrance to the caves is situated a short distance outside the village, so special trams/trains transfer visitors from the reception building, where tickets are purchased, in the centre of the town, to the caves, where multilingual guides lead the way on foot through a progression of caverns, which are adorned with quite outstanding limestone formations: the Salle de Trophée, the Gallery Lannoy, Les Mystérieuses and the Salle d'Armes, where the Lesse reappears after a journey of a kilometre underground (it disappears at the Gouffre de Belvaūx, near to a point visited on Walk 9). Soon after visiting the huge Salle du Dôme, which is partly filled with a small lake, the tour finishes with a boat ride out of the cave system on the River Lesse and so back to Han.

Han caves are usually open from March to December. The opening times are generally from 10am to 4pm in March, November and December, 10am to 4.30pm in April, September and October, 9.30am to 5pm in May and June and 9.30am to 6pm in July and August. Allow a couple of hours for a visit. The caves are closed in January and February.

An explanation of how the caves were formed is provided in the display in the Musée du Monde Souterrain at Place Théo Lannoy 3 in the centre of Han. Besides an exhibition of the geology of the area, the museum includes the archaeological remains, dating from the Neolithic period to the end of the Middle Ages, found during the scientific explorations of the caves. The museum is open from April to September.

The Speleotheme is a relatively new addition to the cave "experience" in Han. It is an audio-visual show on a giant screen displaying the limestone formations which are found in the cave system. The Speleotheme is open from March to November.

The other main tourist attraction in Han-sur-Lesse is the safari park or "wildlife reserve". Covering an area of 620 acres, the reserve is home to 17

Sunlight through the trees of the forest

species of animals found in the Ardennes, not only today (deer, wild boar, etc) but also in prehistoric times (bison, tarpan, lynx, brown bear). A special bus, or "safari car", takes visitors around the park: a visit takes about 1½hrs. The opening periods and times are similar to those of the Grottes de Han.

Those wishing to visit both the caves and the safari park should buy a combined ticket, which gives entry to the caves, the Musée du Monde Souterrain, the Speleotheme and the safari park, at a somewhat reduced rate.

Also in the area is the Belgian Space Satellite Telecommunications Centre, outside the village of Lessive. Those following Walk 10 pass close by and can easily combine their walk with a visit to the centre. The centre, which receives and transmits information by satellite and broadcasts TV programmes, has an interesting exhibition and museum, the display including a full-scale model of a communications satellite. Refreshments are available on site. The centre is open to the public from Easter to November, usually from 9.30am to 5pm. Guided tours are in a number of languages, including English.

Finally, for the more athletic it is possible to descend the Upper Lesse by kayak, and combine this with a cycle ride. There are three options on offer: Han to Lessive (6kms by kayak + 4kms by bicycle), Han to Villers-sur-Lesse (9kms + 6kms) or Han to Wanlin (19kms + 13kms). The hire of both kayak and cycle is included in the price.

Accommodation

There are at least seven hotels in Rochefort: La Fayette, La Malle Poste, Le Central, Le Limbourg, Les Falizes, Le Vieux Logis and the Trou Maulin. Han-sur-Lesse has the Hôtel du Luxembourg, Hôtel des Ardennes, the Henry IV and the Hôtel des Voyageurs et Lesse. There are also a few *chambres d'hôte* in both Rochefort and Han-sur-Lesse.

There are *gîtes d'étape* in both Han-sur-Lesse (signposted from near the church in the centre of the town) and in Rochefort (near the campsite). The modern and well-appointed *gîte d'étape* in Han-sur-Lesse is only 100 metres from the High Street and is passed on Walk 10.

Rochefort has a pleasant campsite: Camping Le Roptai. There are two campsites in Han-sur-Lesse, both on the banks of the river: Camping Le Pirot and Camping de La Lesse. There is also a campsite (Le Caillou) in Belvaux, again close to the Lesse, and passed on Walk 9.

Transport

This walking centre is reached fairly easily by train, although note that trains do not actually run to either Rochefort or Han-sur-Lesse. The key is the railway station at Jemelle, a couple of miles north-east of Rochefort. Jemelle is on the main line between Namur, Arlon and Luxembourg City (see map *Belgian Railways in the Ardennes and Surrounding Areas*). There is a bus connection to Rochefort. Jemelle can also be reached by train from Liège.

Bus services operate between Rochefort, Han-sur-Lesse and Lessive, and these are convenient for the walks described in this chapter. Contact the tourist offices in either Rochefort or Han for the latest bus timetables.

Rochefort can be reached with ease by motorists, for the most part on modern, fast roads: take the N4 from Namur to Marche-en-Famenne where you turn onto the N836 to drive south-west to Rochefort. Han-sur-Lesse is best reached from the E411 (A4) motorway: from junction 23 it is only about 6kms to Han and a further 6kms on the N86 to Rochefort.

Both bicycles and kayaks can be hired in the Han-sur-Lesse.

Official Walking Trails in the Region of Rochefort and Han-sur-Lesse

There are 27 official circular walking trails in the area, from 3kms to 12kms in length. These walks, identified by both a name and a number, are marked on the 1:25,000 scale map entitled *Rochefort - à Pied, à Cheval, à Bicyclette* available from local tourist offices. Each trail starts from the church in the respective town or village and all are waymarked throughout their length. In the list below, the number of the trail (identified on the map) is given, followed by its name and the length of the walk.

From Han-sur-Lesse:
    Walk No. 1 -   Belvédère - 4.5kms.
    Walk No. 2 -   Turmont - 6.0kms.
    Walk No. 3 -   Fond de Tion - 8.5kms.
    Walk No. 4 -   Grotte d'Eprave - 5.5kms.
    Walk No. 5 -   Les Grignaux - 5.5kms.
    Walk No. 6 -   La Grande Tinemont - 8.0kms.

From Rochefort:
    Walk No. 7 -   Lorette - 3.0kms.
    Walk No. 8 -   Rond de Roi - 5.0kms.
    Walk No. 9 -   Fond des Vaux - 10.0kms.
    Walk No. 10 - Abbaye - 8.0kms.
    Walk No. 11 - Chapelle du Maquis - 7.0kms.
    Walk No. 12 - Résurgence d'Eprave - 12.0kms.
    Walk No. 13 - Belvédère de Han-sur-Lesse - 9.0kms.

From Jemelle:
    Walk No. 14 - Les Chavées - 3.0kms.
    Walk No. 15 - Thiers - 6.0kms.

From Belvaux:
    Walk No. 16 - Les Pinsons - 3.0kms.
    Walk No. 17 - Les Martinets - 8.0kms.
    Walk No. 18 - Les Rouges-Gorges - 10.0kms.
    Walk No. 19 - Les Bouvreuils - 5.0kms.

From Auffe:
    Walk No. 20 - Les Etourneaux - 8.0kms.

From Ave et Auffe:
    Walk No. 21 - Les Geais - 5.0kms.

From Eprave:
    Walk No. 22 - Les Roitelets - 10.0kms.
    Walk No. 23 - Les Bergeronnettes - 5.0kms.

From Lessive:
    Walk No. 24 - Les Pics Epeiches - 7.0kms.
    Walk No. 25 - Les Hirondelles - 8.0kms.

From Jamblinne:
    Walk No. 26 - Les Vanneaux - 3.0kms.

From Villers-sur-Lesse:
    Walk No. 27 - Les Rossignols - 4.0kms.

Walks

Six walks are described from this centre, two from Rochefort, three from Han-sur-Lesse and one from the small village of Belvaux, south of Han-sur-Lesse.

WALK 6:
The Rond Du Roi (Sentier Roi Albert)

Description: The most popular walk from Rochefort, and, as the name indicates, a favourite of King Albert I of Belgium (who was killed in a climbing accident in the Ardennes in 1934). Although only 5kms in length the ramble passes a superb viewpoint over Rochefort and the Lhomme (occasionally spelt "Lomme") valley, and traverses a hillside area of mature woodland which is a delight to walk in any season, but particularly in the early autumn when the leaves are a kaleidoscope of changing colour. It is highly suitable for family walks, for both young and old, whilst the experienced walker may wish to stroll the circuit on a summer's evening, when staying in Rochefort to walk longer trails during the main part of the day.

Location: Along a high wooded ridge above the Lhomme valley, south-west of the small town of Rochefort.

Start/Finish: The major junction of the N86 (Liège road), the N949 (Dinant road) and the N803 (Bouillon road) in the centre of Rochefort.

Distance: 3.1 miles (5.0kms).

Time: Allow 2hrs.

Maps: Either:
Rochefort - à Pied, à Cheval, à Bicyclette. A crude, but satisfactory map at an approximate scale of 1:25,000. Available at the tourist offices at Rochefort and Han-sur-Lesse.
      Or:
Promenades Balisées - La Haute Lesse et Rochefort - Carte No. 2, at a scale of 1:25,000. A better but more expensive map than the alternative above. Published by the Syndicat Régional de la Haute Lesse and available at the tourist offices at Rochefort and Han-sur-Lesse.
      IGN 1:50,000 series: sheet number 59.

Waymarking: Waymarking is by a number of metal signposts, some indicating the Sentier Roi Albert and others the Rond du Roi. For a short distance the red and white waymarks of the GR LL (GR of the Lhomme et Lesse) accompany the trail.

Terrain: Although there is a climb at the start of the walk, the round offers mainly easy and relaxed walking (it is a popular route for local dog owners exercising their pets).

Footwear: Trainers or stout shoes are all that is required, except during wet conditions, after a period of heavy rainfall. Boots, of course, would also be required when the trail is covered in snow or ice.

Option: This short circuit could be combined with the long walk

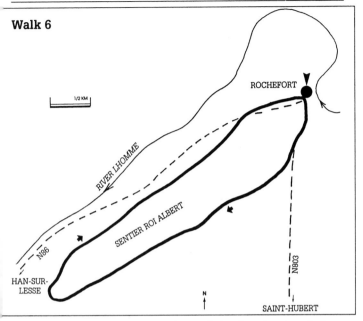

Walk 6

ROCHEFORT

1/2 KM

RIVER LHOMME

SENTIER ROI ALBERT

N86

N803

HAN-SUR-
LESSE

N

SAINT-HUBERT

between Rochefort and Han-sur-Lesse (see Walk 7) at the point where the latter crosses the Sentier Roi Albert on its return towards Rochefort.

Places of
Interest: The Château Comtal in Rochefort, passed en route. The ruins this feudal castle are open to the public for a small entrance fee (open generally from 10am to 6pm). Note the monument nearby which commemorates the arrest here of La Fayette in 1792.

Refreshments: Ample refreshments of every kind are available in Rochefort at the start and end of this short ramble.

Route

From the N86/N949/N803 road junction in the centre of Rochefort, head south on the N803 in the direction of Bouillon and Saint-Hubert, following the signs to the Sentier Roi Albert. Pass the Château Comtal on your right; 80 metres after the entrance to this château, turn right on the Avenue du Rond Point, again signposted as the Sentier Roi Albert. Climb the hill to reach a church on your right. At this point the red/white waymarked GR trail (the GR LL = GR of the Lhomme et Lesse) that has accompanied our journey, heads off to the left, but our route, the Rond du Roi, takes the right fork.

The narrow surfaced lane climbs to reach the Parc National de Lesse et Lhomme. Ignore a fork off to the left at a park signpost, but continue ahead, the track soon levelling out to reach an open area where there are seats, a wooden shelter and a fine viewpoint to the north and east over the Lhomme valley to Rochefort, the twin-towered church of the town being easily visible from here.

After admiring the view, follow the green arrow waymark for the Rond du Roi, directing walkers to the left. The waymarking is a little confusing at this point, but take the woodland track heading gently downhill in a south-westerly direction. The trail eventually swings round first to head northwards for a short while, and then east-north-east (ignore any tracks heading uphill on the right, keeping left always on the main woodland track). Mature deciduous woodland clothes this hillside: it is a particularly beautiful area in autumn when the golden yellows, browns and reds of the turning leaves make this walk a most attractive one. The Rond du Roi eventually emerges on the road on the outskirts of Rochefort at the Rue des Falizes, by an elegant brick-built château, the Château des Falises. Cross this main road by the pedestrian crossing and then bear to the right on the Rue Sous Le Château. This leads to the Avenue de Forest, which when followed will take the walker back to the N86/N949/N803 junction in the centre of town, where the ramble began.

WALK 7:
The Rochefort and Han-sur-Lesse Grand Circuit

Description: This walk is possibly the best circuit in the area between the Lhomme and Lesse valleys, linking the popular small towns of Rochefort and Han-sur-Lesse. Starting in Rochefort (optional visit to the Rochefort Caves), the walk passes the interesting old Chapelle de Lorette, after which there is fine walking through the woodland separating the Lhomme and Lesse valleys. Time can be taken in Han-sur-Lesse, the halfway stage of the walk, to visit the famous Han Caves (recommended) and/or possibly have lunch in one of its many restaurants. The most interesting and scenic section of the walk is perhaps on the return route from Han, when the Eprave Cave is passed, and the crags and rock arches above the River Lhomme can be explored.

Location: Between the small towns of Rochefort and Han-sur-Lesse, in the woods and hills above the Lhomme and Lesse valley, in the Province of Namur.

Start/Finish: The major junction of the N86 (Liège road), the N949 (Dinant road) and the N803 (Bouillon road) in the centre of Rochefort.

Distance: 10.4 miles (16.7kms)

Time: Allow 6hrs (plus a couple of extra hours if a visit to the Han

Caves is planned). If the Rochefort caves are also visited then this will be a very full day.

Maps: Either:

Rochefort - à Pied, à Cheval, à Bicyclette. A crude, but satisfactory map at an approximate scale of 1:25,000. Available at the tourist offices at Rochefort and Han-sur-Lesse.

Or:

"Promenades Balisées - La Haute Lesse et Rochefort - Carte No. 2", at a scale of 1: 25,000. A better but more expensive map than the alternative above. Published by the Syndicat Régional de la Haute Lesse and available at the tourist offices at Rochefort and Han-sur-Lesse.

IGN 1:50,000 series: sheet number 59.

Waymarking: Distinctive signposts waymark the walking trails in the Rochefort/Han-sur-Lesse/Eprave/Lessive region, but unfortunately these always assume that one is following the route in a particular direction. The trails are numbered, but care should be taken when following these numbered routes, as the numbering system of the trails in the area was revised "on paper" a few years ago, but unfortunately all the necessary alterations were not made on the ground. Consequently one can sometimes see the old numbers of the trails on trees and fenceposts, etc, and it is not always easy to determine which belong to the old numbering system and which to the new. However, the signposts now in use do, on the whole, solve any doubts that could possibly arise.

Some red/white GR waymarks will be seen occasionally: these refer to the GR LL (Lhomme et Lesse).

Terrain: Woods, hills, riverbanks, caves and two popular tourist centres. A moderate amount of ascent and descent.

Footwear: Boots are recommended for this walk, except after a long, dry spell during the summer, when trainers or stout shoes might suffice, although special care would then be required on the paths in the area of the Grotte d'Eprave.

Option: A 4km extension to the walk could be made by fit and keen walkers, by following the Sentier Roi Albert (see Walk 6) when this is encountered just before the final descent into Rochefort.

Places of
Interest: The walk can be combined with visits to either or both the Han and Rochefort Caves (admission charges to both cave systems). Note that there is also a safari park in Han-sur-Lesse. See the introductory section on Han-sur-Lesse and Rochefort for further details, and consult the tourist offices in these towns for more information.

Refreshments: There are abundant refreshments of all types available in the

Walk 7

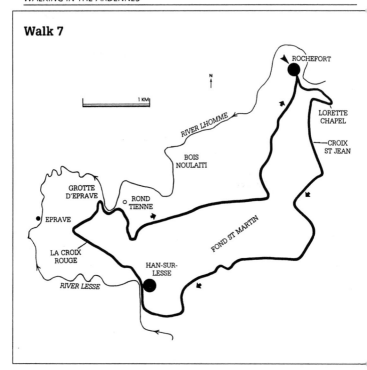

tourist towns of Rochefort and Han-sur-Lesse, but note that no places of refreshment are passed en route between these two centres.

Route

From the N86/N949/N803 road junction in the centre of Rochefort walk uphill on the minor road named Rue Beauregard, heading south. Ignore side turnings and continue to a T-junction where bear left, following walk signposts to Lorette and the Belvédère de Han. In 150 metres turn left on a footpath signposted to Lorette. Follow this pleasant trail past a shelter (view over Rochefort town) and seats, following the metal signposts indicating Lorette, to descend steeply on a narrow footpath to reach a brick-built barn and a stony track. Turn right on the latter for 100 metres before turning right off it up a series of wooden steps, and then left along a footpath. Climb more steps to reach a seat and a narrow surfaced footpath.

Turn right along this footpath, again signposted to Lorette. Climb to pass the small church of Notre Dame de Lorette. This building is usually locked, but note the coat of arms above the doorway and the reference to Josine de la Marck, Comtesse de Rochefort, who died in 1626. Continue ahead, heading west to reach a crossroads. The Lorette route continues ahead on the Avenue des Tilleuls, but we leave it here, turning right along the road signposted to Belvédère de Han. Climb on this road to reach the Rue Croix-Saint-Jean and continue ahead along this lane. There are more seats in the vicinity of the old stone cross of Saint-Jean, which is often decorated with flowers during the spring and summer (note the engraving of a male figure on the cross which is dated 1605).

At the cross of Saint-Jean continue ahead on the track signposted to the Belvédère de Han, heading south. This grassy/stony track leads to a lane at a T-junction by a small stone building. Turn right along this lane. On reaching the main road continue ahead on an unsurfaced track (*) to reach a minor road at a crossroads (@) of track and surfaced lane (note that if the track * is obstructed, eg. by barbed wire, turn left along the main road for 100 metres and then right along the minor road to reach the crossroads @). At the crossroads (@) take the grassy track which begins a few metres east of the crossroads (*not* the wider stony dirt track heading south-west, signposted to the Belvédère de Han). Our trail first passes a back garden and then to the left of a copse of tall fir trees, as it follows a course in line with the main road over to your left. After about 600 metres the path turns to the right to enter woods, and in so doing now bears away from the road.

Remain on the path through the mixed woodland (and look out for blackberries during the early autumn) until a track T-junction is reached. Here turn right, now heading towards the west. Continue ahead at a crossing track following Bridleway B 1. Descend on this forest track until it emerges from the trees to reach a narrow surfaced lane at a T-junction. Turn right here (Fond de Tion signpost). Follow this track as it bends to the right and then to the left. The track, the Rue de la Fontaine Saint Martin, becomes concreted and our trail follows it to a road at a T-junction. Turn right here to walk along the Rue des Grottes to enter Han-sur-Lesse, where cafés, restaurants, hotels and shops abound.

Pass to the left of the church, which is opposite the entrance to the Han Caves reception building. Before passing, note the interesting Arbre à Clous which stands outside the church door. Continue ahead to reach the east bank of the River Lesse, in front of the road bridge. Do not cross the bridge, but turn right here signposted to Eprave. Head north along the east (right) bank of the River Lesse (benches line the riverbank for those in need of a rest, or seeking a lunch spot). Immediately after a lefthand bend in the road, at a large shrine to the Virgin Mary, leave the river by turning right along the Rue des Masures. Bear left at a T-junction onto the Rue Malispre. Remain ahead as the lane becomes the Rue Derrière Herleux and loses its surface to become a stony track.

Continue along this track until it meets a road at a seat and a wooden cross (La Rouge Croix). Bear left along this road for about 200 metres to reach a large tree under which is a bench on the right-hand side of the road. Turn right on the surfaced track immediately beyond this tree, heading up towards the woods. About 50 metres after the track reaches the edge of the trees fork to the right at a Y-junction. The track narrows, loses its surface and enters the trees, where it soon climbs to the left to reach a pair of seats at a fine viewpoint high above the River Lhomme.

After admiring the picturesque rural scene below, descend a steep path and a series of concrete steps down to a dramatic overhanging crag and the entrance to a cave (the Grotte d'Eprave) overlooking the river (the entrance to the cave is barred and entrance is forbidden). Continue the descent through a most impressive rock arch and so down to the left bank of the river, where turn right to follow it up-stream, at first beneath high crags covered with vegetation. The path becomes a track which swings to the right in front of the tree-covered hill of Rond Tienne. Remain on this track, eventually ascending on it to reach the Rue du Beau Sejour and the main Rochefort to Han road.

Cross straight over the main road (care!) to follow the stony track opposite, which climbs steeply into the woods. The path levels out to give a straight line route through this pleasant woodland (keep to the main track avoiding any side turnings). About 400 metres after emerging from the woods the track reaches and crosses a metalled road; keep straight ahead on the dirt track as it meanders over the gentle rise ahead (285m above sea level). About 250 metres before reaching the next road, turn left on a track heading north between fields. This leads to an interesting old church, a farm dated 1661, and the Rue Hamerenne. Turn right onto the road at the T-junction ahead (red/white GR waymark) and left 50 metres later, following the signpost Belvédère de Han. The lane eventually descends towards Rochefort, reaching a T-junction in front of a large church. Turn right onto the Rond Point and descend on this road (now on the reverse of the Sentier Roi Albert - see Walk 6) to meet the main road opposite a stone monument to La Fayette. Turn left along the N803, noting the ruins of the Château Comtal above and to the left, and descend into the heart of Rochefort to the N86/N949/N803 crossroads, where the walk began.

WALK 8:
Han-Sur-Lesse, Belvaux and the Niau & Grignaux Nature Reserves

Description: A figure-of-eight walk linking the popular tourist town of Han-sur-Lesse, famed for its caves, with the village of Belvaux, south of Han, providing an opportunity to visit the two nature reserves in the area, those of Niau and Les Grignaux.

Location: South and south-west of Han-sur-Lesse and the Lesse valley. Han-sur-Lesse is 6kms south-west of Rochefort.

Start/Finish: The road bridge over the River Lesse in the centre of the small town of Han-sur-Lesse, south-south-west of Rochefort. Those with cars can conveniently park them in the car parking spaces near to the church in the High Street, or alternatively in the large car park opposite the modern gîte d'étape, which is situated about 100 metres north of the High Street (turn off the High Street where indicated at the church in the centre of Han).

Distance: 6.5 miles (10.5kms).

Time: Allow 4-4¹/₂hrs (plus a further couple of hours if the Han Caves are visited at the start or end of the walk).

Maps: Either:
Rochefort - à Pied, à Cheval, à Bicyclette. A crude, but satisfactory map at an approximate scale of 1:25,000. Available at the tourist offices at Rochefort and Han-sur-Lesse.
          Or:
Promenades Balisées - La Haute Lesse et Rochefort - Carte No. 2, at a scale of 1:,25,000. A better but more expensive map than the alternative above. Published by the Syndicat Régional de la Haute Lesse and available at the tourist offices at Rochefort and Han-sur-Lesse.
          IGN 1:50,000 series: sheet number 59.

Waymarking: See the note under "Waymarking" for Walk 7.

Terrain: Wooded hills and nature reserves. There is a stiff climb into the Bois de Niau and a steep descent from Les Grignaux woods, but otherwise the gradients are relatively gentle.

Footwear: Boots are recommended, except after a long dry spell during the summer months, when trainers or stout shoes with good grips may suffice.

Options: 1. The 6km Bouvreuils walk from Belvaux could be sandwiched between the outward and return portions of this ramble, to give a full day out (see Walk 9).

          2. The Pinsons (Trail No. 16) 1.9 mile (3km) circuit could be added to the present itinerary. The start and finish of this short, pleasant, well waymarked trail is passed on our ramble, a few hundred metres before reaching the village of Belvaux (see text of the route description for details).

*Places of
Interest:*   A visit to Han-sur-Lesse provides an excellent opportunity to visit the most famous cave system in the Ardennes. See the introductory section on Han-sur-Lesse and Rochefort for further details, and consult the tourist offices in these towns for more information. A visit to the Han Caves can be highly recommended.

Refreshments: There are refreshments of every kind available in Han-sur-Lesse at the start and end of the walk, and there is also a restaurant and a café in Belvaux, which, at the halfway stage of the walk, is a convenient place to stop for lunch.

Route

From the road bridge over the River Lesse in Han-sur-Lesse head westwards on the Rue de Charleville. Ignore turnings off to the left but, at a small stone memorial indicating the limit of the German advance during the winter of 1944-45, turn right on the Rue de la Source, following a signpost to Les Grignaux (red/white waymarks of a GR trail). Fifty metres after crossing a small bridge over a narrow tributary of the Lesse, turn left following the signpost for the GR LL (GR of the Lhomme and Lesse) towards Lavaux Ste Anne via Ave-et-Auffe (*not* via Lessive).

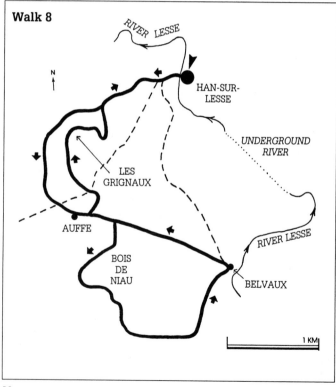

Walk 8

RIVER LESSE

N

HAN-SUR-LESSE

UNDERGROUND RIVER

LES GRIGNAUX

AUFFE

RIVER LESSE

BOIS DE NIAU

BELVAUX

1 KM

Follow the fenced track across fields to the edge of the wood where there is a track junction (point x - see below). Our route lies ahead, signposted to the Pics Epeiches. The track climbs to the right of the wood and narrows to a footpath enclosed between hedges. When the hedges thin out look for a track off to the left (south) following the red/white markings of the GR trail. Soon the buildings of the village of Auffe come into view. On reaching a surfaced lane at a T-junction turn left along the Tienne d'Aise to enter Auffe, still following the red/white markings.

Cross the main road taking the lane opposite, the Rue de Resteigne, signposted to Belvaux. Pass the small village church on your left. The GR trail takes a right fork, but we leave it here crossing the bridge over the stream (the Ave), thereby leaving Auffe. Make a note of the path (B1) turning left off this road a few hundred metres after the bridge (point y). This is the figure-of-eight crossing point to which you will be returning later. But for now continue uphill on the lane, soon ignoring a track off to the left. Twenty-five metres after the lane becomes concreted at a road sign, turn right off the road onto a earthen track heading towards the woods. On reaching the edge of the woods bear right on the track, at first with the wood on your left and grassy fields to your right, but soon the track swings to the left to climb steeply up into the woods of the Bois de Niau.

Keep to the main path during the ascent, ignoring any side turnings to left or right. When the path levels out ignore the first waymarked track on the left and, a few hundred metres later, ignore yet another path on the left (both of these trails are signposted as Martinets). Instead continue ahead (eastwards) on the main track to reach the edge of the forest at a seat and signboard indicating Bois Domanial des Gauderées. Bear right with the track here, now heading south. Ignore any further side turnings until reaching a complex junction of several tracks and a signpost indicating the walking trails of Martinets and Etourneaux. Turn left here, heading eastwards on a stony track. Remain on this main track, ignoring any side-turnings off to the right or left, to reach a minor road at a T-junction. Turn left, heading north downhill towards Belvaux on the Rouges Gorges trail.

On reaching the outskirts of the village, another short, optional walking circuit presents itself, ie the trail named Pinsons (Trail No. 16). To walk this circuit (3kms in length) follow the waymarks which point the walker along the "no through road" on the left. If a decision is made to follow this circuit, then after completing it return to Belvaux before continuing with our trail.

Descend through the village of Belvaux (restaurant and café and rooms available) to take a left turn in its centre, signposted to Han-sur-Lesse and Rochefort. A hundred metres later bear left, signposted to Ave-et-Auffe, on the Route des Onais. Remain on this minor road until reaching point "y" (see text above). Here turn right onto the enclosed footpath which at first follows the course of the Ave stream, which is on your left. The path leads to a semicircular spur of the main road to Han, at a point where the stream passes under the road. Turn left onto the tarmacked spur to join the main road for 30 metres, after which take the track on the right which bends to the right and then to the left to enter the Les Grignaux Réserve Naturelle. Keep ahead at the footpath sign indicating Trail No. 5R, Les Grignaux.

The trail soon narrows to a footpath which skirts the side of the wood, with fields to the left. Eventually the trail swings towards the east to penetrate the wood. On reaching a track junction where there are two Les Grignaux signposts it is most important to turn left (north) downhill at this point (otherwise Trail No. 5, being a circular one, will deposit the walker back at the main road by the Ave stream!). Therefore turn left onto this woodland path which descends steeply to a track junction (point x - see text above). Return to Han-sur-Lesse by retracing your steps of the outward route.

WALK 9:
Bouvreuils

Description: One of the most pleasant short walks in the area. A circuit of the woods to the north-east of the village of Belvaux is sandwiched between a there-and-back stretch alongside the River Lesse. The river is most interesting at this point as it disappears underground at the Gouffre de Belvaux and remains a subterranean watercourse for just over a kilometre, before it re-emerges a few hundred metres before Han-sur-Lesse, after which it continues its flow above ground heading north-westwards towards Dinant.

Location: The village of Belvaux which is situated on the River Lesse, a couple of miles south of Han-sur-Lesse. The trail follows a route to the north-east of the village.

Start/Finish: The centre of the village of Belvaux. An alternative start, which shortens the walk by about a mile, is at a small parking place (indicated as * in the text of the route description below) near to the bank of the River Lesse, north-east of the village. The latter option, of course, is a possibility only for those with private cars.

Distance: 3.7 miles (6.0kms).

Time: Allow 2hrs.

Maps: Either:
Rochefort - à Pied, à Cheval, à Bicyclette. A crude, but satisfactory map at an approximate scale of 1:25,000. Available at the tourist offices at Rochefort and Han-sur-Lesse.

Or:

Promenades Balisées - La Haute Lesse et Rochefort - Carte No. 2, at a scale of

Walk 9

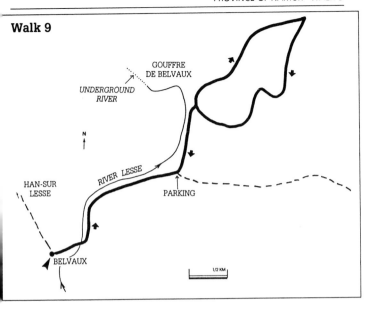

1:25,000. A better but more expensive map than the alternative above. Published by the Syndicat Régional de la Haute Lesse and available at the tourist offices at Rochefort and Han-sur-Lesse.

IGN 1:50,000 series: sheet number 59.

Waymarking: The route is well waymarked with small signposts indicating the name of the trail, viz. Bouvreuils. See also the note under "Waymarking" for Walk 7.

Terrain: Surfaced lane alongside the River Lesse, followed by pleasant woodland tracks.

Footwear: Boots or bogtrotters are preferable during wet conditions when the forest tracks become muddy, but trainers or stout shoes would be suitable during prolonged dry spells.

Options: 1. The walk can easily be combined with Walk 8, which starts in Han-sur-Lesse and reaches the village of Belvaux at its halfway stage. Lunch could then be taken in Belvaux, either before or after undertaking the Bouvreuils circuit, after which the return to Han could be made by following the second half of Walk 8. This would make a full day's outing of 10.2 miles (16.5kms).

2. Those visiting or staying in Belvaux might like to combine this walk with the local Pinsons (Trail No. 16) circuit, which starts 250 metres

south-west of the centre of Belvaux. See Walk 8 for further details. It is 1.9 miles (3kms) in length but involves some ascent and descent.

3. Those who have a car with them have the option of shortening the walk somewhat by parking as indicated by * in the text (see "Start/Finish" above).

Refreshments: There are a couple of restaurants and cafés in Belvaux, but no food shops. A restaurant and a campsite is passed en route, a little outside the centre of Belvaux.

Route

From the road junction in the village of Belvaux, by a wooden crucifix, take the road signposted to Bure and Tellin, following the River Lesse downstream. Immediately after crossing the river bear left, still following the Lesse downstream, now heading towards the prominent crag seen ahead above the river. Pass a restaurant and a campsite, leaving Belvaux on the Rue du Gouffre. Continue beside the river until, 50 metres after the lane bends to the right, turn left on a track signposted Bouvreuils (note that there is a space, *, for parking a car here, for those who wish to shorten the walk by starting and ending at this point).

The track climbs steeply at first, passes a few small rock outcrops and then descends, providing glimpses of the river below to your left (soon after this point the river disappears underground, not to reappear again until just before Han-sur-Lesse). The track levels, bends to the right, crosses a dried-up (usually) stream bed (point x - see text below) and then turns to the left, signposted as Bouvreuils - Aller.

The circuit of these wooded hillsides, which is well waymarked and always obvious to follow, begins with a climb to a spot height of 260m, at which point the trail changes direction by turning to the right to begin a descent and its homeward journey. In the latter stages of the circuit the route follows the dried-up stream bed of the Ruisseau d'en Faule to return to point x. Return to Belvaux by the route used on the outward journey.

WALK 10:
Han-Sur-Lesse, Lessive, Eprave and Les Bergeronnettes

Description: A circuit of the forests of the Bois de Bestin and the Bois de Famenne to the west of Rochefort, the walk linking the popular Han-sur-Lesse with the neighbouring villages of Lessive and Eprave. This excellent woodland walk also provides an opportunity to visit the Lessive Space Satellite Telecommunications Centre, a most interesting tourist attraction.

Location: To the north-east of Han-sur-Lesse, and east of Rochefort.

Start/Finish: The road bridge over the River Lesse in the centre of the small town of Han-sur-Lesse, south-south-west of Rochefort. Those with cars can conveniently park them in the car parking spaces near to the church in the High Street, or alternatively in the large car park opposite the modern *gîte d'étape*, which is situated about 100 metres north of the High Street (turn off the High Street where indicated at the church in the centre of Han).

Distance: 12.6 miles (20.2kms).

Time: Allow 6hrs (plus at least an extra 1hr 30mins for a visit to the Lessive Space Satellite Telecommunications Centre).

Maps: Except for the first 200 metres at the start of the walk in Han-sur-Lesse and for the last couple of kilometres back into the town at the end of the day, the trail is covered by the 1:10,000 map entitled *Carte Promenades: Lessive, Eprave, Jamblinne, Villers/Lesse* published by the local tourist office and available at their offices in Rochefort and Han-sur-Lesse. This is the best map to use for the walk. Alternatively, and to cover the sections missing from the above map, the rather crude but adequate *Rochefort - à Pied, à Cheval, à Bicyclette* map at a scale of approximately 1:25,000 can be used. This is also available at the Rochefort and Han-sur-Lesse tourist offices.

IGN 1:50,000 series: sheet number 59.

Waymarking: A short part of the trail follows the GR LL, so is waymarked in the standard way for long distance paths, ie. with red/white paint waymarkings. Several of the bridleways used on the walk carry signposts and waymarks indicating their number (B 2, B 3, etc) which can be found on the 1:25,000 map mentioned above. See also the note under "Waymarking" for Walk 7.

Terrain: Forest roads and tracks form a large part of this walk. The trail explores a section of the extensive woods which stretch for many miles to the west of Rochefort. There is not a great deal of ascent and descent on the circuit.

Footwear: As some of the forest tracks can be very wet and muddy, especially outside the summer season, boots or bogtrotters are the footwear of choice.

Option: Those wanting a short ramble can easily short-cut the trail when it approaches the outskirts of Eprave on the outward portion of the route. Simply walk through the village of Eprave to cross the road bridge over the River Lhomme, so joining the latter stages of the walk back into Han-sur-Lesse. This reduces the distance by about a half.

Places of Interest: 1. The trail passes close to the Lessive Space Satellite Telecommunications Centre (Station Terrienne de Télécommunications), which is open to the public and well worth a visit (see the introductory section for Rochefort and Han-sur-Lesse above for further details).

2. As with all walks from Han-sur-Lesse, a visit to the town provides an excellent opportunity to visit the Han caves, either at the beginning or end of the walk. As this is quite a long walk, particular note should be made of the opening times of the caves before setting out on the ramble.

Refreshments: Opportunities for refreshments are plentiful on this ramble. Han-sur-Lesse has an abundance of facilities, but there is a restaurant and a café in Lessive, on the outward stage of the walk, and also a café and restaurant in Eprave, which are passed on the return. Finally, a hotel-restaurant is passed on the final section of the walk when heading back towards Han.

For those who like to enjoy a picnic on their day out, then this walk could not be more suitable, as a large picnic and barbecue area is passed en route, ideally situated for a lunchtime stop. There are tables and benches in the open, but also some under cover in open-sided wooden huts, so that a rest and a meal can be enjoyed even if it is raining. Please leave any rubbish in the bins provided. The location of this facility is indicated in the text of the route description.

Route

From the road bridge over the River Lesse in Han-sur-Lesse, follow the Rue de Charleville westwards following the red and white waymarks of the GR LL (GR of the Lhomme et Lesse). Turn right at a small stone war memorial onto the Rue de la Source. Fifty metres after crossing a small bridge over a small tributary of the Lesse, turn right following the GR LL signposted to Lavaux Ste Anne via Lessive (*not* via Ave-et-Auffe). This narrow lane passes through grassy fields where cattle graze in the summer, before climbing gently and becoming an unsurfaced earthen track, and then a path enclosed between fences. Once over the rise the large satellite dishes of the Lessive Satellite Telecommunications Centre will be visible over to your left (a visit to the centre is possible - see "Places of Interest" above, and the introductory section on Rochefort and Han-sur-Lesse at the beginning of this chapter).

The track eventually becomes a surfaced lane (named Sur Le Ban) which passes a number of houses. At the point at which the GR LL (red/white waymarks) turns to the left, our route keeps straight ahead to reach a road T-junction within 100 metres. Bear to the right along the road heading towards the church of Lessive, whose spire should be clearly visible ahead. About 80 metres before the church, follow the road as it bends to the right, signposted to Rochefort and the old mill (*vieux moulin*), soon passing a restaurant on your left. Cross two bridges, the first over the main river and the second over an arm of the Lesse, remaining on this lane to head towards the buildings of Eprave seen ahead.

On reaching the shrine known as Notre Dame des Champs on the outskirts of Eprave, continue ahead on the Rue du Baty for 15 metres and then turn left onto a poorly surfaced drive. Cross the road ahead by a walled cemetery and maintain direction along the track known as the Rue des Boscailles. Remain on

Walk 10

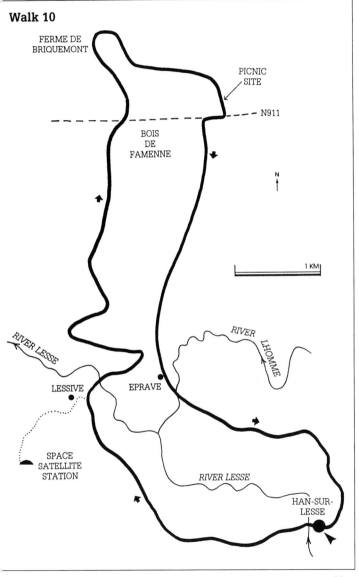

FERME DE
BRIQUEMONT

PICNIC
SITE

N911

BOIS
DE
FAMENNE

N

1 KM

RIVER LESSE

RIVER
LHOMME

LESSIVE

EPRAVE

SPACE
SATELLITE
STATION

RIVER LESSE

HAN-SUR-
LESSE

this track as it first heads west-north-west and then turns quite sharply to the north-east, before curving further to the right to head eastwards. The trail leads to a narrow lane at a T-junction. Turn left here heading towards the trees of the Bois Domanial de Bestin. Remain on this quiet lane as it first heads north-north-west and then bends to the right to head north-north-east, climbing gradually whilst traversing Bestin woods. The gradient increases as the trail penetrates deeper into the woods. At the top of the climb take a track (often muddy) on the right, to pass through an area of fir trees (the track begins opposite a small wooden hut and stony track on the left-hand side of the road - point x). This becomes a somewhat overgrown path which leads to a narrow surfaced lane: turn left for 50 metres to reach a main road (point y). [Note: walkers wishing to avoid this rather muddy and overgrown section can remain ahead on the lane at point x to reach the main road: turn right along this for approximately 200 metres to reach point y, where turn left (north) to continue the route.]

Cross the main road heading north on the gravel track ahead. Remain on this track for about a kilometre to reach a Y-junction of tracks where there is a signpost indicating the B 2 bridleway and the Bergeronnettes walking trail. Turn right (north) here, heading downhill towards the woods. After about 200 metres turn right off this track onto a grassy path beside trees (B 3 signpost), now heading east. After about 150 metres bear right into the woods, still on trail B 3. On reaching a metal barrier the trail bears to the right to head towards the south, soon passing through a dark, enclosed section of wood, before climbing towards the east in more open woodland. Continue ahead on trail B 3 at the point where the track comes in from the left. A few hundred metres after passing another metal barrier the trail reaches a cross-tracks in front of a high gate. Turn right (south) here as indicated by the mauve B 3 bridleway/cyclepath signpost. This forest track leads to a large picnic and barbecue area, an ideal spot for lunch.

Pass to the right of the car park to reach the road ahead. Turn right on this road (B 3 signpost) continuing for about 250 metres until reaching a point at which unsurfaced tracks leave the main road to left and to right at a bridleway and walking trail signpost. Take the track on the left, crossing a cattle grid and heading south. Cross a second cattle grid and continue ahead following signs for the B 1 and B 3 trails. The trail runs alongside the edge of a wood for a while (wood on the right, open fields on your left), then passes to the right of a saw mill before crossing a bridge over a disused railway line. Bear to the right immediately after this bridge, but 150 metres later leave the road by taking the grassy track on the right (field on your right and hedgerow on your left). This leads to a track T-junction, where you turn left. Twenty metres later a walking trail waymark indicates the Roitelets route off to the right, but we ignore this, continuing instead on the main track as it swings to the left, soon passing an interesting small chapel, which is half hidden amongst trees on the right-hand side of the track. Forty metres after this chapel the track meets a lane at a T-junction. Bear right along this narrow road, the Rue Saint Roch, to enter the village of Eprave.

Bear right on reaching another T-junction to walk along the Rue de la Gare, continuing ahead in the direction indicated to Han-sur-Lesse. On reaching the church and water mill in the heart of the village bear left following the stream, which is on your left, down-stream along the Rue du Treux. Leave the village, cross the River Lhomme by the stone road bridge and continue to a crossroads by a white cross on which is mounted a black Christ. Continue ahead at this crossroads heading east-south-east. Ignore the turning on the left by a large tree, bench and parking sign, but stay on the road as it swings to the left at another seat and a wooden cross (La Rouge Croix). Remain on this road until reaching the T-junction with the main Rochefort to Han road, opposite a hotel-restaurant. Turn right along this road, keeping within the cycle lane (and later along the parking and picnic area) to descend to Han. Turn right at the sign indicating the way to the *gîte d'étape* and on reaching this establishment (car park opposite the gîte), turn left to reach the High Street (more car parking spaces). Turn right here to return to the bridge over the River Lesse, the day's starting point.

WALK 11:
The Fond de Tion

Description: A fine figure-of-eight circuit of the steep wooded hillsides to the east of Han-sur-Lesse. After a rather steep climb into woodland, the trail reaches an excellent viewpoint above a precipitous drop. Later in the walk there are wider and more distant views from a high-level plateau above the Fond de Tion. An attractive war memorial is passed en route, yet another reminder of the tragic events that occurred in this area of the Ardennes half a century ago.

Location: The hills and woods to the east of Han-sur-Lesse, south of Rochefort.

Start/Finish: The road bridge over the River Lesse in the centre of the small town of Han-sur-Lesse, south-south-west of Rochefort. Those with cars can conveniently park them in the car parking spaces near to the church in the High Street, or alternatively in the large car park opposite the modern *gîte d'étape*, which is situated about 100 metres north of the High Street (turn off the High Street where indicated at the church in the centre of Han).

Distance: 6.1 miles (9.8kms).

Time: Allow 3$^{1}/_{2}$-4 hours.

Maps: Either:

Rochefort - à Pied, à Cheval, à Bicyclette. A crude, but satisfactory map at an approximate scale of 1:25,000. Available at the tourist offices at Rochefort and Han-sur-Lesse.

Or:

Promenades Balisées - La Haute Lesse et Rochefort - Carte No. 2, at a scale of 1:25,000. A better but more expensive map than the alternative above. Published by the Syndicat Régional de la Haute Lesse and available at the tourist offices at Rochefort and Han-sur-Lesse.

IGN 1:50,000 series: sheet number 59.

Waymarking: Waymarking is by a series of signposts, indicating the Fond de Tion trail. This is also local Trail No. 3 and so this digit will be found on trees and fenceposts along the way (except for the last mile or so of the route which deviates from the official line of the Fond de Tion trail, taking an alternative and superior route back to Han). For a short distance the red and white waymarks of the GR LL (GR of the Lhomme et Lesse) accompany the trail.

See also the note under "Waymarking" for Walk 7.

Terrain: A good mixture of open country, woodland, wide flat valley, high-level plateau and steep hillsides. The walk involves both a stiff climb into and a steep descent from the woods, but both are relatively short. A variety of trails including footpath, woodland track, and quiet, meandering country lanes.

Footwear: The tracks and paths are often muddy, even in summertime, and some of the steeper sections could be slippery in wet or icy conditions. Therefore boots are recommended.

Option: Those wanting a quick return to Han-sur-Lesse after exploring the Fond de Tion can retrace their outward steps from the Airmen's War Memorial. The full route described below is, however, very worthwhile.

Places of
Interest: The Han Caves are recommended for those who have not yet visited them. The reception building where tickets may be bought is located opposite the church in the high street of Han-sur-Lesse. A visit to the caves lasts approximately 1hr 30mins - 1hr 45mins.

Refreshments: Refreshments are only available in Han-sur-Lesse at the start and end of the walk, but as the latter can be accomplished within half a day, this should not present a problem.

Route

From the road bridge over the River Lesse in Han-sur-Lesse, walk east along the High Street of the village, following the red and white waymarks of the GR LL and the walking trail signpost indicating the Fond de Tion. Leave the village behind, ignore the Rue de la Fontaine Saint Martin on the left, but instead continue ahead towards the farm buildings. The lane climbs gently amidst fields until it reaches a "no entry" sign (exit for safari cars!). Forty metres before this road sign bear left on an unsurfaced track heading east (signpost Fond de Tion). Remain on this stony path between wire fences to reach a T-junction at the edge of woodland by a metal crucifix (point x - the trail will return to this point later - see text below). Bear right here at the Fond de Tion signpost along a dirt track. Head south-east along this track until a fence corner and another Fond de Tion sign is reached. At this point (point y - see later below) leave the track to climb up the field on the right (ie. heading south towards the woods), keeping to the left of the fence. This field is sometimes ploughed and therefore one can expect muddy boots.

At the top of the climb bear left in front of the trees, remaining in the field to reach another Fond de Tion signpost which directs to the right into the woods. The route climbs gradually on a muddy track before leaving this at a signposted footpath on the left of the track. This footpath climbs steeply through the woods: its route is never in doubt as waymark number 3 on the boles of trees indicate the way. The path levels and soon reaches a viewpoint perched on the cliff edge overlooking the valley to the west.

From the viewpoint do *not* take a thin unwaymarked path heading east (it peters out after about 1/2km), but rather it is important to retrace your steps for about 40 metres to locate the continuing waymarked trail (Fond de Tion) heading east between tall pine trees. The path turns to head south after a while, eventually emerging from the trees onto a narrow, poorly waymarked track. Turn left (east) along this track.

The way passes through an area of trees again before emerging onto an open grassy plateau, from which there are extensive views. About a kilometre after joining the track a cross-tracks is encountered. Our route takes the track to the left heading west-north-west. After 150 metres fork right at a Y-junction of tracks to descend a straight, narrow track between fields, heading towards the distant wood. The track ends on meeting the trees and the trail continues steeply downhill on a stony and often muddy path, which can be slippery in wet or icy conditions. Descend to a track junction where you bear left to reach point

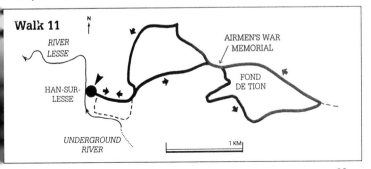

93

y once again. Retrace your steps to point x (see text above).

Turn right at the metal crucifix to reach within 30 metres a war memorial, erected in 1970, dedicated to those American, Russian and Belgian airmen who fell between 1940 and 1945. Continue past the memorial on the narrow winding lane with the wooded hillside to the right and a large flat grassy area to the left. After about 800 metres, where this lane bends to the left, leave the Fond de Tion route which follows this lane, but instead turn right on a stony/grassy track between wire fences, climbing northwards towards the trees. The track narrows and enters the wood, soon after which you arrive at a wooden footbridge over a (usually) dried-up stream on the left. Turn left to cross this footbridge and continue along the path at its far side. This most pleasant, undulating path, which is far preferable to the lane taken by the official Fond de Tion circuit, follows the edge of the woods, just within the trees for the most part, crossing four plank bridges in all (care when wet), before it ends at a tarmacked lane. Turn right at this road, the Rue de la Fontaine Saint Martin, to reach a T-junction. Turn right here, passing the *Sortie Grotte* to walk back into the centre of Han-sur-Lesse.

VRESSE-SUR-SEMOIS AND ALLE-SUR-SEMOIS

General Information and Places of Interest

This area of the Semois is an open air paradise, a mecca for those who want to spend their holidays pursuing quiet, peaceful, outdoor pursuits, such as walking, camping, canoeing, cycling, fishing or cross-country skiing. There are few tourist attractions as such, which is perhaps the great appeal of the area, a place to get away from it all, even in this crowded part of Europe. Alle-sur-Semois has a small museum devoted to the geology and industry surrounding slate (Galerie et Musée d'Ardoisière), and also the Récréalle Recreation Centre (see "Places of Interest" under Walk 13). Vresse has a Tobacco Museum (the area was once important in the tobacco industry). Apart from visiting these, the main reason for holidaying in the area is to enjoy and explore the river valley and the steep and wooded hills in this most tranquil of locations. Canoeing down the Semois is one of the more popular activities in the area, but even with this activity the crowds of kayak enthusiasts often seen on the Lower Lesse at Anseremme and on the Ourthe at La Roche are seldom a problem here.

The tourist office has a very good walkers' map of the area for sale, one of the better ones to be found in the Ardennes. The map has been produced by the Belgian IGN and is very well contoured. Those who have enjoyed the two walks in this area might wish to sample more of the excellent walking available in the Semois region. If that is the case then consult the six walks covered in the chapter on "Bouillon and the Semois" under the Province of Luxembourg.

Accommodation

There are several hotels in both Vresse-sur-Semois and Alle-sur-Semois, and also in Bohan (Walk 12). The tourist information centre in Vresse (Centre Touristique et Culturel - see Appendix 3), housed in a large smart building in the High Street, has details of all hotels in the area, and will book rooms on your behalf on request. There is no youth hostel or *gîte d'étape* in the vicinity.

The area is an excellent one for camping, there being many sites along the tranquil, rural Semois. There are two sites in Vresse-sur-Semois, along the banks of the river: Camping La Gué and Camping Pré Sainte Marie, both on Rue Albert Raty. At Alle-sur-Semois there is Camping Ami Pierre on the Rue de Liboichant. There are also two campsites in Mouzaive-sur-Semois, passed on Walk 13 (Camping Le Héron and Camping Communal de la Lingue), and no less than five sites at Bohan, passed on Walk 12 (Camping de la Douane, Camping des Bouleaux, Camping La Rivette, Camping Confort amd Camping La Besace).

Transport

This centre is one of the more difficult to reach by the walker relying on public transport. The most useful train line is that heading south from Namur to Dinant, Houyet and Beauraing. After Beauraing the line continues to Bertrix and Florenville. Before reaching Bertrix there are stations near to the villages of Gedinne and Paliseul. These stations are the nearest that the railway comes to the area, but they are still some 10-15kms from Vresse. Note also that this is a local, rather than a main line, so trains are not that frequent. There are buses from Bouillon to Rochehaut, Alle and Vresse, but again the service is not a regular one. Contact the tourist offices in Bouillon and Vresse for up-to-date details of services and timetables. An option, for those with sufficient time and energy, would be to walk the trails from Bouillon to Vresse along the Semois valley, making use of both the Bouillon/Dohan and the Vresse/Alle walkers' maps. This would require several days, but would provide a most satisfying holiday, exploring the Semois district in some depth.

The motorist can approach the area on fast, modern roads, except for the last 15-20kms, which are on much slower, single carriageway roads. Follow the E411 (A4) motorway south from Namur to junction 25; leave the motorway here in favour of the N89, a dual carriageway. Remain on this to the village of Menuchenet, where turn right on the single carriageway N819 to Rochehaut, Alle and Vresse. An alternative road south is the N95 from Dinant, eventually leaving this in favour of the N945 which leads to Vresse.

Mountain bikes can be hired from both Vresse and Alle.

Official Walking Trails in the Region of Vresse-sur-Semois and Alle-sur-Semois

There are 7 official waymarked trails from Vresse and 11 such trails from Alle. These are all clearly marked on the 1:25,000 *Carte des Promenades de Vresse-*

sur-Semois available from local tourist offices. The trails are identified and waymarked by number. They are as follows:

Vresse-sur-Semois

    Trail No. 28 - Du Pont de Claies - 2.5kms.
    Trail No. 80 - Chemin du Blanc - 1.5kms.
    Trail No. 81 - Les Viperes - 3.0kms.
    Trail No. 82 - Des Cretes - 4.5kms.
    Trail No. 83 - Trou des Fées - 3.0kms.
    Trail No. 84 - Du Terne - 4.0kms.
    Trail No. 85 - Maquis -7.0kms.

Alle-sur-Semois

    Trail No. 1 - Le Petit Monceau - 1.3kms.
    Trail No. 2 - Récréalle - 2.4kms.
    Trail No. 3 - Nancrète - 8.0kms.
    Trail No. 4 - Jeune Bois - 4.0kms.
    Trail No. 5 - Frahan - 11.0kms.
    Trail No. 6 - Gros-Fays - 11.0kms.
    Trail No. 7 - Sacre-Coeur - 6.0kms.
    Trail No. 8 - Pic de la Girouette - 2.7kms.
    Trail No. 9 - Cornimont - 7.0kms.
    Trail No. 10 - Naglémont et Pont de Claies - 13.0kms.
    Trail No. 11 - Virée des Malheurs - 19.0kms.

There are also other waymarked trails from neighbouring villages in or above the Semois valley which are also marked on the Vresse-sur-Semois walkers' map: 13 walking trails from Bohan (110kms in total), 8 from Sugny (60kms in total), 5 from Chairière (30kms in total), 4 from Laforêt (15kms in total), 3 from Orchimont (25kms in total) and 3 from Nafraiture (22kms in total).

Walks

Two walks are featured in this area of the Semois, one from Vresse and one from Alle.

WALK 12:
Vresse, Bohan and the River Semois

Description: A hilly circuit above the Semois valley to the west of Vresse-sur-Semois. After a steep climb out of Vresse the walk follows a series of tracks and paths to the north of the River Semois before a descent leads south to the pleasant village of Bohan on the Semois. Two steep climbs to viewpoints south of the river take the walker to the village of Laforêt, from where a path leads

The tranquil River Semois between Bouillon and Alle-sur-Vresse (Walks 12-19)

The River Semois at its junction with the Grand Ruisseau north-west of Bouillon (Walk 14)

The château above the River Semois at Bouillon
The view of the River Semois and Dohan from Charmes (Walk 18)

back to Vresse. Several local walking trails are used in the walk, as well as a section of the GR AE, a long distance trail that links the Ardennes with the adjacent range of the Eifel in Germany.

Location: To the west of Vresse-sur-Semois, both north and south of the meandering River Semois.

Start/Finish: The bank of the River Semois in the centre of Vresse.

Distance: 9.9 miles (16.0kms).

Time: Allow 5hrs 30mins - 6hrs.

Maps: The map entitled *Carte des Promenades de Vresse-sur-Semois* at a scale of 1:25,000. It is published by the tourist offices of Alle, Bohan, Nafraiture, Sugny and Vresse-sur-Semois. The best tourist office in the area is the large, modern Tourist and Cultural Information Centre in Vresse-sur-Semois High Street.

IGN 1:50,000 series: sheet number 63.

Waymarking: The local trails are numbered from 1 to 85, and these numbers occur on small waymarks along the trails that are indicated on the tourist office's walkers' map (see "Maps" above). Several of the local trails used on this circuit lacked waymarks at the time of research, but if the route as described in this book is followed carefully, then no navigational problems should be encountered.

Terrain: The River Semois is highly meandering in this region and its banks are very steep sided. Consequently the walking hereabouts is fairly arduous in nature, but the steep woodland paths are often a delight and the views of the surrounding area of hills and woods and of the deep-cut, winding river valley, are marvellous. There are three steep and relatively long climbs on this circuit, so it is quite a strenuous round.

Footwear: Boots are recommended as the majority of the walk follows forest tracks and paths which can be muddy. Some of the paths are steep requiring a good tread on the boots.

Options: Those looking for alternative paths to complete the circuit should take special note of the fact that there are only three bridges across the wide River Semois between Vresse and Bohan: one each at Vresse and Bohan and a third in between these two villages, at Membre.

Refreshments: There are several cafés, restaurants, shops and hotels in Vresse-sur-Semois where the walk begins and ends. The village of Bohan on the Semois, a little over halfway round the circuit, but immediately before two of the steepest climbs on the walk, is very conveniently placed for a lunchtime stop. Bohan, a popular small centre on the riverside, has several cafés, restaurants and shops.

Route

From the north side of the River Semois in Vresse take the road heading north-west, signposted to Membre. Within 100 metres turn right onto a minor road. On reaching the small chapel/shrine of Notre-Dame de Walcourt turn right in front of the shrine up the Chemin des Blaireaux..At the entrance to a house take the track on the far side (Trail Nos 84 and 85) which climbs to the side of the house. Climb towards the north on this track: continue ahead uphill on reaching a cross-tracks, and again proceed ahead at a second cross-tracks, where Trail No. 80 crosses our route, now climbing steeply. At the top of this tiring climb ignore Trail No. 85 on the right, but continue ahead on the track. This crosses the high-level plateau, soon swinging to the left (west-north-west), becoming surfaced as it does so, and then descending to a T-junction by a house and barns (Le Terne).

Turn right on the road, but within 20 metres turn right onto a track (waymarked as Trail Nos 70 and 85) which climbs between hedgerows, with fields either side, heading north-east. On reaching the corner of a wood turn left, now heading north-west, still on Trail Nos 70 and 85, and alongside the edge of the plantation. The trail enters the wood and is accompanied by red/

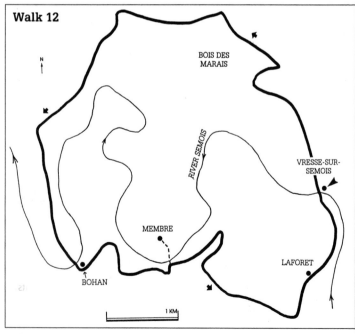

Walk 12

N

BOIS DES MARAIS

RIVER SEMOIS

VRESSE-SUR-SEMOIS

MEMBRE

LAFORET

BOHAN

1 KM

white GR markings for a while, until a cross-tracks is reached. Here our way goes straight ahead on Trail No. 70 to meet, within 100 metres, a metalled lane. Bear left along this following the direction of the Trail No. 70 waymark. Pass the charming stone built Chapel du Flachi (alas it is usually kept locked) and continue ahead on the lane.

About 100 metres after the chapel, at a "70" waymark, turn left on a track between tall trees, climbing to reach a hill-top farm at Orchimont. Here we leave Trail No. 70 (which turns left along the road) but instead take the grassy track ahead (west). Later follow the line of power cables downhill (ie. ignoring both a track off to the left before the descent and another cross-tracks 80 metres later). Descend on the track, following the line of pylons to reach a narrow metalled lane. Turn left along this for about 250 metres until, at the top of the hill, take a track which turns very sharply back to the left. The track heads through the trees, soon swings to the south, and then to the south-west. Ignore a sharp turn to the left at a small bench, and continue ahead. The trail soon becomes a path that descends through the wood along the side of a valley (babbling water should be heard over to your left). The path, a delightful one, descends gently at first, passing several small rock outcrops, before descending very steeply (care), but only for a short distance, to reach a crossing path. Do not continue downhill here, but bear right on a gently climbing path (Trail No. 54) heading south-south-west. Remain on this track until it reaches a road (the N973) by a barrier. Turn left along the road (waymark for Trail No. 54) and descend on it, heading south. Descend on this road for about 1.5kms to the village of Bohan.

Cross the River Semois by the road bridge in the village. Bear right after crossing this bridge, but after 50 metres turn left on the Rue Fernande Pierard (red/white waymark of the GR AE). Continue ahead at the first junction and bear right, uphill on a narrow lane, at the second junction, following the red/white waymarks. Bear right at a third junction, now climbing on an unsurfaced track. The trail climbs very steeply to reach a house. Climb past the house, bearing right into the woods, following the waymark for Trail Nos 49 and 50, now climbing towards the south. The path climbs very steeply to reach a path T-junction at the top of the hill. Turn left, heading east and following the red and white waymarks of the GR AE. The descent is a very steep one and care should be exercised, especially when the conditions are wet or icy.

Descend to a road and turn right along it. Follow the road as it bends to cross a bridge over a small river and reaches a T-junction. Turn left here, signposted to Dinant, but before crossing the bridge over the River Semois turn right (waymarks for Trail Nos 72 and 26) on a track between the two houses that stand on the south side of the bridge. Walk along this attractive stretch of the river to reach a campsite, where you fork right. Before reaching the end of the campsite fork right, uphill, on Trail No. 72 signposted to a *belvédère*. The path climbs first to the north-east and then turns sharply to the right. Follow the track as it levels for a while and then be on the lookout for a path that bears left off the track that you are on, and climbs quite steeply. On reaching the top of the hill, turn right at a path T-junction to reach in a few metres a seat and lookout point (the view is better appreciated during the winter months when the trees are leafless), or turn left to continue the walk, now heading towards the south-east on Trail No. 26.

There are good views to the right, of hills totally blanketed in trees, as the track continues on to reach a junction of seven tracks, where there are two small seats. Continue ahead on the track, signposted to Laforêt, which initially heads east but within 100 metres swings to the right to head south-east. The track leads to a road at a hairpin bend. Turn left along this road. Forty or so metres after the bend in this road, and before a house on the right, turn left down a grassy track through trees. Descend to reach a large hotel-restaurant at a crossroads. Continue ahead, descending through the village of Laforêt, bearing right at the next junction and continuing on to reach the church.

Fifty metres after the church turn right on a descending lane and bear left at the T-junction ahead. A few metres after the road loses its surface be sure to turn left off it onto a footpath waymarked as Trail No. 28 to Vresse. Follow this path, muddy at times, to reach a main road by Vresse road bridge over the River Semois. Turn right to cross the bridge, so returning to the centre of Vresse.

WALK 13:
Alle, the Virée des Malheurs and the Grand Opimont

Description:　　　This walk nicely combines a stroll along a section of the normally tranquil River Semois with a walk in the extensive woods to the south and west of Alle. The ramble follows sections of a number of local trails, principally numbers 10, 11, 60 and 3, and also samples a stretch of the Chemin de Sedan forest trail, before returning to Alle along a part of the long distance GR AE. The way passes through the Virée des Malheurs, the Bois de la Falijle, the Bois des Godrîses, and the Grand Opimont, areas where intricate systems of deep, steep-sided tortuous wooded valleys lie in the heart of this immense forest. The area round Sedan to the south of here is of macabre historical interest as it was the scene of terrible fighting during the Second World War.

Location:　　　A circuit to the south of the River Semois, south-east of Vresse, a few miles from the French border, north of Sedan.

Start/Finish:　　　The church in the centre of the village of Alle-sur Semois.

Distance:　　　11.2 miles (18.0kms).

Time:　　　Allow 6hrs 30mins - 7hrs.

Maps:　　　The map entitled *Carte des Promenades de Vresse-sur-*

Semois at a scale of 1:25,000. It is published by the tourist offices of Alle, Bohan, Nafraiture, Sugny and Vresse-sur-Semois.

IGN 1:50,000 series: sheet numbers 63 and 66 (the walk is awkwardly situated in a corner where four IGN 1:50,000 maps meet, viz numbers 63, 64, 66 and 67).

Waymarking: Four systems of waymarking will be found in the Alle region, in addition to the universal red/white of the GR system: 1. small white waymarks carrying the number of the trail in black and having a red-tipped arrow indicating the suggested direction to walk the trail. 2. small blue and white signs showing a walking stick. 3. white trail numbers on a green background. 4. a separate numbering system of promenades waymarked by the organisation known as the Amis de Alle (Friends of Alle). All this is rather confusing. The other problem is that the trails in the area are waymarked on the assumption that one is travelling in a particular direction along them: it can be quite difficult at times to follow a trail the "wrong way" round (note that this is also a problem with the waymarking in the neighbouring Vresse region). Some of the trails indicated on the Vresse/Alle/Semois map are not waymarked on the ground, and just a few are waymarked in situ along routes other than those shown on the map. All this is not very user-friendly, but with the aid of this guidebook it is hoped that no problems will be experienced on the routes described herein.

Terrain: The wide, graceful flowing River Semois, followed by the extensive forest to the south of the Semois valley. There are a few steep ascents and descents, but generally the walk is not too strenuous.

Footwear: With the exception of the first few kilometres from Alle to Mouzaive which are on a surfaced lane, the majority of the walk follows forest tracks and footpaths, some of which are fairly steep and several of which are muddy after rain. Therefore boots are recommended.

Option: Those who become fatigued on the walk will be comforted to know that once in the Bois de la Falijle there is a shorter return route to Alle from the one described below. This is along waymarked Trail No. 11, heading north-eastwards directly back to the village. This will cut a couple of miles off the route.

Places of Interest: The Récréalle Recreation Centre in Alle offers a number of facilities, from fishing and bathing in the river, to volleyball and *pétanque*. Mountain bikes can be hired, but the most popular activity during the late spring, summer and early autumn is to descend the River Semois by canoe. One and two seater canoe-kayaks can be hired from here and transport provided for descents of the Semois between Bouillon and Alle (27kms), Alle and Bohan (22kms) and Poupehan, Vresse and Membre (24kms).

Refreshments: There are no possibilities for obtaining refreshments en

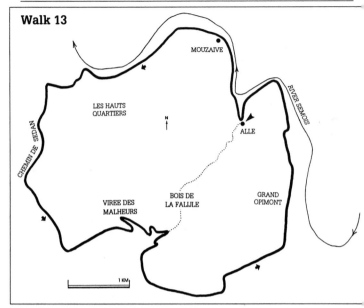

Walk 13

MOUZAIVE

RIVER SEMOIS

LES HAUTS
QUARTIERS

CHEMIN DE SEDAN

N
↑

ALLE

BOIS DE
LA FALIJLE

GRAND
OPIMONT

VIREE DES
MALHEURS

1 KM

route, only at the start and finish at Alle. Therefore the wise will take food and drink along with them. Alle has hotels, several cafés, restaurants and shops. There is a bar-restaurant (Les Pierres du Diable) in the Récréalle Centre on the outskirts of Alle (passed on the return to the village - see "Places of Interest" above).

Route

From the church and war memorial in the centre of Alle head west-north-west across the Place George Mongin for 100 metres to reach the Rue La Ringe. Turn right, north, along this road until a few metres *before* the road bridge over the River Semois, turn left on the lane signposted to Mouzaive. Walk along the River Semois to enter the village of Mouzaive. Pass to the right of the village church and follow the road as it bends to the left past a crucifix. Halfway up the hill ahead, fork right at a Y-junction onto a narrow lane (Rue de Lingue) passing to the right of a small walled cemetery.

Remain on this lane to reach a campsite. Here, at a junction with a track on the left, leave the surfaced lane (which descends to the campsite) by bearing left onto the track, to head very gently uphill into the wood. The track climbs only a little before it descends equally gently. Remain on the main stony track, ignoring a grassy track along the way which climbs to the left, until the track approaches the river again, and then stay on the track as it changes direction to head south-south-west. The track finally swings to the right to reach a track T-junction at a rather novel, small triangular shelter with two seats (a godsend in the rain!). Turn left (south) on the track to pass a metal barrier. About 100 metres after the barrier, at a small wooden seat, turn right off the track onto a narrow path that climbs the hillside to the west. Continue ahead at a crossing track, now following red/white waymarks. At the top of the steep climb the trail reaches a good track, the Chemin de Sedan, at a T-junction.

Turn left (south) along this chemin. Remain on this prominent track, following white & blue "walking stick" waymarks and ignoring all side turnings for about 1.9 miles (3kms) as the track follows a woodland ridge, first to the south-south-west and then to the south-south-east. Eventually you will reach a path on the left at a metal barrier on the left where there is a sign inhibiting motor vehicles *excepté service forestier*. Take this path, Trail No. 60, now heading east-north-east. The trail soon begins to descend. Follow it until it reaches a track at a hairpin bend in the latter. Turn left to follow the track downhill, now heading north-west. Lower down the track takes another hairpin bend, then descending to the south-east to reach a river in the valley bottom. Remain on the main track here as it bends to the left, and climb on it for about 200 metres, to reach a point where two tracks go off acutely to the right. Take the second (upper) of these two tracks, and climb for about 350 metres, first to the south-east and then towards the east, to reach a path junction of Trail Nos 3 and 11 at a small stream in the heart of the Bois de la Falijle. Turn right here on Trail No. 3 (also the Amis de Alle Promenade No. 23) heading south-west downhill, with the stream on your right. Descend to a path junction and here turn left, now leaving the stream, but still following Trail Nos 3 and 23. The path crosses another small stream and then soon swings towards the south to follow the course of yet another woodland stream (the Ruisseau de Rebais) which is running down the valley over to your right. Continue on the path to reach a cross-tracks. Here turn left (east), following the waymark for Trail No. 3, and now climbing up the valley.

Climb on this path until, at the top of the hill, the track approaches a main road and bends to the left to run parallel with and just below the road for about 200 metres, before joining the road. Bear left on this road for a further 200 metres before turning right onto a track. Five metres later, at a small seat, turn right again onto a second track which doubles back to run parallel with the road (NB. do not miss this second turn, ie. do not proceed east-north-east downhill on the track ahead). Our track, waymarked as Trail Nos 3 and 11, bends to the left away from the road within 40 metres, and then after a further 150 metres reaches a track junction, where you follow the direction of waymark No. 3 to the left (east). Continue ahead at a cross-track (waymark 3), and then soon reach a Y-junction where you bear to the left (3 waymark once again), now heading north over another cross-track. The trail soon becomes a path descending fairly steeply between encroaching trees. A little before the bottom of the descent a red/white waymark of the GR AE should be noticed as we pick up this trail: the GR AE is to be followed from here back to Alle.

Descend on the path to reach a main road. Turn right (north) along this road, following the waymarks for Trail Nos 3 and 5. When halfway round the hairpin bend in the road, turn right onto a minor lane (waymarks 3, 5 and red/ white) to enter the outskirts of Alle. Soon the town comes into view below and to the left. Continue along this lane to reach a crossroads, where you proceed ahead around a sharp right-hand bend (ignore a gravel track on the left at this bend). A few metres before reaching a solitary building on the right, turn left off the lane onto a narrow, steeply descending path (red/white waymarks). The path zigzags downhill and then levels before approaching a track down to your right. Do not drop down to this, but follow the narrow path as it now climbs steeply to the left. This delightful path undulates around the hillside above the river Semois, finally dropping down very steeply (care required when wet or icy) to reach the left bank of the river. Turn left to follow it downstream. Follow the grassy bank or the lane beside the river, heading towards Alle road bridge, but before reaching the latter bear left with the lane. About 100 metres after the bend, ignore the left turn taken by the GR AE (red/white waymarks) at a restaurant, but continue ahead to reach the Rue La Ringe and the centre of Alle.

Province of Luxembourg

It is important not to confuse the Province of Luxembourg, part of Belgium, with the Grand Duchy of Luxembourg, a separate country which lies to the east of the Belgian Province. Rather confusingly both the capital of the Grand Duchy and the country itself are commonly referred to as Luxembourg, as too is the Belgian Province of Luxembourg. To avoid any confusion in this book the term Luxembourg, when used, will always refer to the Belgian Province of Luxembourg; the country will be referred to always as the Grand Duchy of Luxembourg and its capital as Luxembourg City.

BOUILLON AND THE SEMOIS
General Information and Places of Interest

Bouillon is one of the author's favourite areas of the Ardennes. The Semois is a greatly meandering river (it is 27kms by canoe from Bouillon to Alle-sur-Semois, but only about a third of that distance by road) and the banks and forests lining the river are very steep sided. The whole area is most picturesque, as is the town of Bouillon itself, built on a tight meander of the Semois. The town, 90kms south of Namur, is dominated by its château, which is well worth a visit: do also view it at night when it is floodlit. Bouillon is very close to the French border and has a very French "feel" to it - indeed it was French territory for a time from 1678.

The River Semois, one of the great rivers of the Ardennes, rises in the Province of Luxembourg, flows through the Province of Namur (see the chapter on Vresse-sur-Semois and Alle-sur-Semois), and then enters France, where it changes its name slightly to the Semoy, before finally draining into the Meuse. The Semois is a more gently flowing river than those of the Lesse or Ourthe. Hence, rather more arm power is required for kayaking on the Semois than on the other rivers, but it provides a very tranquil experience in beautiful surroundings. It is possible to canoe from Bouillon to Poupehan and on into the Province of Namur, to Alle, Vresse and Membre. But walking in the area is an even more rewarding activity.

The map sold at the tourist office in Bouillon (situated in the château) is one of the best walkers' maps that the author has encountered in the Ardennes. Contours are clearly shown, as too is the detailed waymarked path network of the area: it is a pity that most of the other regional Ardennes maps are not of this standard.

No walker who visits the area should leave without exploring the beautiful town of Bouillon itself, the most important settlement in the Semois valley. The

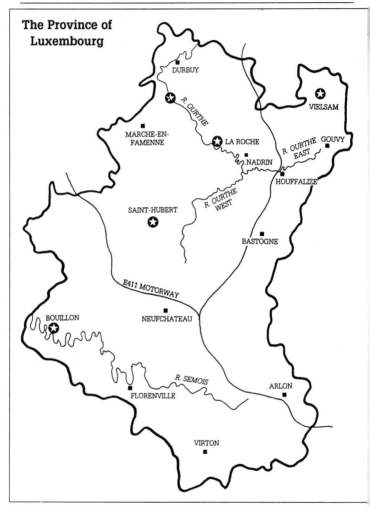

The Province of Luxembourg

DURBUY

R. OURTHE

VIELSAM

MARCHE-EN-FAMENNE

LA ROCHE

R. OURTHE EAST

GOUVY

NADRIN

HOUFFALIZE

R. OURTHE WEST

SAINT-HUBERT

BASTOGNE

E411 MOTORWAY

BOUILLON

NEUFCHATEAU

R. SEMOIS

ARLON

FLORENVILLE

VIRTON

town, which only has a population of about 4000, is dominated by two features, one natural and the other man-made: the wide, gently flowing River Semois, and the château which stands on a high ridge above the river and the houses of the town. The castle dates from the 8th century and is one of the oldest and most interesting to visit in Belgium. The present buildings date from the 15th century, but the fortress was also considerably modified by Vauban, the great French military architect, when the French held the town from 1678. The castle was used for military purposes until 1830. A walk around the numerous courtyards, battlements, towers and dungeons is worthwhile: there is an explanatory leaflet in English. One of the most interesting features is the Chair of Godfrey, a lookout cut out of the solid rock. The castle is open daily from the end of March to the end of November. In December it is closed on Mondays and Tuesdays; during January and February it is open only at weekends; it is open during the Christmas holidays and at Bouillon Carnival time.

The most important figure in the history of Bouillon was Godfrey (Godefroid de Bouillon), the fifth and last count of Bouillon, who was one of the leaders of the First Crusade in 1096. His story is told in Musée Ducal, which is housed in an 18th century house in the town. Apart from a room devoted to Godfrey, the Crusades and weapons of this and later periods, there are other exhibits relating to life in the 16th century, with displays on hunting, clogmaking, lacemaking, weaving and other crafts: there are explanations and a taped commentary in English. A part of the museum is also devoted to folklore and the history of the town; this section includes a model of Bouillon as it was in 1690. This interesting museum is open daily from April to the end of October, and at weekends in November and December.

Chanteraines Animal Park is about a mile (1.5kms) from the centre of Bouillon: here will be found several species of animal found in the Ardennes forests, including roe and fallow deer, moufflon and wild boar. A carnival is held annually in March in the town.

Dohan is a charming village set on the banks of the River Semois, amidst steep, wooded hillsides. Dohan is an excellent centre for walking, so much so that three routes have been described from there in this guidebook. There is an excellent viewpoint of the village, nestling in the deep valley beside the river, from the main Noirefontaine/Bouillon road (N816), about a mile outside Dohan (space for parking a couple of cars), but even better ones are to be had from Charmes on Walk 18 and from the Roche Lecomte on Walk 16.

Rochehaut is a small village (population 300) which owes its name to its location high above the River Semois, where it towers high above the slate roofs of the houses and the 17th century church of tiny Frahan, situated on an ox-bow bend in the River Semois. There are also the castle ruins of Montragut and Lyresse to see at Frahan. Rochehaut is situated at 344m above sea level (compare this with Bouillon which stands at 230m on the River Semois).

Accommodation
Bouillon, as might be expected, has a reasonably large selection of hotels (14 are listed in the latest brochure) including the Hôtel au Vieux Moulin, the Hôtel de France, La Tannerie and the Central Duc de Bouillon. There are also some private rooms available in Bouillon (contact the tourist office for details - see

Appendix 3). The first-rate Auberge du Moulin Hideux is passed en route on Walk 15. Even the smaller village of Dohan (Walks 16, 17 and 18) has three hotel-restaurants. There is one hotel in Rochehaut (Walk 19) and another in nearby Laviot, with several more in the neighbourhood.

Bouillon has a large modern youth hostel (see Appendix 4).

Campsites abound in this popular outdoor centre. In the neighbourhood of Bouillon there are several sites including Camping Halliru, Camping de l'Eauwez, Moulin de la Falize, Les Gouttelles and Camping Pré de la Scierie. In the vicinity of Rochehaut will be found Camping Le Sagittaire, Camping de la Vallée, Camping du Melli, Camping du Ban de Laviot and Camping Le Palis. Poupehan (Walk 19) has the Camping du Vieux Moulin, Camping d'Houlifontaine, Camping Les Gouttelles and Camping La Glycine. Finally there are two small campsites in the village of Dohan (Walks 16, 17 and 18).

Transport

The nearest reasonably sized train station is at Bertrix, unfortunately several kilometres to the north-east of Bouillon. The best plan is to take a train to either Paliseul or Libramont from where a bus may be taken to Bouillon. For Rochehaut take a train to Carlsbourg, then a bus. Bus services serve Bouillon town and the neighbouring villages of Dohan and Rochehaut, both featured in the walks in this chapter. For details of all the services available in the region, contact Bouillon Tourist Office (see Appendix 3).

For the motorist there is fast and easy access to Bouillon from the more northerly regions of the Ardennes. From Namur and Dinant follow the E411 (A4) motorway to junction 25, from where the dual carriageway of the N89 leads directly down to Bouillon. The fast N89 also gives easy access from La Roche and Saint-Hubert. From Liège take the E25 motorway south to the point where it meets the E411: follow the latter to junction 25 and so on the N89 to Bouillon. The roads between Bouillon and Dohan, Rochehaut, Alle-sur-Semois and Vresse-sur-Semois are a different matter, being often steep, narrow and winding, consequently allowing relatively slow progress.

Bicycles and kayaks are for hire from Bouillon.

Official Walking Trails in the Region of Bouillon and Dohan

There is a grand total of 99 official waymarked walking trails in and above the Semois valley in the region of Bouillon and Dohan! These vary in length from 1.5kms to 23kms, and start from a number of towns and villages in the area: Bouillon, Corbion, Dohan, Les Hayons, Noirefontaine, Bellevaux, Poupehan, Rochehaut, Frahan, Ucimont-Botassart, Vivy and Menuchenet. The trails, identified by number, are marked on the excellent 1:25,000 scale walkers' map entitled *Carte des Promenades du Grand Bouillon*, available from Bouillon Tourist Office. The official trails from Bouillon, Dohan and Rochehaut, the three main locations in the area covered by this book, are as follows:

From Bouillon:

Trail No. 10 - Promenade de la Ramonette - 1.5kms.
Trail No. 11 - Promenade de la Gernelle - 7.0kms.
Trail No. 12 - Promenade de l'Arboretum - 4.0kms.
Trail No. 13 - Promenade du Moulin de l'Epine - 8.5kms.
Trail No. 14 - Promenade Cordemois, Belvédère - 6.0kms.
Trail No. 15 - Promenade des Points de Vue de l'Epine - 8.0kms.
Trail No. 16 - Promenade de Chantereine - 5.0kms.
Trail No. 17 - Promenade de Buhan - 11.0kms.
Trail No. 18 - Promenade Roche des Fées - 2.0kms.
Trail No. 19 - La Longue Promenade de Dohan - 23.0kms.
Trail No. 20 - Promenade des Quatre Chemins - 16.0kms.
Trail No. 21 - Promenade du Gros Chêne - 11.5kms.
Trail No. 22 - Promenade du Dos de Loup - 7.5kms.
Trail No. 23 - Promenade de la Falize - 5.0kms.

From Dohan:

Trail No. 40 - Promenade du Rivage de Marion - 5.5kms.
Trail No. 41 - Promenade de la Schevauchée - 6.5kms.
Trail No. 42 - Promenade du Rocher Lecomte - 4.0kms.
Trail No. 43 - Promenade de la Dampirée - 7.5kms.

From Rochehaut:

Trail No. 80 - Promenade des Corbeaux - 3.0kms.
Trail No. 81 - Promenade de Laviot - 6.0kms.
Trail No. 82 - Promenade de Goéchamps - 8.5kms.
Trail No. 83 - Promenade du Moulin de Liresse - 8.0kms.
Trail No. 84 - Promenade des Echelles - 5.0kms.

Walks

Six walks are described from this centre, two from Bouillon itself, three from the village of Dohan to the east, and one from Rochehaut to the north-west of Bouillon. The River Semois is a major feature of all of these walks.

WALK 14:
Bouillon, Sensenruth, the Grand Ruisseau, the Tombeau de Géant and the River Semois

Description: A superb walk which combines a ramble through the rich forests that cover the steep slopes of the Semois valley, with a stroll along the graceful River Semois: if you only have time for one walk in the Bouillon area then this is the one to try. After a steep climb out of the Semois valley, open country is reached as the trail passes through a couple of farming villages to the north of Bouillon. Later the route follows the stream of Le Grand Ruisseau down to the Semois, a beautiful section of the walk through mature woodland. The meandering course of the River Semois is then followed all the way back to Bouillon, sometimes closely, at other times in the woods to the east of the river, passing the well-known locations of the Tombeau de Géant, the Moulin de l'Epine and the Abbey Convent of Clairefontaine. The first third or more of the walk follows the GR 14, a long distance path (see Appendix 5), from Bouillon north to the village of Sensenruth. The remainder of the circuit makes use of a number of local waymarked trails.

Location: To the north and west of Bouillon.

Start/Finish: The Pont de Liège, over the River Semois, in the centre of Bouillon.

Distance: 9.3 miles (15.0kms).

Time: Allow 6hrs 30mins.

Maps: The walkers' map, at a scale of 1:25,000, entitled *Carte des Promenades du Grand Bouillon (Wandelkaart van Groot-Bouillon)* is published by and available from Bouillon Tourist Office (situated in the château of the town). Possibly the best of all the tourist office walkers' maps in the Belgian Ardennes.

IGN 1:50,000 series: sheet number 67.

Waymarking: A note on waymarking in the Bouillon/Dohan/Rochehaut areas: The trails are all numbered and appear as black numbers painted on a white background, often circular, and mainly on trees or concrete telegraph poles. The GR AE and GR 14 are both, of course, waymarked with the standard red and white waymarks of the national GR trails. The numbers of the walking routes marked on the local walkers' map (see "*Maps*" above) correspond to those of the waymarks found along the trails. However, some of the forestry markings on the trees in the Semois area are quite similar to some of the "Promenade" waymarks. For example, numbers other than those of the walking trails appear on trees, and also red/white forestry markings, which do not refer to walking routes, also appear in some areas, so leading to confusion. In the latter case it is important to remember that the GR waymarks are generally smaller than the forestry red/white markings, and that the GR markings are *always* horizontal. Walkers should learn to distinguish between the walking trail waymarks and the forestry markings in this area.

Terrain: Woodland mixed with some open country to the north and east. The meandering and steep-sided Semois valley. There are one or two steep climbs on the walk, the most strenuous being the climb up from the Pont de Cordemois to the Belvédère, on leaving Bouillon soon after the start of the walk.

Footwear: Nearly all of the walk is on paths or tracks which can be muddy and slippery in wet or icy conditions, so boots are recommended.

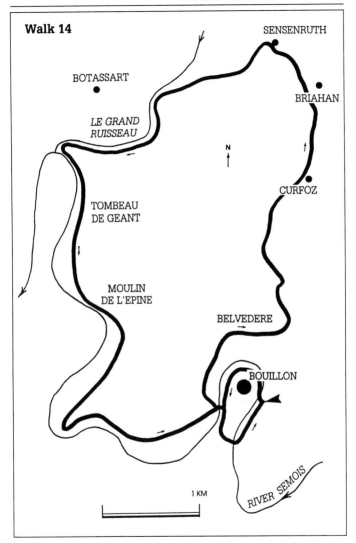

Walk 14

SENSENRUTH

BOTASSART

BRIAHAN

LE GRAND
RUISSEAU

N

CURFOZ

TOMBEAU
DE GEANT

MOULIN
DE L'EPINE

BELVEDERE

BOUILLON

1 KM

RIVER SEMOIS

Option: For a much shorter circuit Trail Nos 14 and 93 could be
followed westwards from the Belvédère, above and to the north of Bouillon, to
the Abbey Convent of Clairefontaine, from where the latter stages of the full

walk could then be traced back to Bouillon (see the walkers' map referred to above).

*Places of
Interest:*   1. Bouillon. An exploration of this picturesque town on the River Semois is highly recommended before leaving the area. A visit to the château is particularly worthwhile. See the introductory section on Bouillon for further details, and consult the tourist office, located in the château, for more information.

2. The Abbey Convent of Clairefontaine. Visits are sometimes possible, but only usually between 12.30 and 1.30pm.

Refreshments: Bouillon, of course, has all facilities: cafés, restaurants, hotels and shops. There is a small café in Sensenruth, a little under halfway round the circuit, but no other place where refreshments can be bought is passed en route. However, there is an excellent picnic spot (picnic tables and seats provided) at the point where the Grand Ruisseau meets the River Semois, after about two-thirds of the walk has been completed. This is therefore a good place to eat a lunch that has been carried in the rucksac from Bouillon.

Route

From the Pont de Liège in the centre of Bouillon, cross to the west (left) bank of the River Semois and turn right along the Boulevard Heynen. Follow the River Semois under two old roofed gateways and continue with the river on your right to reach the Pont de Cordemois. Cross the bridge, so joining the GR 14 and GR AE (red and white waymarks). On the opposite bank of the river immediately turn right to climb a flight of steps, following Trail Nos 14 and 15, and the GR route. Climb the steep hillside by a series of zig-zags, keeping to the well waymarked path so as not to exacerbate the problems of erosion on this hillside, which are already in evidence. Before reaching the top be very careful to follow the waymarks (black painted numbers 14 and 15 on a white painted background, plus the red/white waymarks) on a path to the right which contours the hillside and gives fleeting glimpses down to Bouillon on your right (there is a better view in wintertime when the leaves are off the trees).

Continue on this balcony path until a path Y-junction is reached. Here bear left uphill (Trail Nos 14, 15 and GR14/AE). The path again climbs steeply on a series of zigzags to reach a large observation tower. From the top of this high tower there would be a superb view of the Semois valley, but at the time of writing access to the tower is sealed off and forbidden due to the unsafe condition of the tower (it may be made safe and reopened some time in the future). Bear right at the tower for 80 metres to reach a track T-junction. Here turn right following the red/white waymarks of the GR 14. Descend on this path, soon following a line of electricity cables, to reach a large wooden crucifix at the start of a metalled lane. Do not follow the latter, but instead turn left on a path, now on Trail Nos 3 and 4 (and still on the GR route). Remain on this trail as it heads to the north, meandering somewhat as it does so. Later take care not to take a track off to the right, but continue ahead at a small wooden signpost indicating the way to Curfoz (still following red/white waymarks). The farming village of Curfoz soon comes into view on the hill ahead to the right. The track and the GR 14 lead to the village. Bear right on the road to enter Curfoz, now on Trail No. 93.

Immediately after the chapel in the centre of the village, turn left onto a descending track (GR 14 and Trail No. 93). This soon climbs again to reach a crucifix and a track junction. Keep ahead (north) here, soon descending on a footpath between hedgerows to cross a small stream and climb to approach the village of Briahan (but note that we do not enter this village). Climb to a road on the outskirts of a second village, that of Sensenruth, and bear left along a lane to reach a T-junction opposite a large chapel in Sensenruth. Turn left here, at the roadsign for Botassart (there is a small café on the left which serves simple food menus). Thirty metres before reaching the village church the red/white waymarks take the GR 14 to the right. We leave this long distance path here.

Continue ahead, passing to the left of the church, but 15 metres before the roadsign indicating the limit of Sensenruth, turn left on a descending, poorly surfaced lane. This soon becomes a muddy track. Ignore a narrow grassy path descending to the right of this track, but remain on the track ahead. Keep to this main track, ignoring any side turnings, following Trail No. 94 (the waymarks show the number 94 in black on a white circular painted background). The track, heading first towards the west and then to the south, descends through the forest to reach a stream. Cross the stream and turn immediately right on Trail No. 92 (*not* on Trail No. 94, which turns right *before* the stream). Now follow the left bank of the stream (Le Grand Ruisseau) downhill through delectable woodland country. The stream and the track descend to meet the River Semois. There are picnic tables here at this most pleasant spot, a good place to relax over lunch before returning to Bouillon.

Our walk joins Trail No. 12 and the GR AE (red/white waymarks) at this point. Bear left to follow the combined GR AE, Nos 12 and 93 trails, upstream along the right bank of the River Semois. Soon after passing the Tombeau de Géant, where the river bifurcates, the route reaches a junction of three tracks: the track ahead, a path dropping steeply to the right, and a narrow track beneath trees between the two. Take this latter track, leaving the river for a while, to follow the GR AE, soon passing beneath tall conifers. The trail passes a few buildings to reach a metalled lane at L'Epine (Moulin de l'Epine). Here the River Semois is rejoined. Do not take the path down to the river at this point (it soon becomes impassable), but head along the lane above the river (red/white GR AE waymarks). Pass a wooden shelter with tables and benches on your left, and continue along the lane, now heading towards a group of large buildings which belong to the Abbey of the Convent of Notre Dame de Clairefontaine (also known as the Abbaye de Cordemois).

Continue past these buildings, remaining on the lane for about another 800 metres until the lane bends to the left as it approaches a campsite. At this point, opposite a small seat, turn left off the lane onto a footpath which climbs a few steps and continues climbing the hillside (this is waymarked as Trail No. 14 and the GR AE). Climb upwards through the trees to a seat, after which the woodland path levels out. The trail reaches a Y-junction where the GR AE (red/white waymarks) takes the left fork, but we follow the right fork on Trail No. 14. Descend on this path until the first apparatus of the *Parcours sportif* is reached. A few metres after this take a footpath (waymarked as Trail No. 14) climbing up on the left. Ascend on this path to reach a path T-junction, where you turn right downhill. Continue ahead at a point where another track joins on the right by a bench, still following Trail No. 14. Bear to the right, downhill, at a path Y-junction just after crossing a small stream (Trail No. 14). Just before reaching a road (seen down to the right) bear right at another Y-junction downhill on Trail Nos 14 and 15. Descend to the road at the Pont de Cordemois.

Cross the bridge and turn right along the road beside the river to reach a road junction. Turn left here, walk through the tunnel to emerge in Bouillon, once again beside the River Semois, this time on the other side of its large meander. Cross the bridge in front of you (the Pont de France) and bear left along the Rue du College to walk through the streets of Bouillon to return to the day's starting point, the Pont de Liège.

The château at Bouillon

WALK 15:
Bouillon, Buhan and the River Semois

Description: A walk to the east of Bouillon, following the course of the River Semois on one of its wide meanders, through the forests to the north of the river, an area known as Buhan. The circuit visits the small Chapelle de Buhan before descending back to Bouillon. The walk utilises the GR AE (a long distance path linking the Ardennes with the German Eifel) for over half of its length, before returning to Bouillon on a number of local waymarked trails.

Location: To the east of Bouillon.

Start/Finish: The Pont de Liège, over the River Semois, in the centre of Bouillon.

Distance: 8.7 miles (14.0kms).

Time: Allow 5hrs 30mins.

Maps: The walkers' map, at a scale of 1:25,000, entitled *Carte des Promenades du Grand Bouillon (Wandelkaart van Groot-Bouillon)*. Published by and available from Bouillon Tourist Office.
          IGN 1:50,000 series: sheet number 67.

Waymarking: See the general note on waymarking in the area under "Waymarking" for Walk 14.

Terrain: Forest tracks and paths and the meandering River Semois. There is some ascent and descent on this walk, but be warned that most of this comes after the River Semois has been left behind, over halfway through the walk.

Footwear: The forests tracks can become very muddy after rain, so be warned and take appropriate footwear.

Places of Interest: If Bouillon hasn't yet been explored then do make time at the end of the walk to do so before leaving the area. See the introductory section on Bouillon for further details, and consult the tourist office, located in the château, for more information.

Refreshments: There is one restaurant that is passed on the walk, the highly starred and expensive Auberge du Moulin Hideux, but nowhere else where refreshment may be obtained other than at Bouillon at the start and finish of the round (this is not quite correct as there is a café about a kilometre from the end of the walk, above the town). There is a picnic shelter and tables by the River Semois just before the river is left for the climb up to the Moulin Hideux. This is encountered somewhat over halfway through the walk and is consequently a convenient spot to enjoy lunch.

Walk 15

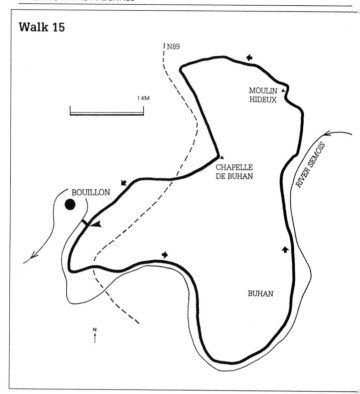

Route

Start the walk at the Pont de Liège in the centre of Bouillon. Walk along the banks of the River Semois to reach a second bridge, the Pont de France. Climb up the steps to reach this bridge, but do not cross it; instead follow the right bank of the river upstream on a grassy path (Trail Nos 17 and 18, and the GR AE). The track soon bends away from the river to follow a small tributary of it, first on your right and then on your left. Do not cross the stream again but soon climb steeply away from the stream to approach a main road, the N89. At the top of the climb bear left on a level path for a few metres to cross the road by a footbridge.

On the other side of this trunk road follow the narrow but well defined path across fields. The trail then descends a little before becoming a level balcony path high above the River Semois, which is down to your right. The trail eventually descends. Remain on the main track as it does so, ignoring side turnings and following the red/white waymarks of the GR AE. However, before the track begins to climb towards the east, it is most important not to miss a minor track/path leaving the main track to the right. This is the route of the GR AE (red/white waymarks) and heads southwards beneath a canopy of trees. When the trail reaches a track at a bend in the latter, do not follow it, but seek out a path to its right (red/white and Trail No. 17 waymarks), although in fact this path soon joins the track, which can become very waterlogged and muddy after heavy rain. Continue along the track, now heading eastwards. Follow both the number 17 and the red and white waymarks carefully as the trail slowly turns to head northwards, eventually reaching a track T-junction at Buhan. The paths and tracks are muddy hereabouts during wet weather.

Turn right at this track T-junction, still heading north. On reaching the area known as Les Enclaves (a small wooden signboard announces the fact) turn left with the red/white and No. 17 waymarks. Follow the track until a waymarked footpath is reached on the right. Take this to cross a small stream, climb briefly and then bear right to descend (buildings seen below near to the river). The path climbs a little and then descends to reach a metalled road. Turn right to descend to the river and a wooden shelter with table and seats, an ideal spot for a picnic. Remain on the lane as it bends to the left to meet another road at a T-junction. At this point we part company with the red/white waymarks of the GR AE, which turn to the right. We turn left onto this lane, now on Trail No. 54 and following the Ruisseau au Moulin Deux, the stream to the left of the road. Climb on this lane to pass two small ponds on the left and then the luxurious Auberge du Moulin Hideux.

Immediately after this hotel/restaurant turn left into its car park (waymarks for Trail Nos 52 and 53). We are to follow Trail No. 53. Cross a small wooden footbridge, pass the side of the hotel to take the waymarked footpath climbing up behind the establishment. Within 150 metres Trail No. 52 turns to the right, but we keep ahead on Trail No. 53. The path climbs through the trees to become a track which continues the climb, until it in turn becomes a surfaced lane which completes the climb out of the woods to reach the Route de la Chapelle at a T-junction in Noirefontaine.

Turn left along this lane and continue for about 1.3kms to reach a crossroads at the small Chapelle de Buhan. Turn right (south-west) here on Trail No. 16. This leads to the main road which is crossed by means of a bridge. At the junction after the bridge, fork right by a café and small go-karting circuit. After about 150 metres ignore another lane on the right, but continue ahead. The houses of Bouillon soon come into view. Descend on this lane into Bouillon. Just before the bottom of the descent, bear right down a flight of steps to reach the bank of the River Semois. Turn left along the river to return to the Pont de Liège where the walk began.

WALK 16:
Dohan, Dampirée, the Côte du Havet and the Rocher Lecomte

Description:　　　A circuit south of Dohan and the River Semois. There are three excellent viewpoints of the River Semois and its valley passed on the walk, at the Dampirée and the Rocher de Dampire in the first stage of the walk, and then from the Rocher Lecomte, just before descending back to Dohan at the end of the day. Rocher Lecomte presents one of the best viewpoints in the region. The crag stands out high above the River Semois and provides a superb view of Dohan village and the Semois valley. The walk is a compilation of sections of several local trails, Nos 43 (Promenade de la Dampirée), 19, 21 (Chemin des Côtes du Havet) and 42 (Promenade du Rocher Lecomte), and offers a mixture of stimulating walking on steep, narrow paths above the river, followed by relaxed rambling through lush forests.

Location:　　　To the south of Dohan and the Semois valley. Dohan is situated on the River Semois about 3.4 miles (5.5kms) east of Bouillon (but considerably farther by either the road network, or by the greatly meandering river).

Start/Finish:　　　The church in the centre of Dohan.

Distance:　　　9.3 miles (15.0kms).

Time:　　　Allow 6hrs.

Maps:　　　The walkers' map, at a scale of 1:25,000, entitled *Carte des Promenades du Grand Bouillon (Wandelkaart van Groot-Bouillon)*. Published by and available from Bouillon Tourist Office.

　　　　　IGN 1:50,000 series: sheet number 67.

Waymarking:　　　See the general note on waymarking in the area under "Waymarking" for Walk 14.

Terrain:　　　Apart from the first few miles along the Promenade de la Dampirée, which is on steep narrow paths above the river, where surefootedness and care in navigation is required, the remainder of the walk offers mainly level walking along *routes forestière*, tracks through the woods, which provide easy navigation and relaxing walking.

Footwear:　　　Because of the steep nature of the footpaths on the Promenade de la Dampirée and the often muddy forest tracks that follow, boots are recommended for this walk.

Option:　　　If you arrive back in Dohan early in the afternoon and still have the energy and enthusiasm for a second walk, then the pleasant Promenade de la Schevauchée (Walk 18) should not be too taxing.

Special Problems: The route along the crags of the Dampirée is steep but without difficulty, *provided* Trail No. 43 (the Promenade de la Dampirée) is

Walk 16

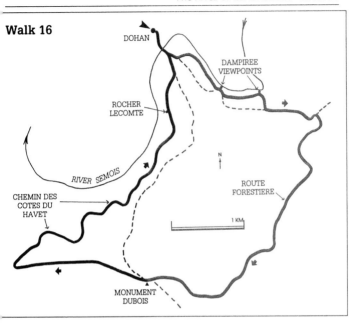

followed without straying from its waymarked route. There are several narrow and steep paths in the vicinity of these crags high above the river, that could soon lead to danger. Follow the route description carefully and do not venture onto difficult unwaymarked ground.

Refreshments: Refreshments are only available at Dohan at the beginning and end of the walk. Therefore it is advisable to take along a packed lunch and something to drink.

Route

From the church in the centre of Dohan take the road signposted to Cugnon, and cross the bridge over the River Semois. Continue along this road for about 350 metres until, about 70 metres after the roadsign indicating the limits of Dohan, you turn left onto a track by the edge of woodland, waymarked as the Promenade de la Dampirée (Trail No. 43). This soon becomes a pleasant path through the woods. It eventually emerges back on the road at a seat and a fine viewpoint (La Dampirée). Bear left along the car parking area to pick up the Trail No. 43 path at its far end. Descend steeply towards the River Semois, taking great care in wet conditions to avoid a slip on the exposed tree roots. The path levels and follows the course of the river which is down to your left.

Climb to a seat and viewpoint above the river. There are several small paths here that could easily lead the unwary into difficulties amongst the small crags in the area. Do not descend towards the river, but seek out a No. 43 waymarked path that soon begins to zigzag steeply up the hillside. The path, albeit steep, is without difficulties (if the path that you are following does not carry frequent waymarks and begins to become tricky, then you must retreat to locate the correct trail). The path climbs to another viewpoint and seat on the top of the crags, the Rocher de Dampire, now high above the river. Head south away from the seat to reach a road and turn left (east) along this.

Remain on this lane for about 800 metres. After the road swings to the left take Trail No. 19 on a *route forestière*, an unsurfaced track on the right of the road. This forest track provides over 2.5 miles (4kms) of pleasant, easy walking on a level gradient. Follow it, ignoring any minor side turnings, all the way to the road at the Monument Dubois. After inspecting the stone memorial on the side of the road, turn right, heading west on the road signposted to Dohan. Within 150 metres, where the road bends to the right, continue ahead on the unsurfaced track (Trail No. 20) signposted to Bouillon. Continue along this more or less level track for 1.2 miles (2kms) until you reach another track on the right (Trail No. 21) signposted to Dohan by the Côtes du Havet.

Follow this track, the Chemin des Côtes du Havet, for about 1.6 miles (2.5kms) until, soon after the track swings towards the south, leave it to take a grassy (at first) track (Trail No. 21) on the left, heading north-north-east (if you reach a metalled lane then you have gone too far: retrace your steps for about 200 metres to locate and follow the above mentioned track). Follow this track, ignoring any side turnings, to reach a track T-junction by a small wooden seat. Bear right along the track (Trail No. 42), heading north-east. After a further 600 metres or so look out for a track on the left, waymarked as Trail No. 42, and signposted to the Rocher Lecomte (*Point de Vue Panoramas*). Follow this track heading north-north-west through the trees. After admiring the view at Rocher Lecomte, from where a Belgian flag often flies, bear right on the narrow path as indicated by the "42" waymark, soon descending steeply. There are several side-turnings off the path, but the correct route is well waymarked. Descend to a path T-junction where you bear left downhill to reach a road on the outskirts of Dohan. Turn left along the road to descend back into the village, so completing the walk.

WALK 17:
Dohan, La Cornette, the Ruisseau des Aleines, Maka and the Roche Percée

Description: A grand circuit to the north-east of Dohan, following a number of local trails, in particular Trail Nos 50 (Promenade de Dohan), 48

(Promenade des Hautes Voies) and 49 (Promenade de la Roche à Colas). A short section of the GR AE is also included. The walk is a rather sporting one and is consequently unsuitable for inexperienced walkers, for young children or for those somewhat unsteady on their feet. There are two principal problems. The main one is crossing the river, the Ruisseau des Aleines. After a long, dry period of weather this would probably be a rather tame affair, although it certainly wasn't when the author researched the walk during a wet week in late September! Secondly, there is some very mild scrambling over rocks and through a rocky defile or gully at the Roche Percée near Maka on the River Semois on the return part of the journey. The walk ends with a gentle stroll along the banks of the tranquil Semois.

Location: To the north of Dohan and the Semois valley.

Start/Finish: The church in the centre of Dohan.

Distance: 8.1 miles (13.0kms).

Time: Allow 6hrs.

Maps: The walkers' map, at a scale of 1:25,000, entitled *Carte des Promenades du Grand Bouillon (Wandelkaart van Groot-Bouillon)*. Published by and available from Bouillon Tourist Office.
                   IGN 1:50,000 series: sheet number 67.

Waymarking: See the general note on waymarking in the area under "Waymarking" for Walk 14.

Terrain: This walk should only be attempted in dry weather, and certainly not after a period of heavy rain, as it involves fording a river at a point where there is no bridge. Those walkers wary of such an activity (or those not wanting to get wet boots!) should not include this walk in their itinerary. The circuit is mainly on tracks and footpaths, with a small amount of walking on quiet lanes. There is some ascent and descent, one short section of which is very steep, but on the whole the walk is not particularly strenuous.

Footwear: The river crossing requires boots with gaiters (or alternatively bogtrotters). Boots with a good grip and ankle support are also strongly recommended for the section over rocks and boulders near the Roche Percée.

Option: If sufficient time is available at the end of the walk, it could be linked to the shorter Promenade de la Schevauchée (Walk 18) which also starts from the centre of Dohan.

Special Problems: Fording the Ruisseau des Aleines:
The stream can be rather fast flowing. If in any doubt whatsoever do not attempt the crossing, but return the way you came, back to Les Hayons. When the author crossed it it had been raining quite heavily for over a week, and the water was about 12-15ins high at its deepest. This presented no real problems, apart from wet boots, but it is conceivable that during heavier and more

121

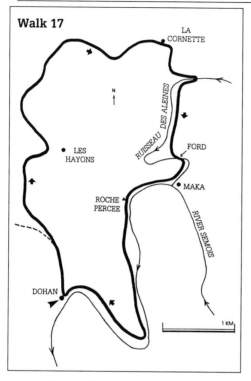

Walk 17

LA CORNETTE

RUISSEAU DES ALEINES

N

LES HAYONS

FORD

MAKA

ROCHE PERCEE

RIVER SEMOIS

DOHAN

1 KM

consistent rain the water could be deeper and faster running, in which case a crossing must certainly not be attempted. It is a good idea to include a spare pair of socks in your rucksac. Gaiters are strongly recommended. Those walking the trail during a long, dry summer will probably wonder why all the above precautions have been emphasised!

Refreshments:
No establishment is passed en route from where refreshments may be purchased. Food and drink must therefore be carried from Dohan. There are three hotel-restaurants, two shops and a couple of cafés in Dohan. Those looking for a picnic sight will find one alongside the river at Maka, after the crossing of the Ruisseau des Aleines. There is a picnic shelter with tables and benches here.

Route

Starting from the church in the centre of the village of Dohan, follow the road (the N816) signposted to Bouillon and Noirefontaine, bending to the left in front of the village war memorial. Follow this road, climbing out of Dohan, for about 800 metres, until the first lane off to the right (a "no through road" for vehicles) is reached. Take this, doubling back above the main road, but after about 150 metres turn sharply to the left, climbing on a grassy track. On emerging at a large grassy pasture on the left, immediately turn right to re-enter the woods on a track. Later, on reaching a Y-junction, take the right fork heading downhill (Trail No. 50). On meeting another track at a bend in the latter bear right to reach another but broader slatey track at a T-junction. Turn left onto this slatey track, heading north, now on a GR trail (red/white waymarks). Remain on this track to reach a road at a T-junction. Turn right (east) along the lane to climb to the village of Les Hayons.

On reaching a small slate-lined chapel on the left-hand side of the road, before the centre of the village, turn left onto a lane waymarked as Trail No. 48 and signposted to Bellevaux. After about 800 metres along this lane, at a point where an unsurfaced track leaves on the left and a narrow surfaced lane goes off to the right, take the latter, waymarked as Trail No. 48. Continue along this lane until its surface ends at a Y-junction of two tracks. Take the left fork signposted as Promenade No. 48 (note that this is *not* the line of Trail No. 48 as marked on some editions of the maps available from Bouillon Tourist Office - on these maps the trail is shown as taking the right fork). Continue on this track to reach a track T-junction where you turn right (east). Remain on this waymarked track which eventually acquires a metalled surface and descends steeply to reach a crossroads in the hamlet of La Cornette. Cross the road and continue ahead in the direction signposted to Auby.

Cross a bridge over the river and bend to the right on the road, ignoring a side road on the left. Follow the lane as it climbs to the south and then bends to the left. A few metres after this left bend in the road, leave it in favour of an unsurfaced track heading slightly downhill into the trees on the right (Trail No. 49). Keep to the main track as it bears to the right around the head of a small valley and then later swings to the left (south) to meet a track Y-junction. Take the right-hand fork here, heading downhill. The track heads south, following the course of the Ruisseau des Aleines, the river seen and heard occasionally about 40 metres below the path on the right. A number of broken, vegetation-covered crags are also seen hanging above this river. On reaching a trail junction where the main track bears to the left (east), leave the track to take the footpath ahead, which descends, gently at first, and then very steeply (care!) to reach a track T-junction. Turn left along this and follow it to a ford across the river. There is no bridge here. At times of heavy rain the water may not be fordable. Do *not* attempt a crossing if the water is high or fast flowing (important: see the note under "Special Problems" above). In this case footsteps will have to be retraced back to the village of Les Hayons and so back to Dohan.

Having waded the river (the Ruisseau des Aleines) walk forward to reach a metalled road. Turn right along this lane, having now joined the GR AE (red/white waymarks). Follow this to reach a campsite at Maka, on the right bank of the River Semois. Follow the track along the bank, heading downstream on Trail Nos 47 and 50, and on the GR AE, soon passing a picnic shelter with tables and benches, a pleasant picnic spot beside the river. On reaching a building leave the track you have been following in favour of a footpath on the left (waymarks for Promenades Nos 47 and 50) which follows the right bank of the Semois, along the water's edge. Follow this most attractive section of river, passing a prominent waterside boulder (La Roche Percée) which is negotiated by means of an interesting narrow gully. An easy scramble past more rocks and boulders leads back down to the path along the tranquil Semois.

Later the trail and the river part company for about 800 metres, the river taking a course 300-400 metres to the left of the track. During this section of the walk the GR AE (red/white waymarks) takes a footpath climbing to the right. Ignore these waymarks, but remain on the level track (Trail Nos 40 and 50) ahead, passing beneath small crags, soon rejoining the Semois. The track eventually becomes surfaced and turns to the right to head towards the north-west, with the river still visible over to the left. Remain on this lane to pass the Moulin de Dohan and reach the war memorial and church in the centre of Dohan.

WALK 18:
Promenade de la Schevauchée

Description: If only a short time is available in the Dohan/Bouillon area then this short walk, which passes a lovely viewpoint of Dohan and the River Semois, will provide a flavour of the Semois valley region, which will no doubt entice you back one day to sample more of the delightful walking in this area. Except for a very short section along a narrow, rather overgrown and somewhat awkward footpath near the beginning, the walk is an easy one, mainly on the level. The ramble follows local Trail No. 41 in its entirety. The walk is only a short one and could even be accomplished by fit walkers wanting a stroll after dinner if staying in Dohan during the long evenings of summer.

Location: To the south-west of Dohan.

Start/Finish: The church in the centre of Dohan.

Distance: 4.0 miles (6.5kms).

Time: Allow 2hrs 15mins.

Maps: The walkers' map, at a scale of 1:25,000, entitled *Carte des Promenades du Grand Bouillon (Wandelkaart van Groot-Bouillon)*. Published by and available from Bouillon Tourist Office.

IGN 1:50,000 series: sheet number 67.

Waymarking: Follow the waymarks for Trail No. 41 throughout the walk.

Terrain: The walk follows one of the large oxbow loops of the River Semois.

Footwear: Trainers or stout shoes would be suitable if the conditions are dry (except perhaps for the short section of awkward footpath referred to above).

Refreshments: There are no refreshments available en route, but sufficient will be found in Dohan.

Route

From the church in the centre of Dohan follow the N865 road, signposted to Cugnon, but only for about 40 metres. *Before* crossing the bridge over the River Semois, turn right onto an unsignposted lane (but it bears a waymarks for Trail No. 41). Continue ahead, soon ignoring a right side-road by houses, to leave the village.

Follow the lane as it bends to the right, but then leave it by turning left in front of a large solitary house. Beyond the house follow the grassy track which soon narrows to a somewhat overgrown footpath, which runs between a hedgerow and the River Semois to the left, and a wire fence to the right. The path eventually bends away from the river to climb beside, and later enter, a wood. Emerge at a track T-junction. Turn left uphill, to the east, on this stony track.

At the viewpoint known as Charmes (excellent view down to Dohan and the River Semois) where there is a seat, the track swings to the right (south) and descends. Stay on this track as it follows the giant meander of the River Semois, but always keeping several hundred metres to the right of the river. Ignore any side turnings from the main track. The trail eventually runs close to the river again. Less than a kilometre after rejoining the river, the track becomes surfaced and climbs before swinging to the right (east) away from the river. Bear right at a T-junction at the main road (N865) and follow this back to the centre of Dohan.

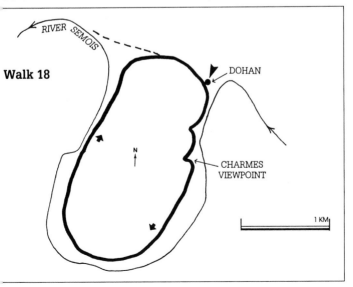

Walking in the Ardennes woods near Rochehaut in springtime

WALK 19:
Rochehaut, Poupehan and Frahan - the Ladder Walk

Description: This circuit, possibly the author's favourite walk in the Ardennes, follows two large meanders of the River Semois south of the village of Rochehaut. There are some fine views of the surrounding countryside, of hills and the steep sided valley, particularly from the *belvédère* near Rochehaut from where the village of Frahan and the oxbow loop of the river around it is on view, one of the most scenic panoramas in the whole of the Ardennes. The ramble makes use of a number of local walks, primarily numbers 84 (Promenade des Echelles), 65 (Promenade des Falloises), 69 (Promenade des Rives de la Semois) and 85 ((Promenade de Laviot).

The walk involves a short section of very steep and difficult terrain which includes the ascent of a long and near-vertical ladder (see "Special Problems" below), above the River Semois, south-east of Rochehaut. Later in the walk near Frahan there is another slightly difficult stretch of trail over a number of footbridges and another ladder. The inclusion of these sections, particularly the former, makes this outing the most thrilling and "sporting" of the Ardennes walks described in this book. It is recommended for experienced walkers only. For suitably equipped and experienced walkers this circuit is most exhilarating, and tremendous fun!

Location: To the north-west of Bouillon, along and above the Semois valley.

Start/Finish: The church in the centre of the village of Rochehaut.

Distance: 9.6 miles (15.5kms).

Time: Allow 6hrs 30mins.

Maps: The walkers' map, at a scale of 1:25,000, entitled *Carte des Promenades du Grand Bouillon (Wandelkaart van Groot-Bouillon)*. Published by and available from Bouillon Tourist Office.

IGN 1:50,000 series: sheet number 67 and 64 (the walk is awkwardly situated in a corner where four IGN 1:50,000 maps meet, viz numbers 63, 64, 66 and 67).

Waymarking: See the general note on waymarking in the area under "Waymarking" for Walk 14.

Terrain: Apart from the relatively short ladder section and the final climb back to Rochehaut, the majority of the walk follows more or less level terrain, alongside the River Semois.

Footwear: Boots with good grips and firm ankle supports are strongly recommended for this sporting walk.

Option: The walk can be shortened by omitting the final loop in the River Semois. From the bridge over the river opposite the village of Frahan climb

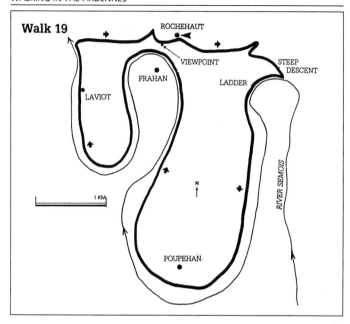

directly back up to Rochehaut on Trail Nos 85 and 86. This reduces the length of the walk by almost 3 miles.

Special Problems: This is the most difficult walk described in the book on account of a relatively short section south-east of Rochehaut, close to the River Semois. This section is on very steep ground and involves not only some mild scrambling, but also the ascent of a long, near vertical ladder to scale a crag above the river. The average mountain walker should experience no great problems, but those walkers unused to steep, loose and slippery terrain may find difficulties. People who suffer from vertigo, a fear of heights and exposure, should not attempt this walk. Because of the nature of the terrain, it is not advisable to attempt the walk in very wet or icy conditions. Furthermore, as sections of the walk venture very close to the riverbank, it is not advisable to set out during or after a period of prolonged rain, as the River Semois can flood to dangerous levels at times in this region.

Refreshments: There are several opportunities for buying refreshments en route, particularly at Poupehan (a café, three restaurants, a hotel and a shop), Frahan and Laviot (see text for details). There is a riverside picnic spot (a shelter with benches and tables) between Frahan and Laviot. Rochehaut has restaurants, a hotel, cafés and a tourist office.

Route

From the church in the centre of Rochehaut walk east, uphill on the Grand Rue, to reach a crossroads. Walk ahead up the Chemin des Falloises (Trail Nos 70, 83 and 84). Bear left at the next junction, now on the outskirts of Rochehaut. Continue ahead at the next track crossroads, signposted to Les Echelles ("the Ladders") on Trail No. 84. Descend on this stony track, but after about 500 metres be sure to look out for a track on the right signposted to Les Echelles (Trail Nos 83 and 84). This track turns very sharply to the right to head south-west, and later, at the head of a small valley, bends to the left at a hairpin bend to head eastwards. Bear left on encountering a track Y-junction. When the trail swings to the right by an outcrop of rock, take the path descending on the left (south-east), signposted to Les Echelles.

If at any time during the following section, marked between asterisks, any member of the party feels unsure of his or her ability to proceed, then the party must retreat and return to Rochehaut. A head for heights and sure-footedness is required. See "Special Problems" above.

* The path descends very steeply over rocks and exposed tree roots. Special care is required here, particularly in wet or icy conditions, when a slip would be all too easy. There is a short section of handrail to assist at one tricky point. Descend on this rather sporting path to reach the right bank of the River Semois. Turn right (west) here to head downstream, still following Trail No. 84, and also now picking up the red and white waymarks of the GR AE. The path soon becomes tricky again, clambering over tree roots and rocks, first along the water's edge (when the river is in flood it may be necessary to make a few footsteps into the water, but normally this should present little problem - in severe flooding conditions, the route is dangerous and should not be attempted) and then climbing on very steep ground which is loose and slippery under wet conditions. Another handrail acts as an aid on this section. It is most important in this area to follow the waymarks for Trail No. 84 very carefully so as to avoid wandering onto dangerous ground. The waymarks lead to the foot of a long metal ladder which climbs a near vertical crag. Climb the ladder and continue on the path beyond until it climbs very steeply again to reach a path junction at a point where there is a steep rocky crag on the left, overlooking the river (a good viewpoint). *

At this point it is most important to head south on trails waymarked as Nos 65 and 71. (Trail No. 84 climbs to the right along with the red and white waymarks of the GR AE - follow this if you want more spills and thrills and ladder sections. Trail No. 84 leads quickly back to Rochehaut.) All difficulties are, however, now over as we head south on an easy, pleasant path, which within less than a kilometre joins a track which comes in from the left. Continue ahead on this track, later ignoring a bridge over an arm of the Semois at a campsite. The track now becomes a narrow surfaced lane which heads south and then west down the Semois valley, about 250 metres to the right of the wide river.

The trail eventually reaches the village of Poupehan. Pass the wooden sheds used for storing timber, and continue to a road T-junction opposite a hotel-restaurant.

Bear right onto the road through the village, passing another restaurant and ignoring the side road leading to the church on the right. Just before leaving the village bear left off the main road onto a narrower lane, signposted to Houlifontaine campsite. After 80 metres ignore a smaller lane on the left and continue ahead, passing a cemetery on your left, heading north-west on Trail Nos 65, 66, 69 and 70. On reaching the above mentioned campsite refreshment can be had at a cafeteria 50 metres to the left, but if not partaking of this then continue ahead, as waymarked, on the same four numbered trails, now following a stony track. This reaches a junction where Trail No. 65 heads off uphill to the right. We continue ahead on Trail Nos 66, 69 and 70. The track soon follows closely to the River Semois and a little above it. At the next junction Trail No. 89 climbs to the right. Once again we ignore this, but continue instead beside the river, on the track signposted to Laviot and Rochehaut. A sign is soon reached which indicates an alternative path to the right. This is for use during periods of flood (*Periode de Crue - Bij Hoog Water*) when the water levels are high. The normal route of Trail No. 69 follows the bank of the river. Our route follows the latter trail, but in periods of high water it is essential to follow the alternative waymarked route. Continue along the trail ahead, following the river downstream.

The path climbs a little above the river before descending back to the banks of the river at a footbridge over the Semois. Refreshments in the form of a Tea Room (sic) are to be had in the village of Frahan, reached by crossing this bridge. We, however, continue ahead on the lower path (*not* the upper track) following the right bank of the river. A most enjoyable path follows, as the trail is taken over a number of metal and wooden bridges and small ladders (not comparable with the earlier long, vertical ladder!) which bridge boulder, rock, crag and gully obstacles. Nowhere is the path difficult, although those people who suffer vertigo may be disturbed at times by the steep drop down to the river on the left. The path drops to the riverside once again to pass a picnic shelter with benches and tables, an excellent spot for lunch.

An easier path and track follows as the trail tackles one final loop of the River Semois. Eventually the track becomes surfaced as it passes a caravan site, which offers refreshments in the form of three site cafés and a caravan site shop (open during the summer season only). The track turns to head north along the valley, towards the village of Laviot. Walk ahead through the village to walk alongside the River Semois as it bends to the left to reach a tributary, the Ruisseau de Hour, where there is a hotel-restaurant/café. We leave the river at this point, to begin the climb eastwards back up to Rochehaut. The trail starts from immediately behind the hotel and is signposted as Trail Nos 81, 82 and 85 to Rochehaut. Climb to a Y-junction, where you take the right fork uphill, soon ignoring a track which climbs sharply to the right, but following the arrow "5" waymark ahead, beneath rock outcrops. Climb to a junction of seven tracks by a rock outcrop and seats. Take the track waymarked to Rochehaut, climbing eastwards and waymarked as Trail Nos 81, 82 and 85, plus a red/white GR waymark. This climbs to a road at a bend in the latter. From here there is a superb view down to Frahan and the loop of the Semois that surrounds it. Turn right along the road, enjoying this magnificent view down to your right, one of the finest in the whole district, to return to the church in the centre of Rochehaut.

SAINT-HUBERT
General Information and Places of Interest
The town of Saint-Hubert, the "capital of hunting and nature", is named after the patron saint of hunters, who on Good Friday AD 683 is said to have undergone a conversion to Christianity, whilst out hunting in the woods nearby. He is said to have seen a stag bearing a crucifix between its antlers, a scene which has been a subject for many painters down the centuries. After his conversion he became a monk in the Abbey of Stavelot, later becoming a bishop, eventually dying in AD 727. A century after his death Saint-Hubert's remains were brought to the abbey which had been built not far from the site of his conversion. It became an important place of Christian pilgrimage, St Hubert's relics (which have since been lost) being said to cure madness, amongst other ailments. The town that grew up around the abbey soon also became known as Saint-Hubert. Saint-Hubert and the surrounding area is still today very much the principal centre of hunting in the Ardennes. The first weekend in September each year sees the staging of the "international hunting and nature days", a good time for walkers *not* to be around, and hunting dogs are still brought to the basilica to be blessed on the 3rd of November, the feast day of Saint-Hubert.

Founded AD 817, the Abbey Church or Basilica Saint-Hubert was rebuilt in 1729. The west facade, Italianate Baroque in design, is the most striking feature of the main central square of the town; the interior of the basilica is Gothic. Parts of the crypt date back to the 11th century. The stalls are carved with the stories of St Hubert and St Benedict (Saint Benoît). The altar is dedicated to St Hubert. Unfortunately, Protestant fanatics destroyed much of the interior in 1568. The secular buildings which surround the basilica now form a cultural centre, housing craft exhibitions and meetings.

The town's other famous son was the painter of flowers, Pierre-Joseph Redouté, who was born here in 1759. There is a bust of Redouté behind the *hôtel de ville* in Saint-Hubert, the P.J. Redouté fountain was erected in his memory, and a museum dedicated to his works will be found at Fourneau Saint-Michel (Walk 20).

Other features of note within Saint-Hubert are the Church of Saint Giles

An old Ardennes barn in the Musée de la Vie Rurale en Wallonie at Fourneau Saint-Michel

(Romanesque, built around 1064) and Saint Roch's Chapel (17th century) passed on Walk 21. In the neighbourhood of Saint-Hubert are a number of places of interest: the *parc à gibier*, or wildlife park, home to deer, moufflon, wild boar and other animals of the Ardennes forests (Walk 20); a monument to King Albert, who was killed in a climbing accident nearby (Walk 20); a small airfield for gliders and light planes (it is possible to take lessons here - Walk 21); the Open Air Rural Museum and the Musée du Fer, both at Fourneau Saint-Michel (Walk 20). All of these places of interest will be visited by following the two walks described below.

Saint-Hubert is situated deep in the heart of some of the most extensive forest and heathland of the Ardennes, at a fairly high altitude of between 435m and 585m. It is perhaps hardly surprising that game dishes feature highly on the menus of the restaurants in the town (especially venison, wild boar and game birds). Prices are generally much cheaper than would be paid for similar dishes in Britain (gastronomic weekends are also on offer at several of the hotel-restaurants). Saint-Hubert makes an excellent centre for a weekend break.

Accommodation

Eight hotel-restaurants are listed for the town. These include the Hôtel de l'Abbaye, opposite the abbey church in the centre of Saint-Hubert. This hotel dates from 1735 and proudly boasts that Ernest Hemmingway was one of its guests in December, 1944 when he was a war correspondent. The author can recommend the Hôtel du Luxembourg in the Place du Marché, also close to the basilica (the food here is of a high quality). There are also a few private rooms available in the town (enquire at the tourist office, which will be found in the abbey complex, next to the basilica - note that it is only open at the weekends from mid-September to Easter). There is a large campsite (Europacamp) just outside the town.

Transport

Take the train from Namur, direction Luxembourg, and alight at Poix Saint-Hubert, a small village about 6kms west of Saint-Hubert. From here a bus may be taken to Saint-Hubert (or a bicycle can be hired from the station). For details of all local bus services contact the tourist office next to the basilica.

Saint-Hubert is situated a kilometre off the main N89 dual carriageway, almost halfway between La Roche and Bouillon, and as such is easily reached by car. Take the equally fast N4 from Namur to the Barrière de Champlon (youth hostel in nearby Champlon - see Appendix 4), the point at which it crosses the N89: follow the latter south-west to Saint-Hubert.

Official Walking Trails From Saint-Hubert

There are 11 official circular walking trails from Saint-Hubert, ranging from 3kms to 16kms in length. These walks, identified by number, from 1 to 9, and 11 and 12, are clearly marked as continuous red lines on the walkers' map, scale 1:25,000, entitled *Carte des Promenades Pédestres*, available from Saint-Hubert Tourist Office.

> Trail No. 1 - Parc à Gibier - 5.0kms.
> Trail No. 2 - La Scaire - 3.0kms.
> Trail No. 3 - Arville - 3.0kms.
> Trail No. 4 - La Blanche Fagne - 7.0kms.
> Trail No. 5 - La Doneuse - 10.5kms.
> Trail No. 6 - Le Pont Mauricy et le Fourneau Saint-Michel - 16.0kms.
> Trail No. 7 - Mémorial du Roi Albert - 8.5kms.
> Trail No. 8 - Hatrival - 8.0kms.
> Trail No. 9 - Vesqueville-Hurtebise - 7.0kms.
> Trail No. 11 - La Borne - Aérodrome - 10.5kms.
> Trail No. 12 - Le Leupont - 6.0kms.

Walks

Two walks are described in this book from Saint-Hubert.

WALK 20:
Saint-Hubert, the Parc à Gibier and Fourneau Saint-Michel

Description: The woods to the north of Saint-Hubert, those of the Roi Albert and Saint-Michel, are famed hunting grounds. There are large herds of deer and wild boar here. The area was a favourite of King Albert, who often visited, the last time shortly before his death in 1934 (a monument to King Albert is passed en route in the forest). This ramble offers a stroll through this most attractive mature woodland, as well as an opportunity to visit a game park (*parc à gibier*) where typical Ardennes fauna can be seen by those not fortunate enough to spot them during their walk. The highlight of the circuit for some will nevertheless be a visit to the splendid Open Air Museum at Fourneau Saint-Michel, conveniently situated at the halfway stage of the walk (see below for details).

The walk is a combination of two of the official local waymarked trails (Nos 6 and 7) as well as the long circuit (2.2kms) around the Fourneau Saint-Michel Open Air Museum.

Location: To the north of Saint-Hubert.

Start/Finish: The large car park outside the basilica in the Place du Marché in the centre of Saint-Hubert.

Distance: The full walk, including the "long circuit" of the Open Air Museum at Fourneau Saint-Michel, but excluding a visit to the game park, is 12.6 miles (20.2kms). By omitting a visit to Fourneau Saint-Michel and the Musée de la Vie Rurale en Wallonie, the walk is reduced to 10.6 miles (17kms). Allow another mile (1.6kms) for a diversion to and walk around the game park (*parc à gibier*).

Time: If both the *parc à gibier* and the museums at Fourneau Saint-Michel are visited then a very full day will be required. Allow about 5-6hrs for the walk plus at least an extra hour if visiting the *parc à gibier*, and at least a further 2-3hrs for the walk around the Open Air Museum and a visit to the Musée du Fer at Fourneau Saint-Michel.

Maps: The walkers' map at a scale of 1:25,000 entitled *Carte des Promenades Pédestres*, sold at the tourist office in Saint-Hubert. The map, which is in black and white, has 11 "official" waymarked walking routes marked on it and is sold with a single sheet leaflet briefly describing these trails in both French and Dutch.

A sketch map of the Open Air Musée de la Vie Rurale en Wallonie is provided on purchase of an entrance ticket to the museum at Fourneau Saint-Hubert.

IGN 1:50,000 series: sheet number 59.

Waymarking: The walking trails in the Saint-Hubert area are waymarked with small, white wooden boards, shaped as arrows, and bearing the number of the official trail together with the letters R.S.I. (Royal Syndicat d'Initiative de Saint-Hubert). The trail numbers are also painted in white on trees, fence posts, etc, with an accompanying directional arrow. Large signposts direct the visitor to the various features of interest in the Open Air Museum.

Terrain: The extensive woodland to the north of Saint-Hubert. The outward walk to Fourneau Saint-Michel is mainly a descending one along pleasant forest tracks for the most part. There are tracks and lanes to follow round the Open Air Museum at Fourneau Saint-Michel after which the return walk to Saint-Hubert is along lanes and surfaced roads and involves a long gradual climb. There are no steep gradients.

Footwear: Only after a prolonged dry spell during the summer would the woodland be dry enough to walk without boots or similar protective footwear. The circuit of the Open Air Museum and the return walk to Saint-Hubert could be safely accomplished wearing trainers or stout shoes.

Options: There are several variations to this walk possible depending on the length of walk required, preferred terrain, interests, and whether visits to the game park and the museums (recommended) are to be included. The main options are as follows:

     1. The full walk including a visit to both the game park and the Open Air Museum. A full and most interesting day.

     2. Omitting visits to either or both game park and the Fourneau Saint-Michel museums. This would save about 3 to 4kms of walking and considerable time. Omitting the *parc à gibier* is perhaps the most sensible option as few would want to miss the Open Air Museum; more time would be saved by following the short (0.6km) rather than the long circuit round the Open Air Museum.

     3. The walk can also be shortened by a kilometre or two by returning to Saint-Hubert all the way along Trail No. 6, thereby repeating part of the outward route, rather than following Trail No. 7 as described. The point at which this option is reached is described in the text below. The return along Trail No. 6 is quite straightforward.

     4. Those wanting only a short walk are thoroughly recommended the long circuit (2.2kms) in the Open Air Museum at Fourneau Saint-Michel.

     5. The outward route from Saint-Hubert to Fourneau Saint-Michel is through most attractive woodland. The return route is less pleasant and some walkers may therefore prefer to retrace their steps back through the forest via Pont Mauricy and the Monument Roi Albert. The distance of the two routes are comparable.

     6. Those travelling by car could start the walk at Fourneau Saint-Hubert where there is a large car park, visiting the Open Air Museum

either at the start or at the finish of the circular walk, possibly having lunch in one of the restaurants in Saint-Hubert at the halfway stage.

Special Problems: Hunting. During the autumn (generally from mid-September until the end of December) these woods and the approach roads are closed to the public, usually on one day per month (sometimes 2 to 3 days in succession), whilst organised shoots are held. During these periods it is not possible to walk the described itinerary. These hunting days are usually known well in advance and details are published locally at the entrances to the tracks, footpaths and roads. The tourist office in Saint-Hubert will be able to advise on these dates. It is generally safe to walk these woods at other times, but special care should always be exercised in this area as it is one of the most famous and well used hunting grounds in the whole of the Ardennes. Keep an eye open for any police or other notices indicating the closure of a trail. The warning notice *Tir à Balles* indicates the possibility of shooting in the area.

Refreshments: There is both a good quality restaurant (the Auberge du Prévost, a reconstructed 18th century inn) and a café (Les Tahons - this boasts 50 different types of beer on sale, many of them local - snacks also available) in the grounds of the Musée de la Vie Rurale en Wallonie at Fourneau Saint-Michel, at the halfway stage of the walk. Note that it is necessary to purchase tickets for the Open Air Museum in order to visit the café in the grounds, but meals and drinks can be taken at the restaurant whether visiting the museum or not. There are picnic tables, where one's own food can be eaten, at Fourneau Saint-Michel by the River Masblette, and also earlier on the walk at the Monument Roi Albert.

There is a cafeteria in the grounds of the *parc à gibier*.

There are several restaurants and cafés in Saint-Hubert offering everything from snacks to *haute cuisine*. There are also several food shops of most types in Saint-Hubert.

Fourneau Saint-Michel:

The hamlet is situated in an attractive woodland setting alongside the River Masblette. There are three museums here:

1. *Musée de la Vie Rurale en Wallonie* - the Open Air Museum.

This occupies a large site, situated at the northern end of the hamlet, on which a number of buildings dating from the 16th to the 18th centuries and from a number of localities within the French-speaking Ardennes have been re-erected and preserved. These buildings represent various aspects of the rural way of life of a largely bygone age: they include cottages, barns, a washhouse, a schoolhouse, a chapel, a printer's and a wheelwright's workshop, and a large 18th century inn. The museum park is well laid out and signposted, several of the buildings having photographic displays within them explaining the various aspects of the old rural life of the region. There is a good children's adventure play area, a café and a restaurant all within the grounds. For most of the year locally made goods and foodstuffs can be purchased from a museum shop.

Contained within the Open Air Museum is a separate museum devoted to Ardennes Shire horses, viz. the Musée Cheval Ardennais. Some of these large working animals are kept on site.

2. *Musée du Fer*

(Ironware Museum - devoted to the craft of iron working).

This is housed in a large building at the southern end of the hamlet. There are examples of all types of ironware and an impressive display of tools: outside there is a reconstructed 18th century forge.

Housed in a nearby barn is a small exhibition on the history of the Ardennes forest.

3. *Musée P.J. Redouté*

This museum is devoted to the works of the 18th century flower painter Joseph Redouté, who was born in Saint-Hubert in 1759.

The museums are usually open from 1st March until the end of December, from 10am until 5 or 6pm. There are small entrance fees to the museums, but it is possible to make a saving by buying a combined ticket to the Rural and Iron Museums. There are information leaflets in English and a sketch map is provided with the entrance ticket for the Open Air Museum which clearly indicates the walking routes for the "long" (2.2kms) and the "short" (600 metres) circuits of the museum.

A good example of an ornate Belgian postbox - this one is at Fourneau Saint-Michel

Route

Start the walk from the large abbey church (basilica) in the centre of Saint-Hubert. With one's back to the facade of the basilica, turn right at the fountain to walk downhill along the Rue de la Fontaine. Reach and cross the main Bouillon/Rochefort road (the N89) and follow the Rue Saint-Michel opposite as

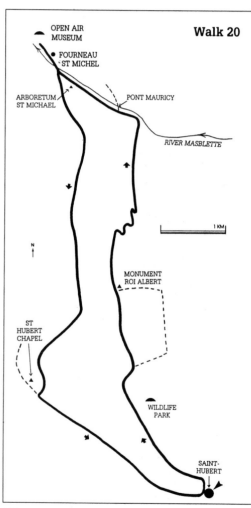

it bends to the left. Climb on the N849 road to leave the town. Several benches line this road from where one can sit to admire the view of the large abbey church and the surrounding pleasing pastoral scene. Pass the Ferme de Chirmont on your left and then the entrance drive to the *parc à gibier* (game park).

The *parc à gibier* is open most days of the year, usually from 9am until dusk. There is a small admission fee to the grounds which also feature a children's adventure playground and a cafeteria.

Continue along the N849 road, now following the direction waymarks

On the map:

OPEN AIR MUSEUM

Walk 20

FOURNEAU ST MICHEL

ARBORETUM ST MICHEL

PONT MAURICY

RIVER MASBLETTE

1 KM

N

MONUMENT ROI ALBERT

ST HUBERT CHAPEL

WILDLIFE PARK

SAINT-HUBERT

for Local Walk Nos 1, 6 and 7 along the Route des Forêts. Cross over the stream in the valley bottom and climb ahead, still on the road. At the top of the hill ignore the track on the right signposted as Trail No. 1, and continue ahead following the signs for Trails Nos 6 and 7. The road gently rises over another brow before dropping down to a stream where the road swings to the left. A few metres before the stream passes under the road, a forest track bears off to the right. Take this track, signposted as Trail Nos 6 and 7, to pass through a tall gate in a deer fence (if the woods are closed because of hunting activities there will almost certainly be a notice to this effect here and a barrier across the track at this point).

Climb on this track for a few hundred metres to reach a cross-track. Here turn left, signposted as Trail Nos 6 and 7, and at this point also picking up red/white (GR 14) and yellow/white waymarks. Follow this track, heading north and ignoring tracks heading off to left and right, until a road is reached. Cross over this road to a picnic spot (benches and tables) and a stone memorial to King Albert. At this point our walk leaves Trail No. 7 which turns left along the road. Instead follow Trail No. 6 by taking the track to the left of the memorial alongside the right-hand edge of the forest, following the painted red/white and yellow/white waymarks.

The trail passes through pleasant woodland eventually dropping to a surfaced forest track. Turn right along this for about 100 metres before forking left on a surfaced track immediately before the bridge over the stream (still following all three sets of waymarks). The trail meanders downhill through attractive woodland, never far from the babbling stream which is at first over to your right and later, after crossing a stone bridge, descends on your left. Soon after this stone bridge ignore a track going uphill to the right, but continue ahead downhill. Cross three more stone bridges on the descent northwards until you emerge at a T-junction of tracks by a ford and plank footbridge. Here the red/white and yellow/white waymarks head off to the right, but we turn left on the track following Trail No. 6 signs, now with the much larger stream (the River Masblette) to your right.

Where the track divides continue ahead and to the left, following Trail No. 6 (do not turn right to cross the river at Pont Mauricy). Before reaching the hamlet of Fourneau Saint-Michel the route passes the Arboretum of Saint-Michel which may be visited (entry by means of a green gate in the fence on your left). The arboretum was created in 1899 and the trees are clearly labelled with their Latin names and year of planting. Information boards provides further details of the arboretum and the management of the forest in general. The trail emerges on the road at Fourneau Saint-Michel. Our route back to Saint-Hubert turns left up the road here, but first you are highly recommended to turn right to explore the historic hamlet of Fourneau Saint-Michel (for details see above).

Leave Fourneau Saint-Michel by climbing on the N849 road heading southwards. Remain on this road for about 3.6kms, climbing steadily for most of the way. Soon after the road flattens out, a little way past the "6km" road mark, a crossroads is reached. Here we leave Trail No. 6 which continues directly ahead to Saint-Hubert (a shortened alternative if required), but instead turn right to rejoin Trail No. 7 (which was left at the the Monument Roi Albert). This narrow lane is signposted to the *Parc à Conteneurs* (rubbish recycling centre). Follow the lane until it descends to another road at a T-junction opposite a bus shelter. Turn left along this road, signposted as Trail No. 7. Follow this road for 2.3kms gently descending back to Saint-Hubert. Bear left on reaching a T-junction on the outskirts of the town to follow the roadsigns for the town centre, so returning to the basilica.

WALK 21:
Saint-Hubert and the Hurtebise Monastery

Description: The walk combines Local Walk Nos 9 and 11 to provide a circuit to the south and east of Saint-Hubert. The trail passes the Monastery of Hurtebise, a working Benedictine monastery in a pleasant rural setting, and later traverses heathland and woods in the vicinity of a small airfield. Small light aircraft may sometimes be seen taking off and landing here and add interest to the walk.

Location: To the east of Saint-Hubert.

Start/Finish: The large car park outside the basilica in the Place du Marché in the centre of Saint-Hubert.

Distance: 8.4 miles (13.5kms).

Time: Allow 4-5hrs.

Maps: The walkers' map at a scale of 1:25,000 entitled *Carte des Promenades Pédestres*, sold at the tourist office in Saint-Hubert (see Walk 20). IGN 1:50,000 series: sheet number 59.

Waymarking: The notes under "Waymarking" for Walk 20, above, apply also for this walk.

Terrain: The first half of the walk is along surfaced lanes, most of which carry little traffic. In the second part of the walk there is a mixture of tracks and footpaths. The landscape includes a small village, a monastery, heathland, woods and a small airfield, used only by small light aircraft. There is relatively little ascent and descent.

Footwear: Trainers or stout shoes would be suitable for the first half of the walk, but the tracks and footpaths used later can be wet and muddy, and the footpath alongside the perimeter fence of the small airfield has a rough grassy surface: hence boots are the recommended form of footwear.

Options: The walk could easily be shortened to about half its length by turning left (west) back to Saint-Hubert on Trail No. 9 on reaching the crossroads immediately before the monastery of Hurtebise (see route description below).

Special Problems: The note under this section in Walk 20 concerning closure of the area due to hunting also applies here, particularly in the woods to the east of the small airfield, although this walk is probably likely to be affected less often than Walk 20.

Refreshments: Refreshments of all types are available in Saint-Hubert at the start and end of the walk, but note that there are no opportunities for obtaining

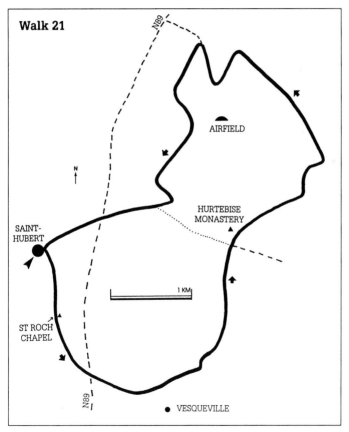

refreshment whilst on the walk, except for the possibility of purchasing yoghurt, cheese, butter and other farm produce from the farm shop attached to the Hurtebise Monastery (open daily except Sunday and Monday).

Route

Starting with one's back to the front facade of the basilica in the centre of Saint-Hubert, turn left at the fountain in front of the church to walk uphill on the Place du Marché, soon bearing to the left at the town hall along the Rue du Mont. Climb on this road to leave the town, reaching the Chapel Saint Roch at the brow of the hill. Continue ahead, now descending on the N849 road. Where the road forks take the left branch signposted as Trail No. 9 (roadsign to Freux and Vesqueville). Cross the roadbridge over the N89 and then immediately take the right fork down the Rue de Mayavaux, still following signs for Trail No. 9.

On the outskirts of the village of Mayavaux (Vesqueville), a few metres before a stream, turn left at a bus shelter onto a narrow surfaced lane, climbing to follow the course of the stream, which is now below to your right. Continue on this lane to a T-junction (bench on left) where you turn left following the waymarked Trail No. 9. Within 100 metres ignore a track off to the left (this is waymarked with red/white, GR 14, and yellow/white paint marks) but instead remain on the surfaced track (Trail No. 9) as it swings to the right, now with a wood on your left and a grassy field on your right. Within a few hundred metres ignore another track off to the right, remaining ahead on the track which follows the line of concrete telegraph poles heading north. The track passes through the wood and then between grassy fields to reach a crossroads. Here our walk leaves Trail No. 9 which turns left along the main road (a short route back to Saint-Hubert - about 2.5kms from here).

Cross the main road to continue ahead now following the signposted Trail No. 11, heading for the monastery buildings of the Monastère des Benedictines d'Hurtebise, which are now clearly visible. Pass the monastery buildings on the Rue du Monastère and remain on this lane to reach a T-junction, where you turn left, still waymarked as Trail No. 11. When a large radar installation comes into view turn left onto a waymarked (Trail No. 11) track, the Chemin de Sainte Ode, heading through the forest. Remain on this main track, ignoring any other tracks to left or right. On emerging from the forest a campsite and a small airfield for light aircraft comes into view on the left. Continue ahead until just before entering trees, where the track loses its rough surface and becomes grassy. Here, at a cross-tracks, turn left along the waymarked Trail No. 11, ignoring a further left turn after 5 metres. This path bends to the right just before reaching the aerodrome access road. Turn right along this lane, still on Trail No. 11 (waymark on tree).

After about 500 metres, before this road swings to the left, turn left (waymark arrows No. 11 on tree) onto a forest track, which can be muddy in wet conditions, now heading south-west. This track, which later narrows to a path, runs in a straight line and is waymarked with Trail No. 11 signs (ignore any turn-off tracks or paths from this straight track). On reaching the tall, green aerodrome perimeter fence turn left (waymark No. 11) to follow a narrow path between this fence on your left and a narrow ditch on your right. Follow this trail, which may be somewhat overgrown in places, to follow the perimeter fence, first to the south-east and then to the south-west.

Leave the perimeter fence at the point where it turns sharply to the left (to head south-south-east), to walk ahead (south-west) still on the narrow path and heading towards the tall conifer trees. On reaching these the trail continues ahead on a path between the forest trees on your left and a grassy field on your right. After a short, steep descent, turn left on reaching a pair of old, large iron gates, and follow this track until it emerges on a caravan site access road. Turn right along this to reach the main road, where you turn right, now heading back towards Saint-Hubert. This road crosses over the main N89 road by a flyover and continues ahead into the town. On reaching the outskirts of Saint-Hubert pass a stone memorial on your left, dedicated on 3rd September, 1994, the 50th anniversary of the Liberation of Saint-Hubert. Continue along the Rue de la Vaux to reach the town hall in the centre of Saint-Hubert. Turn right to return to the basilica.

HOTTON AND THE OURTHE
General Information and Places of Interest
Hotton is a small (population 4300), attractive town in the Ourthe valley, situated beside the river, beneath a rock escarpment nowadays much frequented by rock climbers. It is perhaps most well known for its beautiful limestone show caves, situated a little outside the town (see Walk 22), which were discovered only in 1958. The area was settled in prehistoric times and the Romans also had a camp here; even the present town has a history going back over a thousand years. The region is a quiet rural one, Hotton and the surrounding villages of Melreux, Fronville, Monville, Monteuville, Deulin, Waharday, Trinal and Werpin being rich in history and possessing a number of ancient churches, manorial farms, water mills and other buildings of historical and architectural interest.

Things to see in the area include the church and the British War Cemetery (1940-1945) in Hotton (Walk 22), Faber Water Mill, also in Hotton (Walk 23), the caves (Walk 22) and crags (Hotton Crags or the Renissart Rocks - Walk 23), St Peter's Church and the nearby castle-farm, both 17th century, at Melreux (Walk 24) and finally the 18th century Deulin Castle (Walk 24). Nearby Hampteau also has a former water mill, dating from 1737, and a castle. There is a fortnightly open-air market at Hotton on Saturday mornings. The wide river valley is most attractive in this region, providing peaceful walks, full of interest.

Accommodation

There are two hotels in Hotton ((Hôtel de l'Ourthe and La Commanderie), another at nearby Hampteau (Le Château d'Heblon) and a fourth at Werpin (La Besace - see Walk 23). There are also rooms available at the café Le Jacquemart in Hotton, the café Au Central in Melreux (near the railway station) and at the restaurant La Vieille Ferme in Hampteau. Finally there are a couple of *chambres d'hôte* in Hotton and one in Hampteau.

A *gîte d'étape*, Auberge des Amis de la Nature, is a few kilometres from Melreux on the Route de Durbuy (tel. (084) 46.62.93).

There are several campsites in the area. At Hotton: Camping Les Fonzays (Walk 24 - along the riverbank), Camping La Foulerie, Camping du Père Andre. At Melreux (Walk 24): Camping Chez Philou, Camping Eclos le Long de l'Eau. At Fronville (Walk 24): Camping La Mayette. At Deulin (Walk 24): Camping du Pont de Deulin.

Transport

Hotton can be reached by train from Liège. The railway station for Hotton is at Melreux (passed on Walk 24), a couple of kilometres north-west of the centre of Hotton.

There are buses from Hotton to Manhay, Marloie (for trains) and La Roche (contact the tourist office, see Appendix 3, for the latest timetables).

Hotton is easily accessible by car. From Namur take the N4 dual carriageway to Marche-en-Famenne, from where the N86 leads to Hotton. From Liège take either the N63 to Marche-en-Famenne, or the E25 motorway to junction 49: from here take the N651 to Manhay followed by the N807 to Erezée and Hotton. Hotton is reached from La Roche by driving along the Ourthe valley on the N833.

Official Walking Trails in the Region of Hotton-sur-Ourthe

There are 25 official circular walking trails in and above the Ourthe valley in the region of Hotton. These walks, identified by number from 1 to 25, are marked on the 1:25,000 scale map entitled simply *Promenades*, published by and available at Hotton-sur-Ourthe tourist office. The official trails start from a number of locations within the valley (all start from the church in the respective village, with the exception of Hotton where all walks begin from the road bridge):

From Hotton:

Trail No. 1 -   Renissart - Camp Romain - 2.6kms.
Trail No. 2 -   Vallée de l'Isbelle - Werpin - Ny - 12.0kms.
Trail No. 3 -   Grotte de la Porte-Aive - 8.5kms.
Trail No. 4 -   Isbelle - Hampteau - Grotte des 1001 Nuits - 6.5kms.
Trail No. 5 -   En Maffe - Menil-Favay - Marenne - 8.0kms.

The bridge over the River Ourthe at Hotton

Trail No. 6 -   Bois de Famenne - Thyne - Gehy - 5.0kms.
Trail No. 7 -   British Cemetery - Menil-Favay - 5.6kms.

From Melreux:
    Trail No. 8 -   Hotton - Les Fonzays - 5.0kms.
    Trail No. 9 -   Hotton - 4.0kms.
    Trail No. 10 - Sur Les Thiers - 5.2kms.
    Trail No. 11 - En Champagne - 8.0kms.

From Fronville:
    Trail No. 12 -   Fronville - Monville - 3.8kms.
    Trail No. 13 -   Reine Pédauque - Monteuville - 8.0kms.
    Trail No. 14 -   Château de Deulin - Point de Vue "Sur Somont" - 8.0kms.
    Trail No. 15 -   Monteuville - Rives de l'Ourthe - 8.6kms.

From Ny:
    Trail No. 16 -   Mélines - Soy - 7.0kms.
    Trail No. 17 -   Biron - 8.0kms.

From Werpin:
    Trail No. 18 -   Trinal - 7.0kms.
    Trail No. 19 -   Champs d'Héblon - 4.5kms.
    Trail No. 20 -   Trinal - Wy - Camping de Mélines - 8.8kms.

From Hampteau:
>   Trail No. 21 - Bois "Sur Waha" - 6.0kms.
>   Trail No. 22 - Hamoul - Waharday - 11.0kms.

From Bourdon:
>   Trail No. 23 - Marenne - Verdenne - 7.0kms.
>   Trail No. 24 - Sur le Gros Hy - 3.8kms.

From Marenne:
>   Trail No. 25 - Haie Abannée - Menil-Favay - 8.2kms.

Walks

Three walks are described in and above the Ourthe valley, all starting from and finishing at Hotton village. By following them, all of the main attractions and places of interest in the area can be visited.

WALK 22:
Hotton, Waharday and Menil-Favay, with an optional tour of Hotton Caves

Description: A mixture of open country and woodland walking. A fairly easy circuit, which provides an opportunity to visit the well-known and spectacular Hotton Caves (see below), as well as visiting a number of villages, both in the Ourthe valley and in the woods and hills to the south-west of the river. The itinerary takes in part of the GR O (GR de l'Ourthe), as well as sections of the local waymarked trails, Nos 4, 7, 21, 22 and 25.

Location: To the south and south-east of Hotton, along the Ourthe valley and in the hills and forests to the south-west of the River Ourthe.

Start/Finish: The church and roadbridge over the River Ourthe in the centre of Hotton village.

Distance: 9.6 miles (15.5kms).

Time: Allow 5¹/₂-6hrs for the walk, plus an extra hour or more for the optional visit to Hotton Caves (the tour of the caves lasts approximately 50mins, but allow for waiting time to the next guided tour, and perhaps time to take refreshments in the on-site café).

Maps: The map, at a scale of 1:25,000, entitled *Promenades*, published by Hotton-sur-Ourthe tourist office. Available from the tourist office in Hotton and from certain others in the Ourthe valley (eg. it should be available at La Roche).

>   IGN 1:50,000 series: sheet numbers 54 and 55.

The church at Hotton reflected in the still waters of the River Ourthe

Waymarking: Waymarks are in the form of yellow paint marks and yellow painted numbers on trees and fences as indicated in the text below. Part of the route is waymarked, where indicated, with the red/white waymarks of the GR O (GR de l'Ourthe).

Terrain: A mixture of quiet lanes and woodland tracks. There are hills to climb and descend, but none is excessively steep. A mixture of woodland and open country.

Footwear: During the summer months trainers or stout shoes could be worn for this walk, as a fair proportion of the trail follows quiet surfaced lanes, and even the unsurfaced tracks through woodland tend to be fairly well drained and free from excessive mud for most of the time.

Option: The walk could be shortened considerably by following Trail No. 22 between Hampteau (a little before Rue Inzefin) and Menil-Favay, thereby cutting off the circuit via Hamoul/Nohaipre and Waharday (see the tourist office map for details).

Places of
Interest: 1. *Hotton War Cemetery.*   This graveyard, kept in immaculate condition by the Commonwealth War Graves Commission, contains the graves of 667 men from the UK, Canada, Australia, New Zealand and Poland, most of whom died in the Battle of the Ardennes in 1945.

2. *Grottes de Hotton* (Hotton Caves).   Discovered only in 1958, the cave system, known as the Thousand and One Nights, has some very beautiful rock formations. There is an underground river in the area, which was responsible for forming the cave. Guided tours are available from the beginning of April to the end of October (generally from 9am to 6pm). There is a moderate entry fee: expect to pay in the region of 200BF. The tour of the cave lasts approximately 50mins. Tel 084 - 46.60.46 for further information.

Refreshments: There are several restaurants, cafés and food shops in Hotton. In addition a number of similar establishments are passed on the first third of the itinerary to Rendeux. These should be visited if required, as after leaving Rendeux-Bas there are no further possibilities for refreshment until returning to Hotton at the end of the walk.

Route

Starting from the church and road bridge in the centre of Hotton, take the road signposted to La Roche and Rendeux, heading south-east. After 50 metres turn right along the Rue du Parc (red/white waymark of the GR O, and yellow No. 7 on concrete telegraph pole). Follow this lane as it bends first to the left and then to the right, and at its end strike off left uphill on a footpath between fences, following the waymarks for Trail No. 7. At a cross-track bear right for a few metres to join a road. Turn left on this lane heading uphill away from

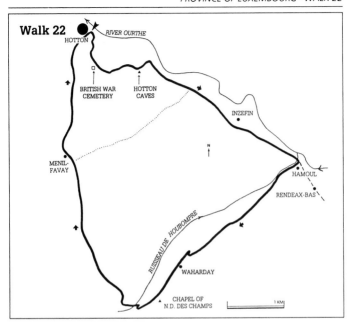

Hotton village. Soon Hotton War Cemetery is reached on the left-hand side of the road (see "Places of Interest" above for details).

Fifty metres after the cemetery, Trail Nos 7 and 4 separate. We take Trail No. 4 which leaves the road on the *second* track on the left (still following the red/white of the GR O trail - note that the "O" here stands for Ourthe). The path passes through a mixture of woodland and open country, eventually reaching a lane (point *). For a visit to the Grottes de Hotton (Hotton Caves) turn right here. The café and entrance to the cave is reached within 5mins.

After a visit to the cave return to the point * (see above) and continue along the lane, heading in a north-easterly direction, following the red-white waymarks down towards the Ourthe valley. On reaching a T-junction turn right at the sign for Bowling Funny Ball(!), along the Chemin du Speleo Club de Belgique. Pass to the left of a large open quarry to meet the main road. Walk along the right-hand side of this road (track and then pavement) passing the entrance to the Château d'Hotton Hôtel-Restaurant and then the Funny Ball establishment (café here). Pass another restaurant and a couple of food shops, ignoring the road (Rue Chavée) on the right signposted to Marenne. Pass more restaurants and cafés and a church on the right. Trail No. 4 goes off to the left along a road signposted to Soy, but we ignore this, continuing instead along the main road

149

until a double bend in the latter is reached. Halfway through this double bend bear right off the main road onto Rue Inzefin (Trail Nos 21 and 22 painted in yellow on a concrete telegraph pole).

Climb the hill ahead, later ignoring the Rue du Bosquet on the right, but 50 metres after this, at a Y-junction, fork left on Trail No. 22 (at this point leaving Trail No. 21 which follows Rue du Cheyeneux uphill to the right). The lane eventually becomes an unsurfaced track beside woodland, with views out to the left of the wooded hills on the far side of the Ourthe valley. When the track begins to descend, at the point where it becomes metalled again, ignore a track forking right, but continue downhill on the lane ahead. This emerges onto the main road opposite a restaurant at Rendeux-Bas (note the old well on the right-hand side of the road). After 50 metres turn right opposite a *boulangerie/ pâtisserie* on the Rue des Hêtres, signposted to Chéoux.

Follow this lane alongside a small stream past the houses of the village of Hamoul/Nohaipre. Ignore any side turnings and remain on the lane as it climbs away from the village. At the point where the road to Chéoux turns sharply to the left, continue ahead on the narrow lane signposted to Waharday, still on Trail No. 22. The lane, the Rue des Bruyères, soon begins to climb, bending repeatedly as it does so, to reach the houses of the village of Waharday, known for its flower-bedecked gardens (and, when the author was there, for its barking dogs!). Remain on the main road through the village. Leave the village and continue ahead until a grassy dirt track is reached which leaves the road on the right at a small metal cross, about 40 metres before a small stone shrine (Notre Dame des Champs). Take this track enclosed between fences and hedges (and *not* the one by the stone shrine). Blackberries abound along this track in the early autumn. The track soon begins a descent to a small stream, after which it bends to the right and then the left on an ascent into the forest, still following the occasional Trail No. 22 waymarks. There follows a superb tract of mature deciduous woodland, the forest floor being richly carpeted with a variety of ferns and mosses, and many mushrooms and toadstools will be seen here during the autumn months.

Ignore any side turnings in the wood, remaining on the main track following "22" signs and the occasional yellow paint mark on trees. The track leads to a narrow surfaced lane at a T-junction. Turn right here along this metalled road, heading north. Continue ahead at crossing tracks, the route now being that of the combined Trail Nos 22 and 25. The forest road eventually descends rather steeply out of the wood to reveal the cluster of buildings of the village of Menil-Favay below, and the distant wooded hills of the Ardennes far beyond. Descend to the village, taking the left fork signposted to Marenne (straight ahead), reaching a water fountain on the outskirts of the village, now re-joining Trail No. 7. Bear left at a second water trough and then right at a third water trough, just before a small chapel on the left, onto the Rue de Maffe, again picking up the red and white waymarks of a GR trail.

Pass farm buildings, ascend a small rise and then begin a descent northwards towards Hotton. The narrow poorly surfaced lane eventually gives out to a grassy/earthen track which crosses a field and enters woodland. The track soon narrows to a footpath which descends to follow the overgrown, dried-up stream bed of the Ruisseau de l'Agauche. This narrow path, which can become a little overgrown during the summer months (beware of stinging nettles if wearing shorts) leads to a concrete track which runs out onto the main road on the outskirts of Hotton. Turn right along this heading towards the village church, the prominent pointed spire of which is seen ahead.

WALK 23:
Hotton Crags: Melines, Trinal, Werpin and Hotton

Description: An opportunity to see the impressive crags and the rock arch above the River Ourthe near Hotton, as well as explore the woods and villages to the north of the Ourthe valley. The walk offers a mixture of woodland walking on pleasant tracks and paths, with more open countryside, mainly on quiet country lanes. The itinerary includes a section of the GR O (GR de l'Ourthe) as well as the following local, waymarked trails: Trail Nos 1, 2, 3, 4, 19 and 20.

Location: To the east of Hotton, in the Ourthe valley and in the hills, woods and villages to the north of the River Ourthe.

Start/Finish: The road bridge over the River Ourthe in the centre of Hotton village.

Distance: 10.1 miles (16.2kms).

Time: Allow 6hrs.

Maps: The map, at a scale of 1:25,000, entitled *Promenades*, published by Hotton-sur-Ourthe tourist office. Available from the tourist office in Hotton and from certain others in the Ourthe valley.
        IGN 1:50,000 series: sheet number 55.

Waymarking: Waymarks are in the form of yellow paint marks and yellow painted numbers on trees and fences as indicated in the text below. Part of the route is waymarked, where indicated, with red/white waymarks of the GR O.

Terrain: Riverbank, woods, hills and villages. The sections near to Hotton and its crags offer some steep paths above the river, but much of the rest of the itinerary presents fairly easy grade walking.

Footwear: Boots with good grips are advised for the initial and latter stages of the walk, which are on steep and sometimes slippery paths, although trainers or good shoes would suffice on much of the rest of the walk during a dry summer period.

Option: The circuit could be considerably shortened by following waymarked Trail No. 2 between Melines and Werpin, thereby omitting the eastern section of the route via Wy and Trinal (see the tourist office map for details).

Places of
Interest: 1. *Moulin Faber.* Visits to this attractive water mill in Hotton are possible during the afternoons of July and August, when the mill, which is still in working order, is usually open to the public between 2 and 4pm.

2. *Hotton Crags.* A well-known rock climbing area, in an attractive setting above the river, near to the village. On most summer days and at weekends throughout the year, the walker is likely to see climbers tackling these popular routes.

Refreshments: A café at the campsite passed en route in the woods near Mélines, but other than this there is no place of refreshment until the village of Werpin, only a few miles before the end of the walk. Hotton, at the start and end of the walk, has several cafés, restaurants and shops.

Route

Start the walk from the right (north) bank of the River Ourthe at the road bridge in the centre of Hotton. Follow the road signposted to Soy and Erezée alongside the narrow arm of the River Ourthe, following red/white GR waymarks. Pass the water mill (Moulin Faber), the wheels of which still turn (for details of a visit see "Places of Interest" above). Fifty metres after the mill, where the main road swings to the left, take the minor right fork, still beside the water. Before this re-joins the main road, locate a narrow footpath at a metal turnstile. This footpath, enclosed between fences and hedges, leads to an impressive crag

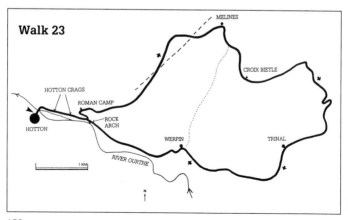

above the river, much used by rock climbers. At the far end of the crag locate a narrow footpath climbing steeply up the hillside (red/white GR waymarks and a yellow paint mark for Trail No. 1). At the top of the steepest part of the climb (point * - see the final part of this route description) our trail, and that of the GR route, swings sharply to the left, still climbing. This excellent hillside path leads to a shelter and a pair of simple wooden seats, the site of a Roman camp.

Turn right at this point, still following the GR O trail, now through an avenue of trees. On reaching a track T-junction leave Trail No. 1, which goes off to the left, but walk to the right to follow the red and white waymarks of the GR O, which is coincident here with local Trail No. 3 (yellow numbers on trees). Follow the clear and obvious path through the woods, generally well waymarked with red/white and yellow waymarks (beware one small area that is often very muddy), to reach a road at a metal barrier. Cut obliquely across this road onto a footpath opposite, thereby maintaining direction, still on Trail No. 3. Follow this to reach another road: here turn right.

Continue to reach and cross the main road, taking the minor road opposite, signposted to Mélines. The road soon begins to bend and to descend, passing a war memorial on the left-hand side which commemorates the loss of an American tank to mines on 3rd January, 1945, during the counter-offensive of the Battle of the Ardennes. Descend to a T-junction at the Rue du Moulin. Turn right here in the direction of Beffe. Cross the bridge over the stream and follow the road as it sweeps to the left. About 40 metres after a new monument commemorating the role of the Americans in the Battle of the Ardennes (unveiled on 10th September, 1994), turn left opposite a cross commemorating John Shields, an American corporal who died here in December, 1944, following the signpost to a campsite and the red/white waymarks of the GR trail. Pass the campsite and its adjacent café, now on Trail No. 20. Cross the small footbridge to the left of the ford and follow the track ahead as it swings to the right. Continue on this track later following the sign indicating the direction to Wy, and then soon passing a stone cross a few metres to the left of the path amongst trees (the Croix Bietle). The trail eventually comes out to a small clearing with fence on left and hedge on right. Shortly after this bear right (south) at a track T-junction, now with a number of tall fir trees on your right-hand side. Climb on this track to reach the farming village of Wy (altitude 325m).

Turn right along Rue Gregoire and in 50 metres follow the road as it bends to the left to climb past the village church. Walk through the village, passing its numerous houses and farms, to descend on the Rue de la Vallée to a T-junction at the edge of the village. Turn right here, downhill. Follow the lane downhill round a right-angled hairpin bend. The minor road begins to reascend after a while. When it levels out look out for a small wooden cross on the left-hand side of the road. Fifty metres or so after this, and about 100 metres before a pylon on the right-hand side of the road, turn right onto a narrow surfaced lane.

Within 50 metres this forks: ignore the left branch heading south, but take the now unsurfaced gravel/grassy track heading west and waymarked with the red/white emblem of a GR trail. Cross the grassy field ahead, then continue down the edge of another field with a wood on your right. Soon the village of Trinal comes into view on the hillside ahead. The enclosed track bears right to reach a gravel track at a T-junction of tracks. Turn left on this track to head downhill. After crossing a stream by an old stone bridge, the lane, now surfaced, climbs to reach a road T-junction on the outskirts of Trinal. Turn left to walk up through the village.

Bear right at a stone shrine onto the Rue du Tier following the direction of the red/white waymarks of the GR O. Near the top of the ascent ignore the lane turning acutely to the right, and also the grassy track curving slightly to the right, but take the lane ahead, waymarked with red/white, and following a line of telegraph posts. Later ignore a turning to the left, but bend to the right with the main lane (red/white waymarks), soon ignoring yet another track down to the left. Our pleasant, little frequented old lane heads westwards and often provides extensive views of the Ardennes forests and hills, before beginning its descent towards the Ourthe valley. During this descent take special care to locate a path (waymarked with red/white paint) that leaves the lane on its right to descend through trees. Emerge from this onto the road to follow it downhill to reach the village of Werpin.

Turn left in front of the small town church with its distinctive pointed steeple. Follow the lane downhill still on the route of the GR O, but also now on Trail Nos 2 and 19. At the Hôtel La Besace (refreshments) do not cross the bridge over the River Ourthe, but instead bear right uphill on the Rue des Champs d'Herlon, leaving the GR trail at this point. A few metres after this lane bends sharply to the right, leave it by descending on an earthen track on the left. This soon narrows to a path enclosed within hedgerows and then enters woodland. This undulating forest path eventually passes a perfect little humpback bridge over a (usually) dried-up stream. Continue ahead on the path eventually reaching a path which descends to the left, indicated as Trail No. 1 (this is about 20 metres before and just below point *, reached on the outward trail at the beginning of the walk (see text above).

Turn left downhill on this path, soon contouring a little to the right, to visit a most impressive rock arch at the far side of which is a view down to the River Ourthe. Retreat from this rock arch (if you wish to explore further a very steep path leads down to the water's edge, but care is required, particularly in wet or icy conditions) and return to point * to rejoin the outward route. Follow this in reverse, passing Hotton Crags once again, to return to the centre of Hotton village.

WALK 24:
Melreux, the Château de Deulin and the Ourthe Valley

Description: A mainly level walk within the valley of the River Ourthe. The ramble offers pleasant views of the tranquil valley of the Lower Ourthe, and visits several interesting villages (Melreux, Monteuville, Deulin, Fronville and Monville) in the region. The walk includes visits to the attractive grounds of the large holiday complex of La Reine Pédauque, and to the 18th century Château de Deulin. The route links up a number of local, waymarked and numbered walking trails, ie. sections of Trail Nos 3, 8, 9, 11, 12, 13, 14, and 15.

Location: The Ourthe valley, north-west of Hotton.

Start/Finish: The road bridge over the River Ourthe in the centre of Hotton village.

Distance: 11.5 miles (18.5kms).

Time: Allow 6hrs.

Maps: The map, at a scale of 1:25,000, entitled *Promenades*, published by the tourist office at Hotton-sur-Ourthe. Available from the tourist office in Hotton and from certain others in the Ourthe valley.
      IGN 1:50,000 series: sheet numbers 54 and 55.

Waymarking: Waymarks are in the form of yellow paint marks and yellow painted numbers on trees and fence posts as indicated in the text below.

Terrain: Mainly in open country and often on surfaced lanes, but the trail also follows some grassy, dirt or stony tracks. The scene is rural and agricultural and there are frequent views of the wide, picturesque River Ourthe. The route offers level walking for the most part, with just a few gentle gradients here and there.

Footwear: Much of the trail follows surfaced lanes, so that trainers or stout shoes would be suitable for most of the year.

Option: The walk can be shortened by starting and finishing in the village of Melreux.

Places of Interest: 1. *La Reine Pédauque.* The walk passes through the attractive grounds of this *centre de vacances* which offers numerous facilities to its guests (tennis, mini-golf, bar, restaurant, etc). The ornamental lake is particularly attractive.

      2. *Château de Deulin.* The castle, built in 1760, is located in an attractive rural setting. The building is private (built and still owned by the Harlez family), but is open for several public events during the year, including concerts in the 18th century Baroque chapel and in the main courtyard, and various exhibitions and fairs. Visits on request may be arranged for groups at

any time of the year (write to M.S. de Harlez, Deulin Castle, 6990 Deulin, or tel 084 - 46.66.16). There are walks in the French Gardens and in the 15 hectare park, which is home to a number of rare species and some ancient trees, including a 200-year-old Virginia maple tree.

Refreshments: Refreshments are available at several locations along the walk: at Hotton, Melreux, La Reine Pédauque and Fronville. In particular facilities of every kind are available in the villages of Hotton and Melreux.

Route

From the road bridge in the centre of Hotton, follow the northern shore of the River Ourthe along the Rue de la Vallée, heading north-westwards. On a clear sunny day note the near perfect reflection of Hotton Church in the water of the River Ourthe. Just before this road bends to the right, turn right off it onto the narrow Rue Saint-Roch (note the shrine to Saint Roch on the left where this lane begins). Continue ahead at the first crossroads, noting the tall, thin spire of Melreux Church over to the left. At the second crossroads (crucifix on the right-hand side) turn left, now heading for Melreux Church along the Rue du Chapelet. Turn right onto the high street in Melreux (cafés, restaurants and shops) and continue along it to turn left signposted to Durbuy, Fronville and the *gare* (station).

Pass under the railway bridge and immediately bear right, signposted to Durbuy. Remain on this lane, the N833 and Trail No. 11, for 2.2kms. This is the least pleasant part of the trail, but it leads to better things, and generally traffic along this road is light. At the 21km road sign refreshments may be obtained at the large complex of La Reine Pédauque, a *centre de vacances* which houses a bar and restaurant. Pass through the entrance gates of the Reine Pédauque, but do not turn to the left towards the reception, but instead, within 10 metres of the entrance gates, bear right along a driveway which leads down to an ornamental lake. Cross the small stone bridge over the lake's inlet stream and follow the drive ahead through the attractive gardens to pass to the right of the large château-like building seen ahead, thereby reaching a car parking area. Here bear to the left along Trail No. 13 which leaves the car park on a gravel pathway heading westwards. In 50 metres, in front of tennis courts, turn right along a track to pass a brick-built tower.

Turn right on meeting a path T-junction in front of a caravan site, now on Trail No. 15. At the corner of the caravan site turn left onto a stony/grassy track, following the waymarks for Trails Nos 13 and 15. Remain on this track ignoring any side turnings to left or right as it gently descends and then reascends on an equally gentle gradient. The track becomes surfaced (the Rue de Holset) and climbs to pass houses before descending slightly to reach a T-junction a few metres after a large house on the right (seated stone lions on the gateway). Turn left at this T-junction walking downhill to enter the village of Monteuville.

Turn left (Trail No. 13) on reaching the main road through the village

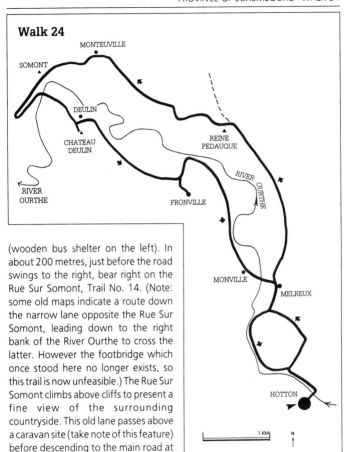

Walk 24

MONTEUVILLE

SOMONT

DEULIN

CHATEAU
DEULIN

REINE
PEDAUQUE

RIVER OURTHE

RIVER
OURTHE

FRONVILLE

MONVILLE

MELREUX

HOTTON

1 KM

N

(wooden bus shelter on the left). In about 200 metres, just before the road swings to the right, bear right on the Rue Sur Somont, Trail No. 14. (Note: some old maps indicate a route down the narrow lane opposite the Rue Sur Somont, leading down to the right bank of the River Ourthe to cross the latter. However the footbridge which once stood here no longer exists, so this trail is now unfeasible.) The Rue Sur Somont climbs above cliffs to present a fine view of the surrounding countryside. This old lane passes above a caravan site (take note of this feature) before descending to the main road at a cemetery. Turn left along this road, now passing beneath the cliffs, until at the far end of the caravan site mentioned above, turn right over the bridge over the River Ourthe to approach the village of Deulin on the N898. On the outskirts of the village, at a shrine to the Virgin Mary, bear right onto a stony dirt track. This leads to a T-junction at farm buildings: turn right in front of the large brick barn (point x), to view, on the left, the impressive Château de Deulin, a classified monument.

Return to the large barn (point x) where bear right to reach a road T-junction (note the statue of Saint Monon mounted within the wall on your right). Turn right here along the Rue du Château, to descend back to the main road. Turn right along this to leave Deulin. Follow this lane, first following an arm of the River Ourthe and heading towards the church of Fronville, the steeple of which should be visible ahead. Pass the roadsign indicating entry into the village of Fronville and, where the road swings to the right, note a lane (Rue Lava) on the left signposted to La Mayette campsite (point z). Continue into the village to visit its fine church (alas it is often locked) or for refreshments (there is a bar opposite the church).

Return to point z to follow the lane towards La Mayette. On reaching a lane junction by some cottages, bear right to follow a narrow surfaced lane which is closed to traffic (except for agricultural vehicles). The River Ourthe is over to your left. This most pleasant lane meanders through the fields and meadows on the fringes of the river, eventually joining its left bank and continuing into the village of Monville. Continue ahead through the small village to reach the main road, where turn left to walk over the bridge above the River Ourthe and pass under the railway bridge to re-enter the village of Melreux. Walk back along its high street, but this time, where the main road swings sharply to the left, continue ahead to pass directly to the left of the church, following Trail No. 9. Where the road bends sharply to the left, turn off it by taking a stony track on the right, which heads towards the railway bridge over the River Ourthe. Turn left along the riverbank to reach the railway bridge (ie. follow the right bank of the river heading southwards, up-stream). Follow the riverbank, first on a grassy track, then a stony one, and then passing through Les Fonzays campsite, finally emerging on the road which leads into Hotton. Follow this back to the road bridge in the centre of the town.

LA ROCHE-EN-ARDENNE
General Information and Places of Interest
The permanent population of La Roche-en-Ardenne is less than 2000, but this figure must be multiplied manyfold during the summer holiday period, when the small, picturesque town is packed with visitors. Situated in the heart of the Ardennes, La Roche is truly its capital, a mecca for holidaymakers and for all lovers of the outdoors. Visit La Roche, if you are able, outside the main tourist season.

The town, situated 70kms from Liège, nestles along one of the many loops of the meandering River Ourthe, below steeply wooded hills. Overlooking the town, on a rocky escarpment, are the ruins of an 11th century castle, said to be haunted by the ghost of one Countess Berthe. The château, from where there is a good view of the town and river, is open in April, May, June and September from 10am to 12pm and from 2 to 5pm. In July and August it is open from 10am to 7pm; from October to March from 10am to 12pm and 2 to 4pm at weekends and 2 to 4pm on weekdays (closed on Tuesdays and in bad weather).

Two other places in the town are worth a visit, especially if the weather is poor. The Museum of the Battle of the Ardennes in the Rue de la Gare has displays on three floors of numerous memorabilia and photographs of the war period. The terrible destruction that took place in the town after the passing of two foreign armies is all too evident from the old photographs. The museum is open from Easter to the end of September from 10am to 12.30pm and from 2 to 6pm. From October to the end of December it is open during afternoons only (closed on Tuesdays except in July and August). At the Crafts Centre, Les Grès de la Roche, it is possible to visit the workshop to watch the famous local blue-grey pottery being made. The centre is open during the Christmas and Spring bank holidays and in July and August, mainly during the afternoons.

Most of the shops along the High Street in La Roche seem never to close. There are many cafés and cake shops selling waffles (*gouffres*). A speciality of La Roche is dried and smoked hams which will be seen on sale in the many delicatessens. The tourist office in the Place du Marché is open all through the winter and on Sundays.

The *petit train touristique* operates throughout the summer months. The journey, which lasts about 45mins, visits several of the outlying areas above La Roche, including the café reached on the latter stages of Walk 30. As it is possible to join and leave the train at various points, it could be used to get some way out of La Roche to join a walk, or you could leave it after a while and make your own way back to La Roche on foot.

Despite a number of places of interest within the town it is the great outdoors that is the main attraction here, the region offering some of finest scenery in the Ourthe valley. It can be enjoyed on foot, by bicycle, by kayak along the river, and, if conditions are favourable, on cross-country skis. Bicycles and mountain bikes can be hired in La Roche, by the hour, half-day, day or longer. There are several marked trails for mountain bikers in the hills and woods above La Roche (a special map showing these trails, as distinct from the walking routes, can be purchased from the tourist office in La Roche). Cross-country ski equipment can also be hired in the town: once again there are many waymarked trails in the area designed specifically for *ski de fond*. The tourist office has details of all firms hiring bikes, kayaks and ski equipment.

One of the main attractions in La Roche is kayaking down the River Ourthe. Beginners should attempt no more than the 12km course which starts upriver at Maboge. Special buses, included in the price, take participants from La Roche to Maboge where the kayak is picked up and paddled back to La Roche. The water level for nearly the whole length of the course is usually only a few feet in depth, so that a drowning accident is unlikely. Indeed the major problem is often one of preventing the canoes running aground on the numerous rocks encountered en route! The current is very gentle and should present no problems to even to the most timid of adventurers. No instruction is given, but the vast majority of first-timers soon master the basic principles and arrive safely back at La Roche two or three hours after leaving Maboge. Single or two-man kayaks are available. More experienced canoeists can opt for longer routes (eg. 25kms from Nisramont to La Roche) and somewhat faster flowing sections. Kayaking operates from May to October. The less intrepid can hire 2 and 4-person pedaloes from La Roche in the summer.

During the winter months, when the rivers are usually much higher and faster flowing, canoeing is more dangerous and impractical, but the companies then offer river rafting. Parties are taken down the river by experienced leaders. River rafting, a more serious affair than canoeing, takes place between November and April, providing conditions are suitable. Inquire at local tourist offices for more information on canoeing and rafting, but it will not be difficult to locate the numerous companies that offer canoeing packages, as their facilities are well advertised locally, and canoe transporters are a familiar site along the roads of the river valleys.

La Roche is an excellent centre for walkers. There are a dozen walking trails around the town (see below) numbered from 1 to 12. These are identified by signposts and waymarks bearing the symbol of a red boot, together with the relevant number. It is important not to confuse these routes with the mountain bike trails which are also numbered from 1 upwards, but which do not bear the red boot symbol. Yet a third set of waymarks refers to cross-country skiing trails. All of these waymarks have been erected by the local tourist office. The local walking trails are supplemented by two long distance paths: the GR 57 or GR O (Sentier de la Vallée de l'Ourthe) passes through La Roche, whilst the GR 14 begins (or ends) in the Place du Bronze in the centre of the town. These paths, of course, are waymarked with the standard red and white paint marks of the GR trails.

Those with extra time available are recommended to make a trip to two viewpoints in the Ourthe valley a little distance from La Roche: the Belvédère de Nisramont and the Belvédère des Six Ourthes. From the latter viewpoint, on a rocky ridge high above the river, near Nadrin on the Ourthe Supérieure, six points of the river can be seen in an area where the Ourthe divides and loops in a complicated fashion. Walking in this area of the Upper Ourthe can also be strongly recommended: a map at a scale of 1:25,000 produced by the Ourthe Supérieure tourist office and entitled simply *Pomenades - Wandelingen* shows all the waymarked trails in the area. The campsite at Nadrin, or a hotel in the village, is a good base from which to explore the Upper Ourthe.

Accommodation

There are about 20 hotels in La Roche and the surrounding area, covering several price ranges, including Les Arcades, Les Ardennes, Le Beau Rivage, Le

---

Negotiating a long ladder up a huge rock boulder on the 'Ladder Walk' near Rochehaut. (Walk 19)

A typical forest stream in the Belgian Ardennes - this one is near Fourneau Saint-Michel (Walk 20)

A view of the Ourthe valley from near La Roche, seen in the evening sunlight of springtime

Bristol, Le Chalet-Hôtel, La Clairefontaine, La Closeraie, Le Corumont, Hôtel de la Place, Les Genêts, Le Majestic, Les Merlettes, Le Midi (recommended), Le Monderne and Les Olivettes. There is also a fairly large selection of private rooms and *chambres d'hôte* in the district. The usual caution about full hotels in the high summer season applies particularly to 'La Roche, a very popular holiday destination.

There are no less than eight campsites in or close to La Roche, a fact which reflects its popularity as an outdoor holiday centre: Camping Benelux, Camping Floreal, Camping Le Grillon, Camping Lohan, Camping de l'Ourthe (recommended), Camping Tempelier, Camping de Vieux Moulin and Camping Le Pont du Tram. Many of these are alongside the picturesque River Ourthe. There is also a campsite (Camping Daco) at Samrée (Walk 25).

Transport
A combination of train and bus is required to reach La Roche by public transport. From Brussels or Namur take a train, direction Luxembourg City, alighting at the village of Marloie. From here there are buses to La Roche, about 22kms away (Bus No. 15, about 10 buses a day, Monday to Friday, but only about 4 buses a day on Saturdays, and 3 a day on Sundays and fête days - the bus journey time is between 40mins and 1hr depending on the bus taken).

From Liège take a train to Melreux (see Walk 24), which is a couple of kilometres north-west of the centre of Hotton. From Melreux buses go to La Roche (Bus No. 13, up to 10 buses a day, Monday to Friday, but only 4 buses a day at weekends - the bus journey time is about 30mins). Alternatively, remain on the train to Marloie (where the Namur and the Liège lines meet) and from here take a bus to La Roche as above.

There are also buses linking La Roche with Houffalize (Bus No. 15 bleu, about 3 times a day, Monday to Friday, very limited service at the weekends and on fête days); with Cens (Bus No. 49 blanc: 3 services a day, Monday to Friday - no buses at the weekends); with Ortho (Bus No. 49 blanc, about twice a day: 2 services a day, Monday to Friday - no buses at the weekends); and with Tenneville (Bus No. 59 blanc, 5 buses a day, Monday to Friday).

There are four bus stops in La Roche, the main ones being by the main parking area in the centre of the town, and at the Place du Bronze.

Motorists driving from Brussels should take the E411 (A4) motorway, leaving it at junction 18 in favour of the dual carriageway N4 (which begins in Namur), heading south-east. Leave this at the Barrière de Champlon for the N89 which leads north-east for about 12kms to La Roche. From Liège head south on the E25 (A26) motorway to junction 50, where you leave the motorway to follow the N89 south-west to La Roche.

Official Waymarked Trails From La Roche-en-Ardenne

Route Number	Distance	Official Time	Direction from La Roche	Official Grade
1	5.3 miles (8.5kms)	2hrs 45mins	North-west	Easy*
2	5.6 miles (9.0kms)	3hrs 30mins	North	Moderate
3	7.8 miles (12.5kms)	5hrs	North	Hard
4	3.9 miles (6.2kms)	2hrs	North-east	Easy**
5	8.1 miles (13.0kms)	5hrs 30mins	East	Hard
6	6.8 miles (11.0kms)	5hrs	North-east	Moderate
7	7.0 miles (11.2kms)	5hrs	South-east	Hard
8	5.8 miles (9.4kms)	3hrs 30mins	South	Moderate
9	7.4 miles (11.9kms)	4hrs 30mins	West	Hard
10	7.1 miles (11.5kms)	4hrs 30mins	South-west	Hard
11	8.2 miles (13.2kms)	5hrs	North-east	Moderate
12	7.5 miles (12.0kms)	4hrs 30mins	East	Moderate

* Mainly on surfaced lanes and tracks
** On surfaced lanes and tracks throughout

Walks

Six walks from La Roche are described below, radiating out from the town at all points of the compass, thereby exploring the neighbourhood fairly comprehensively.

WALK 25:
La Roche and Samrée

Description: A walk through the wooded hills above La Roche and a visit to the village of Samrée.

Location: A circular walk to the north-east of La Roche-en-Ardenne.

Start/Finish: The main car park at the Place du Bronze in the centre of La Roche.

Distance: 9.5 miles (15.3kms).

Time: 5hrs 15mins.

Maps: The walkers' map at a scale of 1:25,000 entitled *La Roche-en-Ardenne*, sold at the tourist office. (The map has the 12 "official" waymarked walking routes marked on it).

IGN 1:50,000 series: sheet numbers 60 and 55.

Waymarking: "Red boot" waymarks carrying a number between 1 and 12.

Parts of Route Numbers 1, 2, 3, 4, 6, 11, and 12 are followed on this walk.

Terrain: A mixture of forest tracks, paths and quiet lanes.

Footwear: Lightweight boots or good, strong walking shoes. Some of the paths are muddy in winter.

Refreshments: There is a small bar in Samrée, at the halfway point in the walk, and a café in the woods, at the junction of Route 6 and Route 11, about a mile from the end of the walk. Both are passed en route.

Route

From the main car park in the centre of the town head north along the High Street. Cross the River Ourthe on the main road bridge, pass the war memorial on your right, and continue ahead on the Rue du Purnalet. If wishing to visit the château (recommended) then take the steps leading up to the right about a hundred metres after the war memorial. Pass the church (worth a quick visit) to reach the end of the High Street, where take the road ahead, alongside the river which is on your left, leaving the outskirts of La Roche. Keep to the footpath on the left-hand side of this road, climbing gently, with a steep, wooded bank down to the left.

About 80 metres after passing a sign for Route No. 1, which descends the bank to the left, take a footpath which leaves the right-hand side of the road, marked as Route No. 6. This climbs by a series of zigzags to reach a forest track, where you turn right. The route is waymarked with red and with yellow paint marks on the trees.

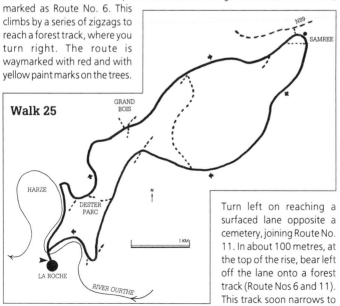

Walk 25

Turn left on reaching a surfaced lane opposite a cemetery, joining Route No. 11. In about 100 metres, at the top of the rise, bear left off the lane onto a forest track (Route Nos 6 and 11). This track soon narrows to

163

an excellent woodland path, which climbs at first before levelling out. The way passes through mature oak and beech woods, delightful in all seasons. After about a mile reach the point at which the waymarked trails diverge: Route No. 3 goes ahead, whilst Route Nos 6 and 11, the way to be taken, bear to the right on a path through the wood. After a further·80 metres turn right on another track at a T-junction. Walk ahead at the next crossing track, but about 100 metres later, at a Y-junction take the right fork, still on Route Nos 6/11 (Route No. 3 takes the left fork). Continue ahead, at first with a steep drop down to the right, before long entering an area of pine trees. On reaching a narrow surfaced lane, Route No. 6 goes to the right. Leave this trail here by walking ahead, over a cattle grid and following Route No. 11 between conifer trees. Keep to the main track ahead, following the No. 11 signs and ignoring any side tracks. Soon after the track levels out the trail crosses a cattle grid and leaves the forest, entering an area of open fields. Continue ahead, with superb views of the wooded hills to the distant left, to join eventually the road in the village of Samrée.

Turn right on reaching a T-junction in the village (left leads in 100 metres to a bus stop on the main road (N89), from where the weary can take a bus (service No. 36) back to La Roche (8kms). Walk downhill passing a small bar/café, until, 80 metres before the church in the centre of the village, turn right on a lane, climbing for 100 metres, before turning left on a poorly surfaced track with hedge on the right and a fence and fields on the left (good view of church and village). When this view disappears at a Y-junction, take the right-hand branch, between fences, with a grassy field sloping up to the right. Remain on the main track, waymarked as Route No. 11, ignoring any side tracks. Soon after this track begins a gentle descent take the right fork at a Y-junction (the point at which Route No. 12 joins Route No. 11). After about 5mins' walking the route reaches a tall fence: pass through the gate to the right of this, continuing ahead on a track through a fir tree plantation. The track begins to descend; go straight ahead at a crossing track. The trail later swings to the right, descending to the left of a couple of small ponds and on to a T-junction, where you turn right. Thirty metres after the point where a stream passes under the track, turn left downhill, at the point where Route No. 6 rejoins our walk. This track descends to the right of a babbling stream. At the bottom of the descent pass to the left of a quarry and cross over the stream to reach a surfaced lane.

Cross over the road to take the surfaced track climbing the hillside ahead (Routes Nos 4, 6 and 11). Thirty metres after passing a large building in the woods (café) bear left on Route No. 6 (ie. leaving Route No. 11 at this point) to enter the Parc Forestière du Dester. Later ignore a track off to the right, but continue the descent, eventually reaching a narrow lane by a house. Turn right on this lane, joining Route No. 12 at this point. Bear right downhill on reaching another lane at a T-junction. There are excellent views on this section of the walk down to La Roche and its château above the River Ourthe, which in this region

The Château and the River Ourthe at La Roche

is contorted into a giant oxbow bend. At the hotel Les Genêts bear left downhill, heading directly towards the château of La Roche. Descend to the Rue Saint Quoilin in La Roche, by the banks of the river. Follow this to the High Street which is reached at the war memorial. Turn left to walk over the bridge to return to the car park.

WALK 26:
La Roche, Maboge and the River Ourthe

Description: Possibly the best walk in the region, to the south and north of the meandering Ourthe valley, visiting the hamlet of Maboge, situated on the river to the east of La Roche. Maboge is the starting point for the 12km canoe route for "beginners" down-stream to La Roche. There will no doubt be several canoeists here of all levels of ability, so you will be able to decide for yourself if you want to try this most enjoyable activity some time later in the holiday.

Location: A circular walk to the east of La Roche-en-Ardenne.

Start/Finish: The main car park at the Place du Bronze in the centre of La Roche.

Distance: 8.4 miles (13.5kms).

Time: 5hrs 15mins.

Maps: The walkers' map at a scale of 1:25,000 entitled *La Roche-en-Ardenne*, sold at the tourist office. (The map has the 12 "official" waymarked walking routes marked on it).
                    IGN 1:50,000 series: sheet number 60.

Waymarking: "Red boot" waymarks carrying the number 5.

Terrain: A mixture of forest tracks, paths and quiet lanes.
The descent to Maboge is on a very steep path.

Footwear: Lightweight boots or good, strong walking shoes (a good grip is required for the steep forest path down to Maboge).

Options: There is no opportunity to shorten this walk, but it could be lengthened considerably into a long day walk by continuing north on Route No. 12 and then Route No. 11 to Samrée, returning south-west to La Roche on Route No. 11.

Refreshments: There is a choice of three cafés (two of which are also restaurants) in the hamlet of Maboge, conveniently situated at the halfway stage of this walk. A café will also be found in the small hamlet of Borzée, north of Maboge.

Route

From the tourist office in the High Street in La Roche take a side street down to the river, where turn left (south) along its bank to reach the main bridge over the river by the war memorial. Cross the bridge over the River Ourthe to take the first turning on the left into the Place du Bronze in front of the car park. Leave the square, but after 25 metres turn right uphill on the Rue du Bon Dieu de Maka, signposted as Route Nos 5 and 7. Follow the lane waymarked with the red/white paint marks of a GR trail. Soon after passing the Hôtel Villa des Olivettes the lane peters out to become an unsurfaced track. Continue ahead on this, climbing gradually into the woods.

On reaching a small stone building (underground reservoir) on the left-hand side of the track, our trail, viz. Route No. 5, along with the red/white waymarked GR trail, takes the track off to the left, parting company with Route No. 7 which continues ahead. Follow the track heading towards the east beneath a tall avenue of trees. Turn right on reaching a Y-junction of tracks within the wood, still following the red/white waymarks. Ignore the next track off to the right, but continue ahead following Route No. 5 and the red and white marks. Ignore further turns to the right and left to reach the edge of the forest at a large open field.

Walk ahead with the forest on your left and the field to the right. At the end of the field, at a T-junction, turn left on a track to re-enter the forest (Route No. 5) still following the GR trail markings. After a few hundred metres take care to follow the right-hand fork, soon heading downhill. The track soon narrows

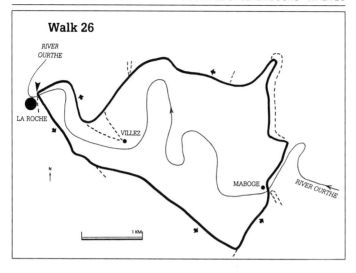

Walk 26

RIVER OURTHE

LA ROCHE

VILLEZ

N

MABOGE

RIVER OURTHE

1 KM

to become a path which descends very steeply to emerge at the bridge over the River Ourthe at Maboge.

Turn left to cross the bridge over the river to enter Maboge (café-restaurant and bus stop). Continue ahead still following red/white GR markings, passing the church, another café-restaurant and a third café, to reach the main road. Continue ahead along the road, so leaving Maboge. Climb gently on this road, making use of the wide footpath on its right-hand side, until reaching the minor road off to the left signposted to Borzée. At this point the GR trail continues ahead for a few metres before turning off to the right, thereby leaving our route. Take the minor road to Borzée, but after a hundred metres or so, just after the road bends to the left, take the track off to the left alongside a stream. After about 250 metres, at a Y fork, take the right-hand branch heading uphill. Keep to the main track soon crossing a stream and continue climbing through the trees, eventually reaching the charming hamlet of Borzée. Turn left to pass in front of the tiny chapel and then left again onto the narrow road, climbing away from the hamlet (a café will be found if you turn a few metres to the right instead).

The road becomes an unsurfaced track on leaving Borzée. Continue climbing on this to a complex junction of five tracks. Remain ahead, following Route No. 5 (on a bearing of 240 degrees magnetic). Later pass a crucifix, follow the sign towards Villez and Lohan and proceed ahead at a crossing track. The trail keeps to this undulating track for about a couple of kilometres. On reaching the second reservoir building after the crucifix, turn left (Route No. 5 waymark)

Canoeists on the River Ourthe at Maboge

on a track which soon becomes a poorly surfaced narrow lane. After about 700 metres take particular care to locate and turn right onto a narrow descending path which is found immediately to the left of a stony gravel track on the right-hand side of the road. Descend on this path to emerge on a road. Turn right along this road, ignore the right turn to the Parc and Carrière Socogétra, but 10 metres after this bear to the right heading uphill (signpost to Les Genêts Hôtel-Restaurant) opposite the Gendarmerie Nationale. This soon becomes a balcony road offering superb views of La Roche and the meandering River Ourthe below. At Les Genêts Hôtel-Restaurant bear left downhill back to La Roche.

WALK 27:
The Vallée des Tombes, Hives and Buisson

Description: The first two-thirds of the walk offers easy navigation on quiet country lanes to visit the villages of Hives and Buisson, both of which have ornate churches. The latter section is along a narrow woodland footpath.

Location: A circular walk to the south of La Roche-en-Ardenne.

Start/Finish: The main car park at the Place du Bronze in the centre of La Roche.

Distance: 8.4 miles (13.5kms).

Time: 5hrs 15mins.

Maps: The walkers' map at a scale of 1:25,000 entitled *La Roche-en-Ardenne*, sold at the tourist office. (The map has the 12 "official" waymarked walking routes marked on it.)
IGN 1:50,000 series: sheet number 60.

Waymarking: "Red boot" waymarks carrying the numbers 8, 10 and 7.

Terrain: Minor country roads for the most path, but the latter stages involves a rather rough and undulating narrow path through woodland.

Footwear: Although trainers would be more than adequate for the section of the walk from La Roche to Buisson, more adequate footwear with good grips is recommended for the return walk north of Buisson, particularly in wet or icy conditions.

Option: The walk can be shortened by taking the combined Route Nos 7, 8 and 10, due north from Hives and so back to La Roche, omitting the village of Buisson.

Refreshments: A café will be found about 150 metres off-route in the village of Hives (the detour can be found in the route description).

Route

From the tourist office head south along the High Street to cross the main bridge over the river. Continue ahead across the Place du Bronze into Rue de Beausaint. After 100 metres take the left fork signposted to Hives. At the next Y-junction take the right fork signposted as Route No. 8. Remain on the lane as it swings to the right to cross over a bridge above a stream. This pleasant lane climbs gently up the valley. After almost 2¹/₂kms take the road turning off to the left to cross over a bridge. Climb gradually on this lane to pass two houses on the left-hand side of the road. Fifty metres after the second house turn left onto a track at the far side of the pond, leaving Route No. 8 at this point to follow Route No. 10 steeply uphill.

The path emerges from the trees onto an open plateau. Walk ahead on the grassy track which soon becomes surfaced and runs between fences. Remain on this, following Route No. 10, until reaching houses at a T-junction on the outskirts of the village of Hives. Here turn right, leaving Route No. 10 which turns to the left. Take the next turning on the left heading towards the church whose steeple is clearly visible. The church is worthy of a visit to admire the rather impressive Stations of the Cross, the stained glass windows and the carved wooden altar pieces. The "garden seat" type pews are also interesting.

At the far side of the church turn left (cemetery on left) and walk ahead at the crossroads to reach a T-junction by a bus stop. Turn right along the lane, now joining Route No. 7 (or first visiting the café-restaurant which will be found 150

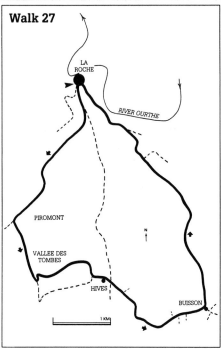

Walk 27

LA ROCHE

RIVER OURTHE

PIROMONT

VALLEE DES TOMBES

HIVES

BUISSON

1 KM

metres down the road to the left). After 100 metres, at a crossroads, turn left on the road signposted to Buisson. Remain on this lane all the way to the church in Buisson, which is again worth a visit (interesting modern-style Stations of the Cross, very different from those in Hives).

Turn left immediately after the church in Buisson. After passing farm buildings the road becomes an unsurfaced track. This descends gently to enter woodland and follows the course of a stream on the left. Take particular care to locate and turn right onto a narrow path (waymarked as No. 7) in a small clearing about 100 metres after passing cross-tracks, and about 150 metres before a small pond on the right of the track. The thin path soon enters a conifer plantation (white No. 10 and yellow No. 7 waymarks on trees). Pass above a mill (note the mill race). On emerging from the conifer plantation cross a small stream and maintain direction along Route No. 7. The path emerges about 100 metres after the stream onto a U bend of a forest track. Take the lower, left-hand fork passing under the high-tension electricity cables to the left of a pylon which is situated on the hill over to the right. A few hundred metres after passing under the HT cables take particular care to locate and follow a narrow path bearing right off the track (there should be a white painted number 10 on a tree trunk at the beginning of the path). This is still Route No. 7 (note that if the track starts to descend steeply then the path off to the right just described has been missed and it will then be necessary to return to locate it before continuing).

The narrow path eventually climbs to a road. Turn left downhill on this road for a few hundred metres until the road bends sharply to the left. Here take a track heading into the trees on the right. Follow this track as it swings to the right (white dot waymarks on the trees) to reach a track T-junction, where turn left. Continue ahead on this track descending gradually, soon joining a red and white waymarked GR trail. The track eventually becomes a surfaced lane which descends back into La Roche.

WALK 28:
La Roche, Hives and Beausaint

Description: A mixture of woodland and high open country on a ramble which visits two of the larger villages in the vicinity of La Roche.

Location: A circular walk to the south and south-west of La Roche-en-Ardenne.

Start/Finish: The main car park at the Place du Bronze in the centre of La Roche.

Distance: 7.5 miles (12.1kms), plus an extra 0.8 mile (1.3kms) if the ford between Hives and Beausaint is impassable.

Time: 4hrs (plus an extra 20mins if the detour around the ford is necessary).

Maps: The walkers' map at a scale of 1:25,000 entitled *La Roche-en-Ardenne*, sold at the tourist office. (The map has the 12 "official" waymarked walking routes marked on it).

IGN 1:50,000 series: sheet number 60.

Waymarking: "Red boot" waymarks carrying a number between 1 and 12. Parts of Route Nos 8, 9 and 10 are followed on this walk.

Terrain: A mixture of forest tracks, paths and quiet lanes.

Footwear: Lightweight boots or good, strong walking shoes. Some of the paths are muddy in winter. Footwear needs to be watertight if the ford is to be crossed.

Special Problems: The circuit involves the crossing of a ford across a river. In times of flood this can be most unpleasant and even dangerous. Therefore it should *not* be attempted under these conditions. There is an easy detour, described in the text, which avoids the ford.

Refreshments: No places of refreshment are passed on the walk (with the exception of a restaurant within a quarter of a mile of the start), but there is a wide choice of cafés, bars and restaurants in La Roche.

Route
From the main car park in the centre of La Roche take the road (Rue de Beausaint) heading south signposted to Saint-Hubert. After only 100 metres, just after the Hôtel du Midi, take the left fork off the main road, signposted to

Hives, following the waymarks for Route No. 8 (in the reverse direction). After a few minutes, on the outskirts of La Roche, do not take the left branch at a Y-junction (signposted to Hives), but rather follow the right branch in the direction of Le Vieux Moulin. Walk to the rear of this restaurant to locate a forest path to the left of the building, which climbs steeply out of the valley, initially above a small caravan site. This route is waymarked with yellow and white paint marks (ie. one horizontal yellow stripe under which is one white stripe). The very steep initial gradient soon eases as the climb continues more gently to a junction of five tracks. Here take the path heading half-right on a bearing of approximately 150 degrees magnetic (yellow/white waymarks). Later ignore both side tracks off to the left and then the right, still following the yellow/white waymarks. Continue ahead, the route eventually becoming a surfaced farm track heading towards the village of Hives with its prominent church seen ahead.

On reaching a Y-junction on the outskirts of the village take the right fork, signposted with the yellow and white stripes. Ignore the first surfaced track leading off to the right (Route No. 10), but continue into the village, in the heart of which you ignore the lane on the left heading towards the church. About 50 metres farther on take the lane on the right at an old rusting village signpost (no sign remains), following the reverse of Route No. 8 and leaving the yellow/

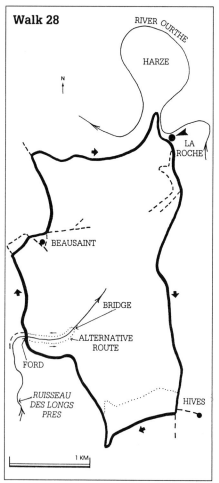

Walk 28

RIVER OURTHE

HARZE

N

LA ROCHE

BEAUSAINT

BRIDGE

ALTERNATIVE ROUTE

FORD

RUISSEAU DES LONGS PRES

HIVES

1 KM

white waymarkings at this point. Descend, eventually crossing a bridge over a stream to reach a T-junction where turn right, still descending, but with the babbling stream now on the right. Remain ahead at the point at which Route No. 10 takes a right turn at a pond by buildings, but a few hundred metres after this, at a point some 40 metres after a chalet style building on the right, and opposite a rock outcrop, take the track climbing up towards the left. At the top of the climb, where the track swings to the left, leave it by walking straight ahead through a dense forest of pine trees. Take great care not to miss a narrow footpath descending sharply back to the right, leaving the track at a point where the latter begins to swing to the left. It is waymarked as Route No. 10, but daydreaming walkers could easily miss it. The correct path descends steeply to the east for about 100 metres to a track; turn left here, still descending but now heading towards the west. The descent soon becomes quite steep down to the river at a ford. Cross this, but *only* if it is quite safe to do so. The current is often fast, and at times it can be of a considerable depth.

If the river is in flood then take the following, alternative route. Immediately before the river there is a track leading off to the right. Take this, following the course of the river down-stream. This leads in about 650 metres to a road. Turn left to cross the road bridge over the river, and then at the T-junction ahead turn left to follow this minor lane back to the ford, but now on the north side of the river. At this point you have joined the GR 57 trail (note the red/white waymarkings).

Take the track opposite the fording point of the river. Climb on this track alongside a tumbling stream to the village of Beausaint. On reaching a road on the outskirts of the village turn right along it to enter Beausaint. Pass through the village, crossing over the main road and continuing ahead between the buildings of the settlement, several of which have interesting architecture, part Dutch and part French in style. Turn left at reaching the first minor crossroads, following in the direction of Route No. 10 (yellow waymark). Keep straight ahead at an unsurfaced cross-tracks (for a shorter route back to La Roche turn right here and follow Route No. 9 which leads directly back down to the valley) still following the red and white waymarks of the GR trail (these are now followed all the way back to La Roche). A superb view of the surrounding hills and the River Ourthe spreads out in front as a gentle descent to the valley begins. Turn right on reaching the tree line on a grassy track immediately in front of the trees (grassy field to the right). The grassy track narrows into an enclosed footpath on approaching the end of the field. Note that this formed part of the old "corpse road" for carrying the dead between La Roche and Beausaint. Continue ahead on this undulating path ignoring any side turnings off to the right, always following the red/white waymarks, with the Ourthe valley down to your left. Soon after passing an excellent viewpoint for the river below (bench provided) a steep descent through trees to La Roche begins. Take care on this descent, especially in wet weather, when the numerous rocks on the path tend to become very slippery. The trail emerges from the trees above the roofs of the town to provide one of the best views of La Roche with its fine church and its château above the banks of the Ourthe. Turn left down a set of steps at the point at which the unsurfaced track becomes a surfaced lane. Follow the road below to reach the High Street of La Roche at the car park.

WALK 29:
La Roche, Vecpré and Beausaint

Description: Certainly the hilliest walk in the neighbourhood of La Roche. The circuit involves three steep hill climbs and one particularly steep descent down to a woodland stream. The terrain is somewhat difficult in places, particularly in bad weather conditions. There is a section of rather busy road to endure, but the quality and views of the rest of the walk render this tolerable.

Location: A circular walk to the west of La Roche-en-Ardenne.

Start/Finish: The main car park at the Place du Bronze in the centre of La Roche.

Distance: 7.5 miles (12.0kms).

Time: 4hrs 30mins.

Maps: The walkers' map at a scale of 1:25,000 entitled *La Roche-en-Ardenne*, sold at the tourist office. (The map has the 12 "official" waymarked walking routes marked on it).

IGN 1:50,000 series: sheet number 60.

Waymarking: "Red boot" waymarks carrying the number 9.

Terrain: Three steep hill climbs. One steep, slippery descent on a narrow path and two other more gentle descents on tracks. The route also entails about 1.5kms of road walking. A mixture of woods and open high country, with walking on forest tracks, paths and quiet lanes.

Footwear: Good boots are recommended.

Option: The route could be considerably lengthened by following Route No. 10 where it is encountered west-north-west of Beausaint. This would lead back to La Roche via the Vallée des Tombes and Hives.

Refreshments: There is a café in Vecpré on the N833. There is also a café at the Camping du Pouhou on the N888, and sometimes a mobile van selling refreshments is situated in the large lay-by outside this campsite.

Route
In the south-west corner of the Place du Bronze in the centre of La Roche locate the narrow road called the Vieille Route de Beausaint, waymarked as Route Nos

9 and 10. Walk uphill on this lane which, after a few hundred metres, becomes unsurfaced (good view to the right of La Roche and its château). Turn left onto an ascending path on reaching an electricity pylon (our trail is coincident with a GR trail at present and as such carries the usual red/white GR waymarkings). A long and stiff climb leads to a good viewpoint down to the Ourthe valley. Continue ahead to reach a wooden cross attached to a tree at a track Y-junction. Take the right fork here to keep along the edge of the escarpment (Route No. 10 and the red/white of the GR trail). Keep ahead for about 1.5kms following the GR trail until reaching a T-junction with a gravel farm track. The GR trail and Route No. 10 both go to the left here, but our walk (Route No. 9) goes to the right downhill on this gravel track.

Descend on the track into the Ourthe valley which is met at the main road, the N833. Turn left along this road for about a kilometre to entre Vecpré (there is a café on the right-hand side of the road here). Turn left onto the N888 signposted to Marche and continue along it from about 500 metres to the lay-by on the left-hand side of the road, immediately after Camping du Pouhou (café). Take the path on the left that leads away from this lay-by (Route No. 9). So begin a long climb out of the valley following once again red/white trail markings.

Climb on the track until a few metres before the trees come to an end on the right of the track. Here climb on the footpath which bears left off the track and is signposted as Route No. 9. The path, which also carries red/white GR markings, climbs even more steeply than the track. Climb to meet a second track where turn left, still heading uphill. Climb to an electricity pylon, where turn left on a narrow, enclosed path by a large wooden cottage, a few metres before a road.

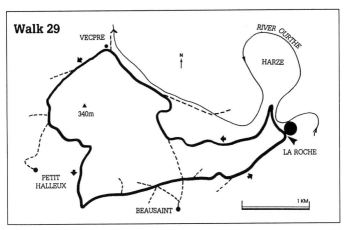

The path bends behind the house to continue as a well-defined line across open hillside. This excellent little path soon enters woodland and becomes undulating, before beginning a long, steep and tortuous descent to the valley bottom (care is required here, particularly under wet conditions; the exposed and slippery tree roots are especially treacherous). Descend to a T-junction in front of a stream. Turn right along a tree-lined path on Route No. 9, still following the red/white trail markings. Continue with the stream to your left, sometimes close and sometimes a few metres above and away from it, until reaching a small log bridge spanning the stream. Cross this bridge to turn immediately to the left, following the red/white and No. 9 waymarks as the path swings away from the stream to follow a small tributary uphill. So begins the third and final steep climb of the walk.

The path climbs to emerge onto open farmland. Continue ahead across this to reach a gravel track. Remain ahead, later ignoring another track off to the right. At a junction of three tracks take the left-hand one signposted Route 9 (also red and white GR markings). On reaching the crossroads on the outskirts of the village of Beausaint, leave the GR trail, which goes off to the left, but instead continue ahead on Route No. 9. In about 100 metres, at a Y fork in the track, take the right-hand branch. Turn right downhill on a path on reaching a pylon at the edge of a field. This path emerges on a road by a terrace of cottages. Turn left to descend on this road all the way into La Roche. Turn right on reaching a T-junction in the town to descend back to the Place du Bronze, your starting point for the walk.

WALK 30:
La Roche, Cielle and Sainte Marguerite

Description: The highlight of this walk is the opportunity to visit the panoramic viewpoint of Sainte Marguerite, which offers the best bird's-eye view of La Roche and the Ourthe valley.

Location: A circular walk to the north of La Roche-en-Ardenne.

Start/Finish: The main car park at the Place du Bronze in the centre of La Roche.

Distance: 8.1 miles (13.1kms).

Time: 5hrs.

Maps: The walkers' map at a scale of 1:25,000 entitled *La Roche-en-Ardenne*, sold at the tourist office. (The map has the 12 "official" waymarked walking routes marked on it).

     IGN 1:50,000 series: sheet numbers 60 and 55.

Waymarking: "Red boot" waymarks carrying the numbers 1, 2 and 3.

Terrain:　　　　Woodland and riverside tracks and paths, plus some sections of quiet surfaced lanes.

Footwear:　　　　Lightweight boots or good, strong walking shoes.

Options:　　　　The walk could easily be shortened significantly by following only Route No. 1 from beginning to end. Those who want a longer walk could follow Route No. 3 when the combined Route Nos 2 and 3 emerge on the N89 road at about the halfway stage of the route described. However, from this point Route No. 3 follows the busy N89 for almost 2kms, and for this reason cannot be recommended.

Refreshments:　　　These are available at the café-restaurant in the village of Cielle and at the café located at the branch point of Route Nos 3 and 6 just under a kilometre before the Sainte Marguerite chapel, on the latter stages of the walk.

Route
From the tourist office in La Roche walk in a north-easterly direction along the main street, leaving the town by the Rue de Cielle. Continue ahead uphill on the main road with the river to your left. After a little under a kilometre take the narrow path descending into trees (prominently signposted on a tree as Route No. 1). The trail descends to a balcony path which runs about 50m above the river. When this path begins to climb, take a path forking left (waymarked as No. 1 with yellow paint on a tree and also with red paint dots), continuing along a balcony above the river, opposite a line of campsites. On reaching a tributary

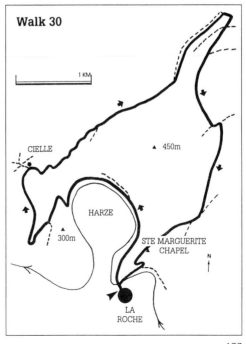

Walk 30

1 KM

CIELLE

▲ 450m

HARZE

▲ 300m

STE MARGUERITE
CHAPEL

N

LA
ROCHE

stream at the edge of the River Ourthe, cross a wooden footbridge and immediately take the path on the right following the bank of the tributary away from the River Ourthe. About 70 metres after the path pulls away from the stream, turn sharply to the left to head uphill, following signs for Route No. 1. The path eventually reaches an open field (good views). Walk round two sides of this field to reach a road. Turn right onto the road and remain on it to the village of Cielle.

On entering the village (café-restaurant) Route No. 1 takes a left turn. Ignore this but continue ahead passing the café to reach the church. At the crossroads at the far side of the cemetery, turn right on a lane heading downhill, rejoining Route No. 1 which has completed a circuit around the village, having visited the Delacolette chapel (you could, of course, walk this route as an additional option). The lane descends to the valley bottom where, at a T-junction, Route No. 1 takes the turn to the right, but our route follows Route Nos 2 and 3 to the left. This lane soon becomes an unsurfaced dirt track. After about a kilometre, soon after passing to the right of a quarry, when the track swings to the left, continue ahead on Route No. 3, leaving Route No. 2 at this point. The route follows a babbling woodland stream gently uphill. The path eventually narrows, crosses the stream and climbs somewhat more steeply to rejoin Route No. 2, which comes in from the left (under wet conditions Route No. 2 would provide a somewhat drier alternative to this point: the two routes are of roughly equal length). Continue ahead on the combined Route Nos 2 and 3 to cross a stream and climb to a track junction. Here turn right to climb up to the main La Roche to Samrée road (the N89).

Cross straight over this rather busy road to take the minor road opposite, heading uphill on Route No. 2. When the lane reaches a left-hand hairpin bend, continue ahead on a woodland track. On reaching a cross-tracks leave Route No. 2, which takes the right turn, but re-join Route No. 3 by continuing ahead downhill. This leads eventually to a narrow surfaced lane. Turn right along this following the combined Route Nos 3 and 11, after 150 metres passing a café on your right. Remain on this road heading downhill towards La Roche.

On meeting a Y-junction take the left fork downhill. Descend to reach the Chapel of Sainte Marguerite, built in 1600. Immediately before the chapel locate a thin path, signposted to the Panorama, which climbs steeply up the hillside to the left. This leads to an octagonal shelter and a superb viewpoint (*belvédère*) overlooking La Roche. This, the best viewpoint in the district, should not be missed. Return by the same route back to the chapel and then continue down the road. About 50 metres before Les Genêts Hôtel-Restaurant, take the series of steps down to the right. Follow the road downhill to return to La Roche.

The church at Commanster, south-east of Vielsalm

VIELSALM AND THE SALM VALLEY

General Information and Places of Interest

Vielsalm is an excellent centre for rambling, offering some of the finest walking in the Ardennes on an extensive network of forest tracks and paths. The area is heavily wooded, but there is also plenty of open country which offers wide vistas of the deeply cut Salm valley and the surrounding hills, ridges and forests. For beautiful woodland, rocky escarpments and deep gorges there is little to beat this fine area. During September the heathlands of the Ardennes are ablaze with the purple flowers of heather, the woods, heaths and clearings around Vielsalm having some of the finest displays.

Vielsalm, with a population of about 7000, is the largest community in the Salm valley. During 1944/45 it was an American headquarters during the horrific Battle of the Ardennes, and temporary home to the 7th American Armored Tank Division. Today one of the squares in Vielsalm is named after General Bruce C. Clarke, in memory of one of the American commanders. There is still a small army garrison based in the town. The artificial Vielsalm Lake, also known as Doyards Lake, is the largest in the Province of Luxembourg (14 hectares) and offers a number of water sports, including kayaking, windsurfing and fishing. There is a cafeteria on the lakeside, only one of the 20 restaurants that the towns boasts.

To gain an idea of what life was like in the Salm valley in former times make a visit to the Museum of History and Life of the Salm Valley, in Vielsalm. Here will be found the interior of a traditional house of the Haute Ardennes, clothing worn in everyday life in centuries past, and a display on the life and works of the local poet Mélot du Dy. In Salmchâteau there is the interesting Musée du Coticule or Stonemasons Museum (see Walk 31) and also, opposite the church, is the Jean Quirin Piette Museum, which displays the arts and crafts of a local stonemason.

In the So Bèchefa area of the Grand Bois (Walk 33) there are nature trails, a keep-fit course and barbecue grills, which can all be used free of charge by the public. A visit to the wildlife park, the Domaine du Monti, which is located in one of highest regions of Belgium (Walk 32), will ensure sightings of the typical fauna of the Luxembourg Ardennes. Nearby are the Hourt Rocks and escarpment which offer dramatic views down to the Salm valley (Walk 32).

Although there are several places of interest to visit in the region, it is the forests, hills and rivers themselves that are the greatest attraction, and these can only be fully appreciated on foot. The three circuits described below give a good overview of the area. The official tourist office map is one of the better walkers' maps of the Ardennes, being fairly accurate with detailed contouring.

Accommodation

There are at least nine hotels in Vielsalm: Les Arcades, Auberge du Carrefour, Belle-Vue, Les Casseroles, Hôtel-Restaurant Le Chalet, Le Gîte Ardennais, Les Hautes Ardennes, Les Myrtilles and the Hôtel-Restaurant Le Val d'Hebron. There are a further two hotels in Salmchâteau (Walk 31), a few kilometres south along the Salm valley: the Hôtel-Restaurant l'Auberge des Grands Prés and the Residence du Vieux Moulin; and another (Les Linaigrettes) at Grand-Halleux, north along the Salm valley (Walk 32).

Vielsalm has two campsites: Camping de la Salm (Walk 32) and Camping Aux Massotais.

Transport

Vielsalm is easily reached by train from Liège, on the Luxembourg City line via Angleur, Poulseur, Aywaille, Coo and Trois-Ponts. The train journey can be recommended as it is on a most picturesque line. Vielsalm railway station is situated at the southern end of the High Street, near to Vielsalm Lake. The line continues up the Salm valley from Vielsalm to Gouvy, after which it enters the Grand Duchy of Luxembourg.

Drivers should make use of either the E25 (A26) or the E421 (A27) motorways. Take the former from Liège, exiting at junction 50 to follow the N89 to Salmchâteau and then the N68 north to Vielsalm. For the E421 (A27) route from Liège and Verviers, drive first to Stavelot (see under "Transport" for the Section on Stavelot and Coo) and from there remain on the N68 to Trois-Ponts and so on to Vielsalm.

Official Walking Trails in and around the Salm Valley in the Region of Vielsalm

There are 17 official circular walking trails in the region, totalling a distance of 106 miles (170kms). They are waymarked on the ground and marked on the official walkers' map, scale 1:25,000, entitled *Carte des Promenades Pédestres - Kaart Voor Voettochten* available from the tourist office in Vielsalm. The trails are identified by a number, shown in blue within a blue circle on the map. These trails start from one of five locations in the area: Vielsalm town, Vielsalm railway station, Grand-Halleux, Hébronval and Baraque de Fraiture.

Walks

Three walks in this book explore the Salm valley and the hills and woods on its flanks. All of them start and finish in Vielsalm.

WALK 31:
Vielsalm, Fârnières, Goronne and Salmchâteau

Description: This long walk, a circuit to the west of the Salm valley between Vielsalm and Salmchâteau, offers a superb forest ramble, one of the best in the Ardennes. There is the perfect mixture of woodland walking with tramping through open countryside, from where there are wide vistas of the Ardennes hills and forests. The walk includes a visit to the tranquil village of Fârnières, situated in a forest clearing and the home of a religious community, whose ecclesiastical buildings are quite outstanding. A number of other small farming villages are visited en route (Goronne, La Comté and pretty Provedroux) which all have a variety of old traditional rural buildings. The trail then descends to the larger village of Salmchâteau in the Salm valley, south of Vielsalm. Here there is an opportunity to visit a unique and interesting museum (see "Places of Interest" below), before a gentle but grand finale to the day is provided by a stroll along the wide Salm valley, past the large Vielsalm reservoir.

The walk follows in its entirety the Vielsalm Tourist Office Official Trail No. 5. This is unusual in its length, as most official local walking trails in the Ardennes are rarely more than 12kms or so long. The local tourist organisation is to be applauded for the development of this superb walking trail.

Location: To the west of the town of Vielsalm.

Start/Finish: The large church and car park at the north end of the High Street of Vielsalm.

Distance: 12.4 miles (20.0kms).

Time: Allow 7-7hrs 30mins.

This walk, one of the longest described in this book, requires a full day if it is to be savoured at a gentle pace, and the various places of interest visited en route.

Maps: The well contoured map, scale 1:25,000, entitled *Carte des Promenades Pédestres - Kaart Voor Voettochten* and published by the Val de Salm Tourist Office. It can be purchased from the Tourist Office in Vielsalm.
IGN 1:50,000 series: sheet numbers 55 and 56.

Waymarking: The route follows official Trail No. 5 throughout. The waymarking once out of Vielsalm is good, but finding the actual way out of Vielsalm requires some care initially, although there should be few problems if the route description given below is followed carefully. It is important to follow the correct No. 5 waymarks: an old waymarking system used numbers on a white and red circle. Do *not* follow a 5 waymark within such a circle, as it will lead to errors, particularly when leaving Vielsalm at the start of the walk. The only waymarks to follow (and there are many others of different types) are those with a black No. 5 on a white square or rectangular background. Follow these throughout the walk.

Terrain: As the trail cuts across several valley systems there is conse-quently plenty of ascent and descent, some of it reasonably steep. Most of the walk is along forest tracks and footpaths. The latter stages of the ramble follow the flat terrain of the wide Salm valley, on quiet lanes and by-ways, and provide an opportunity at the very end to stroll along the shore of the peaceful, albeit manmade, Vielsalm Lake.

Footwear: The trail follows a number of woodland tracks and paths, several of which can become very wet and muddy, so boots are recommended.

Options: 1) The walk can be shortened by just over a kilometre by omitting the village of Provedroux, and following Trail No. 3, rather than Trail No. 5, to Salmchâteau. This alternative trail is marked on the official tourist office map of the region (see "Maps" above) and the point where it leaves the route described in this book is pinpointed in the text of the route description below.

          2) Part of Trail No. 3 can also be used by those who want a walk of only about half the length of that described here. Follow the text below until Trail No. 3 is first encountered, in the wood to the north of La Comté. Here follow Trail No. 3 first to the north-east and then to the east to descend to the Salm valley, which is reached a little to the south of Vielsalm railway station. The route is once again clearly shown on the tourist office 1:25,000 map.

Places of
Interest: 1. *Fârnières Religious Retreat*. Situated in a forest clearing with dominating views of the surrounding woods and valleys, the area pervades an atmosphere of calm and tranquillity. The buildings are elegant and appear rather unexpectedly in this quite vast and lonely area of forest. The Retreat is private, so please do not intrude, but an unobtrusive look from a distance will raise no objections.

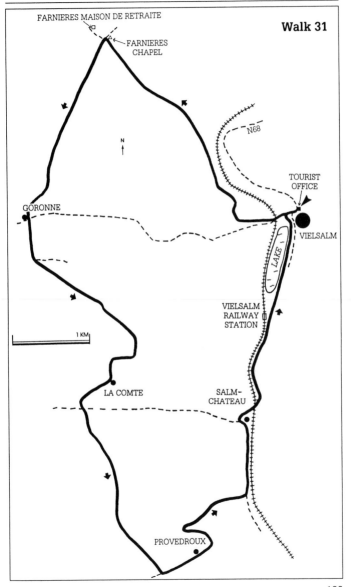

Walk 31

FARNIERES MAISON DE RETRAITE

FARNIERES
CHAPEL

N68

TOURIST
OFFICE

GORONNE

VIELSALM

LAKE

VIELSALM
RAILWAY
STATION

1 KM

LA COMTE

SALM-
CHATEAU

PROVEDROUX

2. *The Castle of the Counts of Salm* in Salmchâteau. The castle, which dates from the 9th century, is now in ruins.

3. *The Musée du Coticule*. The Stonemasonry Museum, located in Salmchâteau and passed on the walk, is largely devoted to the quarrying and preparation of hone or razor stone, a major industry in the Salm valley in the 19th and early 20th centuries. Markets for these products dried up during the second half of this century and as a consequence quarrying declined in the region. The Salm valley quarries eventually ceased operation in 1980. Today the museum tells the story of this type of quarrying and explains the geology of the region. There is a modest entrance fee to the museum, which is open from 1st April to 31st October, 10am - 12pm and 1 - 5pm, Tuesdays to Saturdays and between 2 - 5.30pm on Sundays. Those interested further should note that some of the old Salm valley quarry workings are passed on Walk 33. Various other aspects of the traditional life of the Salm valley are highlighted in the associated Museum of History and Life of the Salm Valley in Vielsalm (see "Places of Interest" for Walk 33).

Refreshments:　　There are plenty of cafés, restaurants, shops and hotels in both Vielsalm and Salmchâteau, but careful note should be made that there are no opportunities for obtaining refreshment once Vielsalm has been left, until the trail drops down into the valley again at Salmchâteau, by which time this fairly long walk is three-quarters completed. It is therefore a good idea to take a picnic lunch on this ramble.

Route

Start the walk from the large church in Vielsalm (there is a large car park adjacent to it and opposite is the tourist office). Locate the bridge over the river behind and below the tourist office building. From this point walk westwards into the village of Rencheux, a suburb of Vielsalm. Cross the railway line and immediately turn right onto a path which climbs a flight of concrete steps and runs alongside a stone wall. Turn left uphill on emerging at a road, the Rue du Château. About 50 metres before reaching a road T-junction, turn right onto a narrow lane signposted to Hydrosalm (waymark No. 5 - a black number 5 on a white background). This lane begins to climb; before reaching another road T-junction, turn right along the Cité de l'Aumônier. Pass alongside rows of terraced houses and a long factory building, picking up the red/white waymarks of the GR 5A. The lane soon becomes a poorly surfaced track which leaves Rencheux and heads north-west towards the forest.

Soon bear right (No. 5 and red/white waymarks) onto another track by a bench (view overlooking the valley) and descend on this to enter the trees. Take the right fork downhill where indicated by the No. 5 and red/white waymarks. Cross the stream ahead, either by fording or on the rather dilapidated wooden footbridge, and then bear to the right to climb on a track (No. 5 and red/white waymarks), heading northwards. The path climbs through the woods to reach

The small chapel at Fârnières, in a forest clearing above Vielsalm

a Y-junction of paths, a point at which our walk, Trail No. 5, parts company with the GR route. The latter takes the right fork, but our trail bears to the left, still climbing and accompanied by waymark No. 5 and, rather confusingly, by red/white/red waymarks (not signifying the GR trail). The path eventually reaches the top of its climb and then continues heading in a north-westerly direction through the wood. There are many path and track junctions, but each is clearly marked with Trail No. 5 painted on trees, but if in any further doubt check the compass direction. The trail eventually emerges at the delightful forest hamlet of Fârnières, where there is a small pretty chapel, which is usually open, and a large Maison de Retraite complex. At this point our trail (No. 5) changes direction by turning left on a No. 5 waymarked track about 20 metres before the chapel is reached, but before continuing on the walk do take a little time to explore the hamlet of Fârnières, which is reached by continuing ahead for a few hundred metres. The religious buildings here are splendid. A strong sense of peace and calm pervades the forest clearing in this area.

Thus refreshed continue on your way, now heading south-south-west back into the wood. Again there are many crossing tracks, but the direction ahead is always clearly marked with a number 5 on trees at every junction, and the way always maintains a direction of south-south-west, as the trail passes through avenues of tall trees. The forest track eventually narrows to become a footpath which crosses a small stream and climbs steeply to exit the wood and reach a metalled lane. Turn left along this to enter the village of Goronne, a farming community. Cross the main road in the centre of the village, passing to the left of the church and walking ahead, towards the south. Ignore a couple of side turnings in the village, always following the No. 5 waymarks ahead.

About 600 metres after crossing the main road in the village our lane swings sharply to the left, after which it forks at a Y-junction. Take the right branch of this fork. This lane soon loses its surface and heads towards the woods to the south-east. There are wide vistas to the left before you reach the woods, although unfortunately the view is spoiled somewhat by the large housing estate clearly seen above Vielsalm. About 150 metres before the wood, the track reaches a T-junction. Turn left here onto a track that can become waterlogged after heavy rain. Bear right at a Y-junction 20 metres before the trees, and enter the wood. The path climbs to reach a Y-junction where you bear right to climb even more steeply beneath the trees. Climb to reach a track T-junction where you turn right, still following, of course, Trail No. 5, but now being joined by Trail No. 3 (the two trails are now coincident for several kilometres, when they eventually go their separate ways a little before Provedroux).

The track descends to a T-junction where our way turns to the right to continue its descent, now out of the forest. The views ahead are wide and charming, tree-dotted green fields and hillsides with farms, hamlets and villages scattered amongst them. The track descends to the valley: turn right on reaching a lane at a T-junction to enter the village of La Comté, which has many attractive old stone farm buildings and cottages. Bear left at a "no through road" sign and continue the descent to the valley bottom. Cross the main Vielsalm to La Roche road and take the quiet lane opposite, climbing towards the wood seen on the brow of the hill ahead. This lane soon loses its surface and climbs to reach a Y-junction of tracks. Bear left here, now walking south-east on a grassy track enclosed between wire fences. The track enters the woods and begins to climb. The ascent ends where a track joins our track from the right. Ignore this, carrying straight on and then staying with the track as it swings to the right to begin a long descent towards the south. Bear to the left at a track T-junction and then in a further 100 metres turn right at a second track T-junction (Trail No. 3 leaves us here, taking the left fork - for those who wish to shorten the walk at this point Trail No. 3 provides a more direct route to Salmchâteau than the one described below). Remain on this narrow surfaced lane to reach a lane at a T-junction by a farm. Turn left along the road to walk into Provedroux, a pretty village with several mellow stone buildings, including both a small chapel and a village church.

Remain on the lane as it passes through the village and snakes down towards the Salm valley below. The lane reaches the main road in the valley bottom on the outskirts of the town of Salmchâteau (or Salm Château). Turn left (north) along the main road for about 250 metres, before leaving it by taking a narrow footpath on the right signposted to the Musée du Coticule.

Cross the footbridge over the river to visit the museum, which is housed in a fine old stone building beside the river.

Pass to the left of the museum and turn left along the narrow, poorly surfaced lane at its far side. Cross a tributary of the main river by a wooden footbridge and continue ahead along the lane to reach the High Street of Salmchâteau. Turn left along this for about 100 metres to the junction of the N68 and N89. Turn right opposite this junction, our trail (No. 5) now rejoining that of Trail No. 3. After about 80 metres keep ahead at the staggered crossroads. Ignore the red and white waymarks of the GR 5A, which are briefly encountered again here, but continue ahead, soon rejoining the river to follow it downstream towards the north, walking under the stout arches of a road bridge as you begin this section of the walk. Pass under a railway bridge and follow this lane alongside the railway line until you reach a bridge over the railway on your right. Cross over this bridge to follow the lane ahead to the main road. Turn left along the latter for about 80 metres, before turning left towards Vielsalm railway station. Turn right along the lane directly in front of the station. Turn left immediately before the bridge over the river and head towards Vielsalm Lake and church, now seen ahead. Cross the bridge immediately in front of the lake and then follow the right-hand (eastern) shore of the lake. There are seats on the lakeside from which to admire the view. Cross the weir at the far end of the lake and continue to the main road, where turn right to return to Vielsalm Tourist Office and church.

WALK 32:
Vielsalm, Grand Halleux and the Rocher de Hourt

Description: An excellent circuit in the forests to the east of the Salm valley, north-east of Vielsalm and east of the village of Grand Halleux. The trail follows sections of several local waymarked trails, in particular those numbered 1, 12 and 2, and it is also coincident with short sections of the GR 5 in two locations. The highlight of the day is undoubtedly a visit to the Rocher de Hourt, one of the best viewpoints in the whole region, from where the layout of the land around and about the Salm valley can be scrutinised, almost from a bird's-eye perch. The visit to the Hourt lookout is a short optional detour from the circuit.

Location: To the north-east and north of the town of Vielsalm.

Start/Finish: The large church and car park at the north end of the High Street of Vielsalm.

Distance: 10.3 miles (16.5kms).

Time: Allow 5hrs to 5hrs 30mins.

Maps: The well contoured map, scale 1:25,000, entitled *Carte des Promenades Pédestres - Kaart Voor Voettochten* published by the Val de Salm tourist office. It can be purchased from the tourist office in Vielsalm.

IGN 1:50,000 series: sheet number 56.

Waymarking: All of the three walks in the Vielsalm area described in this guidebook follow the official tourist office waymarkings for the region: ie. black numbers (1, 2, 4, 5, 12 etc) plus a black directional arrow on a rectangular or square white background. There are many other painted waymark symbols in the area, but these should be ignored.

Terrain: The countryside is hilly hereabouts, so you can expect a fair number of climbs, some of them moderately steep in gradient.

Footwear: The walk follows mainly forest tracks and rides which can be very muddy after heavy rainfall, so that boots or bogtrotters are the recommended footwear.

Option: *The Rocher de Hourt*. The detour to the viewpoint will take about 25mins there and back, plus additional time to admire the view. Care should be taken to follow the route described in the text as the viewpoint can be a little tricky to locate in the forest. The view from the Hourt rock is very extensive, down to the railway line and road that run along the Salm valley, and over to the green fields and long wooded Ardennes ridges to the west. Recommended.

Place of
Interest: *Domaine du Monti Wildlife Park*. Set at an altitude of 465m, this 50 hectare park exhibits all the typical fauna of the Ardennes forest, including deer and wild boar. There are a number of facilities at the park, including lake fishing and a restaurant (the speciality is boar roasted on a spit over a wood fire). There is a small entrance fee to the park, which is open all year.

Refreshments: Vielsalm has many shops, cafés and restaurants, but on the route of this walk there is only one opportunity for obtaining refreshments, ie. there is a restaurant at the Domaine du Monti *parc à gibier*, about three-quarters of the way around the circuit. However, reliance should not be made on this to be open, so it is best to take one's own packed lunch and drinks. For those in desperate need of sustenance, there is the possibility of a detour to the village of Grand Halleux in the Salm valley (about a mile there and back) before turning south on our route for the walk back to Vielsalm.

Route

Start the walk at the car park by the large church in Vielsalm, almost opposite the tourist office, which is housed in a separate detached building. Take the narrow lane, the Chemin de la Vallée, opposite the tourist office: this descends

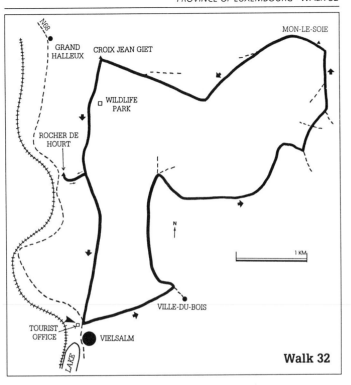

GRAND HALLEUX

N68

CROIX JEAN GIET

MON-LE-SOIE

WILDLIFE PARK

ROCHER DE HOURT

N

1 KM

VILLE-DU-BOIS

TOURIST OFFICE

VIELSALM

LAKE

Walk 32

and heads towards the east, signposted to the Camping de la Salm campsite. Pass the entrance to the campsite and continue ahead to a point where the lane bends to the right. Bear left here on an unsurfaced track (waymark for Trail No. 1). On reaching the far corner of the campsite turn right onto another track. Continue along this track until you reach a road at a T-junction. Turn left along this lane to walk up through the village of Ville-du-Bois.

On leaving the village the lane becomes a rough track. Continue ahead uphill on this track, heading north. Remain on the main track, ignoring any others off to the right or left, to reach a Y-junction. Take the left fork here and within 100 metres ignore a track on the left, but continue ahead soon entering the wood. The forest track climbs gently, gaining height gradually in the forest. Near the top of the ascent ignore the first cross-tracks, but within 100 metres, at the top of the rise, turn right (south-east) as indicated by the Trail No. 1 waymark. Descend, ignore a cross-tracks within about 150 metres, but continue ahead downhill to reach a track T-junction, where you turn left (east). Ignore

189

a descending cross-track within a few hundred metres, but continue ahead, contouring the hillside on the edge of the forest (this track can be rather muddy and waterlogged after heavy rainfall). Bear right at the next Y-junction, and right again at the second Y-junction, this time descending away from the wood. However, after only about 50 metres, turn left on a grassy track with trees to your left and a field to your right. Cross an area of heathland (masses of broom on your right) and ignore a track heading uphill on your left. Continue ahead to enter conifer woods. The track climbs gradually through the trees, eventually swinging to the right to reach another track at a T-junction by the edge of the woods, near to a small open-fronted wooden building on the left. Turn right at this T-junction and follow the track to a minor road by a collection of stone-built houses. Leave Trail No. 1 at this point (it turns to the right) by turning left uphill on this road.

Continue ahead at a crossroads, now joining Trail No. 12. Ignore a lane descending to the right. On reaching the edge of the woods turn left (north) following the direction indicated by the No. 12 waymark on a tree. The path climbs steeply up through the woods to meet a metalled lane. Continue ahead, uphill, on this road to reach a small wooden crucifix (the Croix de Mon le Soie) at the top of the hill. Ignore the cross-tracks here but continue downhill on the surfaced lane, still on route No. 12. Remain on this road as it swings to the left to pass the buildings of the Mont-le-Soie complex.

Keep to the metalled lane as it enters a wood and picks up the red and white waymarks of the GR 5. About 150 metres after entering the wood Trail No. 12 takes a track off to the right, but we ignore this, remaining ahead on the metalled road, following the GR 5 and heading downhill. After about 600 metres leave this road by taking a track off to the left, waymarked with red/white and signposted to Vielsalm. Continue along this forest track for about 800 metres until reaching a major cross-tracks. Here turn right, leaving the GR 5, to head downhill towards the west. Keep on this main forest track, part of Trail No. 12 once again, to descend to a road, the one which you left earlier and which leads to Grand Halleux. Continue downhill on this road, still heading westwards. After about 200 metres a junction of the road with three tracks is encountered. Take the forest track on the left, heading south and signposted to Monti (Trail No. 9 plus red/white waymarks). The track soon begins to descend to reach the car park of the Domaine du Monti (a restaurant will be found by detouring a little distance to the left). Our trail, still No. 9 and heading south, now climbs a red-brown dirt track towards the woods. At the top of the hill the track forks at a Y-junction. It is important to take the right fork here. A few hundred metres after this Y-junction reach a point (point x) where another track leaves on the right. There is a *Parc à Gibier* signboard at this point. This is the start of the optional detour to visit the Rocher de Hourt, a superb viewpoint (see "Option" above). If omitting this detour, then skip to the asterisk (*) in the text below. The detour will take about 25mins there and back.

To reach the Rock turn right down this path (Trail No. 2) and descend on it to a track T-junction. Turn right, now on a more stony path which ascends. Remain on this track as it climbs, until when near the top bear off to the left to reach the Rocher de Hourt. There is a precipitous drop to the west, down to the Salm valley, so take care at this point, particularly if there is a high wind blowing. Four rather strange, stubby blocks of concrete adorn the summit, these being overtopped by even odder short metal ladder-like structures, the remnants of some sort of manmade construction that once stood here. After admiring the view return to point x - see text above - by the reverse of your outward route (*).

Resume the walk along the track heading southwards, continuing along Trail No. 2. The track climbs initially before descending to reach a metalled lane at a cross-tracks (the GR 5 joins us again at this point: red/white waymarks). Continue ahead on this surfaced lane, ignoring a track off to the left at a Y-junction reached after only 20 metres. The lane descends to a cross-track. Continue straight ahead (red/white waymarks) down a narrow grassy path between hedgerows. Descend on this path, passing a rather large shrine on your right, to reach a narrow, poorly surfaced lane. Continue downhill on the lane to reach a road at a hairpin bend. Turn right down this road to reach the main road in Vielsalm. Turn left along this to return to the church and tourist office.

WALK 33:
Vielsalm, Bèche and the Grand Bois

Description: This walk explores just a part of the huge Grand Bois ("Large Wood") or So Bèchefa which stretches for many miles to the east of Vielsalm. The walk follows the route of the local official Trail No. 4 for the most part, although it deviates from it for a little while to take a footpath route through the forest in preference to a main road section.

Hone or razor stone was an important product from the quarries around Vielsalm during the 19th century and early 20th century (see the Musée du Coticule in Salmchâteau passed on Walk 31) and evidence of the once productive quarries can be seen during the initial stages of this walk, several sections of which follow tracks on which slate is much in evidence. The return to Vielsalm is an easy stroll along a country lane, in open countryside, where the views of the surrounding hill country are very fine.

Location: To the east of Vielsalm and Salmchâteau.

Start/Finish: The walk can be started either from the church and tourist office at the north end of Vielsalm town, or at the Vielsalm railway station, at the south end of Vielsalm Lake. It will be described below as if starting from Vielsalm church. If commencing the walk from the railway station begin by following the trail from the asterisk (*) below.

Distance: 8.7 miles (14.0kms).

Time: Allow 4hrs 30mins - 5hrs.

Maps: The well contoured map, scale 1:25,000, entitled *Carte des Promenades Pédestres - Kaart Voor Voettochten* published by the Val de Salm tourist office. It can be purchased from the Tourist Office in Vielsalm.

IGN 1:50,000 series: sheet number 56.

Waymarking: Follow the official tourist office waymarkings for the Trail No. 4, viz. black number 4 plus a black directional arrow on a rectangular or square white background.

Terrain: A walk in the forests and open countryside to the east of Vielsalm. The initial climb out of Vielsalm is a steep one, but after that the gradients are quite gentle.

Footwear: Once again several of the forest tracks and paths can be expected to be wet and muddy after rain, so that boots or bogtrotters are the order of the day.

*Places of
Interest:*   1) *Museum of History and Life of the Salm Valley.* Located at Tienne Messe 3, in the oldest part of Vielsalm, the collection is housed in a building dating from the late 18th century. The museum is open from 1st April to 31st October, from 10am - 12pm and 1 - 5pm, Tuesdays to Saturdays and from 2 - 5.30pm on Sundays.

2) The War Memorial in the car park beneath the church in Vielsalm commemorates the members of the Ardennes Secret Army who operated during the Second World War.

Refreshments: There are no opportunities for obtaining refreshments on this walk, so it is advisable to take food and drink along with you. Vielsalm has every facility, of course.

Route

From the church/car park/tourist office at the northern end of Vielsalm town walk along the N822, signposted to Lierneux, for about 200 metres to reach the railway line. Do not cross the line but turn left a few metres before it on a wide gravel track which leads to Vielsalm Lake (Reservoir). Turn left along its short north shore, heading towards the church. Cross the weir and continue on the footpath alongside the eastern shore of the lake. On reaching the end of the lake, cross the footbridge on the right, over the river and follow the latter upstream to a road bridge, where bear right to reach Vielsalm railway station. Turn left at the station to reach the High Street (*).

On a forest path above La Roche. (Walk 25)

The Falls of Coo after heavy rain (Walks 42 and 43)

The procession of Blancs Moussis in the Stavelot Carnival (note the sacs bulging with confetti and the balloons used to batter the spectators!)

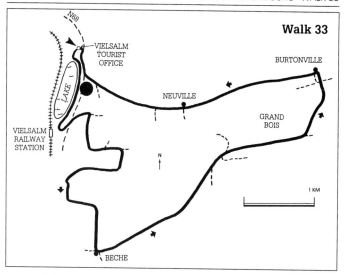

Turn left on this main road for 100 metres before turning right up the Rue des Chars-à-Boeufs. Climb on this road until, just after rounding a right-hand bend, turn right into the Rue des Ardoisieres and continue climbing. The lane climbs steeply to reach a junction by a house whose upper story is wooden. Continue straight ahead here, now climbing on a slatey unsurfaced track. A few metres after passing under telegraph wires, turn left in front of a disused quarrying area, still on a slatey track. Bear left on reaching a complex track junction (6 tracks converge here) to take the track enclosed between hedgerows (waymark No. 4). The grassy path passes behind the back gardens of a row of houses and then the trail turns right on another slatey track to climb up towards the wood to the south (ignore any tracks leading off to the left into the old quarry area). There follows a very steep climb until the track reaches a track T-junction (tall radio communication tower visible ahead). Turn right for 20 metres to a Y-junction by a stone cairn. Bear right here to pass a second cairn amidst broom bushes.

There are occasional glimpses of views down towards Vielsalm as this path is followed westwards along the edge of the escarpment between bushes and trees. Further stone cairns are passed and then the trail begins to swing towards the south-west, then the south, and finally round to head eastwards. Soon after the route begins to head in this direction it is important to take the right fork on reaching a Y-junction, still heading eastwards and descending. The purple heather hereabouts is most attractive in the early autumn. The track ends at a T-junction. Now turn right on a track which descends south to the valley seen below, first between low banks and later between fences. The track descends to the village of Bèche.

Bear left on reaching the road by a wooden bus shelter in the village. Climb out of the village on this lane. A few metres after the last house the lane loses its surface and reaches a Y-junction: take the left branch here. The track soon forks again: this time take the right branch on a narrow stony track which runs between banks with grassy fields to your right. Continue ahead, heading east-north-east, at the next track junction. The track, which now carries red/white waymarks, climbs gradually into the woods, levels out and maintains direction ahead, eventually meeting a road at a bend in the latter.

Trail No. 4 turns right on this road for about a kilometre, but we leave it here, so avoiding this main road section. Therefore turn left along the road for about 150 metres to a sharp left-hand bend. A few metres before the bend turn right uphill on a stony track. Within 100 metres this track narrows to a rock-strewn footpath. Climb for about 40 metres to a path junction where you bear left through conifer trees (Trail No. 1 waymarks, but pointing in the reverse direction). Reach another (better) path at a T-junction and turn left along this, heading east-north-east. The trail, soon becoming a track which can be muddy and wet after heavy rain, continues ahead until it reaches a cross-tracks which lies under a power line cable (two concrete poles bear this cable at either side of the junction - it is important not to miss this junction: it is the point where Trail No. 1 meets Trail No. 4). Turn left here (No. 4 on concrete pole) heading north-east, having regained Trail No. 4. The route follows the power cable all the way down to the valley (ignore any side turnings leaving the line of the cables). Reach and cross a lane, continuing downhill, still following the power line, to pass the church in the village of Burtonville.

Turn left at the T-junction at the bottom of the hill, leave Burtonville and continue along this lane for about 4kms, heading west back towards Vielsalm. There are wide views along this most picturesque valley, scenery somewhat reminiscent of the Yorkshire Dales. The way passes through the village of Neuville (note the interesting old stone crucifix set into slate on the left-hand side of the road in the village). The lane descends gradually all the way back to Vielsalm. Turn right, downhill, at the T-junction on the outskirts of the town, along the Rue des Combattants, and later continue ahead at the traffic lights (in the direction of Stavelot) down the Rue Général Jacques to Place Paulin Moxhet. Turn right on reaching the High Street to return to the church and the tourist office. Those who started the walk at Vielsalm railway station should now return to the front of this route description to follow the trail back to their starting point.

Province of Liege

SPA

General Information and Places of Interest

Spa, the "Pearl of the Ardennes", is *the* original Spa town, having lent its name to many other health resorts around Europe. The medium sized town (population 9000), the world's oldest spa, has been famous since the 13th century for its mineral springs. In its heyday, in the 18th and 19th centuries, it was a very fashionable resort, patronised by royalty, the aristocracy and the extremely rich and famous. Among its more distinguished visitors were Henry VIII and Charles II of England, Henri III of France, Queen Christina of Sweden and Peter the Great of Russia. It was much favoured by the British aristocracy, a fact that can be gleaned from some of the street names still in existence, for example the Route de Balmoral (Walk 37) and the Boulevard des Anglais. Today, there is a hint of the town's former elegance in some of the now rather faded buildings of the baths, the casino and some of the grander hotels.

The heart of the town is the Place Royale where the tourist office is housed in a rather prominent and elegant building: useful free town maps are available

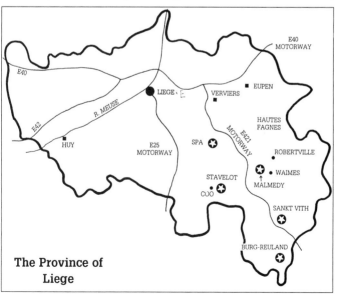

The Province of Liege

from here. *Pétanque* is played nearby. *Boules* is a game really more suited to the dry, warm climate of the south, but problems of inclement weather have been overcome by playing indoors, within the summerhouse at the far end of the wrought iron gazebo (interesting flea market here on Sunday mornings) that leads from the tourist office building. Nearby is the thermal baths complex, the Etablissement des Bains (visits, which include an audio-visual show, are possible - enquire at the tourist office). It is still much frequented by those "taking the waters", an activity particularly popular with the French and the Walloons. Also in the centre of town is the casino, originally built in 1763, but rebuilt in 1919, after the First World War (the town had been a headquarters for the German army in the last days of that war - the top brass were housed in the Hôtel Britannique, and even the Kaiser lived nearby).

The main spring, and the only one in the centre of the town, is the Pouhon Pierre-le-Grand (open Easter to September), named after Peter the Great who received a successful cure here in 1717. The large building in which the spring is now housed was built in 1880. There are five other springs in the area (Sauvenière (the oldest), Géronstère (Walk 39), Groesbeek, Tonnelet and Barisart), all of which can be visited by means of a special type of tram called a *baladeuse*: these should be found waiting around the Place Royale during the summer months. This Tour of the Fontaines takes about an hour. Spa water is rich in iron, sodium bicarbonate and other minerals, and has been said to be useful, over the centuries, for the treatment of rheumatism, high blood pressure, various respiratory problems and even sterility. It is today mainly used for drinking, the bottling and distribution of Spa water being a major industry (the Spa Monopole water bottling factory, sited near the railway station, can be visited every working day, from 9am to noon and from 1 to 4pm - it is closed at weekends).

The Musée de la Ville d'Eau is a small museum in the town which tells the history of Spa (limited opening hours). The attractive Lac de Warfaaz, located some distance from the town (Walk 37), is artificial, the result of a dam built in 1890.

The Parc à Sept Heures (Walks 34, 35 and 36), originally laid out in 1758, soon became a fashionable meeting point for local and visiting dignitaries. Today it is a small pleasant park, ornamented with a fountain and a number of small monuments. One of these is dedicated to the creators (rich noblemen in the 18th century) of the magnificent footpaths and promenades in the wooded hills behind Spa. Several of these *Promenades* are named after the various nationalities of the rich, famous and aristocratic who came here, particularly during the Belle Epoque, to take the waters and stroll around the town, displaying both their finery and social position. For instance, on the walks in this book you will come across a Promenade des Français, a Boulevard des Anglais and a Promenade des Americains. These fine old byways, amidst mature woodland, nowadays form part of the elaborate network of local walking trails around the town. This is complemented by a couple of long distance trails that pass through Spa, the GR 5 and the GR 573 or GR V (see Appendix 5). The paths in the area are clear and well waymarked, but unfortunately the walkers' map of the Spa district (*La Carte du Promeneur* at 1:20,000) is rather poor, showing neither contours nor the routes of the numerous numbered and waymarked trails in the area.

The athletic visitor to Spa can try out the *Parcours Sportif*, called the *Parcours Spa Reine*, located less than a mile from the Place Royale. To reach it follow the route description of Walk 37, past the Sol-Cress complex to the Promenade des Orimièles. This course has a number of stopping stations, each of which has the usual variety of gymnastic equipment designed to work out various muscle groups. Those keen on cross-country skiing may wish to visit Spa, one of the nearest skiing centres from Britain, but it should be emphasised that snow conditions are far from reliable here.

Not far from Spa is the Belgian Grand Prix motor racing circuit at Francorchamps. This is a rather strange town to drive through as there are permanent motor racing stands lining the roadside. There are several race meetings a year including a 24hr race. It is best to avoid the area when a race meeting is taking place, as some of the public roads are sealed off on these occasions: they are used as part of the race track! This will be evident when driving through the town, as several of the public roads are highly banked. The history of motor racing at Francorchamps is told in the Musée Circuit de Spa-Francorchamps at Stavelot (see the section on Stavelot and Coo).

Accommodation

There are many hotels in and around Spa, covering most categories and prices, including L'Auberge, Chalet du Lac (Walk 37), Chalet du Parc (Walk 37), Chemin de Fer, Cardinal, La Détente, Dorint Hôtel, Spa Balmoral, Gai Séjour, La Heid des Pairs, Hôtel de la Gare, Hôtel de l'Avenue, Pension des Sources (Walk 37), Le Relais (recommended), Relais de la Poste, Les Sorbiers and Source de la Géronstère (Walk 39). There are also a fair number of private rooms and smaller *pensions* available, but bear in mind that Spa is very popular during the main summer holiday period; at other times of the year there should be few problems of accommodation (the possible exception being at weekends in winter at a time when there is sufficient good snow for skiing).

There is a *gîte d'étape* at Hockai, 3.5kms north of Francorchamps on the GR 5 (Auberge Amis de la Nature, Les Hautes Fagnes - 50 places, tel. (087) 275147).

Two campsites serve Spa: the small Camping de la Havette (Walk 38) in the town and the larger and more expensive Parc des Sources, a little way out of Spa on the Rue de la Sauvenière. There are also two campsites at nearby Sart-les-Spa and one at Polleur.

Sol-Cress Complex:

Walkers may also like to consider staying at the large Sol-Cress establishment in the woods above Spa (Walks 35, 36 and 37). Rooms and meals can be obtained here. Sol-Cress is a large, purpose-built holiday complex, particularly suitable for those who wish to follow one or a number of outdoor pursuits, especially rambling and mountain biking. It is no cheaper to stay here than in the average hotel, although the complex has every amenity and is particularly suited to family and other groups, who can hire rooms with a kitchen and lounge included in a suite or unit. Further details, together with a brochure, can be obtained by calling at the reception (*Accueil*) when in Spa - some of the staff speak English - or by contacting Sol-Cress by phone (087) 77 23 53, fax (087) 87 78 93, or in writing to Sol-Cress Spaloumont 5, B-4900 Spa.

Transport

Spa is easily reached by train from Liège or Verviers via Pepinster. The railway station lies to the west of the town centre.

The railway line to Spa is a spur of the Liège to Cologne line, ie. it leaves this main line at Verviers. The timetable number for the Verviers to Spa branch line is No. 44. Trains stop at the following stations: Verviers, Pepinster, Pepinster-Cité, Justenville, Theux, Franchimont, Spa and Géronstère (end of line). Several of these small stations are situated along the GR 573 (GR V), so this train service could be used to accomplish a number of linear walks along this long distance trail, whilst staying in Spa.

There are bus services from Spa to Sart, Hockai and Stavelot and on to Trois-Ponts, where there is a railway station for trains to Liège (Service No. 44 - about 9 a day on weekdays and 6 a day at weekends: journey time Spa to Stavelot is just under an hour, plus about 10mins extra to Trois-Ponts). There is a frequent bus service from Spa to Theux, Pepinster and Verviers (Service No. 388 - about 8 to 10 a day on weekdays, about 8 a day on Saturdays and 5 a day on Sundays: journey time is about 1hr from Spa to Verviers). Bus service No. 395 operates between Spa and Malmédy, Sankt Vith and Burg-Reuland (about 6 a day on weekdays, about 5 a day on Saturdays and 3 a day on Sundays: journey time is about 1hr 30mins from Spa to Sankt Vith and 2hrs to Burg-Reuland). Service No. 399 between Spa, Roanne and Coo is very infrequent. Finally, bus service No. 38 (388a) takes a circular route around the environs of Spa (several bus stops for this service will be encountered on the walks described in this book). The service starts from and finishes at the railway station (*gare*) and visits the Chemin du Bahy, Avenue Jehin, Boulevard Chapman and Place Royale (frequency: about 6 times a day and 5 on Sundays).

The easiest and quickest approach by car is via the E421 (A27) motorway, which leaves the E40 (A3) motorway east of Liège. Spa is about a 5km drive from junction 8 of the E421. A more direct, but slower, drive from Liège is along the N61 to Pepinster and then the N62 via Theux to Spa.

With its easy access and abundance of accommodation, Spa is a very good base for walking and exploring this part of the Ardennes.

Official Waymarked Trails From Spa

There are two sets of waymarked trails from Spa, the official tourist office trails and those devised and waymarked by the Sol-Cress organisation (see above). The former trails, well waymarked with signboards, are as follows:

Route No. & Waymark Colour		Title	Distance kms	Official Time hrs mins
1.	grey	Annette et Lubin, Montagnes Ruses, Lac de Warfaaz and the Fontaine du Tonnelet	7.5	2 30
2.	red	Promenade Reickem, Fontaine aux Yeux, Pavilion Renard and Promenade Grande Duchesse	7.5	2 30
3.	sky blue	The Promenade Princesse Clémentine & the Etang de Chawion	7.0	2 30
4.	pale green	Itinerary to Spa Golf Club	7.0	2 30
5.	beige	The Feuillée Jean d'Ardenne and the village of Creppe	7.5	2 30
6.	dark green	The Promenade Meyerbeer, and the Barisart & Géronstère Springs	7.5	2 30
7.	sea blue	The Promenade des Artistes	7.0	2 30
8.	red	The Promenade d'Orléans and the Fontaine de la Sauvenière	6.0	2 30
9.	black	Géronstère and the Fagne de Malchamps	9.0	3 00
10.	brown	The Crosses of Pottier and Bérinsenne	11.5	3 30
11.	orange	Sauvenière and the Fagne de Malchamps	9.0	3 30
12.	red arrow	A Balmoral Itinerary	5.0	3 00

Cress Waymarked Trails (from the Sol-Cress Complex above Spa)

The routes of the Sol-Cress designed, numbered and waymarked trails are shown on a simple sketch map, which is nevertheless easy to interpret and follow, obtainable from the Sol-Cress establishment.

Route No.	Title/Destinations	Distance kms	Time hrs	Time mins
1.	Reickem - Delvaux - Orimièles	5.5	1	45
2.	Chawion - Servais	6.5	2	15
3.	Balmoral - Golf	6.5	2	15
4.	Balmoral - Maraifagne	6.5	2	15
5.	Warfaaz	8.0	2	45
6.	Marteau - Chawion	9.0	3	00
7.	Golf - Ligné - Anglais	10.0	3	30
8.	Chencul	10.0	3	30

Walks

Five walks are described from Spa in this book, three to the north of the town, and two to the south. The last walk from this centre starts and finishes at Géronstère, a couple of miles south of Spa.

WALK 34:
Feuillée Jean d'Ardenne and Creppe

Description: A walk along a narrow, steep-sided sylvan valley and a visit to the village of Creppe, south of Spa.

Location: South-west of Spa.

Start/Finish: The tourist office in Place Royale in the centre of Spa.

Distance: 5.6 miles (9.0kms).

Time: 2hrs 45mins.

Maps: The walkers' map at a scale of 1:20,000 entitled *La Carte du Promeneur*, sold at the tourist office in Spa.
IGN 1:50,000 series: sheet number 49.

Waymarking: The walk follows the route of the official Circuit No. 5, waymarked on yellow signboards, bearing the number 5 within a beige box.

Terrain: Promenades, forest tracks and paths. A narrow, wooded valley. Note that the path up the Feuillée Jean d'Ardenne is steep in a few places and care should be taken under wet, slippery conditions, particularly when the path is covered by wet leaves.

Refreshments: There is ample choice in Spa.

Route

From the tourist office head in a westerly direction under the wrought iron gazebo and through the Parc de Sept Heures. Pass the four Roman columns to leave the park at the junction of the Avenue des Platanes and Rue Hanster. Turn right for 20 metres to turn left onto the unsurfaced Promenade des Français. Follow this uphill (you are also on the red and white waymarked GR trail to Theux). In 150 metres the GR route takes the right fork, but our trail goes left, passing a small shelter on a balcony path, a little way above the buildings of Spa. This pleasant path eventually descends to a road. Cross at the zebra crossing, turn left for 30 metres on the Avenue Reine Astrid (bus stop for service No. 38 here), before turning right on the Chemin de la Fagne Raquet. Pass over the river and soon bear right to cross over the railway line. Turn left along the Avenue du 12ème de Ligne Prince Leopold.

At the top of the hill turn right on the Chemin des Botteresses, and at the T-junction opposite a military base, turn right heading towards La Feuillée Jean d'Ardenne. Continue ahead at the Brasserie Salmon on the descending road. Where this swings to the right, turn left opposite an isolated house, on the path

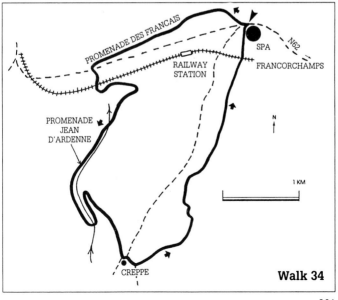

Walk 34

signposted as the Feuillée Jean d'Ardenne. This is a most pleasant, undulating path which follows the course of a babbling brook, up-stream. The steep, twisting, wooded valley is typical of this region of the Ardennes. The route, which is always obvious, is waymarked in this area by triangular-shaped yellow paint marks on the trees. The trail is steep in a places and some care should be taken when the path is wet and slippery.

On reaching the edge of the wood near the top of the gorge, cross over the stream by means of a log bridge and follow the path ahead on the opposite bank, signposted to the village of Creppe. After about 400 metres along this, be sure to turn right, away from the river in the direction indicated by the yellow signpost, Route 5 to Creppe. A narrow path between fences leads to a track where turn right, following this fenced track across fields. On beginning a climb be sure to look back for a superb view over the distant wooded hills of the Ardennes. Keep ahead at a cross-tracks by a wooden cross and crucifix. The track becomes surfaced at the signpost for the Chemin des Essarts, by another crucifix. Continue ahead to enter Creppe, where at the T-junction (church on the right), turn left following the sign to the Promenade des Americains.

In 50 metres turn right along the Avenue Andre Guillaume in the direction of Coo. In 100 metres turn left along the earthen track of the Chemin du Pouhon. This descends gently to a viewpoint and wooden cross where it (and you) swing to the left, following the sign to the Promenade Gustave Dewalque. The track descends to meet and join the GR 5 (red/white waymarks) at a track bend. Take the ascending branch ahead. Turn right at a T-junction, still following the red/white marks of the GR trail signposted to the Promenade Gustave Dewalque. The track soon begins to descend towards Spa, following a line of pollarded trees. Descend to a main road, where turn left to follow this back into Spa, passing a number of impressive 19th century villas on the way. Pass under a viaduct and walk down the Rue de la Mer(!) to reach Place Royale and the tourist office.

WALK 35:
Spa, the Bois du Chincul and the Val du Broxou

Description: A circuit in the woods above Spa. This pleasant walk includes a visit to the picturesque Val du Broxou and to the *belvédère* (viewpoint) above it from where the wooded hills and valley to the west of Spa are seen to good effect. Before returning to the town the trail visits the old Bernard pavilion which is located on the edge of the escarpment facing south, and this too offers a splendid viewpoint. The walk follows sections of two of the local Sol-Cress waymarked trails, Nos 8 and 6, but eventually leaves these to return to Spa along the wide Promenade de Grande Duchesse, and provides another opportunity to stroll through the elegant Parc de Sept Heures in Spa, with its fountain and stone columns.

A small square in the elegant town of Spa

Location: North-west and west of Spa.

Start/Finish: The tourist office in Place Royale in the centre of Spa.

Distance: 7.1 miles (11.5kms).

Time: Allow 4¹/₂-5hrs.

Maps: The walkers' map at a scale of 1:20,000 entitled *La Carte du Promeneur*, sold at the tourist office in Spa.

IGN 1:50,000 series: sheet number 49.

Waymarking: The route is waymarked with Sol-Cress numbered path waymarks (the red figures 8 and 6 painted on trees, etc) although some care is needed in places if crucial path junctions are not to be missed. The waymarking should be followed in conjunction with the detailed route description given below to avoid any possible navigational errors being made. The area is also well waymarked with the familiar yellow signboards of the Spa Tourist Office.

Terrain: Extensive mature woodland, hills and wooded ridges and escarpments. There are a couple of delightful sylvan valleys replete with babbling brooks.

Footwear: There are several steep ascents and descents on this walk and the paths can be muddy. Hence boots are recommended.

Option: A thorough exploration of the whole of the northern forest expanses above Spa, from the north-west to the north-east, could be made by combining this walk with the Lac de Warfaaz Grand Circuit (see Walk 37).

Special Problem: A few less agile walkers may find the very start of the narrow footpath that leaves the Promenade Princesse Clémentine at about the halfway stage of the walk to be a little awkward, particularly in wet or icy conditions, although most walkers should have no real trouble here.

Refreshments: No places of refreshment are passed on this walk, so it is prudent to take along food and drink. Spa, however, where the walk starts and finishes, has an abundance of cafés, restaurants and shops.

Route

From the tourist office building in the heart of Spa walk towards the north-east to the right of a small windmill to locate the path, marked with red/white waymarkings, which climbs the wooded hillside by a series of zigzags. This is the GR 5 (which, if followed to its end, leads to the Mediterranean at Nice). Follow the red/white waymarks to ascend past a viewpoint over the town and a number of seats, to reach a large building, Annette et Lubin, at the top of the climb. Pass to the right of this, still following the red/white waymarks, and on reaching a number of yellow signposts on a tree, bear left on Walking Trail Nos 2, 3 and 4, signposted to Spaloumont; within 100 metres or so bear left again on the Rue des Platanes. You will soon reach the large complex of Sol-Cress.

Pass to the left of the buildings and at their far end turn right on an

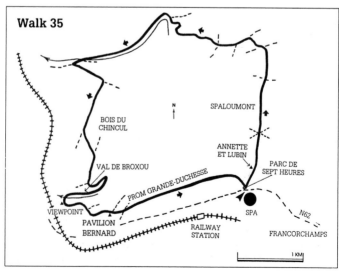

ascending lane signposted to Fratlinfaz and Golf. This leads to a major junction of 5 tracks and lanes. Continue ahead (north) past the metal barrier onto the forest track signposted as the Promenade du Pré des Cerf (Trail No. 3). This forest ride descends to a T-junction, where you turn right towards the Pré du Cerf (Trail No. 3 and Sol-Cress Trail Nos [red numbers] 3, 5, 7 and 8). The trail soon narrows to a path. Follow the above waymarks to reach a cross-tracks at the Avenue Princesse Clémentine. Proceed straight ahead here along the Promenade Foxhalle, following, amongst other coincident trails, Sol-Cress Trail No. 8 towards Feuillée Servais. The forest track descends to a footbridge: turn left at the track T-junction on the far side of this, the way still signposted to Feuillée Servais. In about 80 metres be sure to bear right off this path onto another climbing uphill and signposted as Sol-Cress Trail Nos 7 and 8. The path climbs to reach a track junction. Here turn left (west) on the Promenade de la Longue Heid (Sol-Cress Trail No. 8). Continue ahead at the next cross-tracks following the signpost to the Rue de Chawion and the Promenade Cailteux.

The track eventually descends and does indeed lead to the signposted Promenade Cailteux at a track T-junction. Turn left along this forest promenade still following Sol-Cress Trail No. 8 (red number 8 on a tree) walking downhill towards the west. Within a couple of hundred metres the trail reaches another track T-junction. Turn right (north) here, once again picking up the red and white waymarks of the GR 5 trail. However, we follow this for only 80 metres or so because it then turns off to the right on its long route to Malmédy, whereas we remain on the main promenade as it swings to the left. This track follows the course of a stream (over to your left) gently downhill, in a most charming sylvan location. Follow this babbling stream down its valley for about a mile to cross it by a bridge (cobbled surface and elaborate metal handrails) at the Sentier du Renard.

Do not take the latter, but instead bear to the right (still heading westwards) along Avenue Princesse Clémentine, now with the stream to your right. After about 300 metres from the bridge it is most important to locate a narrow footpath on the left which leaves the promenade and climbs, very steeply at first, the wooded ridge to the south (there should be a red number "8" on a tree to locate the start of this path - if you reach a railway line then you have gone too far along the Promenade Princesse Clémentine, in which case you will have to retrace your steps to find the path up the hillside). The first few footsteps on this path are very steep and somewhat eroded, so care is required, particularly in wet or icy conditions. The path climbs towards the south-east, pulling away from the stream in the valley bottom to attain the ridge, where the path levels, soon reaching a track junction (note that the area to the right, from this junction to the railway line in the west, has been designated as a conservation area and as a consequence there is no public access).

Bear left for 15 metres to a Y-junction, where our route (still Sol-Cress Trail No. 8) takes the right-hand branch heading east-south-east on the Sentier du

Fossé-Limite. However, after only about 100 metres the trail turns to the right (south-south-west) on meeting a cross-tracks. This track, the Promenade du Chincul, descends to pass into the Bois du Chincul, but then reascends to reach a cross-tracks. Here turn left (south-east), still on the Promenade du Chincul, now heading towards C.F. Maisonette and Spa. Climb on this track to reach a track T-junction at an altitude of 300m. Here turn right to head south-west. Continue to the point at which this main track turns to the left at a hair-pin bend. Here is the junction between Sol-Cress Trail Nos numbers 6 and 8. Leave Trail No. 8 (which you have been following all the way from Spa) at this point, and instead walk ahead to take the less prominent track waymarked with a red No. 6. This soon bears left through the trees to head towards the south-east and later towards the north-east. Within a few hundred metres of it attaining this direction the trail reaches a junction, where our route (No. 6) turns downhill sharply to the right, on the Promenade Delvaux, signposted the Val du Broxou. Head south-west down into this beautiful sylvan valley.

About 200 metres before reaching the river which lies at the bottom of the valley, look out for a narrow path which traverses the gully on the left (it is waymarked with a red No. 6). Take this (it is easily missed) to climb on it as it zigzags up the hillside, passing a number of small rocky outcrops to reach a shelter and viewpoint above the railway line in the valley below. After admiring this fine view take the path which heads east away from the precipitous drop (ignore the other path which heads in a southerly direction). This path heading east leads in a couple of hundred metres to the Promenade Reickem. Turn left heading eastwards on this major forest track. Pass a shelter and seat, which is on your right, and continue for 300 metres or so farther along the Promenade Reickem, until you reach a yellow signpost which indicates a path on the right leading to the Pavilion Felix Bernard. Leave Sol-Cress Trail No. 6 at this point.

The pavilion is reached within 75 metres. There are seats at this now rather dilapidated old stone pavilion, as well as a stone tablet on which are inscribed some lines of verse by Felix Bernard. A fine view overlooks the valley from the pavilion. From this panorama take the narrow path heading downhill, signposted to the Promenade de la Grande Duchesse. Descend the zigzags to reach this prominent track and bear left (east-north-east) along it, heading back towards Spa, now once again following the red/white waymarks of a GR route. The trail descends to the Promenade des Français. Follow this ahead in the direction of the Parc de Sept Heures. Cross the metalled road (the Avenue des Platanes) to enter the park. Walk past its stone columns and waterfall to return to the tourist office.

WALK 36:
Spa and the Etang de Chawion

Description: A visit to the small, attractive tarn, the Etang de Chawion, buried deep in the woods behind Spa.

Location: North-west of Spa.

Start/Finish: The tourist office in Place Royale in the centre of Spa.

Distance: 6.0 miles (9.5kms).

Time: 3hrs.

Maps: The walkers' map at a scale of 1:20,000 entitled *La Carte du Promeneur*, sold at the tourist office in Spa.

IGN 1:50,000 series: sheet number 49.

Waymarking: The walk follows the route of the official Circuit No. 3, waymarked on yellow signboards, bearing the number 3 within a light blue box.

Terrain: Promenades, forest tracks and paths. Lakeside.

Option: The route may be shortened by about a couple of miles (about 3kms) by taking a short cut on reaching the Etang de Chawion (this is indicated in the route description).

Refreshments: There is ample choice in Spa.

Route
Walk east from the tourist office along the Place Royale, keeping to the left-hand side of the road. A few metres after the thermal baths (which are over on the right-hand side of the road) walk ahead on the Rue Delhasse. This soon bends to the left to become Rue Storheau. Within 50 metres this becomes a narrow lane climbing steeply between houses. On reaching Rue Brixhe at a T-junction, turn left to reach a yellow signpost within 50 metres. This indicates Route No. 4 and Route No. 3 to the left. Follow this signpost towards the Annette et Lubin and Spaloumont, climbing on a track which soon provides views of the roofs of Spa below to the left. On reaching the large building of Annette et Lubin (SNCV) bear right in front of it following Route Nos 2, 3 and 4 towards Spaloumont, having now joined the route of the GR 5 (red/white waymarks). Continue ahead on meeting a Y-junction at a surfaced lane by an ornate red post box and pass a bus stop (service No. 38). At the far end of the Sol-Cress establishment turn right on a surfaced drive signposted to Fratlinfaz and Golf, Pré du Cerf.

On reaching a T-junction, with the Sol-Cress complex to the right, walk ahead on the forest track signposted to the cemetery (a bearing of 30 degrees magnetic), leaving the GR 5 at this point. After a descent turn right at a T-junction of tracks, signposted as Route No. 3 to Pré du Cerf (note: ignore the

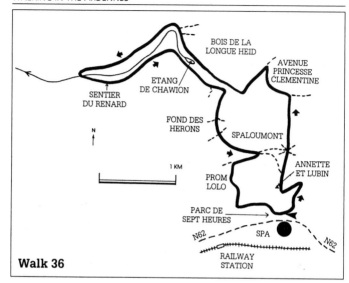

Walk 36

smaller numbered waymarks [red numbers and letters on a white background] - these refer to Sol-Cress routes - see "Waymarking" under Walk 37). The track narrows to a footpath: cross a small stream and continue ahead with field to the right and wood to the left. Soon reach a cross-tracks where turn left on the Avenue Princesse Clémentine, signposted to the Etang (tarn) de Chawion and Sentier Renard. Remain on this broad pleasant avenue between tall trees, soon descending to follow a small stream which eventually runs into the lake. Continue on the track to the right of the tarn. The small dam at the far end of the water, where the GR 5 is rejoined, has seats and a small shelter which is a good place for a picnic. Those ramblers wishing to shorten the walk can cross the dam at this point, turning left on the track above the opposite shore, to resume the walk at the point marked by the asterisk (*) below. About 50mins' walking time will be saved by taking this shorter alternative.

At the point at which the GR 5 turns sharply to the right, continue ahead, bearing to the left on the GR F, which is also the GR 573A signposted to Franchimont, Theux and Pepinster. Where the latter turns off to the right, remain ahead on the main track signposted to the Sentier du Renard, Route No. 3. Eventually cross the now reasonably sized river by means of a stone bridge bearing metal railings, but immediately turn left, still on the Sentier du Renard (fox's path). This track climbs gently above the river, but when it forks take the left-hand (lower) branch on the Sentier des Etangs. Remain on this track as it climbs, ignoring another track off to the right, but follow the main track as it swings to the right above the stream to pass above and to the right of the Etang de Chawion. At this point the GR 5, now heading back to Spa, is rejoined (*).

Follow the red and white waymarks of the GR 5, later taking the left fork at a Y-junction, and after a further few hundred metres, turn right uphill, still following the red/white markers. Pass a picnic table on the left and follow the sign towards Reickem, later ignoring a track to the left, but continuing ahead on the Avenue Maraifagne. On reaching the cemetery turn right on the Promenade Reickem, heading towards the Promenade Lolo, now on the GR 573V (to Marteau, Theux, Pepinster and Nessonvaux). Ignore a track off to the right opposite a covered picnic table, but 30 metres later, opposite a bench, turn left downhill on a woodland path signed Promenade Lolo to the Fontaine des Yeux ("Fountain of Eyes") and the Avenue des Plantanes. Descend to a road at the Fontaine des Yeux where turn right downhill. Just before a road sign for Rue Hanster bear left into the park (Parc de Sept Heures) to return to the tourist office in the centre of Spa.

WALK 37:
The Grand Circuit of the Hills of Spa - the Lac de Warfaaz

Description: This is probably the finest circular walk in the wooded hills above Spa. There is plenty of variety on the trail, from broad promenades to forest tracks, narrow steep footpaths and babbling brooks to follow and cross. A visit to the picturesque Lac de Warfaaz, the largest lake in the area, is one of the highlights of this tour.

Location: North-west of Spa.

Start/Finish: The tourist office in Place Royale in the centre of Spa.

Distance: 8.1 miles (13.0kms).

Time: 4hrs 30mins.

Maps: The walkers' map at a scale of 1:20,000 entitled *La Carte du Promeneur*, sold at the tourist office in Spa.
                  IGN 1:50,000 series: sheet number 49.

Waymarking: The walk follows parts of three of the Sol-Cress waymarked trails, viz. Nos 7, 3 and 5. These numbered trails are waymarked throughout, and it is important not to confuse this waymarking with that of the official tourist office routes. Whereas the latter are waymarked with numbers (from 1 to 12) on relatively large yellow boards, the Sol-Cress waymarks are on small white cards which bear small red arrows which point in both the forward and reverse directions, and which also carry the number of the trail (from 1 to 8). These signs carry a distinguishing emblem of the letter S within a larger letter C (for Sol-Cress). Follow *only* the Sol-Cress waymarks on this walk.

Terrain: Promenades, forest tracks and paths. Lakeside. There is considerable ascent and descent. A stream has to be forded at one point, but it is usually shallow and easy to cross (but the walk is not recommended, for this reason, after heavy rain).

Options: The route may be shortened at several points by making use of several of the other numbered and waymarked Sol-Cress trails. A number of options can be chosen back to the Sol-Cress establishment above Spa by reference to the sketch map indicating the Sol-Cress routes, obtainable from Sol-Cress (see the introduction to this section). If Sol-Cress Circuit No. 7, with which this route commences, is followed all the way back to Spa, without linking up with Sol-Cress Routes 3 and 5 as described below, the total distance is only 6.2 miles (10kms).

Refreshments: There is a café and two hotels at the Lac de Warfaaz.

Route

From the tourist office locate the steps behind the small ornamental windmill to the right of Le Chalet du Parc Hôtel-Restaurant. Take the path that begins here, climbing on zigzags above the town: it is the red/white waymarked GR 5 signposted as the Promenade Maréchal Foch. Ignore the Promenade Gérard Borckmans off to the left whilst on this ascent, but continue climbing, following the red and white paint markings. Probably the best view of the town is to be had from this well-constructed path. Follow the zigzags until the building of the Annette et Lubin comes into view, at the point where Route No. 1 bears off to the right. Remain on the GR 5 to pass to the right of the buildings, picking up Route No. 2 to Spaloumont. Continue on the track and then lane ahead to reach the Sol-Cress complex on your right. Here continue ahead along the Promenade Reickem, picking up the first Sol-Cress sign for their Route No. 7 (see "Waymarking" above).

Remain ahead, crossing a main track at an off-set track junction, still following red and white paint markings (GR 5, GR F and GR 5731). Keep ahead on the main track until reaching a gate across it, where turn left uphill, leaving the GR trail at this point, following Sol-Cress Route Nos numbers 1 and 7 on the Promenade des Orimièles. A parcours sportif is soon encountered. At station No. 11 of this circuit turn right onto the Promenade des Anglais. Keep ahead at the next cross-tracks, but bear to the left at a Y-junction, still following Sol-Cress Route No. 7. On reaching a main crossing track (Coupe-feu [fire-break] de la Maisonette), turn right along it. This track later descends. Keep straight ahead downhill at the point where Sol-Cress Route No. 6 joins from the left, but 50 metres farther on, where the main track swings to the left, continue ahead on a path downhill marked as Sol-Cress Route Nos 6 and 7. This path descends quite steeply. At a Y-intersection take the right fork to descend to a track, where Sol-Cress Route No. 6 turns right on this track. However, our route continues ahead

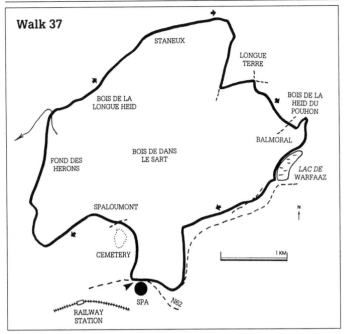

Walk 37

STANEUX

LONGUE
TERRE

BOIS DE LA
LONGUE HEID

BOIS DE LA
HEID DU
POUHON

BALMORAL

BOIS DE DANS
LE SART

LAC DE
WARFAAZ

FOND DES
HERONS

SPALOUMONT

N

CEMETERY

1 KM

SPA   N62

RAILWAY
STATION

on a footpath, following Sol-Cress Route No. 7; 40 metres later take the right fork heading downhill to reach and cross the stream in the valley bottom. There is no bridge at this point, but the stream should be easily fordable unless there has been heavy rain preceding the walk. Do not attempt to ford the water in the unlikely event of the river being in spate; in this case it will be necessary to return to Spa by one of the other numbered trails.

Turn left on the track on the opposite bank of the river (right leads to the Etang de Chawion - see Walk 36), rejoining the red and white markings indicating a GR route. After only about 80 metres take the track bearing to the right (GR 5 and Sol-Cress Route No. 7). Where this track swings to the left, leave the GR 5 by taking the path to the right which crosses the culvert. Continue on this pleasant path above the river, which is on your right, until reaching a stream at a Y-junction. Here take the right fork to cross the stream and head uphill towards the lookout post. Continue ahead on the widening track, crossing straight over at the next two cross-tracks. On reaching a T-junction (house to the left), turn right in the direction of Ligne, heading downhill. Bear right in front of the river in the valley bottom and in 50 metres cross a small footbridge over the stream. Climb the hill ahead, now heading in a southerly direction. At the

211

top of the ascent meet at a bend, and turn left along a country lane signposted to Arbespine and Tiege (Sol-Cress Route No. 3). Turn right at the next junction, still on a surfaced lane, with open fields to the left and a golf course to the right. Continue ahead to the main road, the Route de Balmoral.

Cross with care, turn left for 10 metres and then right on a path heading downhill towards the Lac de Warfaaz. The path soon swings to the left continuing its descent through attractive woodland following Sol-Cress Route No. 5. Note the château on the hill over to the right. Later on the descent be sure to take a thin path forking left, signposted as the Sentier de la Fourche, descending to the lake. On reaching the shoreline turn right on a surfaced drive which hugs the lakeside. A number of benches will be passed along the lakeside: here is a good spot for a picnic.

Turn right on the Avenue Amedée Hesse at the far end of the lake (note: those seeking refreshment should turn left here to continue around the lakeside to the second white building, which is a café). Leave this road within 80 metres by taking the path up to the right, which bends back to the right and climbs. When level with the white house on the lakeside, where paths fork, take the left branch uphill, but after 10 metres, at cross-tracks, turn left (Sol-Cress Route No. 5) on the Promenade H. Peltzer. Follow the path, also labelled as the GR V (573), gently uphill. Reach and cross a main road to rejoin the red/white waymarked path, still on the Promenade H. Peltzer. This is a most pleasant balcony path, following the line of the road below, heading back towards Spa. Continue ahead at a crossroads, still on the balcony path which is now called the Promenade Arago. Where the path ahead forks, take the left-hand, downhill path signposted to the Boulevard des Anglais (Route No. 1), leaving both the GR trail and the Sol-Cress Route No. 5 at this point. The path descends to the main road opposite a large supermarket on the outskirts of Spa. Turn right along the main road (footpath to its edge) to re-enter the town.

WALK 38:
The Promenade des Artistes & the Arboretum de Tahan

Description: This ramble, official Circuit No. 7, is, in the author's opinion, the best short walk from Spa. On its outward section it takes what is probably the most picturesque footpath in the district, the Promenade des Artistes, which follows a rocky, bouldery stream uphill, crossing the brook several times by means of a number of well-constructed footbridges. Secondly, the ramble provides an opportunity to visit the interesting and well-tended Arboretum de Tahanfagne, which contains a variety of tree species, both native and intro-duced to the Ardennes Hautes Fagnes region. Finally, the return to Spa is made along a superb, centuries-old trail, the Chemin d'Andrimont. So altogether an excellent walk, one of the finest in the Ardennes. A delight which should not be rushed.

Location: South-east of Spa.

Start/Finish: The tourist office in Place Royale in the centre of Spa.

Distance: 4.4 miles (7.0kms).

Time: Allow 2hrs 45mins.

Maps: The walkers' map at a scale of 1:20,000 entitled *La Carte du Promeneur*, sold at the tourist office in Spa.

IGN 1:50,000 series: sheet number 49.

Waymarking: The waymarking is generally clear throughout, by means of the yellow signboards familiar to all who walk in the environs of Spa. Follow Circuit No. 7.

Terrain: Footpaths, tracks and quiet country lanes.

Footwear: Boots are recommended to negotiate the rough stony paths.

Options: 1. Those wanting a short stroll, or who are less interested in the arboretum, may shorten the walk by turning right (to head south-west) when first reaching the Route des Fontaines. Walk along this road for 600 metres to the point where the lane from the arboretum (the Chemin de Tahanfagne) meets the Route des Fontaines. Turn right here to take the Coupe Feu du Thier de Statte, so rejoining the ramble for its final descent back into Spa.

2. Walkers wanting a full day's walk can combine this ramble with the longer Géronstère and the Hautes Fagnes (see Walk 39). This itinerary is particularly suitable for those based in Spa without their own transport, as it provides an interesting and picturesque route out of Spa to join the Géronstère circuit. On reaching the Route des Fontaines, after a visit to the arboretum, turn left along it for 250 metres to join the route of the Géronstère walk at point x: continue along the Route des Fontaines to reach the restaurant at the Font de la Géronstère, where Walk 39 actually begins. Follow the Géronstère circuit until point x is once more encountered: here turn right to walk the 250 metres back to the point where the present ramble was abandoned. Turn left here to resume the walk, descending back to Spa on the Coupe Feu du Thier de Statte. The total distance of this combined walk is 12.1 miles (19.5kms).

Place of
Interest: *The Arboretum de Tahanfagne*. Entry is free and the gate is usually left open for passing visitors. The trees are labelled with small plaques on which is printed the name of the tree species in French, the Latin name of the species, together with the country and region of origin. Visitors who require further information are advised to purchase the guide to the arboretum before undertaking the walk. Copies of the guide are available from the tourist office in the centre of Spa.

Refreshments: There is no possibility of obtaining refreshments en route,

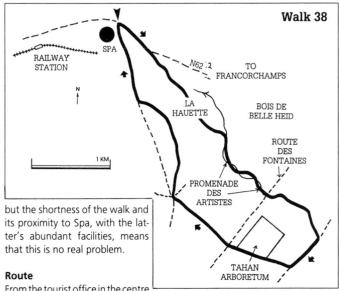

Walk 38

RAILWAY STATION

SPA

N62 : 2
TO FRANCORCHAMPS

LA HAUETTE

BOIS DE BELLE HEID

ROUTE DES FONTAINES

1 KM

PROMENADE DES ARTISTES

TAHAN ARBORETUM

but the shortness of the walk and its proximity to Spa, with the latter's abundant facilities, means that this is no real problem.

Route

From the tourist office in the centre of Spa head east along the Rue Royale, passing the baths and the casino, which are on your right. Begin the walk out of town on the N62, signposted to Malmédy, passing the Fontaine Monumentale des Arcades. The road soon begins its climb out of town. On reaching the sign for the Camping de la Havette, at a point where the remnants of an old railway bridge are still visible at the side of the road, turn right along a road which leads to a roundabout at the Square de la Resistance. Cross obliquely to the left to follow Rue Chelui. Fifty metres after the entrance to the campsite turn right at a yellow signboard indicating Trail No. 7 and the Chemin Havette. This lane climbs out of the town to reach the edge of the woods at a most attractive area by two wooden footbridges over a stream.

Ignore the yellow signboard for Trail No. 8, but follow the direction given for Trail No. 7, along the Promenade des Artistes to the right, a route which is accompanied by the red/white waymarkings of a GR trail. Do not cross either of the first two footbridges, but follow the red/white waymarks as they head uphill to the right of the streambed, through an area of trees and small boulders. When sunlight is streaming through the trees onto the jumble of rocks lining the babbling stream one can understand how this most picturesque trail achieved its name. The path crosses the stream at the third wooden footbridge, so that then one continues uphill but now following the right bank of the stream. There are occasional benches on which a rest can be taken whilst enjoying this most peaceful area. A fourth wooden bridge by a shelter and seat deposits the walker on the left bank of the stream once again. Continue the climb on the path. Three more well-constructed wooden footbridges are crossed before this delightful path comes to an end at the Route des Fontaines.

Cross straight over this road to cross another wooden footbridge and so reach the Promenade Dolez, a similar path to the Promenade des Artistes, still in beautiful surroundings. Follow this trail, still climbing with the stream and still following the red/white GR waymarks on the trees. Several more wooden footbridges and plankwalks lead the walker to a shelter known as Pouhon Delcor, at which is a pure water source. Continue past the shelter to reach a track T-junction. Turn right (south) along the Chemin des Sables, still following the GR trail, to reach a cross-tracks within about 300 metres. Turn right (south-west) here on the Chemin Forestière Nélis, a perfectly straight lane through the woods. At the next crossroads turn right onto the Route de Tahanfagne, signposted to the arboretum. On reaching the entrance to the latter walk through the gate into the arboretum - it is generally left open at all times (see "Place of Interest" above).

After enjoying a wander around the paths in the arboretum return to the gated entrance and descend the lane for 100 metres to reach the Route des Fontaines once again, at a point to the south-west of where the road was first crossed on the outward journey. Cross the road to descend on the Coupe Feu du Thier de Statte, a stony track, to Belleheid, a junction of roads and forest tracks. Turn right onto the Route de la Géronstère for 20 metres: ignore the first turning on the right, the Avenue Belheid (sic), but take the second turning on the right, the Vieux Chemin d'Andrimont, a descending grassy track between hedgerows and fences. Bear right on reaching a track junction, remaining on the signposted Chemin d'Andrimont, which now narrows to a footpath between old hedgerows. Eventually this path becomes a narrow surfaced lane which continues the descent towards Spa. Soon a lane T-junction is encountered. Turn left here downhill on the Chemin de la Roche to reach a second T-junction, this time with the Route de la Géronstère. Turn right downhill on this road to descend back into the centre of Spa. The road changes its name once it reaches the town to become the Rue du Waux-Hall. Follow this downhill to reach Spa's large church. Descend to the left of the church to reach Rue Royale, where you turn left to return to the tourist office where the walk began.

WALK 39:
Géronstère and the Hautes Fagnes

Description: A walk on the Hautes Fagnes (High Fen Country) to the south of Spa and a visit to the springs of Géronstère. Several of the tracks used on the walk were the ancient routes across this rather hostile landscape, used for many centuries before the modern road system was engineered. Two old crosses are encountered, both of which were important landmarks hereabouts in days gone by.

Location:　　　　La Géronstère, south of Spa.

Start/Finish:　　　　The car park outside the hotel-restaurant, the Source de la Géronstère, a few miles south of Spa. The easiest way to drive to here from Spa is as follows. Leave Spa heading east on the Francorchamps/Malmédy road. After about 2kms from the centre of Spa (ie. c500 metres after the large Camping des Sources campsite) turn right on the small road signposted to Géronstère. Drive along this straight lane for about 3kms to a T-junction where the large car park and hotel-restaurant is situated for the start of the walk.

Those without private transport can also tackle this walk by reaching the starting point on foot. This can be achieved by leaving Spa on the Route de la Géronstère. The starting point is reached after a walk of about 3.2kms, but note that there is a considerable ascent involved, and this route will have to be reversed at the end of the walk, making a total extra distance of over 6kms. A much better option for those without private transport is to combine this circuit with Walk 38 (for details see under "Option No. 2" of Walk 38).

Distance:　　　　7.5 miles (12.0kms).

Time:　　　　4hrs.

Maps:　　　　The walkers' map at a scale of 1:20,000 entitled *La Carte du Promeneur*, sold at the tourist office in Spa.

　　　　IGN 1:50,000 series: sheet number 49.

Waymarking:　　　　The walk follows the route of the official Circuit No. 10, waymarked on yellow signboards, bearing the number 10 within a brown box.

Terrain:　　　　Long promenades, fire breaks and forest tracks. High fen country which is often wet and muddy, and somewhat difficult underfoot in places. This is particularly so during the autumn, winter and spring along the section between the Bérinsenne and Pottier crosses. There is relatively little ascent and descent, unless the start and finish of the walk is made from Spa.

Options:　　　　The walk can also be commenced from the car park situated along the road to the south of the Font de la Géronstère, at the point where the Piste de Ski du Thier des Rexhons leaves it. This is a smaller car park than the one at the Source (or Font) de la Géronstère, but is an alternative if the latter, popular car park is full. The short but not particularly pleasant road walk would then be left to the end of the circuit, after first, no doubt, having secured refreshments at the Source de la Géronstère.

An optional there-and-back detour may be taken from the Ferme de Bérinsenne to a monument commemorating the role of the RAF in the Second World War. This walk along a signposted track to the Monument de la Royal Air Force is about 3kms in length, there and back (allow about an hour for the return journey which should provide a little time for contemplation at the monument).

Footwear: Bogtrotters or waterproof boots are recommended, unless the weather has been exceptionally dry.

Refreshments: These may be had at the hotel-restaurant Source de la Géronstère either before setting out on the walk or when returning to the car park at the end of the day.

Route

From the car park at the Source de la Géronstère head south along the road signposted to Coo. Ignore the left turn to Creppe, but look for a stone memorial on the left-hand side of the road opposite this junction. This monument, erected by the Touring Club of Belgium, is said to mark the limit of the German advance in the "Last Big Push" of the winter of 1944/45, but its siting here is somewhat controversial as the actual advance reached the hamlet of Borgoumont, 5kms further south. Continue ahead on the road signposted to Stavelot. About 250 metres after the Creppe turn-off, where the Stavelot road swings sharply to the left, turn right, through the car park (the alternative start for the walk), and

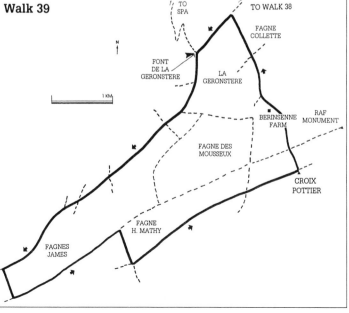

along the forest track signposted as the Piste de Ski du Thier des Rexhons.

The route passes through the Forêt de Plein Fays Les Aunais. Later ignore a track on the right, continuing ahead towards the Petite Vêquée on Route No. 10. On reaching open country, about 3kms after leaving the road, bear left with the main track signposted to Fagne James. Turn left at the next major crossing tracks (Route No. 10 to Fagne James). After about 1.5kms leave this wide forest track to take a signposted (Route No. 10) grassy track heading slightly uphill towards the Croix Jacques de Bérinsenne. This stone cross, dated 1696, is only about 3ft high, and is situated under high-tension electricity cables close to a pylon.

Turn left at the cross, following the line of pylons to the north-east. This is typical Hautes Fagnes country, rather marshy, and wet and muddy underfoot, particularly outside the relatively dry summer period. Progression along this track is likely to be rather slow. Follow the trail, always a little to the left of the line of overhead power cables, eventually crossing the Route de Bérinsenne (Berinzenne on the road sign here). Continue ahead, still following the power lines, along the old route of La Vêquée (Vecquee on a signpost here) until the prominent Croix Pottier is reached. The present cross, made of stone and about 12ft high, commemorates Maurice Pottier, a painter of this region. Next to this large cross is a smaller wooden cross, Poteau d'Andrimont, which itself replaces a much earlier cross which served as an important landmark before the modern road network was constructed across this wild, high fen country.

Turn left at the two crosses onto the SR 5, waymarked with red/white markers, following the sign for Spa. At a cross fire-break keep ahead on Route No. 10 (the ancient Chemin de Stavelot, the old road linking Spa to Stavelot), signposted to the Ferme de Bérinsenne, and 100 metres later also keep ahead, ignoring the left fork. The trail leads to the Ferme de Bérinsenne, where an optional detour may be taken, along the track to the right, to the Monument de la Royal Air Force (see "Options" above). Keep ahead at the farm buildings, still on Route No. 10, following the Route Forestière Nélis downhill. Where the gravel track swings to the left, keep ahead on a grassy track through the trees. Descend to a narrow surfaced forest road, the Chemin Forestière Nélis. Cross this to continue ahead on the Vieux Chemin d'Andrimont et Stavelot, descending gradually to reach the Route des Fontaines. Here turn left along this lane to return to the car park and restaurant at the Font de la Géronstère.

STAVELOT AND COO
General Information and Places of Interest
The town of Stavelot in the Amblève valley is famous both for its abbey and for its annual carnival, but it also happens to lie in some of the most delectable walking country in the whole of the Ardennes. The town has a long and rich history, going back to the 7th century when its abbey was founded by Saint

Remacle. The abbots of Stavelot Abbey were powerful local rulers from the 7th to the 18th centuries. Stavelot's history in the first half of the 20th century is the unhappiest of all, when it and the neighbouring region of Trois-Ponts were witness to some of the worst civilian atrocities in the Second World War, during the Battle of the Ardennes, just before Christmas, 1944.

There are few reminders today of this terrible period in Stavelot, a charming town (population 5000) of narrow winding streets filled with 18th century houses. The abbey buildings are extensive and house the town's three museums, which are all quite different in content and appeal. The Musée Régional d'Art Religieux et de l'Ancienne Abbaye contains a number of beautiful pieces of religious art dating from the 14th to the 18th centuries. Displays describe the story of the abbey from its beginnings to the present day. The museum is open from Easter to November, usually from 10am to 12.30pm and 2 to 5.30pm. In the abbey cellars is the Musée Circuit de Spa-Francorchamps, which has displays of motor cars describing the history of the famous 14km Belgian Grand Prix circuit, situated a few miles from here. Its opening dates and times are similar to those of the previous museum. Finally there is the Musée Guillaume Apollinaire devoted to the life and works of the Franco-Polish writer (1880-1918) who spent the summer of 1899 in Stavelot (open July and August only). It is possible to buy a combined ticket for all the abbey museums. The 18th century market square of the town is attractive (Walk 40) and the Eglise Saint-Sébastien has some richly decorated shrines.

The best time to visit Stavelot is for the weekend of the famous carnival. Held every year during the third weekend before Easter, the Laetare attracts many visitors from far and wide. The main procession is held on the Sunday when hundreds of participants wearing white cloaks, hoods and masks with long red noses, the Blancs Moussis, parade through the streets. There are floats and the whole place seems to go wild. The carnival has its origins many centuries ago: in 1499 the Abbot Guillaume de Manderscheidt issued an edict forbidding his monks from taking part in carnivals. The townsfolk of Stavelot poked fun at this pompous act by attending their carnival dressed as White Monks. The first Laetare took place in 1502 and since 1820 it has taken place annually (with the exception of the war years of this century). The Blancs Moussis now take part in carnivals abroad, in Germany and in France, so acting as ambassadors of Belgian culture and tradition. The author can thoroughly recommend a visit to the Laetare Carnival (don't wear your best clothes, and prepare to be battered by balloons and covered in great quantities of confetti - it is difficult to avoid spectator participation!).

The waterfall at Coo, a result of the labours of monks from Stavelot Abbey in the 18th century, is a popular tourist attraction. Unfortunately, apart from the falls there are rather too many other tourist trappings in this small village: cafés, snack bars and souvenir shops abound, and there is a mini-golf course, a *petit train touristique*, a chair lift, a game park (*parc à gibier*) and other "attractions" to lure the tourists away from the one thing that they have supposedly come to see: the most impressive waterfalls. It is possible to hire canoe-kayaks at Coo for use on the Amblève (descents of the river are possible to Cheneux, 9kms, and to Lorcé, 23kms).

The large village of Trois-Ponts to the south of Coo is situated at the point where the Amblève and the Salm valleys meet: head south up the Salm valley from here to cross into the Province of Luxembourg to reach Vielsalm (see the section on Vielsalm and the Salm valley).

Accommodation

There are at least a dozen hotels in Stavelot and the neighbouring towns and villages. These include in Stavelot the Hôtel du Mal-Aime, the Hôtel d'Orange, the Hôtel-Restaurant Le Relais, La Maison du Crouly, and the Hostellerie Le Val Amblève. The Vieux Moulin de Lodomez is 4kms from Stavelot on the road heading to Refat. In Coo there is the Auberge Le Vieux Sart, the Hôtel-Restaurant Le Baron and the Hôtel-Restaurant Val de la Cascade. Trois-Ponts has the Hostellerie Doux Repos and the Hôtel-Creperie des Trois Vallées. Finally, in the somewhat more distant Francorchamps will be found the Hôtel Beau Site, the Hôtel Belle Vue, the Hostellerie Le Roannay and the Hôtel Moderne. There are several private rooms, *chambres d'hôte* and the like, also available in the area. Contact the tourist offices in Stavelot (located in the abbey complex), Coo or Trois-Ponts (see Appendix 3) for further details and to place bookings. Note that if a hotel room is required during Stavelot Carnival (the third weekend before Easter) a booking will have to be made well in advance.

There are two campsites serving Stavelot: Camping de Charles (2kms from the centre) and Camping l'Eau Rouge. At Coo there is the Camping de la Cascade site, whilst nearer to Francorchamps is Camping Francopole. Just outside Trois-Ponts, at Basse-Bodeux, there are two campsites: L'Ancienne Barrière and Le Plein Sud.

Transport

The area is easily reached by train from Liège. Take a train, direction Luxembourg City, alighting at Trois-Ponts. A bus from here links the railway with Stavelot, a distance of about 4kms. Also, it is only a couple of kilometres from Trois-Ponts to Coo, a journey that can be made on foot or by bus.

The most direct route to Stavelot for motorists is via the E421 motorway (the A27) which leaves the E40 (A 3) motorway east of Liège. However, it should be realised that an important section of the E421 motorway has never been built, viz. the section between junctions 10 and 11. The motorway passes Verviers and then Spa, but shortly afterwards comes to an abrupt end. This is shown on some road maps, but not on others. It is then necessary to follow the roadsigns for the E421 and Stavelot carefully, through the motor racing circuit town of Francorchamps, a distance of about 7kms. Do not rejoin the motorway where it recommences, but instead follow the signs for the N68 to Stavelot. To reach Coo from Stavelot drive west along the N68 to Trois-Ponts and then north on the N633 to Coo. It has still not been decided whether the missing section of the motorway will ever be constructed, but in the meantime the only option is to follow the rather tedious, but well-signposted route via Francorchamps. The abrupt end of the motorway can come as rather a shock to the unprepared.

An alternative is to take the E25 motorway from Liège, leaving at junction 48 for the N66 which leads to Trois-Ponts. From here take the N68 east to Stavelot, or the N633 north to Coo. To reach Stavelot from Spa follow the N62 via Francorchamps.

The Official Walking Trails in the Region of Stavelot and Coo

There are 14 official walking trails in the area, mostly circular in nature. They are all clearly marked, as red continuous lines, on the 1:20,000 scale map entitled *Carte des Promenades de Stavelot (Stavelot et Coo)*, available from local tourist offices. They are identified and waymarked by a variety of symbols, particularly those representing a specific bird or animal:

Promenade du Lièvre - 13.5kms -	"hare"	waymark - S.
Promenade de la Croix-Collin - 13.0kms -	"Christian Cross"	waymark - S.
Promenade de la Truite - 12.0kms -	"trout"	waymark - S.
Promenade du Hibou - 8.5kms -	"owl"	waymark - S.
Promenade du Merle - 8.5kms -	"blackbird"	waymark - C.
Promenade du Cerf - 8.0kms -	"stag"	waymark - S.
Promenade du Faisan - 7.5kms -	"pheasant"	waymark - S.
Promenade de l'Ecureuil - 7.0kms -	"squirrel"	waymark - B.
Promenade de la Chauve-souris - 6.5kms -	"bat"	waymark - S.
Promenade du Loup - 6.5kms -	"wolf"	waymark - S.
Promenade du Point de Vue de Ster - 6.0kms -	"forest lookout post"	waymark - C.
Promenade de la Passerelle - 5.5kms -	"footbridge"	waymark - S.
Promenade du Magiru - 5.0kms -	"?"	waymark - S.
Promenade du Canard Colvert - 3.0kms -	"duck"	waymark - C.

S = start/finish point is the Parc de l'Abbaye in Stavelot
C = start/finish point is the church in Coo
B = start/finish point is the village of Beaufort east of Stavelot

Walks

Four walks are described from this centre, 2 from Stavelot and 2 from Coo. All of the main features of the area are covered in the 4 walks, from high heathland and forest to waterfalls and lakes, and there should even be time available to explore Stavelot itself.

WALK 40:
Stavelot, Amermont and Renardmont

Description: A circular walk to the north-west of Stavelot, mainly on tracks and footpaths, but also following the course of an old disused railway line for a considerable distance (the line has been lifted, but the resultant path is still lined with ballast). The circuit follows, in part, three of the waymarked local walks: the "stag" or "deer" trail, the "wolf" trail and the "bat" trail.

Location: To the north of Stavelot.

Start/Finish: The tourist office near the town hall in the centre of Stavelot.

Distance: 6.8 miles (11.0kms).

Time: Allow 4hrs 30mins.

Maps: The walkers' map, at a scale of 1:20,000, entitled *Carte des Promenades de Stavelot (Stavelot et Coo)*. Available from Stavelot Tourist Office.

     GN 1:50,000 series: sheet number 50.

Waymarking: Stavelot district has a unique system of waymarking its footpaths and walking trails: it uses a number of animal and other symbols. These appear, rather infrequently, painted on trees and fences, as a white symbol on a green background. They are easily missed, perhaps because the dark green paint used blends well into the background. It is also evident that, mainly due to tree felling, some of these waymarks are now missing. Symbols include fish, birds, various animals (squirrel, hare, wolf, bat, deer, etc), a cross and a footbridge.

Terrain: A disused railway line converted to a walking trail, fields, woods and heathland. A mixture of paths, forest tracks and quiet country lanes. There are some hills to contend with, but nothing too strenuous.

Footwear: The stony nature of some of the paths and tracks, and the fact that it can be wet underfoot at times, means that boots are recommended for this walk.

Options: Use could be made of the "deer" or the "wolf" waymarked trails to make an earlier return to Stavelot for those wanting a somewhat shorter walk than the one described below (these are both marked on the tourist office walkers's map of the area - see "*Maps*" above).

Places of Interest: This ramble is not a long one and so there should be time, either before or after the walk, to explore Stavelot, one of the more interesting towns in the Ardennes. See the introductory section on Stavelot for further details, and consult the tourist office in the town for more information.

Refreshments: There are no possibilities for obtaining refreshment en route,

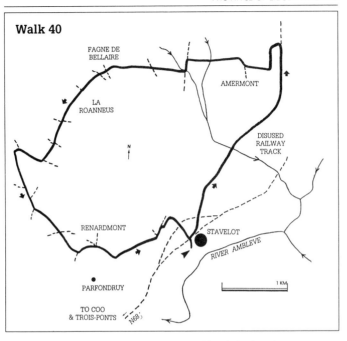

Walk 40

FAGNE DE
BELLAIRE

AMERMONT

LA
ROANNEUS

DISUSED
RAILWAY
TRACK

N

RENARDMONT

STAVELOT

RIVER AMBLEVE

PARFONDRUY

1 KM

TO COO
& TROIS-PONTS

N68

but Stavelot has shops, cafés, restaurants and hotels in abundance.

Route

From the tourist office in the centre of Stavelot locate the Avenue Ferdinand
Nicolay on the north side of the Parc de l'Abbaye. Leave this Avenue on the Rue
du Général Jacques to enter the Place Saint-Remacle. Leave this by the first
street on the right to reach a crucifix in a small square (Place Prume). Bear to
the left to walk along the street called Devant les Capucins. Cross the main road
ahead and continue uphill on the Route de Spa, so leaving the limits of Stavelot.
Cross over the railway line and then about 15 metres after the drive leading to
the Château des Montys, turn right along a narrow footpath enclosed by tall
hedgerows. This superb trail follows the route of an old disused railway line, as
will be evident from the considerable quantity of rock ballast underfoot.

Continue along the old trackway until reaching a barrier across it. Divert to
the right on a footpath at this point, pass a house, cross a road and rejoin the
disused railway. The old line passes through a rock cutting, and then, about a
kilometre after the road crossing, reaches a solitary house. Here we leave the
disused railway line by turning left in front of the house. Fifteen metres after the

house, at a Y-junction of footpaths, take the left-hand branch. This woodland path climbs and so swings to the left, thereby heading towards the south. The path leaves the wood, skirts the right-hand edge of a field, and arrives at a path junction by a field corner. Turn right here (west) along a stony/grassy path enclosed within wire fences. The views to the south, over the area covered by Walk 41, are extensive. The path becomes a track. Bear round to the left on this at a farm (ignore track on the right here) to reach a metalled lane. Turn right, uphill, along this road. At the top of the hill remain on this lane as it swings to the left behind a house and a farm. Later ignore a lane heading off to the right, but remain on the lane ahead towards the west to enter woodland.

Turn left on reaching a T-junction with the Stavelot to Francorchamps road, and follow the latter downhill for about 250 metres to a stony track on the right-hand side of the road. Follow this track, once again heading westwards. Later ignore a track off to the left, as our track climbs to reach a cross-tracks. Walk ahead here, now on a grassy footpath. Continue along this (it is perhaps somewhat indistinct in places, but with a little care no problems should be encountered) to reach a track T-junction within the forest. At this point the GR 5 (red/white waymarks) is encountered. Cross over the track and follow the footpath ahead (yellow paint stripes on trees) which within 120 metres reaches a ditch and cross-track. Turn right along this to pass a metal barrier and reach a metalled lane at a bend in the latter. Turn left along this road heading south-west.

After about a kilometre, at a point where this surfaced lane bends sharply to the left, continue ahead (south-west) on a stony track (ignore another track at this point which heads to the right). Continue to the next cross-tracks where there should be a small, plain wooden cross. Turn right along the track here, now heading west-north-west. After about 450 metres it is important not to miss a footpath that leaves this track on the left. It is marked by a "bat" trail symbol (white bat on a green background) painted on a tree on the left. This is a footpath, not a track (if you reach a track on the left then you have gone too far down the hill and will have to return to locate the start of the footpath). This footpath through the trees leads within about 100 metres to a path T-junction (another "bat" waymark). Turn left onto the path here, now heading towards the south. Follow this footpath as it leads to a solitary house and continue where it joins a narrow metalled lane. Continue ahead along this road for about 250 metres until you reach a crucifix on the left-hand side of the lane. Here turn left onto a grassy track, an excellent example of a green lane, lined with hedgerows. Descend on this track passing fields, now on the return route to Stavelot.

Cross straight over a metalled lane and 20 metres before the house ahead bear to the left down a grassy path with trees on your right and a field on your left. Descend to a second metalled lane. Turn left on this to cross a small bridge over a stream. Follow this lane to a crossroads where turn right along another lane (motor traffic prohibited *excepte circulation locale)*. Descend steeply on this lane, a splendid panorama of Stavelot soon coming into view. Continue the descent on this lane, ignoring side turnings, to reach the railway line. Cross this at the "crossing point", then bearing left with the lane to continue the descent into Stavelot. Swing round to the right near the bottom of the hill on the road called La Collerie, cross the main road ahead to take the cobbled road back into the Place Saint-Remacle. Descend ahead to cross the Rue du Général Jacques, pass through the Parc de l'Abbaye to return to Stavelot Tourist Office.

WALK 41:
Stavelot, the Magiru Stream and the Croix Collin

Description: A walk along the high-level heaths and forests to the south-west of Stavelot. The walk starts with the finest footpath in the Stavelot area, a steep, interesting climb beside a tumbling stream, which finishes with a visit to a memorial to the famous Belgian cyclist Eddy Merckx, a national hero who, among other victories, won the Tour de France on five occasions. Then a series of tracks and footpaths takes the walker across high-level heath and moorland to visit the old Croix Collin. A return is made primarily through woodland, before Stavelot is seen in panoramic view, spread out below in the valley of the Amblève. The route of the walk first follows a local trail up the Magiru (or Magéru) stream, then follows a section of the GR 5, before joining the Croix Collin local trail to reach the eponymous cross that lies to the south of the Bois de la Ronue Haie. The walk back to Stavelot follows the return leg of the Croix Collin waymarked trail. In good, clear conditions the views down to Stavelot and of the hills and valleys to the north and east are very fine indeed.

Location: To the south-east of Stavelot.

Start/Finish: The tourist office near the Hôtel de Ville in the centre of Stavelot.

Distance: 8.7 miles (14.0kms).

Time: Allow 6hrs.

Maps: The walkers' map, at a scale of 1:20,000, entitled *(Carte des Promenades de Stavelot et Coo)*. Available from Stavelot Tourist Office.
IGN 1:50,000 series: sheet numbers 50 and 56.

Waymarking: "Owl" waymarks accompany the early stages of the walk. The outward walk, from the farm known as La Bergerie until just before the Croix Collin, follows the red and white waymarkings of the GR 5. From the Croix de la Belle Femme, south-east of Stavelot, the "Christian Cross" waymark symbol is followed all the way back to Stavelot (sometimes a green cross on a white background and elsewhere a white cross on a green background). Yellow paint waymarks on rocks and trees are an aid to navigation in a few locations, as indicated in the text.

Terrain: A very steep but short path beside a stream, followed by high heathland and forest, on tracks, footpaths and quiet lanes.

Footwear: Because of the nature of the terrain, a steep rocky path that ascends close by a stream, followed by tracks across heathland that can be very muddy, boots are recommended.

Option: Those wanting only a short walk, but a beautiful and most interesting, albeit quite strenuous one, can easily return to Stavelot after ascending the footpath along the Magiru stream. The best way to do this is to take the lower of the two roads from the Eddy Merckx memorial, descending towards the north. About 50 metres after the memorial turn left onto a narrow path enclosed between trees. Follow the "owl" waymarks through this wood until you reach a road by a solitary house, from where there is a splendid panorama down to Stavelot. Turn left to descend back to the town. This walk is only a couple of kilometres in length, but it generally takes longer to complete than its distance might suggest. Strongly recommended.

Places of
Interest: Stavelot should certainly not be missed, although there may not be much time available after today's walk to do it justice.

Refreshments: There are no possibilities to buy refreshments en route, so as this is a long walk, it is advisable to take a picnic lunch and plenty to drink with you. Stavelot has, of course, a wide choice of cafés, restaurants and shops.

Route

Pass through the archway to the left of the entrance to the tourist office in the centre of Stavelot, and turn left down the Rue du Châtelet, bearing left at Place Wibald down the Rue Gustave Dewalque, to cross the bridge over the River Amblève. On the south bank of the river there is a junction of five roads. Take the second road on the right, signposted as the GR A, and with a white "owl" symbol on a green background. When the river comes into view down to your right, the GR A (red/white waymarks) leaves our route by descending towards the river on a track on the right. We, however, remain on the lane as it bends to the left to reach a bench in a small area recessed from the road and on the bank of a stream.

Locate a path (yellow paint marks on a boulder) just behind the bench. This path climbs on the right (north) bank of the stream. Follow this delightful path up amongst boulders and rocks, with the constant sound accompaniment of the stream descending the hill by a series of small cascades. This path has similarities with the Promenade des Artistes outside Spa (see Walk 38), but it is steeper, albeit shorter than the latter. There is an abundance of Fly Agaric and other fungi along this splendid trail during the autumn months. Follow the

Walk 41

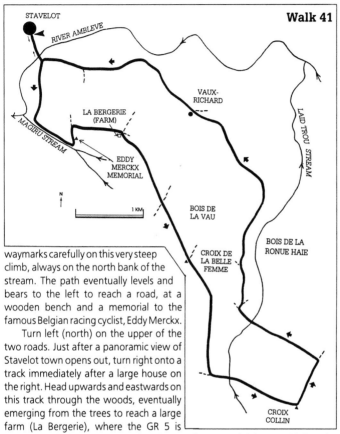

waymarks carefully on this very steep climb, always on the north bank of the stream. The path eventually levels and bears to the left to reach a road, at a wooden bench and a memorial to the famous Belgian racing cyclist, Eddy Merckx.

Turn left (north) on the upper of the two roads. Just after a panoramic view of Stavelot town opens out, turn right onto a track immediately after a large house on the right. Head upwards and eastwards on this track through the woods, eventually emerging from the trees to reach a large farm (La Bergerie), where the GR 5 is encountered. Those wanting only a short walk can turn left here and follow the GR 5 red and white waymarks back to Stavelot. However, for the complete walk turn right, passing between the farm and a house to bend left with the stony track, following the red/white GR 5 waymarks heading south-east. On reaching a cross-tracks continue straight ahead (red/white waymark), now on a sunken path beneath pine trees. This leads to the Croix de la Belle Femme at another cross-tracks. Continue ahead now following both the red and white waymarks of the GR 5 and a series of small wooden waymarks depicting a Christian cross (a green cross on a white background).

The trail becomes a footpath which crosses high-level heathland (it is 540m [1770ft] above sea level in this area). Continue ahead at the next cross-tracks, still heading south. Later, when the track bends to the right, leave it for a footpath on the left (waymarked with the cross symbol and with the GR red/ white marks). The next 100 metres (which can be very muddy after heavy rain) lead to a cross-tracks where our trail continues straight ahead (yellow paint marks on trees). On reaching the next track junction (the crossing point of five tracks) our trail (signposted with the cross symbol) turns left (east), by so doing leaving the GR 5 route which is on its way to Vielsalm. Remain on this main track, ignoring any side tracks, until an old, plain wooden cross is encountered on the left-hand side of the trail. This is the Croix Collin, after which the local trail waymarked with the cross symbol, and that which we are following for a large part of our walk, is named.

The Croix Collin is the point at which we begin our return journey to Stavelot, following the cross symbols all the way. Turn left and head north-north-east through an avenue of trees. At the next cross-tracks turn left, now heading north-west. The track descends out of the forest to cross a stream. About 250 metres after the stream, at a cross-tracks, turn right along a track with a wood to your right and a field to your left. In about 150 metres ignore a track off to the right as our trail swings to the left to head north. Ignore any side-turnings, passing through an area of woodland and then reaching a small clearing where the grassy track divides at a Y-junction. Take the right fork (cross symbol) continuing ahead through this large section of woodland. Walk straight ahead at the next cross-tracks where, once again, there should be a cross symbol waymark. The trail eventually becomes a path which skirts the edge of woodland and then follows a line of trees across a grassy field, from where there are expansive views of hills, woods and fields to the right (north-east). Pass through a (permitted) gap in the fence at the far side of the field to join a track. Turn right on this track and bear left with it after 10 metres, ignoring another track on the right. Our trail quickly becomes a path enclosed within hedgerows, then an enclosed track which descends to an elaborate war memorial. Continue past the memorial to reach a lane at a T-junction.

Turn right here, downhill into the village of Vaux-Richard, where you bear left again at a large wooden cross onto the road that passes through the village. Bear right at a Y-junction by a Virgin Mary and an old water fountain. Descend now towards the Amblève valley, with marvellous views ahead and to the right, of hills, woods and valley. On rounding a left-hand bend a panoramic view down to Stavelot unfolds. Continue along the lane to descend steeply into Stavelot, to reach once more the road bridge over the River Amblève. Cross this and retrace your outward steps back to the tourist office in the centre of Stavelot.

WALK 42:
The Falls of Coo, the Promenade du Point de Vue de Ster and Coo Reservoir

Description: This excursion is really two walks, each starting and finishing in Coo village. The first and major part of the walk is a circuit of the hills and woods to the east of Coo, visiting the villages of Ster and Biester and the Six Moines area, north of Trois-Ponts. The view of Coo and the Amblève valley is a particularly attractive one on the descent from Six Moines to Biester. The walk starts with a steep and fairly long climb up the hillside east of Coo to reach the *belvédère* above Coo and the Point du Vue de Ster. A return to Petit Coo is made along the wide River Amblève, after which those who wish to see the large artificial lake of Coo can follow the circular local walk known as the Promenade du Canard Colvert.

Location: Two circuits, the main one to the east of Coo and the Amblève valley, and the other to the west of Coo, within the "horseshoe" of Coo Reservoir.

Start/Finish: The Falls of Coo, situated between the adjacent villages of Grand Coo and Petit Coo, about 2.5 miles (4kms) due west of Stavelot. There is a large car park here at this popular tourist attraction.

Distance: 6.5 miles (10.5kms).

Time: For the complete walk allow 5hrs 30mins. 1hr - 1hr 30mins is sufficient for the circuit to Coo Lake (the second, and shorter, of the two circuits described).

Maps: The walkers' map, at a scale of 1:20,000, entitled *Carte des Promenades de Stavelot (Stavelot et Coo)*. Available from Stavelot Tourist Office.

IGN 1:50,000 series: sheet numbers 49 and 50.

Waymarking: The trails used in the walk are waymarked by various symbols (forest lookout tower, pheasant and duck) as indicated in the text.

Terrain: Steep wooded hillsides, villages, the wide Amblève valley, and finally the large, semi-circular Reservoir de Coo. After the steep, long and tiring climb from Coo, the gradients encountered are only moderate.

Footwear: There are two places on the walk where boots with a good grip would be invaluable: the steep climb at the start of the day, and for the return on the Promenade du Canard Colvert towards the end of the second circuit, where the path can sometimes be quite slippery.

Options: 1. It is not necessary to complete both of the circuits described below, although to do so would allow a full appreciation of the whole area. Either of the circuits taken alone would provide a good walk.

2. Those who wish to avoid the initial steep climb from Coo can take the chair-lift. The trail passes very close to the upper chair-lift station. The chair-lift operates from mid-March to mid-November, from 9am to 8pm.

Places of

Interest: The walk starts from the Falls of Coo, a large, wide and spectacular waterfall. If seen after heavy rain the waterfall is a huge raging, angry torrent. Apart from viewing the waterfall, a visit to the small church of Coo, a few metres from the falls, can also be recommended before setting out on the walk.

Refreshments: The many cafés, restaurants and open-air snack bars in the vicinity of the Coo Falls are there to meet the needs of the tourist trade, but the walker will find them equally useful. Note that refreshments are available nowhere else along the route.

Route

After viewing the waterfall leave the crowds behind by crossing the bridge above the falls and then bearing left on the road signposted to Liège. Fifty metres after the roadsign indicating the limit of the village of Coo, turn right up steps signposted as the Promenade du Point de Vue de Ster. The waymark symbol of a "forest lookout post" is given as your reference on this noticeboard. The way is also marked with the red and white marks of a GR trail. The path climbs the steep hill to the east of Coo by a series of zigzags. Follow the waymarks which show the forest lookout symbol in purple on a white background. There are benches on which to rest on the climb up this rock- and boulder-strewn hillside; you may well need them for it is a fairly strenuous climb. Keep to the zigzags on this ascent as signs of erosion are already much in evidence as a result of walkers short-cutting the path. The trail climbs to reach the chair-lift station, which, of course, could have provided the alternative means of attaining this high point above Coo.

Turn right just below the chair-lift station, following both the purple and the red/white waymarks, now contouring the hillside, and soon ignoring a track descending on the right. On reaching a cross-tracks turn left on a track for 5 metres and then be sure to take the footpath on the right climbing into the trees (purple waymark). About 60 metres later take the right fork at a path junction. The rocky path climbs amongst small boulders. More zigzags lead to a shelter with seats. This will be a welcome sight for most, a good place to rest after the not inconsiderable exertions of the ascent. The viewpoint would be far superior were it not for the trees that obscure the view; a wintertime visit is best, when the trees are devoid of leaves.

Pass to the right of the shelter and within 100 metres of it, after a short rise in the path, turn left off the purple and red/white waymarked path onto another less obvious path heading east through the wood. The tree-root strewn

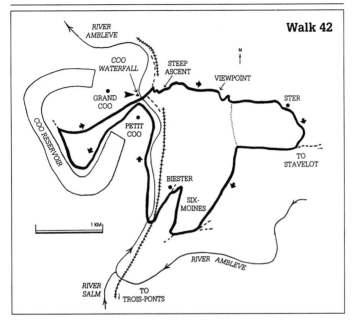

Walk 42

path (care is required in wet conditions) soon becomes clearer as it passes through a near tunnel of densely packed conifers. It swings to the right and then quickly to the left on emerging from these trees, and then passes between fields to become a track once more, still heading east through an avenue of trees. On reaching a track T-junction turn right to descend to the village of Ster.

Follow the lane as it bends to the left in the village and 25 metres later, at a bench and crucifix, turn right downhill. Pass farm buildings and continue, now on a track enclosed between wire fences. There are fine views of the valley and wooded ridges to the east. The track meanders and descends, now between hedgerows. Descend on this ancient track to reach a track junction. Here turn right, now heading west. On reaching a Y-junction by a seat, bear left to cross a metalled lane and continue ahead, still heading west on a stony/grassy track, with trees to the left and a field to the right. At the field corner, about 150 metres after the metalled lane, be sure to locate and follow a footpath on the left, heading downhill into the trees. At this point you are rejoining the red/white and the purple "forest lookout" waymarks.

Descend to a lane and turn right (south) along this, but after less than 100 metres bear left off the road onto an unsurfaced track, still following the two sets of waymarks. The track later rejoins the lane, the Chemin des Masures: bear left along it to continue the descent. The trail reaches a shelter with seats, at a T-junction. Cross the road to take the footpath ahead, signposted to the Croix des Six Moines. Descend on the main path, ignoring side-turnings, following the red/white and purple waymarks, to reach the crucifix (ie. the Croix des Six Moines) at a track junction, where there is a pair of seats. At this point leave the red/white waymarks, but follow the purple "forest lookout" waymark, down a track to the right, which is also signposted to Coo village. This track descends first towards the west and then swings to the right, as indicated by a purple waymark, to continue the descent, now heading north. Coo village and the wooded hills and ridges that surround it soon come into view, a really superb scene. The track snakes downhill to the hamlet of Biester.

Turn left on reaching the lane in the hamlet, to descend on it towards the south-west. Bear left on reaching a main road and pass under the railway line. Twenty-five metres later turn right to cross the bridge over the wide River Amblève. Twenty metres before reaching a junction with a lane on the left, turn left off the road onto a grassy track which doubles back towards the river. Cross a narrow footbridge and then bear left to follow the left bank of the River Amblève. Cross the grazing pasture (* - see note below) that lines the edge of the river, soon bearing to the left away from the river aiming for a telegraph pole in the field and at the far end of a line of tall conifers. Here locate a waymarked squeeze stile which gives access to a footpath enclosed between hedgerows. This path leads to a lane, the Chemin des Faravennes, which is followed ahead to reach Petit Coo.

It is possible, of course, to end the walk here, but those wishing to complete the whole itinerary should walk ahead, following the River Amblève to reach the bridge over the tributary of this river, about 40 metres before the falls. Do not cross this bridge, but rather turn left along the road immediately before it, following the tributary downstream on its left bank. Pass the information centre (where details of all the waymarked trails around Coo will be found) and later pass a wooden noticeboard that indicates that you are following the Promenade du Canard Colvert ("duck" waymarkings in white). Where the lane bends at right angles to the left, locate a path on the far side of the solitary building on your right. Follow this to climb a flight of steps which leads to the large retaining wall of Coo Reservoir.

Follow the track along the right (west) shore of the lake. The track soon becomes a path which passes between a wooded bank on the right and the lake on the left. On reaching a Y-junction of paths take the right fork uphill and continue ahead at a white waymark. The path begins to climb, at first gently and then quite steeply (care is required in wet or icy conditions when the path can be very slippery) to attain the wooded ridge above the reservoir. Turn sharp right (south-east) here to continue climbing on a track along the ridge. The trail levels, becomes a footpath, and soon begins its descent, which is slippery in places (be particularly on the lookout for wet, exposed tree roots which could cause a nasty slip). The path descends to meet a road opposite Coo cemetery. Turn right along this lane to return to Coo church and waterfalls.

* Note that there was a bull, with cows, in one of these fields when the author researched this route. If this is the case on your visit you may wish to be more prudent and return to Coo along the road.

WALK 43:
A Circuit of Coo Lakes

Description: The walk starts from Coo, about 2.5 miles (4kms) due west of Stavelot, which is well known not only for its waterfall, popular with tourists, but also for the huge semi-circular reservoir that surrounds the village, which itself is rather artificially divided into Grand and Petit Coo. The walk, to the west of Coo, encircles not only the main lake of Coo, but also the smaller but higher *Lac Supérieur* to the east of Coo Lake. There is considerable hydroelectric industry in the area which will be evident from the array of HT pylons visible on certain sections of the walk. There is considerable ascent and descent on the trail, although no undue difficulties are encountered until near the end of the walk, when there is a very steep descent to the shores of Coo Lake (there is an easier, albeit longer waymarked alternative for those who prefer to avoid this "sting in the tail" towards the end of the day). There are good views of the Amblève valley and surrounding hills whilst on sections of the walk, and in the latter stages Coo Lake is seen to good effect. Lovers of woodland walking will enjoy the sections through the Bois de Rahier and the Bois de Stalons.

Location: West of Coo village and north of Trois-Ponts, near to the point where the Salm and Amblève valleys meet.

Start/Finish: The large car park at the Falls of Coo, about 2.5 miles (4kms) due west of Stavelot.

Distance: 7.5 miles (12.1kms).

Time: Allow 5hrs 45mins.

Maps: The walkers' map, at a scale of 1:25,000, published by the tourist office of Trois-Ponts, entitled *Trois-Ponts en Ardenne - Promenades, Wandelingen*. The map is available from Trois-Ponts Tourist Office and also usually from the tourist office in Stavelot. This map covers the whole route of the walk.

    The eastern half of the circuit, east of the Lac Supérieur, is covered by the walkers' map, at a scale of 1:20,000, entitled *Carte des Promenades de Stavelot (Stavelot et Coo)*, the map used for the other walks in the Stavelot/Coo area.
               IGN 1:50,000 series: sheet number 49.

Waymarking: The walk uses part of the waymarked "Blackbird" trail on the outward and return sections (blackbird waymarking symbols), whilst in between it strays into the Trois-Ponts district, where the trails are marked with the letters of the alphabet (Trails B, C, E, etc) and carry yellow signposts and waymarks. The red and white waymarks of a GR trail are followed in places along the route as indicated in the text below.

Terrain: Woods, hills and two large artificial lakes. A generally hilly route, with one very steep descent at the end of the day (see "Special Problems" below).

Footwear: Most of the walk is along tracks and footpaths which can be muddy and wet after rain. Furthermore if the steep descent to Coo Lake at the end of the walk is to be attempted then boots with a good grip are definitely required.

Option: Those who finish this walk with time and energy to spare could combine it with a walk within the inner "horseshoe" of Coo Lake, viz, the Promenade du Canard Colvert, the second circuit described in Walk 42 above.

Places of Interest: See under "Places of Interest" for Walk 42.

Special Problems: There is a very steep, and rather slippery descent down to Coo Lake at the end of the day, on a footpath that can be rather difficult to follow and which is often somewhat overgrown. This can be avoided by taking a longer waymarked route towards the south, and so eventually back to the lake and Coo village, where indicated to do so in the text below. Any person unsure of tackling this steep descent is strongly advised to take the longer, easier route.

Refreshments: No establishments where refreshments can be purchased are passed en route, so take food and drink with you, although of course there will be adequate opportunity for refreshment of all kinds in Coo village at the start and end of the walk.

Route

From the Falls of Coo cross the smaller of the two bridges to enter Petit Coo. Follow the River Amblève up-stream to a large hotel where bear right with the road (ignoring the Chemin des Faravennes on the left) to reach the Chemin Sur Les Fosses, also on the left. Take this lane, following both red/white GR waymarks and local white waymarks depicting a blackbird. Climb on this lane to reach a main road, where there is a wooden signboard indicating the Promenade du Merle, waymarked with a blackbird symbol in red (*merle* is French for blackbird) and the Promenade des Papillons, waymarked with a butterfly symbol in yellow (*papillon* is French for butterfly). Cross the road and ascend ahead on the track, following the direction indicated for these two walks.

After a few hundred metres fork left following the waymarks climbing up

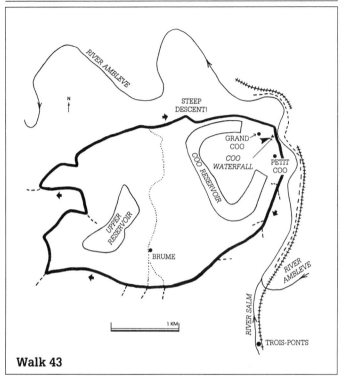

Walk 43

through the wood. Later at a Y-junction fork left again, to reach a signpost for Trois-Ponts and Brume. Here bear right (south-west) uphill on a muddy track, leaving the red/white waymarks of the GR trail at this point (they head for Trois-Ponts), but following the blackbird waymarks. Climb steeply to a Y-junction where the red (blackbird) and the yellow waymarks part company. We follow the red waymarks to the left, but after 25 metres we bear left again, uphill on another track. Climb to the top of the hill to reach a squeeze stile by a gate, which gives access to a grassy hilltop field. Follow the path ahead across this field. This path is rather indistinct, but if in any doubt aim for the small low building seen ahead (a small barn) and from there head for the corner of the wood ahead. Enter the wood and bear right at a junction of tracks by a seat, once more picking up the red/white waymarks of a GR trail, as well as continuing to follow the red blackbird waymarks.

Emerge from the woods, pass an electricity generating station and continue along the dirt road, following the line of HT cables, to reach a metalled lane by

235

a seat. Bear right here to reach a wooden cross and a bench at a Y-junction of lanes on the outskirts of Brume. At this point we part company with the "blackbird" trail (we will resume it later on the return to Coo) by turning left, following the red and white GR waymarks heading west, uphill, and following the line of HT cables. Continue ahead at the next cross-tracks, ignoring the waymarked trail (Trail B) to Trois-Ponts and later bear right (Trail B5) on reaching another electricity station at the top of the hill. Reach a T-junction about 300 metres farther on, and here bear left, still heading towards the west, now leaving the power lines behind, but still following the red/white GR waymarks. Continue ahead on the metalled lane, ignoring any tracks off to the right, until you reach a junction where a road bears to the left, signposted to Basse-Bodeux. There is a crucifix on the right at this junction. Turn right here on a track (Trail E), heading north-north-east through the forest, signposted to Monceau, and carrying the red/white GR waymarks.

Keep to the main track to descend to a cross-tracks where you turn right, still following the waymarked Trail E and the GR trail. Turn left on reaching a track T-junction opposite a tall perimeter fence. About 150 metres later leave the fence to descend on the track ahead. The track bends to the left, after which you ignore tracks off to the right and left at a staggered cross-tracks, but continue ahead towards the north-north-west, downhill on the GR waymarked trail. A few metres after the track swings to the left (west) leave the track by taking a footpath off to the right waymarked as Trail E and with the red/white waymarks of the GR trail. Descend on this path to meet a narrow surfaced lane at a T-junction. Turn right here, now on Trail E1, heading north-east.

There are good views of the Amblève valley and the hills and ridges to the north and west as the trail contours the hillside, soon becoming an unsurfaced track. Bear to the right on reaching farm buildings on a grassy track that soon becomes enclosed between tall hedgerows and leads to a track junction by a stream. Continue ahead here, uphill on the waymarked Trail E1. Keep to the main track as it climbs to meet and cross another track, holding a bearing of east-north-east. Climb through the forest on this track to reach a Y-junction. At this point the "blackbird" trail is rejoined (red and white blackbird waymark on tree). We now follow this trail back to Coo. Take the left fork at the Y-junction, heading east and downhill. Descend to reach a noticeboard which indicates that the "blackbird" and "butterfly" trails take a track on the right. However the "blackbird" trail has an alternative waymarked route which continues ahead.

We take this latter route, leaving the track after about 100 metres on a narrow footpath on the right, which begins just before the large pylon carrying HT cable. Within a few paces a glorious panorama opens out of the semi-circular Coo Lake a long way below. The path that follows is very steep, rather overgrown and slippery, particularly in wet or icy conditions. Hence care and concentration is required on the descent. Be particularly careful not to lose the path (if any member of the party experiences difficulties here then a return should be made to the noticeboard referred to above, from where the longer route which heads to the south should be taken to reach eventually the shore of the lake and so return to Coo). The trail descends very steeply through trees and bushes to reach a narrow lane. Turn left along this and in a few moments reach a bench from which there is a pleasant view of the lake. Rutting deer can be heard here in the autumn time, from animals in the surrounding forests, but also more likely from deer in the game park in nearby Coo. Continue along the lane, with the lake to your right, heading towards the dam. Do not cross the dam, but continue ahead down the lane to reach the bank of the River Amblève in Coo. Turn right to follow the river upstream so returning to the Falls of Coo.

Sunlight through the trees of the forest

Crags in the Hautes Fagnes, near Malédy

Cantons de l'Est

MALMEDY AND ENVIRONS

General Information and Places of Interest

Malmédy is a medium-sized town (population 10,000) situated at the confluence of the Rivers Warche and Warchenne, both of whose valleys feature in our walks. In all there are some 48 waymarked trails in this area, not counting the two long distance trails that pass through the Cantons de l'Est, the GR 5 and the GR E, so it is obvious that walking is a popular activity in the region. Above the town rises the extensive region of high heathland, bog and forest known as the Hautes Fagnes. The highest point in the Belgian Ardennes, and indeed in all Belgium, is to be found here, the Signal de Botrange, at 694m (2275ft) above sea level. Winters can be bleak up here, with considerable snowfall, making cross-country skiing a popular activity.

Malmédy suffered severe damage from Allied bombing during the Second World War, so that there is unfortunately little to see there except for the cathedral. This is dedicated to no less than three saints (Peter, Paul and Quirinus), the present building dating from the late 18th century. A succession of abbey churches stood on the site previously, Malmédy being as important an ecclesiastical centre as nearby Stavelot. Perhaps the most interesting items in the cathedral are the busts of four Roman soldiers, some very early Christian martyrs. Like Stavelot, Malmédy also has a famous carnival. The annual event, called the Cwarmê, is described in detail in Malmédy's Carnival Museum, open daily in July and August, at weekends throughout the year and during the Christmas and Easter holidays (afternoons only).

Robertville is smaller than Malmédy (population 5600) and, situated at a much higher altitude, is a good centre for walking (there is a small tourist office in the village where further information is available). Its two main attractions are the large and beautifully situated artificial lake, and the Castle of Reinhardstein. The latter, owned by the local Metternich family for three centuries, fell into ruin until it was beautifully restored in 1969. The castle is still inhabited, and although visiting times are somewhat restricted (open, afternoons only, in July and August on Tuesdays, Thursdays and weekends, and on Sundays and public holidays during the second half of June and the first half of September) a visit is well worthwhile. Beyond Robertville the road ascends further to reach the highest parts of the Hautes Fagnes. Here, 7kms north of Robertville on the road to Eupen, will be found the Botrange Nature Centre which houses permanent and temporary exhibitions on the surrounding Hautes Fagnes and Eifel regions. Nature films and a multi-vision slide show on the Hautes Fagnes can be seen at this centre, where there is also a cafeteria and picnic spot. The centre is open daily from 10am to 6pm.

Walkers who have use of a car, or who are prepared to walk a considerable distance from Robertville, might like to explore the wilds of the Hautes Fagnes on foot. Maps showing the walking trails in the Hautes Fagnes are available locally (there is a choice of a 1:25,000 scale map of the Hautes Fagnes published by IGN, and a 1:20,000 scale map produced by Les Amis de la Fagnes, A.S.B.L.).

Accommodation

There is no shortage of hotels in the Malmédy district, the local tourist authority boasting that there are 1800 hotel beds available in Malmédy and the surrounding towns and villages. Hotels in Malmédy include the Hôtel-Restaurant Albert 1, the Auberge de la Fagne, Hôtel au Sorbier, Hôtel au St-Esprit, Hôtel Camarine, Hôtel La Forge, Hôtel Le Floreal, Hôtel de Spa, the Hôtel du Tchession and Willem's Hôtel. A few kilometres from the town, on the GR 5, the Hôtel-Restaurant Ferme Libert can be recommended (excellent food). In addition there are 400 beds available in private rooms in the area. The tourist office in Malmédy can supply further details and book accommodation on your behalf if required. The town of Malmédy itself obviously has the widest selection of hotels, but both Robertville (Walk 46 - Hôtel Auberge du Lac, Auberge Au Vieux Hetre, Hôtel International, Hôtel La Frequence, Relais de Poste, Hôtel Residence du Lac) and Waimes (Walks 47 and 48 - Auberge de la Warchenne, Hôtel Cyrano, Hôtel des Bains, Hôtel-Restaurant Hotleu) have several hotels. There are also hotels in several of the smaller villages passed en route on some of our walks, eg. at Ligneuville (Walk 44) and at Géromont (Walk 45).

Youth hostellers will be pleased to discover that there is a youth hostel in Malmédy (see Appendix 4).

Campsites are plentiful in the Canton. Just outside Malmédy there are two sites, Camping du Moulin and Camping Familial. At Robertville there is Camping de la Plage (highly recommended), Camping du Lac and Camping Les Charmilles. Waimes also has two campsites nearby, Camping Anderegg and Camping Belle-Vue.

Transport

The best way to reach Malmédy by public transport is first to take the train from Liège to Spa (see "Transport" in the section on Spa) and then take a bus on to Malmédy. Buses are reasonably frequent between these two major towns. Alternatively take the train from Liège to Verviers, from where a bus may be taken to Malmédy. A bus service also operates between Stavelot and Malmédy. Local buses run between Malmédy and Waimes and between Malmédy and Robertville (consult the tourist office in Malmédy for up-to-date details of services).

The main access for the motorist is via the E421 (A27) motorway, but note that this ends abruptly at junction 10 (see the note under "Transport" in the section on Stavelot and Coo). The route is essentially as described for Stavelot, via Francorchamps, but at the point where the motorway is about to recommence, turn left to follow the N 62 to Malmédy. Waimes is reached from Malmédy by leaving the town on the N62 and later taking the N632 to Waimes. Robertville is connected to Malmédy by the N681 which climbs steeply to reach the village.

Official Walking Trails in the Region of Malmédy, Waimes and Ligneuville
Forty-eight circular walking trails are to be found in this region. They are all clearly marked, as red continuous lines, on the 1:50,000 scale map entitled *Promenades : Malmédy-Waimes*, available from local tourist offices. They are classified as woodland or forest walks (Type W), country walks (Type C) and riverside walks (Type R).

They are identified by a letter of the alphabet (usually signifying the start/ end points) followed by a number:

F2 Faymonville - Wegifat - Bouhémont - Faymonville: 5kms,   Type C.
F3 Faymonville - Mon Antône - Sur l'Ak - Faymonville: 5kms,   Type C.
F4 Faymonville - Bouhaye - Stephanshof - Crope - Faymonville: 7kms,   Type C.
F5 Faymonville - Sur l'Ak - Schoppen - Stephanshof - Faymonville: 9kms,

           Type C.
L1 Ligneuville - À la Haye - Ligneuville: 4.2kms,   Type C and Type W.
L2 Ligneuville - Houyire - Baugnez - Hedomont - Lamonriville -
   Ligneuville: 9.5kms,   Type C and Type W.
L3 Ligneuville - Reculémont - Pont - Ligneuville: 5kms,   Type C and Type R.
L4 Ligneuville - Pont - Val de Roba - Ligneuville: 5kms,   Type C and Type R.
L5 Ligneuville - Roba - Wolfsbusch - Ligneuville: 10kms,   Type C and Type W.
L6 Ligneuville - Vallée de l'Amblève - Ligneuville: 8kms,

       Type C, Type W and Type R.
L7 Pont - Bois Magis - Pont: 5.2kms,   Type C, Type W and Type R.
L8 Bellevaux - Lasnenville - Planche - Bellevaux: 5kms,   Type C.
L9 Bellevaux - Lamonriville - Floriheid - Hurdebise - Bellevaux: 10kms,

          Type C and Type W.
L10 Bellevaux - Cligneval - Rocher de Falize - Rocher de Warche - Bellevaux: 10kms,
       Type C, Type W and Type R.
M1 Malmédy - Chôdes - Vallée de la Warche - Lac de Robertville: 10kms,

          Type W and Type R.
M2 Malmédy - Ferme Libert - Trô Marets - Bernister - Malmédy: 13kms,   Type C.
M3 Malmédy - Gohimont - Géromont - Arimont - Malmédy: 10kms,

          Type C and Type R.
M4 Malmédy - Ligneuville - Pont - Lamonriville - Préai - Malmédy: 17kms,

           Type C.
M5 Malmédy - Otaimont - Falize - Cligneval - Préai - Malmédy: 12.5kms,   Type C.
M6 Vallée du Bayehon - Baraque Michel: 10kms,   Type W and Type R.
M7 Ferme des Bruyères - Rocher de Falize - Rive Gauche de la Warche -
   Ferme des Bruyères: 2kms,   Type W and Type R.

| M8 | Xhoffraix - Vallée de la Warche - Vallée du Bayehon-Hargister - Trois Hêtres - Xhoffraix: 14kms, | Type W and Type R. |

M8 Xhoffraix - Vallée de la Warche - Vallée du Bayehon-Hargister -
   Trois Hêtres - Xhoffraix: 14kms,   Type W and Type R.
R1 Robertville - Bains: 1km,   Type C.
R2 Robertville - Gonayheid - Bains: 2kms,   Type C and Type R.
R3 Robertville - Pont - Airheid - Walk - Barrage - Robertville: 6kms,
        Type C, Type W and Type R.
R4 Barrage - Vallée de la Warche - Walk - Barrage: 6kms,
        Type C, Type W and Type R.
R5 Robertville - Noirthier - Outrewarche - Robertville: 6kms,   Type C.
R7 Robertville - Sacre-Coeur - Cheneux - Ovifat - Robertville: 6kms,   Type C.
R8 Robertville - Sacre-Coeur - Cheneux - Carrières - Reinhardstein -
   Robertville: 8kms,   Type C, Type W and Type R.
R9 Barrage - Reinhardstein - Warche - Bayehon - Moulin - Ovifat - Barrage:
   10kms,   Type C, Type W and Type R.
R10 Barrage - Nez de Napoléon - Chemin des Chevaliers - Warche -
   Reinhardstein - Barrage: 10kms,   Type W and Type R.
R11 Ovifat - Pont de Bayehon - Cascade - Longfaye - Ovifat: 12kms,
        Type C, Type W and Type R.
R12 Ovifat - Piste de Ski - Fagne - Botrange: 7kms,   Type C and Type W.
R14 Robertville - Ovifat via the Chemin des Haies: 6kms,   Type C.
S1 Sourbrodt - Bosfagne - Petite Roer - Bosfagne - Sourbrodt: 5kms,
        Type C, Type W and Type R.
S2 Sourbrodt - Les Censes - Noirthier - Sourbrodt-Gare - Sourbrodt: 7kms,
        Type C.
W1 Waimes - Fayai - Moulin - Waimes: 2kms,   Type C.
W2 Waimes - Libomont - Espérance - Boussîre - Trô des Poyes - Waimes: 8kms,
        Type C, Type W and Type R.
W3 Waimes - Chivremont - Grosbois - Rue - Waimes: 7kms,   Type C, and Type W.
W4 Waimes - Remacreux - Grosbois - Rue - Waimes: 6kms,   Type C.
W5 Waimes - Faymonville - Rtier - Belair - Thioux - Bouhémont - Waimes:
   8kms,   Type C.
W6 Champagne - Pont de Lanonweye - Outrewarche - Champagne: 6kms, Type C.
W7 Champagne - Camping Bellevue - Pont de Haelen - Barrage - Walk -
   Airheid - Champagne: 9kms,   Type C, Type W and Type R.
W8 Bruyères - Hokgniez - Agister - Morfat - Bruyères: 8kms,   Type C and Type W.
W9 Thirimont - Hauts Sarts - Thirimont: 8kms,   Type W.
W10 Ondenval - Crope - Bouhaye - Steinbach - Remonval - Ondenval:
   7kms,   Type C.
W11 Ondenval - Rurbusch - Croix de Sarts - Wolfsbusch - Faye - Ondenval:
   10kms,   Type C, Type W and Type R.
W12 Ondenval - Faye - Ondenval: 3kms,   Type C and Type R.

Walks

Five walks are described for this region, two from Malmédy itself, one from the higher village of Robertville to the north-east of Malmédy, and two from Waimes, a small town to the east of Malmédy. There is considerable variety in the five walks.

WALK 44:
Malmédy and Ligneuville

Description: A walk mainly on quiet and narrow country lanes, visiting a number of attractive villages and farming hamlets south of Malmédy. Much of the ramble is in open country, but there are some sections which follow tracks and paths through woodland. The circular route uses part of the M4 (Malmédy Trail No. 4), L4 (Ligneuville Trail No. 4) and also follows a considerable length of the GR E long distance trail. The walk visits the charming upper valley of the Amblève, a river which rises in the hills to the north-east of Ligneuville, a pleasant village with a most attractive church situated at its heart.

Location: To the south of Malmédy.

Start/Finish: Place Albert 1 in the centre of Malmédy.

Distance: 11.8 miles (19.0kms).

Time: Allow 6hrs.

Maps: The map at a scale of 1:25,000 entitled *Promenades Malmédy - Waimes* available from local tourist offices.
       IGN 1:50,000 series: sheet number 50.

Waymarking: Waymarking of the route is generally good.
Note that the waymarking system in the Malmédy/Ligneuville/Waimes/ Robertville area is unique to that region. The trails have each been assigned a letter of the alphabet followed by a number. Six alphabetical letters are used, each standing for one of the principal towns or villages in the area, viz. M = Malmédy, L = Ligneuville, W = Waimes, R = Robertville, F = Faymonville, S = Sourbrodt. The present walk follows M and L waymarked trails (Malmédy district and Ligneuville district walks). The waymarking of the Malmédy (M), Ligneuville (L), and Robertville (R) walks is generally of a reliable standard (the trails, eg. M2, L3, R4, etc, are marked with yellow paint).

Terrain: A good mixture of gentle hills, woodland, open countryside, rivers, valleys, villages and hamlets.

Footwear: As much of the walk follows surfaced lanes and tracks, many walkers would find that good quality trainers or stout shoes are adequate, except during wet weather or after a period of persistent rainfall.

Option: The walk can be shortened by 2 - 3 miles by omitting the village of Pont and the Rôbe valley. This is achieved by taking a short cut along the GR E to Ligneuville, soon after passing the village of Lamonriville (details of this short cut are given in the route description below - see the two asterisks [*] in the text).

Refreshments: Refreshments are available at Ligneuville, which is conveniently situated just over the halfway stage of the walk. There are shops here and the trail passes the Hôtel du Moulin, which is also a restaurant open to non-residents. Malmédy, where the walk starts and finishes, has numerous cafés, restaurants and shops.

Route

From the east side of Place Albert 1 in the centre of Malmédy, locate the narrow Ruelle des Capucins. Follow this narrow passage heading south to pass the Academie de Musique and cross a footbridge. Turn right at the T-junction on the Rue Abbé Peters to reach a large stone crucifix on the left. Turn left here following the sign on a lamppost for the M4 and the M5 (rural walks, not motorways!). Bear to the right at the Place du Parc following the red/white waymarks of the GR E. Pass under a railway bridge to turn left, and then turn right in 25 metres, following the sign to the gendarmerie. Pass the latter and begin a steep climb out of Malmédy on the Route de St Vith heading southwards (use the footpath along the bank to the left of the road - a bench with a view over the town will be found along here).

At a right-hand bend in the lane locate a footpath which leaves the road on its left-hand side to climb at the far side of a house, bending to the right to continue the climb, following signs M and L painted in yellow and the red/white waymarks of the GR trail. Bear right onto the lane reached at the top of the ascent. Remain on this lane until reaching another more minor road on the right at the far side of a house (point "x" - see text below). Turn right here (waymarks M4, L and red/white of the GR E), bearing to the left with it in about 100 metres (ignore trail off to the right here). Continue ahead on this pleasant narrow lane to a crossroads. Here the M5 route takes the right fork, but we continue ahead on the M4, L9 and GR E trails, still on a narrow peaceful lane, the surface of which gradually deteriorates until it becomes a stony track which descends into woodland. On reaching a field on the left-hand side be sure to take the left fork at a path junction, following the red/white waymarkings. A hundred and fifty metres or so after this junction ignore the M4 trail which takes a path on the left, but continue ahead on the L9 and GR E. This is a most attractive woodland path.

On leaving the woods the trail continues ahead on a track to cross a stream by a culvert and continues ahead towards the farm buildings, soon reaching a metalled lane on a bend in the latter: bear to the left uphill and in 100 metres or thereabouts, when the lane bends to the left, bear right continuing the

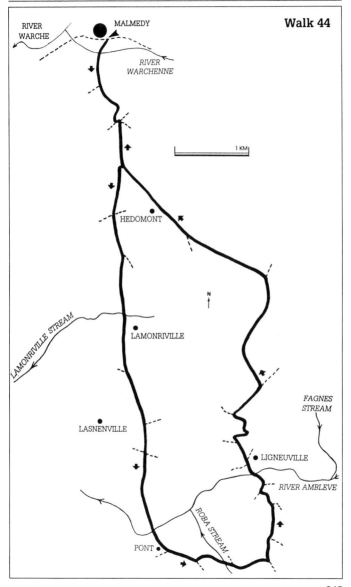

Walk 44

RIVER
WARCHE

MALMEDY

*RIVER
WARCHENNE*

1 KM

HEDOMONT

N

LAMONRIVILLE STREAM

LAMONRIVILLE

LASNENVILLE

FAGNES
STREAM

LIGNEUVILLE

RIVER AMBLEVE

ROBA STREAM

PONT

ascent past the houses of the hamlet of Lamonriville. Remain on this lane when it levels out, still heading south on the GR E, later ignoring the L9 route which turns off to the right on a stony track. At the next staggered road/track junction the GR E branches off to the left to take a more direct route to Ligneuville (this can be taken by those who wish to shorten this walk - continue with the text at * below).

Our route continues ahead along the lane heading south. On reaching a T-junction (signpost to Bellevaux to the right) turn left for 5 metres and then right along the lane signposted to Pont, following the M4 and L3 trails. Continue ahead on the lane at the top of a rise by a seat and a track crossing point. Descend on the lane towards Pont, the impressive motorway bridge which spans the valley ahead soon coming into view. The lane enters the outskirts of Pont and becomes the Thier de la Principaute. Descend steeply on the lane ignoring the L3 route which turns off to the left 100 metres or so before the bottom of the hill, at this point picking up the red/white waymarks of the GR trail once again. Bear left at the bottom of the hill to cross the River Amblève on the road bridge.

Remain on this lane, the Thier d'Amblève, as it bears to the left, but a few metres after doing so take the right fork signposted as the L4 trail. Climb to a crossroads at a small war memorial and follow the Route Saint Donat ahead, signposted to the chapel dating from 1752. After a visit to the chapel (good stained glass windows, but alas it is often locked) continue ahead uphill on the lane following the L4 and L 7 trails (but leaving the red/white waymarks at this point). At the top of the hill turn left onto the Route du Rôba, following the L4, but leaving the L7 at this point. Descend into the Val du Rôba, cross the stream (the Rôba) at its bottom, and continue to the road. Turn right along this for 100 metres to turn left in front of a large commercial building, as indicated for the L4 and L5. Climb the hill to reach a lane T-junction. Turn left here on the L4 trail (the L5 leaves us here by turning to the right). After a further, more gentle ascent, the trail reaches another T-junction by farm buildings. The return loop of the L5 rejoins us at this point. Turn left on the Vers La Croix lane heading downhill towards the north into Ligneuville. Descend on the Rue Saint-Clair, bending to the right at a water trough, following the L5 waymarks and continuing the descent. Later ignore the L1 and L6 routes, which head off to the right along the Route de Montenau, but continue the descent, now on the Rue W. Egan. On reaching the river (the Amblève again) turn right across the road to walk along the High Street of Ligneuville.

Ignore the left turn onto the Rue de la Laiterie opposite the attractive village church, in front of the Hôtel du Moulin (it is also a restaurant), but continue along the road for a further 50 metres to reach a pair of war memorials. Turn left between these memorials on the lane named as La Coulee, following the waymarks for the L3 and M4 trails and the GR E, direction Malmédy. Climb the hill, later ignoring Chemin Thomas on the left, but follow the waymarks ahead to reach a junction (* - see the short cut mentioned in the text above) between the GR E and the L2, L3 and L4 trails. We turn right (east) to take the latter route. On reaching farm buildings turn very sharply to the left on the Route Napoleon. Climb on this lane as it bends first to the right and then to the left to reach a junction of trails. L2 and L3 continue ahead but we take trail M4, which follows Route Napoleon to the right. This straight lane passes a bench and reaches the edge of woodland. Here take the M4 which leaves the Route Napoleon by turning left onto a stony track entering the wood. Take the right fork at a track Y-junction 10 metres later. Cross two open clearings (good views to the left) and re-enter the wood, this time for just over a kilometre to reach its northern edge.

Bear left (M4 waymark) at a track T-junction near the edge of the woods, and a few hundred metres later, just after a right bend in the track, turn left onto a narrow path (the M4) which skirts the very edge of the woods. The path becomes a grassy track within a few hundred metres, and this continues ahead, leaving the wood as it heads west-north-west, now enclosed between fences. Grass soon gives way to a poor surface as the narrow track descends gently, heading towards the buildings of the village of Hedomont seen ahead. Bear left on reaching a road at a T-junction, and right at a second T-junction, following the signposted direction towards Malmédy to enter the village of Hedomont. Walk through the village and remain on the lane ahead as it descends to pass point x (see text above). Reverse the route taken on the outward journey, following M4 waymarks, to return to Place Albert 1 in the centre of Malmédy, a distance from point x of about 1.2 miles (2kms).

WALK 45:
Malmédy, Géromont and Arimont

Description: This circuit is one of the finest walks from Malmédy. It follows a series of footpaths, tracks and lanes to the south-east and east of the town. The homeward section along the Warchenne valley is particularly attractive. The route uses the local M3 waymarked trail, as well as a considerable section of the GR E long distance path.

Location: To the east of Malmédy.

Start/Finish: Place Albert 1 in the centre of Malmédy.

Distance: 6.2 miles (10.0kms).

Time: Allow 3hrs 15mins.

Maps: The map at a scale of 1:25,000 entitled *Promenades Malmédy - Waimes* available from local tourist offices.

IGN 1:50,000 series: sheet number 50.

Waymarking: Follow the M4 waymarks on trees, fence posts, etc. Once the railway line is encountered in the Warchenne valley our route is also waymarked with the red/white paint markings of the GR E. See also the general note on waymarking in this region under "Waymarking" for Walk 44.

Terrain:　　Woods, a series of villages, and the prominent valley of the River Warchenne.

Footwear:　　Boots are recommended for this route, although trainers or stout shoes may be acceptable if conditions underfoot are very dry.

Option:　　The circuit, at its far eastern point, where it first meets the railway line in the Warchenne valley is only 100 metres or so west of the route of Walk 48, near the Trô des Poyes. It is thus possible for those wanting a full day out to combine these two walks, to form a circuit between the two principal towns in the region, Malmédy and Waimes. This would create a figure-of-eight walk of approximately 11.4 miles (18.3kms) in length.

*Places of
Interest:*　　As the walk is not a particularly long one there is ample time in a day's visit to explore the town and cathedral of Malmédy (see the introductory section on Malmédy for further details, and consult the tourist office for more information).

Refreshments:　　These are available at the village of Géromont (hôtel-restaurant) and at the Val d'Arimont establishment passed en route by the River Warchenne (restaurant and bar). There is also a small bar where the railway line and the GR E are both first encountered, where the trail begins its homeward journey back along the Warchenne valley.

Route

Leave the Place Albert 1 in the centre of Malmédy by walking eastwards along the Rue du Commerce. Bear right at the Place du Commerce and right again on rejoining the two-way traffic. Head out of Malmédy at the road signposted to St Vith and Luxembourg, but only 50 metres after the traffic lights turn right on a minor road signposted to the Institut Notre-Dame (Trail M3). Bear right to cross the old railway line and then bear left (ignoring the first, sharper turn to the left) on a lane which begins to climb rather steeply out of the town. About 80 metres after the roadsign which indicates the limit of Malmédy turn left off the road, at a point where it bends to the right, onto a surfaced lane signposted to Socoma (M3). After passing a small car park on the left the lane becomes a stony track which soon narrows to become a footpath enclosed between hedgerows. This leads to a narrow lane by a seat and a most unusual pair of trees, two of whose branches are fused together to form an archway.

Turn right onto the lane and in 80 metres bear left at a fork in the road. Descend to farm buildings, after which the lane reverts to a stony/grassy track. The trail gradually ascends through thin strips of woodland. Take particular care not to miss a path on the left that eventually leaves this track: it is waymarked

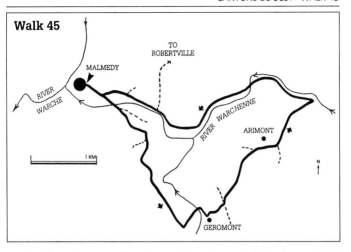

M3 (in yellow paint, as usual) and passes through a gap in the hedge on the left of the track. The path, which heads north-north-east, is narrow and is enclosed by wire fences as it passes to the right of grazing pasture. It leads to a group of buildings on a narrow lane. Turn right here to walk uphill. Bear left at the junction near the top of the hill onto the Chemin des Poumreux, and follow this lane to reach the church with the rather unusual tower and the main road at Géromont, opposite a hotel-restaurant.

Turn left along the main road for 30 metres to turn right off it onto a drive at the far side of the hotel-restaurant. Descend past a scattering of houses to locate an M3 waymarked footpath which begins at the side of a house. This footpath, enclosed between low wire fences, descends to cross a stream and then reascends steeply to become a narrow surfaced track. Bear to the left on reaching a lane junction, to walk along the Chemin de la Terre d'Aneu, so entering the village of Arimont.

Turn right on reaching a T-junction in the village, walking in the direction of Camping Familial. Ignore the Chemin du Château on the left, but continue up the hill. However, before reaching the top of the hill turn left along the Chemin du Val. Later ignore the Rue des Bruyères on the right, but continue ahead in the direction of the Val d'Arimont restaurant and sporting complex, still on the Chemin du Val. The lane descends into the valley bottom to cross an old railway line in front of a pond and bar (refreshments), at which point the trail joins the GR E which has come in from the east. This GR trail, with its red and white waymarkings, is now followed back all the way into Malmédy.

Cross the railway line and immediately turn left along the lane at its far side. The lane crosses back over the railway line and continues its gentle descent. A few metres before the sign for the Val d'Arimont Hôtel-restaurant-bar bear left off the lane onto a woodland path which runs beside a babbling brook. This is, in fact, the River Warchenne. In a few hundred metres be sure to take the right waymarked branch when the path forks. This path keeps alongside the river, but a little above it. The path later leaves the river to pass beneath a canopy of trees. The path reaches the railway line again. Do not cross it this time, but follow the line for 20 metres before bearing left on a path (M3 and red/white waymarks) which leads to the river. Cross the river by means of the wooden footbridge (there is a bench here, a pleasant spot to relax for a while).

The path continues now along the right bank of the river, following the latter on its journey downstream. Meet the railway line yet again and this time cross it, continuing ahead on the path to the left of the woods. Later ignore a path off to the right into the woods, continuing on the path with fields to the left. This very pleasant path finally becomes a narrow surfaced lane as it nears the main road. Continue ahead downhill at a point where another lane joins from the right near a house. Descend beneath an avenue of tall old trees which have an interesting array of exposed roots. This quite fascinating lane sinks beneath a bank of old trees and shattered crags to reach the road that links Malmédy with Robertville. Forty metres before reaching this road do not cross over the stone bridge on the left, but locate a narrow footpath on the far side of it. This path leads down to the right bank of the river which it follows to emerge on the Malmédy/Robertville road. Bear left along this road to head back into Malmédy. Cross the Warchenne for the last time and turn right at the traffic lights ahead to return to Place Albert 1 in the centre of Malmédy.

WALK 46:
Robertville and the Vallée de Bayehon

Description: A very fine circuit which visits the large Lac de Robertville and later follows the dramatic gorge of the Vallée de Bayehon, the route including some of the finest walking available in the area. The trail also provides an opportunity to visit the most aptly named place in Europe for a rambler: the village of Walk, near Waimes. The walk includes considerable sections of the GR 56 or GR E (GR of the Cantons de l'Est) as well as sampling many of the waymarked local trails: sections of numbers R5, W6, W7, R3, R4, R10, R9, R11, R7, R14.

Location:	Robertville is 5.6 miles (9kms) north-east of Malmédy.
Start/Finish:	The centre of the small village of Robertville.
Distance:	10.3 miles (16.5kms).
Time:	Allow 5hrs 30mins - 6hrs.
Maps:	The map at a scale of 1:25,000 entitled *Promenades Malmédy*

- *Waimes* available from local tourist offices.
IGN 1:50,000 series: sheet number 50.

Waymarking: The local trails bear a number preceded by a letter of the alphabet, either the letter R (for Robertville) or W (for Waimes). In addition the red and white waymarks of the GR E are also followed on this walk where indicated in the text. In the Vallée de Bayehon there are a number of smart wooden signposts indicating a number of local trails and their destinations.

Terrain: Steep-sided wooded valleys and gorges to the west and north-west of Robertville, coupled with quiet country lanes and villages farther east. The trail crosses the large reservoir of the Lac de Robertville south of Outrewarche.

Footwear: Boots are recommended for this walk to negotiate safely the sometimes rough footpaths in the steep-sided valleys to the west and north-west of Robertville.

Option: On reaching the Moulin de Bayehon there is the possibility of taking a very worthwhile optional detour to the Bayehon waterfall. The direction to walk to reach the waterfall (*cascade*) is clearly indicated by a wooden signpost at the Moulin.

Places of Interest: 1. The *Reinhardstein Château* or Château Rénastène is situated just outside the village of Robertville, and is reached by a short detour from our trail. Dating from 1354, the Château of the Hautes Fagnes, the highest in Belgium, was completely restored in 1969, and is well worth a visit.

2. The *Lac de Robertville*. Formed by a dam, the Barrage de la Warche, this large reservoir, beautifully situated, offers various outdoor activities including fishing, canoeing and swimming.

Refreshments: There are refreshments available en route in the form of a café at the Moulin de Bayehon and another in Ovifat village (there is also a shop here where foodstuffs may be bought), but the widest selection of cafés and restaurants will be found in Robertville, where the circuit begins and ends.

Route

Starting from the centre of the village of Robertville take the road heading south signposted to Waimes. Pass the village church and descend to a "village green" with seats. Here turn left on the road (Rue du Thier) signposted to Outrewarche, following the red/white waymarks of the GR E. Where this lane bends to the right leave the GR E to take Trail No. R5, which follows the dirt track ahead. Pass between fields. Turn left at a T-junction and 20 metres later, immediately before the bridge over the stream (Ruisseau de Quarreux), turn right along another track to follow the water up-stream. On reaching a culvert over the stream turn right on a track between fences which turns away from the stream, waymarked

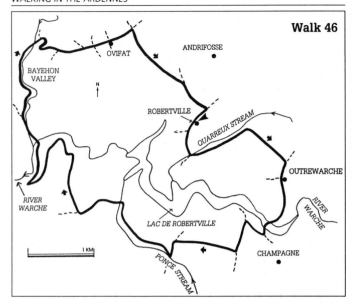

Walk 46

ANDRIFOSSE

OVIFAT

BAYEHON VALLEY

N

ROBERTVILLE

QUARREUX STREAM

OUTREWARCHE

RIVER WARCHE

RIVER WARCHE

LAC DE ROBERTVILLE

1 KM

CHAMPAGNE

PONCE STREAM

as R5. This emerges onto a lane at a bend in the latter: continue ahead along this lane. On reaching a T-junction leave Trail No. R5, which goes off to the left, but instead turn right to walk through the village of Outrewarche, soon picking up the red/white waymarkings of the GR E once again, as well as R6 markings.

Head south on the lane in the direction of Champagne. Descend to cross the Lac de Robertville by a bridge and ascend on the lane ahead for about 200 metres until another lane is reached on the right-hand side. Take this, now following white triangle waymarks heading north-west. Turn left on reaching the entrance to the Belle Vue campsite to walk towards the south on the narrow lane to reach a staggered crossroads. Turn right here following the white triangle and R6 waymarks. Walk along this lane heading westwards between fields, passing a small stone cross on your right and continuing to reach a main road. Turn left along this road, the N676 (leaving Trail No. R6 at this point), and descend to reach a stream (the R du Poncé). Do not cross the stream, but immediately before it turn right on a track (7W waymark) which passes in front of the Anderegg campsite. Remain on this main track, later ignoring a path which climbs into the wood to the right. The track passes through woodland heading north-west, later bearing more towards the north. When it reaches a metalled lane near a small pond on your left, turn left onto this lane heading now towards the west. At the top of the hill, the lane, part of Trail No. R3, reaches the main Malmédy to Robertville road in the aptly named village of Walk.

Turn left along the road in the direction of Malmédy, now following the red and white waymarks of the GR E and soon passing the village church. About 80 metres before reaching the roadsign indicating the limit of Walk, leave the GR E, which turns to the left on its way towards Waimes, but turn right on a poorly surfaced track waymarked as Trail No. R4. Continue ahead at a cross-tracks, heading north, now on a grassy dirt track. Remain on this track, enclosed between fences and hedgerows as it meanders downhill to reach the edge of woodland. Here turn left on Trail No. R10, also picking up the red and white waymarks of the GR E once again. This most pleasant woodland path soon climbs to reach a rocky viewpoint high above the steep-sided wooded valley to the north.

Continue along this fine path, following carefully the waymarks for the GR E and also the yellow marks of the R10, to descend to a path junction. Leave the GR E at this point, turning sharply to the right, continuing the descent towards the valley on the R10 trail, now heading north-eastwards. The trail descends to the river in the bottom of the valley. Do not attempt to wade across this, but instead walk down-stream to the left for about 50 metres to locate a wooden log bridge stretching across the river. Cross over the river on this bridge, taking special care in wet weather when the surface is very slippery.

Turn right on the opposite bank of the river, following the path up-stream as indicated by the wooden footpath signpost (direction Robertville, R10). Reach a pair of shelters within 100 metres and a second wooden signpost by another bridge over the river. Do not cross this bridge, but take the track heading uphill, signposted to Ovifat on Trail No. R9, along the Vallée de Bayehon. The route is also following the red and white waymarks of the GR 56. The trail follows the river up-stream through a most impressive rocky and wooded gorge. The water comes rushing down this river in great haste in times of spate. On reaching a third wooden signpost at a track junction, cross the wooden footbridge over a tributary of the main river and follow the GR 56 waymarks in the direction indicated to the Moulin de Bayehon and Ovifat, continuing to follow the river up-stream. The stream is soon crossed by a wooden footbridge (again take care in wet conditions). Continue up-stream on the left bank of the river for 150 metres or so before crossing another wooden footbridge back over to the right bank of the river. Continue up-stream on the path, but again cross another footbridge to return to the left bank of the river, still following the red and white waymarks, eventually emerging at the Moulin de Bayehon (refreshments available at the café) and another wooden signpost.

Leave the GR 56 at the Moulin de Bayehon by taking the path heading uphill to the right, signposted to Ovifat on the R9 and R11. The path climbs steeply, crosses a road and continues uphill at the same gradient to reach a second road on the outskirts of the village of Ovifat. Turn left, heading east to enter the village (shop and a café-bar). Walk through Ovifat heading straight on in the direction indicated to Verviers, passing the church to reach a crossroads on the outskirts of the village, about 40 metres before a roadsign which indicates the limit of Ovifat. Turn right here onto the Rue du Cimetière, now following Trail Nos R7 and R14. Pass the cemetery and continue ahead downhill, later ignoring a side road on the right. At the bottom of the hill the lane enters the outskirts of Robertville, where it changes its name to the Rue de la Machurée Fontaine. Continue ahead, climbing on the R7 and R14 to reach the main road in Robertville. Turn right along this to return to the village centre.

WALK 47:
Waimes, Chivremont, Grosbois and Remacreux

Description: A circular walk on lanes and forest tracks to the south-west of Waimes, which is the second most important settlement in the area after Malmédy. An exploration of the mature woodland of the Grosbois (large wood) is one of the main features of the walk; here will be found a fine and varied collection of mushroom and toadstool fungi during the autumn months. The walk follows parts of the local Trail Nos W3 and W4, as well as sampling a section of the GR E, the long distance trail through the Cantons de l'Est.

Location: Waimes is 4.7 miles (7.5kms) east of Malmédy. This circuit is to the south-west and south of Waimes.

Start/Finish: The centre of the village of Waimes.

Distance: 5.0 miles (8.0kms).

Time: Allow 2hrs 45mins to 3hrs.

Maps: The map at a scale of 1:25,000 entitled *Promenades Malmédy - Waimes* available from local tourist offices.

IGN 1:50,000 series: sheet number 50.

Waymarkimg: An assortment of waymarks: W3 and W4; a white triangle and two blue dots; red/white GR waymarks (the latter are only found on the last stage of the walk, back into Waimes). The waymarking, at least at the time of the author's visit, was not of a high standard.

The waymarking of the Waimes trails is generally less good than that of the Malmédy, Ligneuville and Robertville walks. Whereas the latter generally use yellow paint marks on trees, etc, there is a different system in operation for waymarking the Waimes walks, ie. use is made of small rectangular waymarks attached to trees and fence posts. These waymarks bear the trail number (W1, W2, W3, etc) in green lettering. Many of these were missing or broken at the time of the author's last visit to the area. Generally more care is required when following one of the Waimes walks, particularly those not featured in this book.

Terrain: A mixture of woodland and open country with wide views from the high points of the two hills, Chivremont and Remacreux, passed en route. There are two or three ascents on the walk, but these are generally on fairly gentle gradients.

Footwear: The tracks in the Grosbois can be very muddy after rain, hence boots or bogtrotters are recommended.

Option: The walk can be shortened by about a kilometre by avoiding the right turn into the Voie des Allemands (see route description below): carry on ahead instead, following M3 waymarks, heading north-east directly back to Waimes.

Refreshments: There are hotels, restaurants, cafés and shops in Waimes, but note that no places of refreshment are passed en route.

Route

Leave the centre of Waimes on the N634, the road to Malmédy. About 200 metres after passing the post office turn left onto the Rue de Chivremont, on the trail waymarked as W3. Keep ahead at the staggered crossroads, climbing on a "no-through road" away from the village of Waimes (white triangle and two blue dots serve as a waymark). The lane climbs gently to reach the summit of Chivremont, where it becomes an unsurfaced track which enters the woods ahead. After a few hundred metres ignore the track on the right, but continue on the track ahead. Remain on the main track, which can become very muddy under wet conditions, as it meanders and gently descends to a road. Cross over this road to continue the trail on the grassy track ahead.

The trail enters an enclosed avenue of conifers, and shortly afterwards reaches a staggered track junction. Turn left for 5 metres and then right, ie. maintain direction (white triangle/blue dots and an arrow on a tree act as waymarks). Remain on the track, later bearing to the left (south-east) at a track T-junction (white painted arrow on stone) and left again (east) on arriving at a second track junction. This track, now enclosed with low wire fences, crosses fields and gradually turns towards the north to return to the road at a point to the south-east of where you first crossed it. Turn left along the road, the Route de Grosbois, for about 100 metres, to reach a lane on the right. Turn along this, the Chemin de Freneux, to head towards the north-east. After 250 metres turn right onto the Voie des Allemands to head in a south-easterly direction towards farm buildings. Pass the farm and continue ahead, climbing gradually towards a second farm seen on the rise ahead. Ignore the left fork opposite the farmhouse, but continue ahead on the Voie des Allemands (waymark of a white triangle with two blue dots on a telegraph pole). The trail reaches a road at a T-junction by a third farm. Here our trail joins the GR E (red/white waymarks) for the return to Waimes.

Turn left onto the road. The lane climbs gently to pass over the rise of

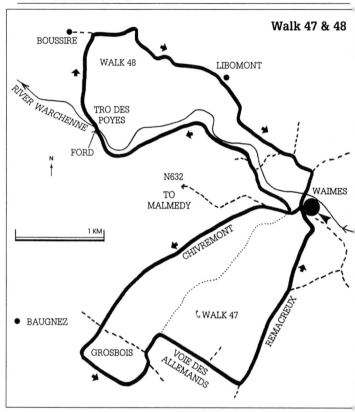

Walk 47 & 48

BOUSSIRE

WALK 48

LIBOMONT

RIVER WARCHENNE

TRO DES
POYES

FORD

N

N632
TO
MALMEDY

WAIMES

1 KM

CHIVREMONT

⸂WALK 47

REMACREUX

BAUGNEZ

GROSBOIS

VOIE DES
ALLEMANDS

Remacreux (bench on the side of the lane). Continue ahead now descending towards the Warchenne valley in which lies the village of Waimes. Pass a crucifix alongside the lane and then, about 600 metres after the above mentioned bench on the top of the Remacreux hill, be sure to locate a track which leaves the road on the left (it was not waymarked the last time the author visited this spot and is easily missed). This unsurfaced track bends to the right within 50 metres and heads southwards between fields. The track leads to an area of playing fields. Continue ahead (red/white waymark) to join a narrow surfaced lane (the Rue de Coirville) which continues the descent towards Waimes. Reach the houses of the village and descend to a T-junction where turn left on the Rue du Marché, later turning right down the Rue du Vinâve, passing the village church to reach the High Street in the centre of Waimes.

WALK 48:
Waimes, Tro des Poyes and Libomont

Description: This pleasant walk, which is best undertaken during a dry summer (see below), follows Waimes local trail No. 2 (W2) to the north-west of the small town. The first half of the walk is along the attractive Warchenne valley following a section of the GR des Cantons de l'Est, after which, once the river has been forded (see "Special Problems" below), there is a fairly stiff climb out of the valley. The trail climbs to a high point above the village of Libomont, from where there is an extensive view of the surrounding countryside, before dropping back down to Waimes for welcome refreshment in one of its cafés or restaurants.

Location: To the west and north-west of Waimes, a village 4.7 miles (7.5kms) east of Malmédy.

Start/Finish: The village centre of Waimes.

Distance: 5.0 miles (8.0kms).

Time: Allow 3hrs.

Maps: The map at a scale of 1:25,000 entitled *Promenades Malmédy - Waimes* available from local tourist offices.

IGN 1:50,000 series: sheet number 50.

Waymarking: The waymarking is good when following the GR E, but much less so once this has been left behind. However, it is hoped that the walker will find few problems if the route description described below is followed carefully.

See also the note on waymarking in the Waimes area under "Waymarking" for Walk 47.

Terrain: Level walking along the Warchenne valley, followed by a river crossing (see below), after which there is a fairly long and sustained climb out of the valley, moderately steep in places. A final long descent back down to the valley.

Footwear: Because there is a ford to cross over the River Warchenne, bogtrotters or boots with gaiters are recommended, although the water level will probably not come over the top of boots during a long, dry summer period. This walk should not be attempted wearing either shoes or trainers.

Option: See "Option" for Walk 45.

Special Problems: A warning must be given of the river crossing that occurs at almost the halfway stage of this walk. Unless a footbridge over the River Warchenne is eventually built in the Trô des Poyes area there is no alternative but to ford it. During a fine dry summer this should present little problem for most people, but after heavy rain it is quite a different matter. The author forded the river at this point during one wet September, when the water level was well

257

above normal boot height and the flow was quite swift. This walk should not be attempted during and after heavy rainfall, nor after a prolonged wet period, as the river crossing would then be dangerous. No attempt whatsoever should be made to ford the river when it is running high and fast; the only alternative then will be retrace your outward steps back along the GR E to return to Waimes, which in any case would be no hardship. A depth of more than about 9ins would be unacceptable. If in any doubt about this river crossing then please do not attempt it.

Refreshments: A café can be visited by a short detour from the route at the point at which the trail leaves the GR E (see text for details). Otherwise there are opportunities for refreshments in Waimes at the start and end of the walk.

Route

From the church in the centre of Waimes walk uphill on the road in the direction of Malmédy for about 100 metres to the point where the main road bends to the right. Here is located the Rue du Moulin, a minor road on the right. Here also should be found the red and white waymarks of the GR E, a trail that is to be followed for nearly half of this walk. Leave Waimes by following the Rue du Moulin which leads to a railway line. Take care here to follow the correct set of red/white waymarks. Do *not* cross the railway line (the red/white waymarks on the opposite side take the GR E to Robertville) but carry straight on along the line, following the GR E in the direction of Malmédy. After another 100 metres or so ignore a path off to the left, but remain on the lane ahead.

This lane follows the Warchenne valley, the River Warchenne being seen occasionally on your right-hand side. Remain on the lane, following the red/white waymarks as the surroundings become more wooded. The GR E remains on this lane until it encounters the railway line once again, at the entrance to a quarry. Bear right following the red/white waymarks to reach the railway line (note the interesting small statue of Sainte Barbe on the left - she is the patron saint of quarrymen). Keep on the left-hand side of the railway line for about 80 metres to locate a narrow footpath which enters the trees to the left. The path soon follows alongside the River Warchenne and then crosses it by a ford (caution: the crossing can be tricky if the river is high, in which case it will be necessary to retrace your steps back to Waimes - do not attempt a crossing if the water level is above about 9ins).

Shortly after the river crossing the trail reaches the railway line once again. At this point our route leaves the GR E. Therefore ignore the red/white waymarks which lead to the left (café in 100 metres), but instead bear right along the railway line for a few metres before crossing it and climbing uphill into the wood on a path which is waymarked with the occasional very faint white triangle/two blue dots waymark. The path climbs quite steeply through the woods, levels and emerges from the trees to drop a little to cross a small stream at a lane on the outskirts of the village of Boussire. Bear right uphill on the lane and climb on this to reach a road. Turn right along this, now heading east. Remain on this lane soon ignoring a track which leaves the lane off to the right (it leads to a dead end at a private property within 150 metres). The lane climbs, bends to the left and then more sharply to the right to cross a small stream and then heads south towards farm buildings. The lane bends to the left in front of these buildings and continues its climb, soon passing to the left of a conifer plantation. A superb view opens out at the top of the hill: Waimes is clearly seen nestling in the valley below. Remain on the lane to descend to the village of Libomont. On reaching a Y-junction in the village bear right on the lane signposted to Waimes. Descend on this lane, the Rue de Vivier, to the outskirts of Waimes, where the red and white waymarks of the GR E are encountered once again. Where these turn left at a perfect circle of grass on which stands a solitary tree at its centre, leave them to turn right instead, then continuing to meet the main road at a T-junction. Turn right here to descend back to the church in the centre of Waimes.

SANKT VITH
General Information and Places of Interest
The thing that strikes the first time visitor to Sankt Vith is how German it all is. The town and surrounding countryside comprise one of the three Belgian Cantons de l'Est, or Ostkantone (the other two Cantons are those of Malmédy and Eupen). Leave the E 421 motorway at junction 10 and all is definitely French in character; leave it a few miles later at junction 14 and the world is now very Germanic in both language and atmosphere. Although some French is understood by most of the inhabitants, German is the main language in Sankt Vith and in the surrounding villages. A glance at the map of the region around here and Burg-Reuland will soon confirm this fact, as the majority of the names of the towns and villages are German (Braunlauf, Lommersweiler, Grüfflingen, etc). And it is, of course, Sankt Vith, not Saint Vith. A visit to this region allows the visitor not only to enjoy this very charming pastoral landscape, but also to experience yet another facet of multi-cultural and multi-linguistic Belgium.

Sankt Vith acquired its name from the relics of Saint Vitus, which, it is said, rested hereabouts for a time around AD 836. It is a bright, pleasant town today (population about 8000), although it was virtually razed to the ground by bombing raids in 1944. Sadly its medieval fortifications are more or less non-existent today. The church, built in the 1950s, as was most of the modern town, is well worth a visit: it is a large, modern, spacious building, rather elegant in style. A small local museum (limited opening times) in the town has displays which highlight the chequered history of the area, and explain the old, rural lifestyle of the region. The Canton lies just to the west of German territory, and was the scene of most terrible fighting during the Battle of the Ardennes, as will be witnessed by the numerous war memorials in the area.

Sankt Vith, unlike several of the towns in the Ardennes, such as Spa and Malmédy, is not geared up quite so much towards tourism. Therefore a stay here can be a very peaceful, tranquil experience. The area is a well-to-do one, the prosperity being plainly evident in the houses and shops in the town. Sankt Vith can be recommended as a base from which to explore the surrounding countryside.

Accommodation

There are at least 8 hotels in Sankt Vith: Hôtel Eden, Hôtel Le Luxembourg (recommended: excellent food), Hôtel Marquet, Hôtel-Restaurant Pip-Margraff, Pension Schulzen, Hôtel-Restaurant Steinweiher, Hôtel-Restaurant St Vither Hof and Hôtel-Restaurant Zur Post. In addition there is a hotel near Crombach (Walk 49) and another at Lommersweiler (Walk 51).

Sankt Vith has a youth hostel (*jugendherberge*) in Rodterstrasse. To reach it from the tourist office, see the beginning of the route description for Walk 49, below.

There is a campsite a few miles to the south-west of Sankt Vith, near Neubrück, and another at Schînberg, north-east of Lommersweiler.

Transport

The nearest railway lines are all some distance from Sankt Vith, so it will be necessary to take a bus if travelling by public transport. The best way of reaching the town by public transport is to first visit Malmédy (see the section on Malmédy and Environs) and from there take a bus to Sankt Vith. Buses run with moderate frequency between the two towns. It is also possible to reach Sankt Vith by bus from Verviers (reached by train from Liège). The relevant bus service for all of the three centres in the Cantons de l'Est featured in this book is line No. 395: Verviers, Spa, Malmédy, Sankt Vith, Grufflange, Burg-Reuland (see "Transport" in the section on Spa for full details).

The services listed below, with the exception of the Sankt Vith to Ettelbruck service, are all operated by the local TEC bus company.

Bus no. 401 blanc: Sankt Vith to Vielsalm. Mondays to Fridays only - there are 3/4 buses per day in each direction. The service links with the railway at Vielsalm. Journey time from Sankt Vith to Vielsalm is about 45mins. The route is Sankt Vith > Hünningen > Rodt > Hinderhausen > Vielsalm (ie. there are stops at some of the villages included in one of the walks described below).

Bus No. 395: Sankt Vith to Burg-Reuland via Neubruck, Oudler, Wemperhardt and Ouren. Monday to Friday only. About 4 per day, but only 1 or 2 go all the way to Burg-Reuland; most stop at Wemperhardt. About 1/2hr from Sankt Vith to Wemperhardt and 1hr from Sankt Vith to Burg-Reuland.

Bus No. 48a blanc: Sankt Vith to Waimes and on to Eupen (railway station for trains to Liège and Aachen). Between Monday and Friday there are about 6 buses a day in both directions to and from Eupen plus 3 extra ones which go only as far as Waimes. At the weekends there are about 5 buses to Waimes, 3 of which go on to Eupen. Journey times: Sankt Vith to Waimes is about 35mins; Sankt Vith to Eupen is about 1½hrs.

Bus No 400 blanc: Sankt Vith to Rocherath via Büllingen. Monday to Friday only. About 5 a day to Rocherath, plus 3 others which go only as far as Büllingen. Journey times: Sankt Vith to Büllingen is about 45mins; Sankt Vith to Rocherath is about 1hr.

Bus No 48b: Sankt Vith to Gouvy (railway station here for trains to Liège) via Crombach, Weisten and Ourthe. Monday to Friday about 6 buses a day; weekends about 2 a day. Journey time: Sankt Vith to Gouvy is about 45mins.

Sankt Vith to Ettelbruck (railway station). Operated by the Company Voyages Simon. Only one bus in each direction per day Monday to Friday (timed with train connections to and from Luxembourg City.

Sankt Vith is very easily reached by car by way of the fast E421 (A27) motorway, which branches off the E40 motorway east of Liège. Note, however, the break in the motorway after the Spa turn-off, between junctions 10 and 11 (see "Transport" in the Stavelot and Coo section). The motorway, after its resumption at junction 11, is rarely busy. Leave the motorway at either junction 14 or junction 15 for the last few kilometres to Sankt Vith.

Official Trails in the Cantons de l'Est

The routes of these trails are all clearly marked, as solid red lines, on the 1:25,000 scale map entitled *St Vith Wanderkarte*, sold in the Sankt Vith Tourist Office. Note that there are a few minor errors concerning the routes of these trails on this map, mainly the result of the incorrect depiction of the route of the new E421/A27 motorway on the map. Note also that that on the occasions of the author's two visits to the area, only the Sankt Vith (SV) walks had been waymarked on the ground. Although the Lommersweiler (L routes), Recht (R routes), Crombach (C routes) and Schönberg (S routes) shown on the map were not waymarked, they were nevertheless quite easy to follow with the aid of the map.

Trails around Sankt Vith:
These all carry the prefix SV followed by a number (SV 1 up to SV 11). They were all waymarked on the ground with red/blue metal waymarks, carrying the relevant number.

Trails around Recht:
These all carry the prefix R followed by a number (R 1 up to R 11).

Trails around Lommersweiler:
These all carry the prefix L followed by a number (L 1 up to L 9).

Trails around Schnönberg:
These all carry the prefix S followed by a number (S 1 up to S 11).
Trails around Crombach:

These all carry the prefix C followed by a number (C 1 and C 2).

The GR E or GR 56:

The GR 56 (the GR des Cantons de l'Est) passes through the area. Part of its rather tortuous route is marked, as a dotted red line, on the map referred to above.

Walks

Three walks are described below, all starting and finishing in Sankt Vith, exploring the areas to the west, north and east of the town.

WALK 49:
Sankt Vith, Neundorf and Kapellen

Description: A walk over gentle open rolling hill country, utilizing sections of the following local walking trails: SV 4, C 1, C 2, GR E (GR 56), SV 11 and SV 2. There are extensive views of the surrounding wooded countryside of the Belgian Ardennes and over the border into the German Eifel. The first third of the route is dominated by a large disused railway line and its prominent embankment.

Location: To the west of the town of Sankt Vith, in the German-speaking south-eastern part of the Belgian Ardennes.

Start/Finish: The tourist office just off the High Street (Hauptstrasse) in the centre of Sankt Vith.

Distance: 12.7 miles (20.5kms).

Time: 6hrs.

Maps: The walkers' map at a scale of 1:25,000 entitled *St Vith Wanderkarte*, sold at the tourist office in Sankt Vith.

IGN 1:50,000 series: sheet number 56.

Waymarking: The Sankt Vith routes (SV 4, SV 2 and SV 11) are waymarked with old metal waymarks, usually red and blue in colour, bearing the letters SV followed by the appropriate number. The GR E (GR 56) is waymarked with the usual red and white paint markings. The Crombach trails (C 1 and C 2), although marked on the 1:25,000 walkers's map described above, are not waymarked on the ground. However navigation is not, on the whole, particularly difficult, and most people should have no difficulty in following the route if the 1:25,000 scale map is used in conjunction with the route description given below.

Terrain: Open countryside throughout. A landscape of gently rolling hills, with no steep gradients. The walk is predominantly on quiet, narrow surfaced lanes and tracks.

Footwear:　　　Trainers or good quality walking shoes are suitable for most seasons, unless conditions are exceptionally wet.

Option:　　　The walk can be considerably shortened to a stroll of a few miles by heading north from Neundorf on route SV 4/C 1, and then east back to Sankt Vith on route SV 4 (see *St Vith Wanderkarte* map).

Refreshments:　　A congenial café (and combined beer museum) is encountered on the walk about two-thirds of the way around the circuit. This establishment is open not only during the summer season, but also during the winter months, particularly at weekends, as it serves the cross-country skiing trade. In cold weather it offers a welcoming log fire. The "museum" consists mainly of an extensive and curious collection of old beer bottles of every description. It also sells coffee, hot chocolate and snacks including delicious hot waffles and cream.

Route

From the tourist office in Sankt Vith cross the Hauptstrasse to walk west along Büchelstrasse. Turn right in front of the round stone tower at the end of this road; where the small park on the left comes to an end, ie. before rejoining the High Street, turn left downhill on a road. Descend to pass a sports hall, cross over a small stream and continue ahead for about 250 metres to a road junction (the way to the youth hostel [*Jugendherberge*] is off to the left before reaching this junction). Take the left fork signposted to Neundorf and Crombach. Remain on this lane to walk through the underpass beneath the motorway (A27/E42). Climb gently away from the autoroute to reach farm buildings on the right and bus stops. Turn left on a surfaced track opposite the farm buildings (note the SV 4 waymark: a white number 4 on a red/blue background, ie. Sankt Vith route No. 4).

　　Continue ahead, eventually crossing over an old bridge above a disused railway. On reaching a crossroads (stone crucifix on the right) turn right onto the narrow lane (another SV 4 waymark) and descend to the village of Neundorf, aiming for the prominent church. Continue ahead through this village, passing the church and war memorial, the latter dedicated to the 30 inhabitants, including two small children, of this tiny village who lost their lives here during World War Two (note the old primitive crucifix to the left of the war memorial). Leave the SV 4 at this point (it goes off to the right immediately before the church) but instead continue ahead towards the west along walk C 1 (not waymarked on the ground). Leave the large and impressive church of Neundorf behind (note the Stations of the Cross made from old sleepers of the disused railway to the right, behind the church).

　　About 300 metres after the church the road swings to the right to pass under the railway embankment. Ignore this, but instead continue ahead on the narrow lane with fields to the left and the tree-lined embankment to the right.

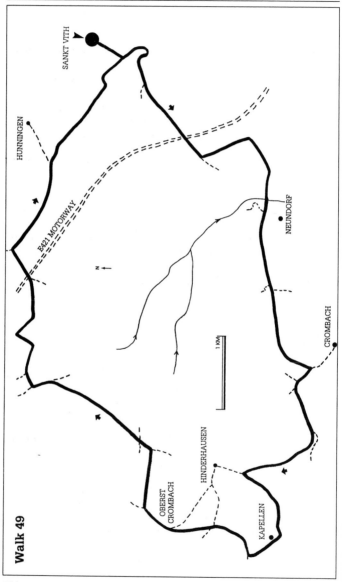

Walk 49

SANKT VITH

HUNNINGEN

E421 MOTORWAY

N

NEUNDORF

CROMBACH

1 KM

HINDERHAUSEN

OBERST CROMBACH

KAPELLEN

Follow the course of the disused railway line ahead, ignoring roads branching off to right and left. Continue to a T-junction on the outskirts of the village of Crombach; turn right to walk past the houses of this sprawling village. Ignore the right turn to Rodt, but instead continue ahead following the road as it forks to the left downhill. Cross a stream and then climb uphill to a Y-fork: take the right branch here. After about 200 metres reach a narrow crossroads, where turn right. Continue to a T-junction on the outskirts of Hinderhausen. Here turn left heading now towards the south-west.

Enter the village of Kapellen. Where the road divides by a small stone crucifix, turn right and immediately right again at the next fork. Climb away from the village to reach a track T-junction, where turn right. At the end of the climb, at a crossroads by a small stone crucifix (extensive view - note Sankt Vith clearly visible over to the east), continue ahead towards the north. Remain ahead at the next cross-tracks. Ignore the next right turn (unsurfaced track on the left), but less than 100 metres later take the right fork (large farmhouse ahead on the left). Turn left on reaching the next T-junction. Continue ahead at the next cross-tracks (small stone crucifix on the left) to reach and cross a main road at a bus stop. About 250 metres after this main road, bear left at a Y-fork waymarked with white arrows on blue and red backgrounds (*ski de fond* waymarks). Head for the prominent white tower. At a T-junction (unsurfaced track ahead) turn left to pass the white tower. Sixty metres after the white tower turn right opposite a wooden building (café and "beer museum"). A stop is recommended at this establishment, which is at a *pavillon de chasse*, at a point where the route C 2 meets the GR E.

The red/white waymarks of the GR trail, as well as white triangle/blue dot waymarks, are encountered here. Where the surfaced lane bends to the left away from the forest, continue ahead on an earthen track alongside the wood, following the red/white GR markings. The track soon bends to the left downhill to rejoin the surfaced track. Here turn right, heading for the buildings seen ahead. Walk past the farm buildings and continue to reach and pass beneath the motorway by its underpass. Continue ahead to a T-junction, where turn right, waymarked as the GR E to Sankt Vith (the route is now also coincident with the local SV 2 and SV 11 trails). Remain on this road as it swings to the right, still following the red/white markings. By a solitary house on the left, before reaching a main road, take a right turning which soon bends to the left (red/white markings and white triangle and blue dots waymarks - SV 2 and SV 11 routes). Cross the main road and take the lane opposite (panoramic view of Sankt Vith). Continue ahead over a cross-tracks aiming for the church of Sankt Vith seen ahead, walking along an old unsurfaced track. This leads to the main road where turn right to enter the town and return to the tourist office in its centre.

WALK 50:
Sankt Vith and Hunningen

Description: A short and pleasant ramble using part of the SV 2 and SV 11 local trails. There are extensive views out to the west from the balcony lane north of Hünningen. Considerable numbers of raptors ride the thermals in this part of the Ardennes.

Location: To the north-west of Sankt Vith, in the Cantons de l'Est.

Start/Finish: The tourist office just off the High Street (Hauptstrasse) in the centre of Sankt Vith.

Distance: 6.1 miles (9.8kms).

Time: About 2hrs 30mins.

Maps: The walkers' map at a scale of 1:25,000 entitled *St Vith Wanderkarte*, sold at the tourist office in Sankt Vith.

     IGN 1:50,000 series: sheet number 56.

Waymarking: The various local routes used on the walk are waymarked with old metal waymarks, usually red and blue in colour, bearing the letters SV followed by the appropriate number.

Terrain: Narrow metalled lanes and surfaced and unsurfaced forest tracks. A mixture of woodland and open country. Only gentle gradients.

Footwear: Unless it is or has been raining heavily, trainers or good quality walking shoes are suitable for this walk.

Refreshments: Sankt Vith has several cafés and restaurants, but no refreshments will be found en route.

Route
From the tourist office in Sankt Vith walk in a north-westerly direction along the High street for about 750 metres. Fifty metres after the memorial to the 2nd Infantry Division of the USA who fought here in 1944/45, turn right along Silvio-Gesell-Strasse. In about 100 metres take the first turn to the left. Where this surfaced track swings to the left, turn right onto a dirt track by a metal building. Continue to the outskirts of the village of Hünningen.

     Bear right at the T-junction to walk up to the main road to the north-east of the village. Turn left along the main road for about 150 metres, until about 50 metres before the traffic lights, turn right along a country lane with good views to the left to the village of Niederemmels and the grassy hills and woods beyond. This eventually reaches a T-junction by a house and farm. Turn right here (ie. leaving the SV 2 but continuing along the SV 11). In about 150 metres turn right (SV 11 waymark) and 20 metres later bear right again, keeping to the surfaced track. At the top of a short climb, by the edge of the wood where the

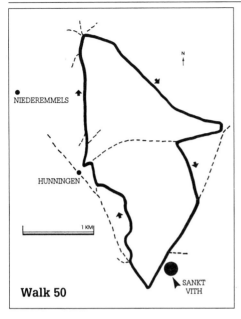

track swings to the left, bear to the right on a forest track. Walk through the wood and continue until just before reaching the main Sankt Vith to Amel road, where turn right along a country lane signposted to Malmédy and Vielsalm.

Take the first turn on the left along a poorly surfaced narrow lane - Sankt Vith comes into view at this point. On reaching the main road turn right along it walking on the pavement to head back into Sankt Vith to the point where you started the ramble.

Walk 50

NIEDEREMMELS

HUNNINGEN

1 KM

SANKT VITH

WALK 51:
Sankt Vith, Lommersweiler and the German Border

Description: A full day's walk to the south-east of Sankt Vith in an area adjacent to the German Eifel. This is possibly the best walk in the Cantons de l'Est region. There are steep hillsides, meandering valleys, woods, and a number of attractive, slumbering villages. The trail passes through the village of Lommersweiler, which has a most elaborate church, and also follows the German border for a while in the vicinity of Steinebrück. The route uses part of the following local trails in the sequence given: SV 6, L 3, L 4, L 2, L 3, L 1, L 6, L 9, and SV 5, plus considerable sections of the GR E (GR 56), which is taken, abandoned and then rejoined on several occasions throughout the walk.

Location: The German-speaking region of the Belgian Ardennes, south-east of Sankt Vith.

Start/Finish: The tourist office just off the High Street (Hauptstrasse) in the centre of Sankt Vith.

Distance: 14.0 miles (22.5kms).

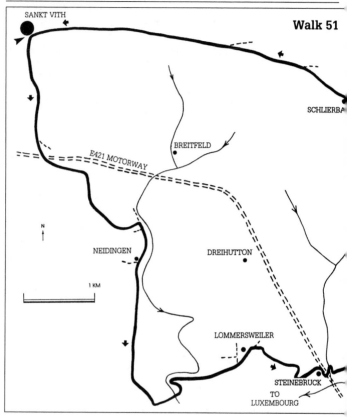

Time: About 7hrs.

Maps: The walkers' map at a scale of 1:25,000 entitled *St Vith Wanderkarte*, sold at the tourist office in Sankt Vith. (Note that there are a few minor errors concerning the marked walking routes on this map, mainly the result of the incorrect depiction of the route of the new E 42/A 27 motorway on the map. This affects the first crossing point of the motorway on the route described below, but no problems should be encountered if the route as described is followed.)

IGN 1:50,000 series: sheet number 56.

Waymarking: The Sankt Vith routes (SV 5 and SV 6) are waymarked with old metal waymarks, usually red and blue in colour, bearing the letters SV

followed by the appropriate number. The GR E (GR 56) is waymarked with the usual red and white paint markings. The Lommersweiler trails (L 1, L 2, L 3, L 4, L 6 and L 9), although marked on the 1:25,000 walkers's map described above, are not waymarked on the ground. There should be few difficulties, however, if the route description below is followed in conjunction with the 1:25,000 walkers' map. The last few miles from Schlierbach are mainly along a quiet, more or less straight road, with few navigational problems to tax the weary rambler at the end of a long day.

Terrain: A mixture of woods and open country. Several steep-sided, meandering valleys, and row after patchwork row of rolling wooded hills stretching into the distance into Germany and Luxembourg. A moderately hilly route; there are a few steep climbs, but it is never difficult. The walk is mainly on unsurfaced tracks and paths, but the later stages are predominantly on surfaced quiet, minor lanes.

Footwear: Lightweight boots are probably the best form of footwear; some may find trainers adequate, but bear in mind that there are several steep ascents and descents.

Options: The route could be shortened by taking routes L 3 and SV 6 back from Lommersweiler (see *St Vith Wanderkarte* 1:25,000 map).

From Lommersweiler onwards, the villages en route are connected to Sankt Vith by bus service 48a blanc. The walk could therefore be shortened by returning to Sankt Vith by bus from one of these villages, but if planning to take this option it would be wise to check on the availability and timetable of the bus service, before setting out on the ramble.

Refreshments: There are two cafés/restaurants in Steinebrück, which is located about two-thirds of the way around the circuit. Steinebrück would therefore make an ideal place to stop for a mid-day meal, but note that an early start from Sankt Vith will have to be made in order to reach Steinebrück in time for lunch. Even if intending to buy a mid-day meal here, it is nevertheless best to bring some emergency food, in case these establishments are closed on arrival. Many seats and benches, often at viewpoints, and a few provided with picnic tables, will be passed en route. These make ideal stopping places for a picnic lunch.

Lommersweiler: This village, passed at roughly the halfway point on the walk, has a most impressive church at its centre, well worth a visit. There is ornate statuary both inside and outside the building. Note, in particular, the painted

Stations of the Cross inside the church and the stained glass windows. The seven painted tableaux between cemetery and church are of interest, whilst the war memorial opposite is a poignant reminder of the tragic events that occurred in the region during the Second World War.

Route

From the tourist office in Sankt Vith, walk south-east along the Hauptstrasse to the town car park/bus station. Take the road opposite signposted to the US Memorial, in 50 metres passing the St. Josef Hospital. Continue ahead along this road to pass the memorial dedicated to the men of the 106th Infantry Division, USA, who died during the Battle of the Bulge in December, 1944. Red and white GR waymarks (the GR 56 E) soon lead across a bridge over the deep embankment of the wide, old disused railway line. Extensive views open out as the route is followed ahead along the narrow country lane.

On reaching a double red/white paint sign on a tree (indicating a change of direction) take the track off to the left, heading for the corner of a conifer wood. The track follows the edge of the wood and leads to the motorway which cuts an impressive swathe through the hills. Leave the GR E here by turning right to pass under the motorway. Immediately after the underpass turn left onto a poorly surfaced track heading towards the edge of a wood. The track bears right at the wood's edge, following the SV 6 route into trees. On re-entering trees after a clearing, take the left fork where the track divides (very old SV 6 sign). This track soon begins a descent into an attractive valley.

Descend to a narrow lane where the GR E is rejoined (on the left at this point is a small grotto cut into the hillside). Turn right to follow the lane on the GR trail (red/white markings). On reaching the outskirts of the village of Neidingen, at a fork by a white cottage and a picnic table, bear right uphill. Near the top of the climb the road forks again; this time take the left fork downhill. In the centre of the village do not cross the small bridge to the church, but instead fork right following the white triangle/blue dot waymarked route which is also part of the GR trail. Leave the village. Where the lane bends to the right by a white cottage and small stone cross, take the track on the left by the cottage and where it forks in 20 metres take the right fork uphill, following the red/white trail markings. Cross over a narrow lane and continue the climb ahead. Near the top of the ascent, walk ahead over a cross-track by a small crucifix. Continue on the track over the high level plateau until reaching the edge of a wood. Here, still following the GR 56, bear to the right for 50 metres and then to the left on a grassy track enclosed between low fences, heading towards a conifer wood. Follow the main red/white waymarked track down through the wood, eventually emerging from it to descend to a stream in the valley bottom. Cross the water on a small footbridge by farm buildings.

Leave the GR trail here by turning left on a narrow lane by a wooden cross. Fifty metres after the last building, at a road junction, bear left downhill

In the Cantons de l"Est near the German border

following the signpost towards Lommersweiler. Remain on this narrow lane as it meanders along the valley bottom and then climbs steeply out of it. Remain on the lane to enter the village of Lommersweiler, with its impressive church. Continue straight ahead through the village, passing to the left of the church (bus stop for route 48a blanc, Sankt Vith to Steinebrück). On reaching a metal crucifix on the left-hand side of the road (white Christ), walk ahead on the narrow lane signposted to Steinebrück. In 150 metres take the right fork heading towards the motorway viaduct. Pass under the latter (an impressive feat of modern engineering) and descend to the village of Steinebrück, just on the Belgian side of the border with Germany.

On reaching the main road, turn right. A few metres to the left at this point will be found a café, Zur Latarne, which provides food. About 80 metres before the bridge over the river, turn left along a road, at this point rejoining the GR trail (red/white waymarks.) There is a second restaurant here. In about 80 metres leave the road by taking a dirt track on the left, signposted as the route of the GR. In 100 metres, where the track divides, take the right-hand (lower) fork. Remain on this track until it descends to a road and river (the opposite bank of the stream is in Germany). Turn left to walk on the road along this pleasant valley bottom, passing through the small village of Weppeler, still following the GR trail markings. At the far, top end of the village, where the lane divides, take the left-hand, upper fork. This climbs, soon becoming an unsurfaced dirt track. After the steepest part of the climb, an extensive view opens out. Where the

271

tracks divide continue ahead towards the trees, still following the red/white GR E waymarks. Continue ahead at a junction of tracks. The track eventually emerges onto a road leading into the village of Schlierbach.

Turn left onto the road to pass through the village. Continue ahead through Schlierbach, following the sign to Sankt Vith. The road climbs gradually above the village. Remain on this road after the climb, heading in a westerly direction. Just over 3kms after Schlierbach, where the road bends sharply to the left, by the memorial stone to the 168th US Engineer Combat Battalion, continue ahead on a forest track, signposted as the SV 3 (and waymarked with red/white GR markings at this point). Descend on this track. Do not follow the GR route after a few hundred metres as it bends to the left. Instead continue straight ahead steeply downhill on the track, to reach and cross the main road. The town of Sankt Vith, with its prominent onion-shaped church spire, is now clearly visible ahead. Descend on the lane towards the town, soon rejoining the main road; turn right on it heading towards the centre of town. The road eventually returns the walker to the bus station/car park where the walk began. Turn right to walk along the High Street of Sankt Vith back towards the tourist office.

BURG-REULAND
General Information and Places of Interest
Burg-Reuland lies in the southernmost part of the Canton of Sankt Vith. It is much smaller than the other centres featured in this book, but is none the worse for that. It is surrounded by delectable countryside, more open than much of the Ardennes, but there are also several mature woods in the region. South of Burg-Reuland lies a narrow wedge of land, part of Belgium which becomes increasingly hemmed in as one proceeds towards the pleasant village of Ouren, by Germany to the east and the Grand Duchy of Luxembourg to the south and west. A kilometre south of Ouren, which can be reached from Burg-Reuland by following the GR 5, the three countries meet at Trois-Frontières, where there is a European peace memorial. The beautiful valley of the Our heads south from here into the Grand Duchy.

Those who visit the Canton de l'Est by car might also like to explore the whole region fully by following the waymarked drive known as the Ourtal-Route. Cyclists would also enjoy this route as, for the most part, it keeps to quiet, rural lanes (cycles can be hired locally). This circular route is 59 miles (95kms) in length and from Burg-Reuland is as follows: Burg-Reuland, Crombach, Neundorf, Sankt Vith, Meyerode, Amel, Heppenbach, Honsfeld, Losheimergraben, Manderfeld, Schönberg, Steinebrück, Dreihütten, Lommersweiler, Bracht, Ouren, Lieler, Weiswampach, Dürler, Oudler and so back to Burg-Reuland.

Accommodation

The only hotel in Burg-Reuland itself is the Pension-Restaurant Burg-Hof (tel 080 32.98.01). This establishment can be recommended. In the neighbouring villages there are hotels in Lascheid (Walk 52), Oberhausen and Ouren (south of Burg-Reuland, on the GR 5 close to the border with the Grand Duchy).

The nearest campsite is at Ouren (Camping International), about 9kms south of Burg-Reuland.

Transport

Burg-Reuland can be reached from Liège by travelling by train to Verviers (a regular service) and from there take a bus (line No. 395) to Burg-Reuland via Malmédy, Sankt Vith and Grufflange (see "Transport" in the section on Spa for full details).

An interesting alternative for those with reserves of both time and energy is to take the train from Liège to Vielsalm (see the section on Vielsalm and the Salm valley) and then, after exploring that area, walk to Burg-Reuland by following the GR 5 via the villages of Commanster, Braunlauf, Schirm-Grufflange and Bract. This is a full day's walk (16 miles; 25.7kms) but not particularly strenuous. The route is well waymarked with the standard red and white GR markings.

Motorists should leave the E421 (A27) motorway (see "Transport" in the section on Sankt Vith) at junction 15. From here follow the N62 south to Oudler and then a minor road for the last few kilometres into Burg-Reuland.

Official Walking Trails in the Region of Burg-Reuland, Thommen and Ouren

The following 35 circular walking trails are all clearly marked, as numbered red continuous lines, on the 1:25,000 scale map entitled *Burg Reuland - Wanderkarte (Cartes des Promenades)* available from local tourist offices. Note that both the GR E and the GR 5 pass through Burg-Reuland. The GR E route is the one marked as red dots on the above map, but rather strangely the GR 5 is not marked on this map.

Route 1:   Ouren - Lieler - Ouren (7.3kms)

Route 2:   Ouren - Harspelt - Sevenig - Ouren (7.1kms)

Route 3:   Ouren - Lützkampen - Welchenhausen - Oberhausen - Ouren (12.5kms)

Route 4:   Ouren - Schiebach - Rehbach - Ouren (8.6kms)

Route 5:   Ouren - Schiebach - Weiswampach - Ouren (11.5kms)

Route 6:   Ouren - Oberhausen - Stoubach - Weweler - Reuland - Lascheid - Richtenberg - Hiereberg - Ouren (16.9kms)

Route 7:   Oberhausen - Welchenhausen - Ouren - Oberhausen (6.8kms)

Route 8:   Oberhausen - Junkersberg - Rodscheid - Stoubach - Oberhausen (6.5kms)

Route 9:   Stoubach - Richtenberg - Junkersberg - Stoubach (6.8kms)
Route 10:   Stoubach - Diepert - Lützkampen - Welchenhausen - Oberhausen
             - Stoubach (8.0kms)
Route 11:   Reuland - Lascheid - Weweler - Reuland (6.9kms)
Route 12:   Reuland - Stoubach (2.5kms)
Route 13:   Reuland - Bracht - Thommerberg - Alster - Reuland (7.4kms)
Route 14:   Reuland - Auel - Steffeshausen - Reuland (9.7kms)
Route 15:   Reuland - Auel - Thommerberg - Bracht - Reuland (9.2kms)
Route 16:   Reuland - Bracht - Maspelt - Hasselbach - Luxhof - Alster - Reuland
             (10.0kms)
Route 17:   Reuland - Alster - Koller - Reuland (5.5kms)
Route 18:   Reuland - Lascheid - Oudler - Koller - Reuland (12.5kms)
Route 19:   Malscheid - Harteknopf - Leishart - Malscheid (8.5kms)
Route 20:   Malscheid - Lascheid - Oudler - Dürler - Malscheid (12.9kms)
Route 21:   Oudler - Espelerberg - Thommen - Oudler (5.8kms)
Route 22:   Oudler - Rüfensberg - Grüfflingen - Thommen - Espelerberg - Oudler
             (9.4kms)
Route 23:   Lengeler - Dürler - Lengelerberg - Lengeler (8.4kms)
Route 24:   Lengeler - Dürler - Espeler - Steinemann - Lengeler (9.8kms)
Route 25:   Lengeler - Dürler - Espeler - Trickchesberg - Leineres - Steinemann
             - Lengeler (12.2kms)
Route 26:   Thommen - Kpperberg - Espeler - Eulenstein - Thommen (5.8kms)
Route 27:   Thommen - Aldringen - Trickchesberg - Espeler - Thommen (10.5kms)
Route 28:   Thommen - Maldingen - Aldringen - Thommen (9.2kms)
Route 29:   Thommen - Maldingen - Braunlauf - Thommen (9.0kms)
Route 30:   Maldingen - Braunlauf - Weisten - Fachweg - Maldingen (7.7kms)
Route 31:   Maldingen - Weistervenn - Maldingen (8.4kms)
Route 32:   Maldingen - Weistervenn - Maldingen (5.7kms)
Route 33:   Hohenbusch - Wlfchen - Wfferberg - Schirm - Hohenbusch (3.2kms)
Route 34:   Hohenbusch - Wlfchen - Neubrück - Galhausen - Bovenknopf -
             Wlfchen - Hohenbusch (8.2kms)
Route 35:   Hohenbusch - Schirm - Braunlauf - Schnborn - Schirm - Hohenbusch
             (7.5kms)

Walks

Two walks are featured, one from Burg-Reuland itself and the second from the
village of Oudler a few miles to the west.

WALK 52:
Burg-Reuland, Lascheid and Durler

Description: A pleasant circuit to the west of Burg-Reuland, passing through the old farming communities of Lascheid, Dürler and Oudler. There are many wide vistas, characteristic of this broad undulating landscape of rolling wooded hills. The walk uses a number of waymarked local trails, principally those numbered 6, 20 and 18. The return walk to Burg-Reuland from Oudler samples a small section of the GR 5 in a delightful rural backwater, south of the village of Alster. The Germanic villages in this area have an atmosphere all their own, all rather idyllic and rural, at least on the surface. Each village has a fine church which should be visited if time is available.

Location: A circuit to the west of Burg-Reuland in the German-speaking district of the Cantons de l'Est.

Start/Finish: The church in the centre of the village of Burg-Reuland.

Distance: 9.0 miles (14.5kms).

Time: Allow 5hrs 30mins.

Maps: The map designed for walkers, at a scale of 1:25,000, entitled *Reuland, Ouren, Burg-Reuland: Wanderkarte, Cartes des Promenades, Wandelingen*. Available from the tourist office in Sankt Vith and elsewhere in the Cantons de l'Est.

IGN 1:50,000 series: sheet numbers 56 and 61.

Waymarking: A general note on waymarking in the Burg-Reuland area: the trails are identified by a number which is indicated (usually) on small red rectangular metal waymarks, pointed at one end. The numbers of the trails, which can be identified on the official walking map of the area, are in white on this red background. They are usually only found at major junctions along the trails and are easily missed, as they are small and often placed inconspicuously (and some are obviously missing). Furthermore the trails are waymarked on the assumption that they are to be followed in one particular direction. Hence they are not particularly valuable waymarks for the walker.

The Burg-Reuland area also has several rather old, but attractive wooden signposts which point the way to the various villages and hamlets in the area, and which are intended for use by the walker, cyclist and horserider.

Terrain: A mixture of open country and tracks through forest. There is some climbing to contend with, but no steep gradients.

Footwear: The forest sections can be very wet and muddy after prolonged rain, so that under these conditions boots or bogtrotters are recommended.

Option: Really fit and enthusiastic walkers could combine this trail with Walk 53, so forming a very long day's walk of 17 miles (27.4kms).

Places of

Interest: 1) *The ruined castle at Burg-Reuland.* A fortification was originally built here in AD 963, but the present ruins date from the castle constructed in the 11th century. A visit to the rather romantic ruins of the castle on the hill above the village should certainly be included before you leave the area.

        2) *The church at Burg-Reuland.* The interior of the church is also worth a visit before leaving: the baroque altarpiece is particularly fine. The church door is usually left open.

Refreshments: Refreshments are available en route at Lascheid (café), Dürler (café) and at Oudler (café-restaurant). There are cafés, restaurants and shops in Burg-Reuland, as well as a pension-restaurant (the Burg-Hof: this establishment is on the outskirts of the village, and is passed on the entry into Burg-Reuland in the last stage of the walk described below - meals are available to non-residents).

Route

From the church in the centre of Burg-Reuland head west for 50 metres and then turn left to head south following waymark No. 6 (white No. 6 on a small red metal arrow waymark) and also the red/white waymarks of the GR 5. Within 80 metres bear left to pass under an old archway between houses. Forty metres later opposite a wayside crucifix (grey Christ on a black cross) the GR 5 bears left on a surfaced lane. However, we leave this to turn right (west) on a footpath between tall trees. Within about 100 metres turn right on reaching a track T-junction (still heading to the west). Descend to meet a narrow lane at a bend in the latter: bear left onto this (ie. straight ahead) following the direction of the waymark for Trail No. 6 uphill. This narrow, quiet rural lane climbs away from Burg-Reuland. Soon a small village appears on the hillside above the valley to the right. This is Lascheid, a farming community and our first destination. The climb out of Burg-Reuland is quite a long one, but when the lane levels it soon reaches a T-junction by a wooden bench. Turn right here (No. 6 waymark) and turn right again on reaching a crossroads by another wooden bench, now heading directly for Lascheid. Descend into the village, later ignoring the road which turns sharply to the left (signposted to Richtenberg).

Bear to the left at a Y-junction in the centre of Lascheid (signpost to Café Schmitz) and head north through the village to reach a T-junction, opposite house No. 38, where you turn left (still signposted to Café Schmitz). Pass this café (which is also a *gasthaus*) and leave the village on this lane, which is heading south-west. After about 500 metres bear right at a Y-junction, and about 250 metres later ignore Trail No. 19 which takes a track on the right, but keep to the surfaced lane instead (Trail No. 20) for a further 150 metres to a point where a second dirt track leads off to the right at a Y-junction of lane and track. Bear right onto this track, heading south-west towards the woods seen

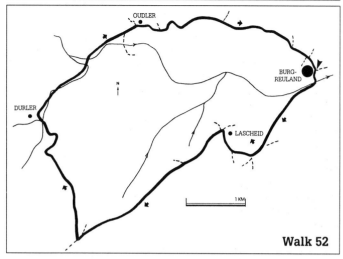

Walk 52

ahead. Walk through the forest on this track which can become very wet and waterlogged in places after heavy rain. Continue ahead (west-south-west) on reaching a cross-tracks in the woods. About 1.5kms after entering the wood the trail comes to an oblique cross-tracks by a wooden seat, a noticeboard/map and a crucifix. Follow to the south-west the track on which the crucifix stands, but only for about 50 metres to a point where two tracks join on the right. Take the *first* of these tracks heading due north through the forest, still following Trail No. 20. Remain on this track as it heads through the woods, passes through a clearing, traverses a further short section of conifer wood and then emerges onto an open grassy hillside.

On reaching the top of a slight rise there is an expansive view of the surrounding hills, dales and forests, and the small village of Dürler lies nestling in the shallow valley ahead. Head towards the village: the grassy track soon becomes a poorly surfaced lane. Remain on this lane as it bends to right and left and passes under the stone arch of an old railway bridge, finally descending to a road on the outskirts of Dürler. Turn right along this road for about 150 metres before turning left at the signpost for Dürler (there is a café at this junction). Bear right at the junction reached within 60 metres to walk past some of the houses of the village (church to your left ahead on a slight rise). After about 150 metres (ie. before reaching the church) turn right (north-west) at a wooden cross, to pass a small row of terraced cottages. Remain on this narrow surfaced lane until it swings to the right to cross the stream in the valley bottom. Do *not* cross this stream, but instead follow a grassy path ahead (north-west) which is enclosed between fences and which always keeps to the north-west side (left bank) of the river. This valley path runs parallel to the main road over to your right. It eventually emerges at a junction with a road. Cross straight over the road and maintain direction, now on a narrow surfaced lane which almost immediately crosses a bridge over a river. Continue ahead along this pleasant narrow lane which runs alongside a grassy bank, now heading for the church and houses of the village of Oudler seen ahead. Keep ahead on this lane to reach the main road in Oudler, opposite a café-restaurant and about 100 metres before the large village church.

Bear left along the road and bear right at the crossroads signposted to Burg-Reuland, now on Trail No. 18. Keep to the pavement whilst walking eastwards through Oudler village. Where the road bends sharply to the right, bear left off of it onto a minor lane (waymark No. 18). On reaching a Y-junction take the right fork signposted to Koller. This quiet, pleasant lane climbs into a delightful rural landscape of lush green grass-covered, rolling hills. At the top of the climb ignore a lane on the left which brings in the GR 5 (red/white waymarks) which are followed ahead towards Burg-Reuland, descending gently with wide vistas all around. The GR 5 is now followed all the way back to Burg-Reuland. Eventually the roofs of the village come into view, the houses of the town nestling in a deep hollow, the ruined castle and the dome of the church being easily recognised. The trail descends more steeply just before the outskirts of Burg-Reuland are reached. Pass a hotel-restaurant and then bend left downhill with the lane to reach a T-junction at a water fountain. Turn right here to descend into the centre of the village. Later bear to the right on the main thoroughfare through the village to return to the church where the day began.

WALK 53:
Oudler, Espeler and Thommen

Description: A circular walk from the village of Oudler west of Burg-Reuland. The walk uses a number of waymarked local trails, principally those numbered 21, 22, 26 and 27. Two more farming villages in the rural Cantons de l'Est are visited on the walk: Espeler and the hilltop town of Thommen. Both have impressive churches. The latter part of the walk consists of a long descent through the large area of forest to the north of Oudler.

Location: In the German-speaking area of the Cantons de l'Est, between the villages of Oudler and Thommen. Oudler is 2.5 miles (4kms) west of Burg-Reuland.

Start/Finish: The church in the centre of the village of Oudler.

Distance: 8.1 miles (13.0kms).

Time: Allow 5hrs.

Maps: The map designed for walkers, at a scale of 1:25 000, entitled *Reuland, Ouren, Burg-Reuland: Wanderkarte, Cartes des Promenades, Wandelingen*. Available from the tourist office in Sankt Vith and elsewhere in the Cantons de l'Est.

IGN 1:50,000 series: sheet number 56.

Waymarking: See "General note on waymarking in the Burg-Reuland area" under "Waymarking" for Walk 52.

Terrain: A mixture of woodland, open country and rural villages. Much of the walk follows quiet, surfaced country lanes. The ascents and descents are mainly gentle in nature.

Footwear: Trainers or stout shoes are quite suitable for much of this walk, except for one section of woodland between Oudler and Espeler where the way is somewhat indistinct, overgrown and rather wet after heavy rain (See "Special Problems" below).

Options: For those without private transport, Oudler can be reached from Burg-Reuland by means of the local bus service. The other possibility, however, would be to walk to Oudler from Burg Reuland using the reverse of the route described for the previous walk (ie. leaving Burg-Reuland on the GR 5 heading westwards). This would add about 2.5 miles (4kms) to the length of the walk (or 5 miles [8kms] if the reverse of the outward walk is made back to Burg-Reuland). As Walk 52 passes through Oudler it is possible for the very fit and enthusiastic to combine both routes (ie. Walks 52 and 53) into one long day.

Special Problems: Totally inexperienced ramblers are warned that the section between the villages of Oudler and Espeler is a little difficult to follow, although hopefully with the aid of this guidebook no undue problems will be experienced. The first part of the walk from Oudler poses no problem, but where Trail No. 21 is left for Trail No. 26 there is a short section which can be rather overgrown and indistinct to follow on the ground. There is a shallow (normally) stream to cross at the end of this section, but the crossing is aided by stepping stones. If in the fairly unlikely event that this river is in flood, no attempt should be made to cross it (Thommen can then be reached by omitting Espeler and following either Trail Nos 21/22 or Trail No. 26, both of which routes are marked on the official tourist office walkers' map of the area - see *"Maps"* above). This somewhat tricky part of the trail is only a small section of the walk, but could be a little disturbing for the inexperienced or unprepared. Experienced walkers should find little to worry them.

Refreshments: Refreshments are available in Oudler (café-restaurant), but not elsewhere en route.

Route

At the crossroads a few metres to the east of the church in the centre of Oudler, take the lane heading north, signposted as the Ourtal Route. Bear to the left on this road as it climbs to head out of the village. Before it leaves Oudler turn left, uphill, on a lane heading south-west and waymarked as Trail No. 21. Continue on this lane, heading towards the woods that lie to the west. Remain on the lane when it is crossed by an unsurfaced track.

About 100 metres before the edge of the forest the lane becomes an unsurfaced stony/grassy track. At the edge of the wood Trail No. 21 takes the track to the right, but we leave this numbered trail here, and instead walk ahead (west-north-west) on a grassy track that enters the forest. However, after only about 80 metres (ie. before entering the densely packed trees) bear to the left (west-south-west) on another grassy track that within 25 metres enters a belt of conifers. This is Trail No. 26. A track soon becomes a path which is rather indistinct on the ground. It can also be somewhat overgrown at times and also quite wet after heavy rain. Do not be tempted to climb the tree-lined banks to the right or left. The route heads down the centre of the valley on a bearing of west-south-west. With a little perseverance the trail will be followed until, nearing the bottom it becomes a clearer path which swings a little towards the north to reach and cross a river (stepping stones - the author's last visit was after a period of heavy rain; there was even then no real difficulty in crossing this water, so that it is probably without difficulty for much of the year).

Reach the opposite bank and a few metres later reach and cross a road, to take the clear track ahead, which starts by a wooden bench. Climb on this track to pass another bench, soon after which, once over the top of the rise, the village of Espeler is attained. Bear right on reaching a track T-junction at a third bench. The track becomes a lane which descends into Espeler. Head for the church in the village and then take the road that heads north-east from it (waymarked as Trail No. 27). Bear right at the junction in the village, by a stone crucifix, telephone box and bus shelter, to continue heading north-east. Descend on this lane to cross a stream (ignore the road on the right to Oudler at this point) and then climb, remaining on the lane, with a wood on a high bank to your right, and the stream and grazing meadows down to your left. The lane heads north, then north-east and finally north again to climb to the hilltop village of Thommen. Once again head for the village church and bear left immediately in front of its tower and steeple.

Walk to the far side of the church to reach a Y-junction north-east of the church. Take the right-hand lane heading east-north-east through the remainder of the village, now once more on Trail No. 22. Continue ahead on the same bearing on reaching a crossroads by the village cemetery. Leave Thommen and descend the hill into the village of Grüfflingen. Cross the main road to take the lane opposite, signposted to Maspelt. Pass the church and its war memorial, heading eastwards out of the village.

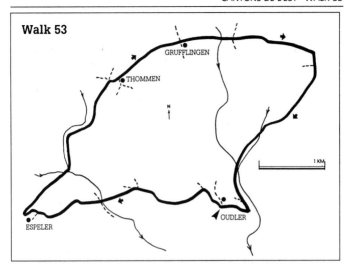

Walk 53

GRUFFLINGEN

THOMMEN

N

1 KM

ESPELER

OUDLER

About 1.5 miles (2.5kms) after leaving Thommen the trail enters a large expanse of woodland. On reaching the edge of these woods ignore a poorly surfaced lane that heads off to the left, but continue straight on, still heading in an easterly direction, now penetrating the forest. Seven hundred metres after entering the wood leave the road by taking a forest track heading south, downhill on the right (NB. this is the *second* track encountered on the right after entering the forest and is further distinguished by leaving the road at the top of the hill and heading south - the first track begins lower down the hill and heads south-west). Ignore a right side-turning after 150 metres and continue ahead, downhill. Remain on the main stony track as it turns slightly to head south-west. Later, on reaching a Y-junction, take the right fork. Remain on the main track, ignore any more side-turnings to follow a long descent out of the wood. The track eventually acquires a poor surface and descends more steeply to cross a stream, before leaving the forest and heading south-south-east along the side of the valley leading back towards Oudler. Turn left on reaching a T-junction at a lane and then right at a second junction with the main road. Keep to the pavement to walk through Oudler to return to the village church where the walk began.

APPENDIX 1

French, Dutch, German and English Place Names in the Belgian Ardennes, and Surrounding Regions

The list of place names given in the table below shows the alternative French, Flemish and German names for the principal countries, cities, towns and villages in the Belgian Ardennes, and in surrounding areas. The list includes the place names that are likely to be encountered on the journey from the channel ports to the Ardennes.

The most important alternative place names to learn, particularly for the British travelling from the channel ports to the Ardennes, carry an asterisk (*) in the following list.

French	Flemish (Dutch)	English	German
Aix-la-Chapelle*	Aken*	-	Aachen*
Alost	Aalst	-	-
Anvers*	Antwerpen*	Antwerp	Antwerpen*
Arlon	Aarlen	-	-
Ath	Aat	-	-
Audenarde	Oudenaarde	-	-
Belgique*	België*	Belgium	Belgien*
Braine l'Alleud	Eigenbrakel	-	-
Braine-le-Château	Kasteelbrakel	-	-
Braine-le-Comte	s'Gravenbrakel	-	-
Bruges*	Brugge*	-	Brugge*
Bruxelles*	Brussel*	Brussels	Brüssel*
Bullange	-	-	Büllingen
Campine	Kempen	-	-
Cantons de l'Est	Oostkantons	-	Ostkantone
Clabecq	Klabbeek	-	-
Comines	Komen	-	-
Courtri*	Kortrijk*	-	-
Dunkerque*	Duinkerke*	-	-
Enghien	Edingen	-	-
Escaut	Schelde	Scheldt	-
France*	Frankrijk*	France	Frankreich*
Furnes*	Veurne*	-	-
Gand*	Gent*	Ghent	Gent*
Grammont	Geraardsbergen	-	-
Hal	Halle	-	-
Hainaut*	Henegouwen*	-	-
Hautes Fagnes*	Hohes Venn*	High Fens	Hoge Venen*

French	Flemish (Dutch)	English	German
Huy*	Hoei*	-	-
Jodoigne	Geldenaken	-	-
La Flandre*	Vlaanderen*	Flanders	-
La Hulpe	Ter Hulpen	-	-
Lessines	Lessen	-	-
Liège*	Luik*	-	Lüttich*
Lierre	Lier	-	-
Lille*	Rijsel*	-	-
Louvain*	Leuven*	-	-
Luxembourg*	Luxemburg*	Luxembourg	Luxemburg*
Lys	Leie	-	-
Malines*	Mechelen*	-	-
Meuse*	Maas*	-	-
Montjoie	-	-	Monschau
Mons*	Bergen*	-	-
Moselle*	-	-	Mosel*
Mouscron	Moeskroen	-	-
Namur*	Namen*	-	-
Nivelles	Nijvel	-	-
Oreye	Oerle	-	-
Ostende*	Oostende*	Ostend	-
Othée	Elch	-	-
Pays-Bas*	Nederland*	Netherlands	Niederlande*
(Hollande)	(Holland)	(Holland)	(Holland)
Renaix	Ronse	-	-
Rénastène	-	-	Reinhardstein
Roulers	Roeselare	-	-
Saintes	Sint Renelde	-	-
Saint Nicolas	Sint Niklaas	-	-
Saint Trond	Sint Truiden	-	-
Saint Vith*	-	Saint Vitus	Sankt Vith*
Soignies	Zinnik	-	-
Termonde	Dendermonde	-	-
Tirlemont	Tienen	-	-
Tournai	Doornik	-	-
Trèves*	-	-	Trier*
Tubize	Tubeke	-	-
Waimes	-	-	Weismes
Waremme	Borgworm	-	-
Wavre	Waver	-	-
Ypres*	Ieper*	"Wipers"	-
Zeebruges*	Zeebrugge*	-	-
-	Nijmegen*	-	Nimwegen*

APPENDIX 2:
Useful French and Flemish Words

French	English
In town	
Accueil	Reception, welcome
Banque	Bank
Brasserie	Café/restaurant
Bureau de change	Money exchange
Crêperie	Pancake restaurant
Eglise	Church
Gare	Railway station
Gare routière	Bus station
Hôtel de Ville	Town hall, in a city or large town (*not* a hotel)
Mairie	Town hall, in a small town or village
Office du tourisme	Tourist office (usually in large town or city)
Porte	Gate
Poste	Post office
Place	Town or village square
PTT	Post office (poste, télégraphe et télécommunication)
Renseignements	Information
Syndicat d'Initiative (SI)	Tourist office (usually in small town or large village)
Zone pietonné	Pedestrianised area
Accommodation	
Abri	Simple or basic shelter
Auberge de jeunesse (AJ)	Youth hostel
Camping à la ferme	Farm campsite
Chambre	Room
Chammbre à deux lits	Room with two beds
Chambre avec (sans) douche	Room with (without) shower
Chambre avec (sans) bain	Room with (without) bath
Chambre avec petit déjeuner	Room with breakfast
Chambre d'hôte	Bed and breakfast (B&B)
Emplacement	A space for a tent at a campsite
Gite d'étape	Simple hostel
Hebergements	Lodgings, accommodation
Relais d'étape	Very simple hostel or shelter/resting place
Tente	Tent
Terrain de camping	Campsite

French	English
Shopping	
Alimentation	Foodshop (often used to refer to an *épicerie*)
Boucher	Butcher's shop
Boulangerie	Baker's shop
Charcuterie	Delicatessen
Epicerie	Grocer's shop
Gaufre	Waffle (a Belgian speciality)
Marché	Market
Pâtisserie	Cake and pastry shop
Pharmacie	Chemist shop
Ravitaillement	Provisions, food supplies
Supermarché	Supermarket
On the trail	
A pied	On foot
Ampoule	Blister
Arrêt	Bus stop
Beau (mauvais) temps	Good (bad) weather
Bois	Wood, forest
Boue	Mud
Bruyère	Heathland
Carrefour	Crossroads, cross-tracks
Centre ville	Town centre
Champs	Field
Chasse	Hunting
Chien méchant	Dangerous dog
Chemin	Track, narrow lane or way
Défense d'entrer	No entry
Eau non potable	Water not suitable for drinking
Eau potable	Drinking water
Etang	Pond or pool
Falaise	Cliff or crag
Ferme	Farm
Fermé	Closed
Forêt	Wood, forest
Grande randonnée (GR)	Long Distance Walking Trail
GR de pays	Regional walking trail
Grange	Barn
Grotte	Cave
Gué	Ford
Hameau	Hamlet
Lacet	Hairpin bend
Ouvert	Open
Moulin	Mill

French	English	French	English
Passerelle	Footbridge	Ville	Town or city
Petite randonnée (PR)	Short, local, walking trail	Route national (RN)	Trunk road
Pont	Bridge	Rue	Street or lane
Pré	Meadow	Ruisseau	Stream
Propriété privée	Private property	Sac à dos	Rucksac
Rocher	Rock	Sentier	Footpath
Route	Road	Table d'orientation	Topograph
		Tour	Tower
Navigation		Est	East
A côté de	Next to	Haut(es)	High
A droite*	To the right	Jusqu'à	As far as
A gauche	To the left	Nord	North
Après	After	Ouest	West
Avant	Before	Pas loin	Not far
Bas(se)	Low	Plus loin	Further
Boussole	Compass	Près	Near
Carte	Map	Sortie	Exit
Derrière	Behind	Sud	South
Devant	In front of	Tout droit*	Straight on; ahead
Entrée	Entrance	Vers	Towards

* care should be exercised when listening to directions in French: the final "t" is not pronounced in *droit*, but the "t" is pronounced in *droite*.

Note that in Walloon French (as in Swiss French) the 70, 80 and 90 are *septante*, *huitante* and *nonante*, although locals do understand the standard French words *soixante-dix*, *quatre-vingt* and *quatre-vingt-dix*.

FLEMISH (DUTCH) WORDS

Dutch (Flemish)	English	Dutch (Flemish)	English
General		Dank u	Thank you
Alstublieft	Here you are; please	Dank u wel	Thank you very much
AUB (or aub)	Here you are; please (frequently used abbreviation for alstublieft).	Een/twee/drie	One/two/three
		Goede morgen	Good morning
		Goed middag	Good afternoon
		Goed nacht	Good night
Bedankt	Thanks	Ja	Yes
Dag!	Hello! Goodbye! (literally "day", but commonly used as the English use "good day")	Ne	No
		Prima!	Fine, OK, good, first-rate
		Tot ziens!	So long, see you, bye

Dutch (Flemish)	English	Dutch (Flemish)	English
In town		Fietspad	Cycle track
Apotheek	Pharmacy	Geen toegang	No access;
Bushalte	Bus stop		no admittance
Centraal station		Heide	Heathland, moor
(usually abbrviated	Central railway	Heuvel	Hill
as CS)	station	Huis	House
Dames	Women (eg. on	Kanaal	Canal
	toilet door)	Kaart	Map
Geopend	Open	Kerk	Church
Gesloten	Closed	LAW (Lange-Afstand	
Gulden	Dutch guilder	-Wandelpad)	Long distance path
	(florin)	Let op!	Attention!
Heren	Men (eg. on toilet		Look out!
	door)	Links	Left
Ingang	Entrance	Linksaf	Turn left
Kamer	Room	Lopen	To walk
Laan	Lane, road	Meer	Lake
Markt	Market	Molen	Mill
Plein	Square (in a town)	Natuur terrein	Nature reserve
Postkantoor	Post office	Natuureservaat	Nature reservation
Rekening	Bill (in restaurant,	Noorden	North
	etc)	Oost	East
Stadhuis	Town hall	Pad	Path
Stadscentrum	Town centre	Pas op!	Attention! Look
Straat	Street		out!
Tankstation	Petrol station,	Recht	Right
	garage	Rechtdoor	Straight ahead
Trein	Train	Rechtuit	Straight ahead
Uitgang	Exit	Rechtsaf	Turn right
VVV	Tourist office	Reisgids	Guidebook
Winkel	Shop	Ruiterpad	Bridleway
		Spoorlijn (weg)	Railway
On the trail		Veld	Field
Akker	Field	Verboden Toegang	Entry forbidden -
Beek	Stream, brook		no admittance
Bezoekerscentrum	Visitor centre	Voetbrug	Footbridge
Boerderij	Farm	Voetpad	Footpath
Boom	Tree	Vrije toegang	Free access
Bos	Wood, forest	Wandelen	Walk, go for a walk
Bromfietspad	Motor cycle track	Wandelpad	Walking trail
Brug	Bridge	Wandelroute	Walking trail
Doorlopen	Walk straight on	Weg	Way, route, trail,
Dorp	Village		road

Dutch (Flemish)	English	Dutch (Flemish)	English
West	West	Pannekoeken	Pancakes (a Dutch/ Flemish speciality)
Zuid	South		
		Poffertje	Small pancake or fritter (a Dutch/ Flemish speciality)
Food and drink			
Appelgebak	Apple tart		
Avondeten	Dinner	Rijst	Rice
Biefstuk	Beefsteak	Rundvlees	Beef
Bier	Beer	Soep	Soup
Broodjes	Sandwiches	Suiker	Sugar
Ei (plural eieren)	Egg (eggs)	Thee	Tea (drink)
Frituur	Snack bar or stall (fried foods)	Uitsmijter	Cheese or ham with eggs on bread (a very popular light meal in Holland and Flanders)
Gebak	Cakes, pastries		
Kaas	Cheese		
Koffie	Coffee		
Kip	Chicken	Varkensvlees	Pork
Lamsvlees	Lamb	Vis	Fish
Melk	Milk	Wafels	Waffles (a Belgian speciality)
Oliebollen	Doughnuts (a Dutch/Flemish speciality)	Wijn	Wine
		Worst	Sausage
Ontbijt	Breakfast		

APPENDIX 3:
Tourist Offices in the Belgian Ardennes

The tourist offices in the 14 centres featured in this guidebook are given below, plus a few other local offices, together with the main tourist offices in the UK and in the Belgian capital, and in the principal cities and large towns of the Ardennes.

Those tourist offices marked with an asterisk (*) are only open during the main summer season. Those not so marked are expected to be open all year (often only at weekends during the winter months), unless otherwise stated.

Belgian tourist office in the UK:
Belgian Tourist Office
29, Princes Street
London, W1R 7RG
Tel. (0171) 629 0230
Fax. (0171) 629 0454

Belgian tourist office in Brussels:
(principal tourist office for the whole of Belgium)
Tourist Information Office
Rue Marché-aux-Herbes 61
Grasmarkt
B-1000 Brussels
Tel (+32) (02) 504 03 90
Fax (+32) (02) 504 03 77

Province of Namur:
Namur
Office du Tourisme
Square de l'Europe Unie
B-5000 Namur
Tel (+32) (081) 22 28 59

Dinant
Syndicat d'Initiative
Rue Grande 37
B-5500 Dinant
Tel (+32) (082) 22 28 70

Rochefort
Syndicat d'Initiative
5, Rue de Behogne
B-5580 Rochefort
Tel (+32) (084) 21 25 37

Han-sur-Lesse
Syndicat d'Initiative
Rue des Sarrasins 1
B-5580 Han-sur-Lesse
Tel (+32) (084) 37 75 96

Han-sur-Lesse *
Syndicat d'Initiative
Place Théo Lannoy
B-5580 Han-sur-Lesse
Tel (+32) (084) 37 75 76

Vresse-sur-Semois
Centre Touristique et Culturel
Rue Albert Raty 112
B-5550 Vresse-sur-Semois
Tel (+32) (061) 50 08 27
(closed January and February)

Province of Luxembourg:
Bouillon
Office du Tourisme Château Bouillon
B-6830 Bouillon
Tel (+32) (061) 46 82 85

Rochehaut *
Syndicat d'Initiative
Rue de la Cense 6A
B-6830 Rochehaut
Tel (+32) (061) 46.69.70

Saint-Hubert
Syndicat d'Initiative, Palais Abbatial
Place de l'Abbaye, B-6870 Saint-Hubert
Tel (+32) (061) 61 30 10 or 61 20 70

Hotton
Maison du Tourisme
Rue Haute 7
B-6990 Hotton
Tel (+32) (084) 46 61 22

La Roche-en-Ardenne
Office du Tourisme
Place du Marché
BP 34, B-6980 La Roche
Tel (+32) (084) 41 23 43

Nadrin (Upper Ourthe)*
Syndicat d'Initiative
S.O.S. No. 30
B-6982 Bérismenil
Tel (+32) (084) 44 42 61

Vielsalm
Tourist Office Val de Salm
B-6690 Vielsalm
Tel (+32) (080) 21 50 52

Province of Liège:
Liège
Office du Tourisme
Feronstrée 92
B-4000 Liège
Tel (+32) (041) 22 24 56

and
Syndicat d'Initiative
Boulevard de la Sauvenière 77
B-4000 Liège
Tel (+32) (041) 22 42 10

Spa
Office du Tourisme
Place Royale 41
B-4880 Spa
Tel (+32) (087) 77 17 00 or 77 29 13
Fax (+32) (087) 77 07 00

Stavelot
Office du Tourisme
Musée de l'Ancienne Abbaye
B-4970 Stavelot
Tel (+32) (080) 86 27 06 or 86 23 39 or
86 23 43

Coo*
Syndicat d'Initiative
Petit Coo
B-4970 Stavelot
Tel (+32) (080) 68 46 39 or 68 43 74

Trois-Ponts*
Syndicat d'Initiative
Place Communale 10
Trois-Ponts
B-4980 Trois-Ponts
Tel (+32) (080) 68 40 45

Malmédy
Office Communal du Tourisme
10, Place du Châtelet
B-4890 Malmédy
Tel (+32) (080) 33 02 50

Cantons de l'Est:
(for *Sankt Vith* and *Burg-Reuland*)
Touristeninformation
Verkehrsamt der Ostkantone
Mühlenbachstrasse 2
B-4780 Sankt Vith
Tel (+32) (080) 22 76 64 or 22 77 64
Fax (+32) (080) 22 65 39

APPENDIX 4
Youth Hostels in the Belgian Ardennes, Brussels and Ostend

For further information and a full list of youth hostels throughout Belgium (there are 32 in total) write to Centralle Wallone des Auberges de la Jeunesse, 52 Rue Van Oost, B-1030 Bruxelles, tel (+32) (02) 215 31 00.

Youth hostels in the Ardennes:
Bouillon
Auberge de Jeunesse
Chemin du Christ 16
B-6830 Bouillon
Tel (+32) (061) 46 81 37
136 beds

Champlon
Auberge de Jeunesse
Rue de la Gèndarmerie 4
B-6971 Champlon
Tel (+32) (084) 45 52 94
72 beds

Herbeumont
Auberge de Jeunesse
Rue de la Hulette 17
B-6887 Herbeumont
Tel (+32) (061) 41 13 68
40 beds

Huy (Tihange)
Auberge de Jeunesse
Rue de la Paix 3
B-4500 Huy
Tel (+32) (085) 23 10 51
66 beds

Liège
Auberge de Jeunesse
B-4000 Liège

Malmédy
Auberge de Jeunesse "Hautes Fagnes"
Bébercé 8A, B-4960 Malmédy
Tel (+32) (080) 33 83 86
178 beds

Namur
Auberge de Jeunesse "F. Rops"
Avenue Félicien Rops 8
La Plante B-5000 Namur
Tel (+32) (081) 22 36 88
114 beds

Sankt Vith
Jeugendeberge
Rodterstrasse 13A
B-4780 Sankt Vith
Tel (+32) (080) 22 93 31
85 beds

Tilff (Liège)
Auberge de Jeunesse
Rue Blandot 4
B-4130 Tilff-Liège
Tel (+32) (041) 88 21 00
66 beds

The following youth hostel is in France, a few kilometres across the Belgian border, south of Dinant:

Givet
Auberge de Jeunesse
Château Mon Bijou
Route des Chaumières
08600 Givet France
Tel (+33) 24 42 10 60
30 beds

Youth Hostels in Brussels:
Jeugdherberg "Bruegel"
• Heilig Geeststraat 2
B-1000 Brussel
Tel (+32) (02) 511 04 36
131 beds

Auberge de Jeunesse "Jacques Brel"
Rue de la Sablonnière 30
B-1000 Bruxelles
Tel (+32) (02) 218 01 87
139 beds.

Auberge de Jeunesse "La Fonderie" or "J. Nihon"
Rue de l'Eléphant 4
B-1080 Bruxelles
Tel (+32) (02) 410 38 58
150 beds

Youth Hostel in Ostend:
Jeugdherberg
Langestraat 82
B-8400 Oostende
Tel (+32) (059) 80 52 97
110 beds

APPENDIX 5
GR Trails in the Belgian Ardennes

Several of the routes described in this guidebook use sections of some of the many GR trails that cross the popular walking region of the Ardennes. For reference the major long distance paths traversing the Belgian Ardennes are listed below, together with the principal towns, villages and areas through which they pass.

GR 12	Sentier Paris - Bruxelles. The trail passes through the western edge of the Ardennes: Montcornet, Moulin-Manteau, Dourbes, Walcourt, circa 68 miles (110kms)
GR 12B	A 31 mile (50km) variant of the GR 12 between Dourbes and Walcourt
GR 121	Sentier du Hainaut Occidental. Hainaut to the Côte d'Opale. Virginal, Ath, Bon-Secours. 57 miles (91kms)
GR 126	Sentier Bruxelles - Semois. 149 miles (240kms). The majority of this trail runs through the Ardennes, from Namur to Membre-sur-Semois via Profondeville, Godinne, Houx, Dinant, Freyr, Walzin, Houyet, Beauraing and Gedinne
GR 129	Sentier Escaut-Meuse (Schelde-Maas). Mons to Dinant. 78 miles (126kms)
GR 14	La Transhubertine. 81 miles (131kms) from Sedan (in the French Ardennes) to La Roche-en-Ardenne, via Corbion, Bouillon, Naomé, Lesse, Transinne, Mirwirt, Fourneau, Saint-Michel, Saint-Hubert, Lavacherie, Tenneville, Champion and Vecmont
GR 5 (E 2)	European Long Distance Path Number 2 from Holland to the Mediterranean. This famous ultra-long distance walking trail passes through the Belgian Ardennes between Kanne near Maastrict and Ouren on the border with Luxembourg, a distance of 118 miles (190kms)
GR 56 (GR E)	Sentier des Cantons de l'Est. Between Baelen, Eupen, Robertville, Butgenbach, Manderfeld, Weveler, Burg-Reuland, Sankt Vith and Malmédy, mainly in the German-speaking eastern fringe of the country. 97 miles (156kms)
GR 563 (GR H)	Tour du Pays de Herve. A circular route between Berneau, Dalhem, Nessonvaux, Walhorn, Gemmenich, Aubel and Berneau. 81 miles (130kms)
GR 57 (GR O)	Sentier de la Vallée de l'Ourthe. Angleur, Esneux, Hamoir, Hotton, La Roche-en-Ardenne, Houffalize, Gouvy. 111 miles (179kms). Has also been termed the Grand Traverse of the Ardennes
GR 57A	Sentier Trans-Femenne. Hotton, Marche-en-Famenne, Humain, Rochefort, Ciney. 32 miles (51kms)
GR 571	GR Amblève. Remouchamps, Quarreux, Coo, Trois-Ponts, Stavlot.

	One of the three Circuits des Vallées de Légendes
GR 572	GR Salm. Trois-Ponts, Vielsalm, Gouvy. One of the three Circuits des Vallées de Légendes
GR 573 (GR V)	Sentier Vesdre - Hoegne-Helle - Hautes-Fagnes. Liège (Angleur), Pepinster, Eupen, Hautes-Fagnes, Hockai, Sart, Polleur, Pepinster, and a variant Pepinster, Theux, Marteau, Spa, Sart, Belleheid. 101 miles (163kms)
GR 574	GR Lembrée. 11 miles (18kms). Along the Lembrée valley between Logne and Harzé
GR 575 (GR GV)	Sentier de la Guerre de la Vache. A circular tour between Jambes, Ciney, Ardenne and Jambres
GR 576 (GR C)	Sentier du Condroz. 31 miles (50kms) between Huy, Modave and Hamoir
GR 577 (GR LL)	Sentier de la Lesse et Lomme. A circular tour between Ciney, Houyet, Han-sur-Lesse, Rochefort and Ciney. 41 miles (66kms)
GR 578 (GR Li)	Sentier de la Lienne. Remouchamps, Lorcé, Chevron, Bra, Lierneux, Hébronval, Gouvy. 68 miles (110kms). One of the three Circuits des Vallées de Légendes
GR 579	Sentier Bruxelles - Liège/Huy. Brussels, Huldenberg, Bossut, Orp, Amay, Esneux. 93 miles (150kms)
GR 579A	A 20 mile (32km) variant of the GR 579 between Hannut and Huy
GR AE	Sentier Ardenne-Eifel. 248 miles (400kms) linking the German Eifel with the Ardennes. Two Topo Guides (AE-N and AE-S) describe the route. Monschau, Eupen, Spa, Aywaille, Werbomont, Houffalize, Bastogne, Tintange, Martelange, Habey-la-Neuve, Florenville, Mortehan, Bouillon, Alle, Membre, Bohan, Sorendal (with a 9km variant between Florenville and Orval). Much of the trail forms part a small section of the European Long Distance Path Number 3 (E 3) which runs for some 8000kms between the Atlantic Coast of Spain and the Black Sea
GR OA	GR Liaison Ourthe - Amblève. Mery, Remouchamps, Nessonvaux-Fraipont. 21 miles (33kms)

There are Topo Guides to all of these trails, mainly in French, but occasionally they are also available in Dutch (alas never in English). For availability and ordering contact either Les Sentiers de Grande Randonnée or Grote Routepaden, the two organisations responsible for long distance paths in Belgium (for addresses see Appendix 6). A *Topographical Map, Sentiers de Grande Randonnée*, published by the Belgian IGN at a scale of 1:250,000, showing the entire GR network in Belgium, can also be purchased from either of the above organisations. For further information about the E 2 and the other European Long Distance E walking trails contact the European Ramblers' Association (see Appendix 6 for address).

APPENDIX 6
Useful Addresses

For the addresses and telephone numbers of the relevant tourist offices see Appendix 3.

1. Edward Stanford Ltd. 12-14 Long Acre, London WC2E 9LP. Tel (0171) 836 1321.
2. The Map Shop. 15, High Street, Upton upon Severn, Worcestershire WR8 0HJ.
   Either of these two specialist map shops should have Belgian IGN maps in stock or will be able to order them on your behalf.
3. British Rail European Enquiries. Tel (0171) 834 2345.
4. National Express Coach Services. Eurolines. Victoria Coach Station, London SW1. Tel (0171) 730 0202 or (0171) 730 8235. Details of coach services between the UK and Belgium.
5. P & O European Ferries. Channel House, Channel View Road, Dover CT17 9TJ. Tel (01304) 203388, or London (0181) 575 8555.
   Cross Channel Ferries: Dover to Ostend, Dover to Zeebrugge, Felixtowe to Zeebrugge, Dover to Boulogne, Dover to Calais.
6. Sealink Stena Line. Charter House, PO Box 121, Park Street, Ashford, Kent TN24 8EX. Enquiries and reservations: Tel (01233) 647047 (Monday to Friday 7.30am to 8.30pm; Saturday 7.30am to 7.30pm; Sunday 9am to 5pm). Cross Channel ferries: Harwich to the Hook of Holland, Dover to Calais.
7. North Sea Ferries. King George Dock, Hedon Road, Hull, N. Humberside HU9 5QA. Tel for reservations and general enquiries (01482) 77177. Cross Channel Ferries: Hull to Rotterdam.
8. Sally Line Ferries. Sally Line Ltd, 81, Piccadilly, London W1V 9HF. Tel (0171) 409 2240 or Ramsgate (01843) 595522. Cross Channel Ferries: Ramsgate to Dunkerque.
9. Hoverspeed. Maybrook House, Queen's Gardens, Dover CT17 9UQ. Tel (01304) 240101. Cross Channel hovercraft and catamaran: Dover to Boulogne and Dover to Calais.
10. Sabena (Belgian National Airlines). 36 Piccadilly, London W1. Tel (0181) 780 1444.
11. Thomas Cook Group Ltd. PO Box 36, Thorpe Wood, Peterborough PE3 6SB. Tel (01733) 63200. Ask for details of their Independent Travellers' Insurance Scheme.
12. West Mercia Insurance Services. High Street, Wombourne, near Wolverhampton WV5 9DN. Tel (01902) 892661. Ask for details of their insurance scheme for "walking, rambling, scrambling and camping".
13. Belgian Tourist Reservations Service (BTR). PO Box 41, B-1000 Brussels 23, Belgium. Tel (+32) (02) 230 50 29.

A free hotel reservation service covering the whole of Belgium.

14.   Centralle Wallone des Auberges de la Jeunesse. 52 Rue Van Oost, B-1030 Bruxelles, Belgium. Tel (+32) (02) 215 31 00.
      Youth hostel organisation for the French-speaking regions of Belgium. Provides a full list of youth hostels, with addresses, telephone numbers and a location map, throughout Belgium, and current list of overnight and meal charges. Alternatively the equivalent Flemish youth hostel organisation (Vlaamse Jeugdherbergcentrale, Van Stralenstraat 40, B-2060 Antwerpen, Belgium), tel (+32) (03) 232 72 18), will send the same information.

15.   Les Sentiers de Grande Randonnée. Rue Katteput 26, bte 64, B-1080 Bruxelles, Belgium. Tel (+32) (02) 465 35 54.
      Information on the Long Distance Path (GR) network in Belgium, particularly in the French-speaking area of the country. The organisation produces a magazine (in French - published quarterly) featuring articles on long distance paths in Belgium and in other countries as well as news and up-to-date information on Belgium LDPs. Topo Guides and Belgian IGN maps can be bought from this organisation.

16.   Grote Routepaden. Van Stralenstraat 40, B-2060 Antwerpen, Belgium. Tel (+32) (03) 232 72 18. Fax (+32) (03) 231 81 26.
      Information on LDPs in the whole of Belgium. This association also produces a quarterly magazine (in Dutch - called *Wandelen*). Topo Guides and Belgian IGN maps can also be bought from this organisation.

17.   European Ramblers' Association. Postfach 10 32 13, D-66032 Saarbrücken, Germany. Tel. (+49) (06 81) 39 00 70. Fax 49-681 3904650.
      Details of the European International Long Distance Footpaths (E routes - including the Ardennes section of the E 2) and general information on walking in Europe.

INDEX

Index of walks listed in order of length

To make it easier to choose a walk based on distance, the 53 walks in this book are listed below in terms of their length. Remember that length is not the only criterion of difficulty: refer to the "Terrain" section of each walk for comments on the amount of ascent and descent and the steepness of the gradients involved, and to the "Special Problems" section (if one is included for the walk) for further advice. The centre where each walk is based (and therefore the section of the Guide) is given in brackets at the end of the walk title.

LENGTH	WALK TITLE (and Centre)	WALK No.	PAGE
14.0 miles (22.5kms)	SANKT VITH, LOMMERSWEILER AND THE GERMAN BORDER (Sankt Vith)	WALK 51	267
12.7 miles (20.5kms)	SANKT VITH, NEUNDORF AND KAPELLEN (Sankt Vith)	WALK 49	262
12.6 miles (20.2kms)	HAN-SUR-LESSE, LESSIVE, EPRAVE AND LES BERGERONNETTES (Rochefort & Han)	WALK 10	86
12.6 miles (20.2kms)	SAINT-HUBERT, THE PARC A GIBIER AND FOURNEAU SAINT-MICHEL (Saint-Hubert)	WALK 20	134
12.4 miles (20.0kms)	VIELSALM, FARNIERES, GORONNE AND SALMCHATEAU (Vielsalm)	WALK 31	181
11.8 miles (19.0kms)	MALMEDY AND LIGNEUVILLE (Malmédy)	WALK 44	243
11.5 miles (18.5kms)	MELREUX, THE CHATEAU DE DEULIN AND THE OURTHE VALLEY (Hotton)	WALK 24	155
11.2 miles (18.0kms)	ALLE, THE VIREE DES MALHEURS AND THE GRAND OPIMONT (Vresse and Alle)	WALK 13	100
10.4 miles (16.7kms)	THE ROCHEFORT AND HAN-SUR-LESSE GRAND CIRCUIT (Rochefort & Han)	WALK 7	76
10.3 miles (16.5kms)	VIELSALM, GRAND HALLEUX AND THE ROCHER DE HOURT (Vielsalm)	WALK 32	187
10.3 miles (16.5kms)	ROBERTVILLE AND THE VALLEE DE BAYEHON (Malmédy)	WALK 46	250
10.1 miles (16.2kms)	HOTTON CRAGS: MELINES, TRINAL, WERPIN AND HOTTON (Hotton)	WALK 23	151
9.9 miles (16.0kms)	VRESSE, BOHAN AND THE RIVER SEMOIS (Vresse and Alle)	WALK 12	96
9.6 miles (15.5kms)	ROCHEHAUT, POUPEHAN AND FRAHAN: THE LADDER WALK (Bouillon)	WALK 19	127

LENGTH	WALK TITLE (and Centre)	WALK No.	PAGE
9.6 miles (15.5kms)	HOTTON, WAHARDAY AND MENIL-FAVAY, WITH AN OPTIONAL TOUR OF HOTTON CAVES (Hotton)	WALK 22	146
9.5 miles (15.3kms)	LA ROCHE AND SAMREE (La Roche)	WALK 25	162
9.3 miles (15.0kms)	BOUILLON, SENSENRUTH, THE GRAND RUISSEAU, THE TOMBEAU DE GEANT AND THE RIVER SEMOIS (Bouillon)	WALK 14	109
9.3 miles (15.0kms)	DOHAN, DAMPIREE, THE COTE DU HAVET AND THE ROCHER LECOMTE (Bouillon)	WALK 16	118
9.0 miles (14.5kms)	BURG-REULAND, LASCHEID AND DURLER (Burg-Reuland)	WALK 52	275
8.7 miles (14.0kms)	BOUILLON, BUHAN AND THE RIVER SEMOIS (Bouillon)	WALK 15	115
8.7 miles (14.0kms)	VIELSALM, BECHE AND THE GRAND BOIS (Vielsalm)	WALK 33	191
8.7 miles (14.0kms)	STAVELOT, THE MAGIRU STREAM AND THE CROIX COLLIN (Stavelot)	WALK 41	225
8.4 miles (13.5kms)	SAINT-HUBERT AND THE HURTEBISE MONASTERY (Saint-Hubert)	WALK 21	140
8.4 miles (13.5kms)	LA ROCHE, MABOGE AND THE RIVER OURTHE (La Roche)	WALK 26	165
8.4 miles (13.5kms)	THE VALLEE DES TOMBES, HIVES AND BUISSON (La Roche)	WALK 27	168
8.1 miles (13.1kms)	LA ROCHE, CIELLE AND SAINTE MARGUERITE (La Roche)	WALK 30	176
8.1 miles (13.0kms)	FALMAGNE AND THE RIVER LESSE (Dinant)	WALK 4	62
8.1 miles (13.0kms)	DOHAN, LA CORNETTE, THE RUISSEAU DES ALEINES, MAKA AND THE ROCHE PERCEE (Bouillon)	WALK 17	120
8.1 miles (13.0kms)	THE GRAND CIRCUIT OF THE HILLS OF SPA - THE LAC DE WARFAAZ (Spa)	WALK 37	209
8.1 miles (13.0kms)	OUDLER, ESPELER AND THOMMEN (Burg-Reuland)	WALK 53	278
7.5 miles (12.1kms)	LA ROCHE, HIVES AND BEAUSAINT (La Roche)	WALK 28	171
7.5 miles (12.1kms)	A CIRCUIT OF COO LAKES (Stavelot)	WALK 43	233

LENGTH	WALK TITLE (and Centre)	WALK No.	PAGE
7.5 miles (12.0kms)	FALMIGNOUL AND THE RIVER MEUSE (Dinant)	WALK 3	58
7.5 miles (12.0kms)	LA ROCHE, VECPRE AND BEAUSAINT (La Roche)	WALK 29	174
7.5 miles (12.0kms)	GERONSTERE AND THE HAUTES FAGNES (Spa)	WALK 39	215
7.1 miles (11.5kms)	SPA, THE BOIS DU CHINCUL AND THE VAL DU BROXOU (Spa)	WALK 35	202
6.8 miles (11.0kms)	STAVELOT, AMERMONT AND RENARDMONT (Stavelot)	WALK 40	222
6.5 miles (10.5kms)	HAN-SUR-LESSE, BELVAUX AND THE NIAU & GRIGNAUX NATURE RESERVES (Rochefort & Han)	WALK 8	80
6.5 miles (10.5kms)	THE FALLS OF COO, THE PROMENADE DU POINT DE VUE DE STER AND COO RESERVOIR (Stavelot)	WALK 42	229
6.2 miles (10.0kms)	MALMEDY, GEROMONT AND ARIMONT (Malmédy)	WALK 45	247
6.1 miles (9.8kms)	THE FOND DE TION (Rochefort & Han)	WALK 11	91
6.1 miles (9.8kms)	SANKT VITH AND HUNNINGEN (Sankt Vith)	WALK 50	266
6.0 miles (9.5kms)	SPA AND THE ETANG DE CHAWION (Spa)	WALK 36	207
5.6 miles (9.0kms)	FEUILLEE JEAN D'ARDENNE AND CREPPE (Spa)	WALK 34	200
5.0 miles (8.0kms)	WAIMES, CHIVREMONT, GROSBOIS AND REMACREUX (Malmédy)	WALK 47	254
5.0 miles (8.0kms)	WAIMES, TRO DES POYES AND LIBOMONT (Malmédy)	WALK 48	257
4.4 miles (7.0kms)	THE PROMENADE DES ARTISTES AND THE ARBORETUM DE TAHAN (Spa)	WALK 38	212
4.0 miles (6.5kms)	PROMENADE DE LA SCHEVAUCHEE (Bouillon)	WALK 18	124
3.7 miles (6.0kms)	BOUVREUILS (Rochefort & Han)	WALK 9	84
3.1 miles (5.0kms)	THE ROND DU ROI [SENTIER ROI ALBERT] (Rochefort & Han)	WALK 6	74
2.5 miles (4.0kms)	NAMUR: A TOUR OF THE CITADEL (Namur)	WALK 1	50

LENGTH	WALK TITLE (and Centre)	WALK No.	PAGE
2.2 miles (3.5kms)	THE FURFOOZ NATIONAL PARK (Dinant)	WALK 5	67
2.0 miles (3.2kms)	NAMUR: A TOWN TRAIL (Namur)	WALK 2	53

*　　*　　*

CICERONE GUIDES

Cicerone publish a wide range of reliable guides to walking and climbing abroad

FRANCE, BELGIUM & LUXEMBOURG

THE BRITTANY COASTAL PATH
CHAMONIX MONT BLANC
- A Walking Guide
THE CORSICAN HIGH LEVEL ROUTE:
GR20
FRENCH ROCK
THE PYRENEAN TRAIL: GR10
THE RLS (Stevenson) TRAIL
ROCK CLIMBS IN BELGIUM &
LUXEMBOURG
ROCK CLIMBS IN THE VERDON
TOUR OF MONT BLANC
TOUR OF THE OISANS: GR54
TOUR OF THE QUEYRAS
WALKING IN THE ARDENNES
WALKING THE FRENCH ALPS: GR5
WALKING THE FRENCH GORGES
(Provence)
WALKING IN THE HAUTE SAVOIE
WALKING IN THE TARENTAISE &
BEAUFORTAIN ALPS
WALKS IN VOLCANO COUNTRY
(Auvergne)
THE WAY OF ST JAMES: GR65

FRANCE / SPAIN

WALKS AND CLIMBS IN THE
PYRENEES
ROCK CLIMBS IN THE PYRENEES

SPAIN & PORTUGAL

WALKING IN THE ALGARVE
ANDALUSIAN ROCK CLIMBS
BIRDWATCHING IN MALLORCA
ROCK CLIMBS IN MAJORCA
COSTA BLANCA CLIMBS

MOUNTAIN WALKS ON THE COSTA
BLANCA
THE MOUNTAINS OF CENTRAL SPAIN
WALKING IN MALLORCA
WALKING IN THE SIERRA NEVADA
WALKS & CLIMBS IN THE PICOS DE
EUROPA
THE WAY OF ST JAMES: SPAIN

SWITZERLAND including adjacent parts of France and Italy

THE ALPINE PASS ROUTE
THE BERNESE ALPS
CENTRAL SWITZERLAND
CHAMONIX TO ZERMATT The Walker's
Haute Route
WALKS IN THE ENGADINE
THE GRAND TOUR OF MONTE ROSA
(inc Italy)
THE JURA - Walking the High Route and
Winter Ski Traverses
WALKING IN TICINO
THE VALAIS - A Walking Guide

GERMANY / AUSTRIA / EASTERN EUROPE

HUT-TO-HUT IN THE STUBAI ALPS
THE HIGH TATRAS
THE KALKALPEN TRAVERSE
KING LUDWIG WAY
KLETTERSTEIG - Scrambles
MOUNTAIN WALKING IN AUSTRIA
WALKING IN THE BLACK FOREST
WALKING IN THE HARZ MOUNTAINS
WALKING IN THE SALZKAMMERGUT

Other guides are constantly being added to the Cicerone List.
Available from bookshops, outdoor equipment shops or direct (send for price list)
from CICERONE, 2 POLICE SQUARE, MILNTHORPE, CUMBRIA, LA7 7PY

CICERONE GUIDES

Cicerone publish a wide range of reliable guides to walking and climbing abroad

ITALY & SLOVENIA
ALTA VIA - High Level Walks in the Dolomites
THE CENTRAL APENNINES OF ITALY
CLASSIC CLIMBS IN THE DOLOMITES
THE GRAND TOUR OF MONTE ROSA inc Switzerland))
ITALIAN ROCK - Rock Climbs in Northern Italy
VIA FERRATA - Scrambles in the Dolomites
WALKING IN THE CENTRAL ITALIAN ALPS
WALKING IN THE DOLOMITES
WALKS IN THE JULIAN ALPS

MEDITERRANEAN COUNTRIES
THE ATLAS MOUNTAINS
CRETE: Off the beaten track
WALKING IN CYPRUS
THE MOUNTAINS OF GREECE
THE MOUNTAINS OF TURKEY
TREKS & CLIMBS IN WADI RUM, JORDAN
THE ALA DAG - Climbs & Treks (Turkey)

HIMALAYA & OTHER COUNTRIES
ADVENTURE TREKS - W. N. AMERICA
ADVENTURE TREKS - NEPAL
ANNAPURNA - A Trekker's Guide
EVEREST - A Trekker's Guide
LANGTANG, GOSAINKUND & HELAMBU - A Trekker's Guide
MOUNTAIN WALKING IN AFRICA 1: KENYA

ROCK CLIMBS IN HONG KONG
TREKKING IN THE CAUCAUSUS
CLASSIC TRAMPS IN NEW ZEALAND

GENERAL OUTDOOR BOOKS
THE ADVENTURE ALTERNATIVE
ENCYCLOPAEDIA OF MOUNTAINEERING
FAMILY CAMPING
FIRST AID FOR HILLWALKERS
THE HILL WALKERS MANUAL
LIMESTONE -100 BEST CLIMBS IN BRITAIN
MOUNTAIN WEATHER
MOUNTAINEERING LITERATURE
MODERN ALPINE CLIMBING
MODERN SNOW & ICE TECHNIQUES
ROPE TECHNIQUES IN MOUNTAINEERING

CANOEING
CANOEIST'S GUIDE TO THE NORTH EAST
SNOWDONIA WILD WATER, SEA & SURF
WILDWATER CANOEING

CARTOON BOOKS
ON FOOT & FINGER
ON MORE FEET & FINGERS
LAUGHS ALONG THE PENNINE WAY
THE WALKERS

Also a full range of British guidebooks to walking - from short family walks, day walks to long distance trails, biking, scrambling, ice-climbing, rock climbing and canoeing

---

*Other guides are constantly being added to the Cicerone List.
Available from bookshops, outdoor equipment shops or direct (send for price list)
from CICERONE, 2 POLICE SQUARE, MILNTHORPE, CUMBRIA, LA7 7PY*

*PRINTED BY CARNMOR PRINT & DESIGN,
95/97 LONDON ROAD, PRESTON, LANCASHIRE*